Microsoft® OFFICE 2010

ESSENTIAL

Gary B. Shelly

Misty E. Vermaat

Contributing Authors

Raymond E. Enger

Steven M. Freund

Mary Z. Last

Philip J. Pratt

Jeffrey J. Quasney

Susan L. Sebok

COURSE TECHNOLOGY
CENGAGE Learning™

SHELLY CASHMAN SERIES®

Australia • Brazil • Japan • Korea • Mexico • Singapore • Spain • United Kingdom • United States

COURSE TECHNOLOGY
CENGAGE Learning™

Microsoft Office 2010: Essential
Gary B. Shelly, Misty E. Vermaat

Vice President, Publisher: Nicole Pinard

Executive Editor: Kathleen McMahon

Senior Product Manager: Mali Jones

Associate Product Manager: Aimee Poirier

Editorial Assistant: Lauren Brody

Director of Marketing: Cheryl Costantini

Marketing Manager: Tristen Kendall

Marketing Coordinator: Stacey Leasca

Print Buyer: Julio Esperas

Director of Production: Patty Stephan

Content Project Manager: Matthew Hutchinson

Development Editors: Jill Batistick, Amanda Brodkin, Deb Kaufmann, Lyn Markowicz

Copyeditors: Foxxe Editorial and Troy Lilly

Proofreaders: Chris Clark and Karen Annett

Indexer: Rich Carlson

QA Manuscript Reviewers: Chris Scriver, John Freitas, Serge Palladino, Susan Pedicini, Danielle Shaw, Susan Whalen

Art Director: Marissa Falco

Cover Designer: Lisa Kuhn, Curio Press, LLC

Cover Photo: Tom Kates Photography

Text Design: Joel Sadagursky

Compositor: PreMediaGlobal

For product information and technology assistance, contact us at
Cengage Learning Customer & Sales Support, 1-800-354-9706

For permission to use material from this text or product, submit all requests online at **cengage.com/permissions**
Further permissions questions can be emailed to
permissionrequest@cengage.com

Library of Congress Control Number: 2010929674

ISBN-13: 978-0-538-74870-4

ISBN-10: 0-538-74870-2

Course Technology
20 Channel Center Street
Boston, MA 02210
USA

Cengage Learning is a leading provider of customized learning solutions with office locations around the globe, including Singapore, the United Kingdom, Australia, Mexico, Brazil, and Japan. Locate your local office at:
international.cengage.com/region

Cengage Learning products are represented in Canada by Nelson Education, Ltd.

Visit our website **www.cengage.com/ct/shellycashman** to share and gain ideas on our textbooks!

To learn more about Course Technology, visit **www.cengage.com/coursetechnology**

Purchase any of our products at your local college store or at our preferred online store **www.cengagebrain.com**

We dedicate this book to the memory of James S. Quasney (1940 – 2009), who for 18 years co-authored numerous books with Tom Cashman and Gary Shelly and provided extraordinary leadership to the Shelly Cashman Series editorial team. As series editor, Jim skillfully coordinated, organized, and managed the many aspects of our editorial development processes and provided unending direction, guidance, inspiration, support, and advice to the Shelly Cashman Series authors and support team members. He was a trusted, dependable, loyal, and well-respected leader, mentor, and friend. We are forever grateful to Jim for his faithful devotion to our team and eternal contributions to our series.

The Shelly Cashman Series Team

Printed in the United States of America
2 3 4 5 6 7 15 14 13 12 11

Contents

Preface   vii

Microsoft **Office 2010 and Windows 7**

Office 2010 and Windows 7: Essential Concepts and Skills

Objectives	OFF 1
Office 2010 and Windows 7	OFF 2
Overview	OFF 2
Introduction to the Windows 7 Operating System	OFF 2
Using a Mouse	OFF 2
Scrolling	OFF 4
Shortcut Keys	OFF 4
Starting Windows 7	OFF 5
To Log On to the Computer	OFF 6
The Windows 7 Desktop	OFF 7
Introduction to Microsoft Office 2010	OFF 7
Microsoft Office 2010 Programs	OFF 8
Microsoft Office 2010 Suites	OFF 8
Starting and Using a Program	OFF 9
Word	OFF 9
To Start a Program Using the Start Menu	OFF 10
To Maximize a Window	OFF 12
The Word Document Window, Ribbon, and Elements Common to Office Programs	OFF 12
To Display a Different Tab on the Ribbon	OFF 16
To Minimize, Display, and Restore the Ribbon	OFF 17
To Display and Use a Shortcut Menu	OFF 18
To Customize the Quick Access Toolbar	OFF 19
To Enter Text in a Document	OFF 20
Saving and Organizing Files	OFF 21
Organizing Files and Folders	OFF 21
To Create a Folder	OFF 22
Folder Windows	OFF 24
To Create a Folder within a Folder	OFF 24
To Expand a Folder, Scroll through Folder Contents, and Collapse a Folder	OFF 26
To Switch from One Program to Another	OFF 27
To Save a File in a Folder	OFF 27
Navigating in Dialog Boxes	OFF 30
To Minimize and Restore a Window	OFF 30
Screen Resolution	OFF 31
To Change the Screen Resolution	OFF 33
To Quit an Office Program with One Document Open	OFF 35
Additional Microsoft Office Programs	OFF 36
PowerPoint	OFF 36
To Start a Program Using the Search Box	OFF 37
The PowerPoint Window and Ribbon	OFF 39
To Enter Content in a Title Slide	OFF 40
To Create a New Office Document from the Backstage View	OFF 41
To Close an Office File Using the Backstage View	OFF 44
To Open a Recent Office File Using the Backstage View	OFF 45
Excel	OFF 46
To Create a New Blank Office Document from Windows Explorer	OFF 47
To Start a Program from Windows Explorer and Open a File	OFF 48
Unique Features of Excel	OFF 49
To Enter a Worksheet Title	OFF 50
To Save an Existing Office Document with the Same File Name	OFF 51
Access	OFF 53
Unique Elements in Access	OFF 54
To Create an Access Database	OFF 55
To Open an Existing Office File	OFF 57
Other Office Programs	OFF 58
Outlook	OFF 58
Publisher	OFF 59
OneNote	OFF 61
Moving, Renaming, and Deleting Files	OFF 62
To Rename a File	OFF 63
To Move a File	OFF 64
To Delete a File	OFF 64
Microsoft Office and Windows Help	OFF 66
To Open the Help Window in an Office Program	OFF 66
Moving and Resizing Windows	OFF 66
To Move a Window by Dragging	OFF 66
To Resize a Window by Dragging	OFF 67
Using Office Help	OFF 68
To Obtain Help Using the 'Type words to search for' Text Box	OFF 68
To Obtain Help Using the Help Links	OFF 70
To Obtain Help Using the Help Table of Contents	OFF 71
Obtaining Help while Working in an Office Program	OFF 72
Using Windows Help and Support	OFF 73
To Start Windows Help and Support	OFF 73

Chapter Summary	**OFF 74**
Learn It Online	**OFF 75**
Apply Your Knowledge	**OFF 76**
Extend Your Knowledge	**OFF 76**
Make It Right	**OFF 77**
In the Lab	**OFF 78**
Cases and Places	**OFF 80**

Microsoft **Word 2010**

CHAPTER ONE

Creating, Formatting, and Editing a Word Document with Pictures

Objectives	**WD 1**
Introduction	**WD 2**
Project — Flyer with Pictures	**WD 2**
Overview	WD 4
Entering Text	**WD 5**
To Type Text	WD 6
To Display Formatting Marks	WD 7
To Insert a Blank Line	WD 7
Wordwrap	WD 8
To Wordwrap Text as You Type	WD 8
Spelling and Grammar Check	WD 9
To Check Spelling and Grammar as You Type	WD 9
Navigating a Document	WD 11
Formatting Paragraphs and Characters	**WD 12**
To Center a Paragraph	WD 14
Formatting Single versus Multiple Paragraphs and Characters	WD 15
To Select a Line	WD 15
To Change the Font Size of Selected Text	WD 16
To Change the Font of Selected Text	WD 17
To Change the Case of Selected Text	WD 18
To Apply a Text Effect to Selected Text	WD 19
To Shade a Paragraph	WD 20
To Select Multiple Lines	WD 21
To Bullet a List of Paragraphs	WD 22
To Undo and Redo an Action	WD 23
To Italicize Text	WD 24
To Color Text	WD 25
To Use the Mini Toolbar to Format Text	WD 26
To Select a Group of Words	WD 27
To Underline Text	WD 27
To Bold Text	WD 28
To Change Theme Colors	WD 28
Selecting Text	WD 30
Inserting and Formatting Pictures in a Word Document	**WD 30**
To Insert a Picture	WD 31
To Zoom the Document	WD 33
To Resize a Graphic	WD 34
To Resize a Graphic by Entering Exact Measurements	WD 36
To Apply a Picture Style	WD 37
To Apply Picture Effects	WD 38
Enhancing the Page	**WD 40**
To View One Page	WD 40
To Add a Page Border	WD 41
To Change Spacing before and after a Paragraph	WD 43
Correcting Errors and Revising a Document	**WD 44**
Types of Changes Made to Documents	WD 44
To Insert Text in an Existing Document	WD 46
Deleting Text from a Document	WD 47
To Delete Text	WD 47
To Move Text	WD 47
Changing Document Properties	**WD 49**
To Change Document Properties	WD 49
Printing a Document	**WD 51**
To Print a Document	WD 51
Chapter Summary	**WD 53**
Learn It Online	**WD 54**
Apply Your Knowledge	**WD 54**
Extend Your Knowledge	**WD 56**
Make It Right	**WD 57**
In the Lab	**WD 58**
Cases and Places	**WD 63**

Microsoft **PowerPoint 2010**

CHAPTER ONE

Creating and Editing a Presentation with Clip Art

Objectives	**PPT 1**
Introduction	**PPT 2**
Project — Presentation with Bulleted Lists and Clip Art	**PPT 2**
Overview	PPT 4
Choosing a Document Theme	**PPT 5**
To Choose a Document Theme	PPT 5
Creating a Title Slide	**PPT 7**
To Enter the Presentation Title	PPT 7
Correcting a Mistake When Typing	PPT 8
Paragraphs	PPT 8
To Enter the Presentation Subtitle Paragraph	PPT 9
Formatting Characters in a Presentation	**PPT 10**
Fonts and Font Styles	PPT 10
To Select a Paragraph	PPT 10
To Italicize Text	PPT 11
To Increase Font Size	PPT 11
To Select a Word	PPT 12
To Change the Text Color	PPT 13
Adding a New Slide to a Presentation	**PPT 14**
To Add a New Text Slide with a Bulleted List	PPT 14
Creating a Text Slide with a Multi-Level Bulleted List	**PPT 15**
To Enter a Slide Title	PPT 16
To Select a Text Placeholder	PPT 16
To Type a Multi-Level Bulleted List	PPT 17
To Select a Group of Words	PPT 19
To Bold Text	PPT 19
Adding New Slides and Changing the Slide Layouts	**PPT 21**
To Add a Slide with the Title Only Layout	PPT 21
To Add a New Slide and Enter a Slide Title and Headings	PPT 23
PowerPoint Views	**PPT 24**
To Move to Another Slide in Normal View	PPT 25
Inserting Clip Art and Photographs into Slides	**PPT 26**
The Clip Art Task Pane	PPT 26
To Insert a Clip from the Clip Organizer into the Title Slide	PPT 27
To Insert a Clip from the Clip Organizer into a Content Placeholder	PPT 30
Photographs and the Clip Organizer	**PPT 31**
Resizing Clip Art and Photographs	**PPT 33**

To Resize Clip Art	PPT 33
To Move Clips	PPT 36
Ending a Slide Show with a Closing Slide	**PPT 38**
To Duplicate a Slide	PPT 38
To Arrange a Slide	PPT 39
Making Changes to Slide Text Content	**PPT 40**
Replacing Text in an Existing Slide	PPT 41
Deleting Text	PPT 41
To Delete Text in a Placeholder	PPT 41
Adding a Transition	**PPT 43**
To Add a Transition between Slides	PPT 43
Changing Document Properties	**PPT 45**
To Change Document Properties	PPT 46
Viewing the Presentation in Slide Show View	**PPT 47**
To Start Slide Show View	PPT 47
To Move Manually through Slides in a Slide Show	PPT 49
Printing a Presentation	**PPT 51**
To Print a Presentation	PPT 51
Chapter Summary	**PPT 54**
Learn It Online	**PPT 55**
Apply Your Knowledge	**PPT 55**
Extend Your Knowledge	**PPT 57**
Make It Right	**PPT 58**
In the Lab	**PPT 59**
Cases and Places	**PPT 70**

Microsoft **Excel 2010**

CHAPTER ONE

Creating a Worksheet and an Embedded Chart

Objectives	**EX 1**
Introduction	**EX 2**
Project — Worksheet with an Embedded Chart	**EX 2**
Overview	EX 4
Selecting a Cell	**EX 7**
Entering Text	**EX 7**
To Enter the Worksheet Titles	EX 8
AutoCorrect	EX 9
To Enter Column Titles	EX 10
To Enter Row Titles	EX 12
Entering Numbers	**EX 13**
To Enter Numbers	EX 13
Calculating a Sum	**EX 15**
To Sum a Column of Numbers	EX 15
Using the Fill Handle to Copy a Cell to Adjacent Cells	**EX 16**
To Copy a Cell to Adjacent Cells in a Row	EX 17
To Determine Multiple Totals at the Same Time	EX 18
Formatting the Worksheet	**EX 20**
Font, Style, Size, and Color	EX 22
To Change a Cell Style	EX 22
To Change the Font	EX 24
To Bold a Cell	EX 25
To Increase the Font Size of a Cell Entry	EX 26
To Change the Font Color of a Cell Entry	EX 27
To Center Cell Entries Across Columns by Merging Cells	EX 28
To Format Column Titles and the Total Row	EX 29
To Format Numbers in the Worksheet	EX 31
To Adjust the Column Width	EX 33

Using the Name Box to Select a Cell	**EX 34**
To Use the Name Box to Select a Cell	EX 34
Other Ways to Select Cells	EX 35
Adding a Clustered Cylinder Chart to the Worksheet	**EX 36**
To Add a Clustered Cylinder Chart to the Worksheet	EX 38
Changing the Worksheet Names	**EX 42**
To Change the Worksheet Names	EX 42
Changing Document Properties	**EX 43**
To Change Document Properties	EX 43
To Save an Existing Workbook with the Same File Name	EX 45
Previewing and Printing a Worksheet	**EX 45**
To Preview and Print a Worksheet in Landscape Orientation	EX 46
Starting Excel and Opening a Workbook	**EX 47**
AutoCalculate	**EX 48**
To Use the AutoCalculate Area to Determine a Maximum	EX 49
Correcting Errors	**EX 49**
Correcting Errors While You Are Typing Data into a Cell	EX 49
Correcting Errors After Entering Data into a Cell	EX 50
Undoing the Last Cell Entry	EX 51
Clearing a Cell or Range of Cells	EX 52
Clearing the Entire Worksheet	EX 52
Chapter Summary	**EX 53**
Learn It Online	**EX 54**
Apply Your Knowledge	**EX 54**
Extend Your Knowledge	**EX 56**
Make It Right	**EX 57**
In the Lab	**EX 58**
Cases and Places	**EX 63**

Microsoft **Access 2010**

CHAPTER ONE

Databases and Database Objects: An Introduction

Objectives	**AC 1**
Introduction	**AC 2**
Project — Database Creation	**AC 2**
Overview	AC 4
Designing a Database	**AC 6**
Database Requirements	AC 6
Naming Tables and Fields	AC 8
Identifying the Tables	AC 8
Determining the Primary Keys	AC 8
Determining Additional Fields	AC 8
Determining and Implementing Relationships Between the Tables	AC 9
Determining Data Types for the Fields	AC 9
Identifying and Removing Redundancy	AC 10
Creating a Database	**AC 13**
The Access Window	**AC 15**
Navigation Pane and Access Work Area	AC 15
Creating a Table	**AC 15**
To Modify the Primary Key	AC 16
To Define the Remaining Fields in a Table	AC 19
Making Changes to the Structure	AC 20

To Save a Table   AC 21
To View the Table in Design View   AC 21
Checking the Structure in Design View   AC 22
To Close the Table   AC 23
To Add Records to a Table   AC 23
Making Changes to the Data   AC 25
Starting Access and Opening a Database   AC 27
To Add Additional Records to a Table   AC 28
To Resize Columns in a Datasheet   AC 29
Previewing and Printing the Contents of a Table   **AC 30**
To Preview and Print the Contents of a Table   AC 31
Creating Additional Tables   **AC 32**
To Create a Table in Design View   AC 33
Correcting Errors in the Structure   AC 37
Importing Data from Other Applications to Access   **AC 38**
To Import an Excel Worksheet   AC 38
Additional Database Objects   **AC 42**
To Use the Simple Query Wizard to Create a Query   AC 43
Using Queries   AC 45
To Use a Criterion in a Query   AC 46
Creating and Using Forms   AC 48
To Create a Form   AC 48
Using a Form   AC 50
Creating and Printing Reports   AC 51
To Create a Report   AC 52
Using Layout View in a Report   AC 53
To Modify Column Headings and Resize Columns   AC 54
To Add Totals to a Report   AC 57
Database Properties   **AC 58**
To Change Database Properties   AC 59
Special Database Operations   **AC 60**
Backup and Recovery   AC 60
Compacting and Repairing a Database   AC 61
Additional Operations   AC 62

Chapter Summary   **AC 63**
Learn It Online   **AC 63**
Apply Your Knowledge   **AC 64**
Extend Your Knowledge   **AC 65**
Make It Right   **AC 66**
In the Lab   **AC 66**
Cases and Places   **AC 72**

Appendices

APPENDIX A
Project Planning Guidelines

Using Project Planning Guidelines   **APP 1**
Determine the Project's Purpose   APP 1
Analyze Your Audience   APP 1
Gather Possible Content   APP 2
Determine What Content to Present to
     Your Audience   APP 2
Summary   **APP 2**

APPENDIX B
Publishing Office 2010 Web Pages Online

Using an Office Program to Publish Office 2010
     Web Pages   APP 3

APPENDIX C
Saving to the Web Using Windows Live SkyDrive

Introduction   **APP 5**
To Save a File to Windows Live SkyDrive   APP 6
Web Apps   APP 8
To Download a File from Windows Live SkyDrive   APP 9
Collaboration   APP 12

Index   **IND 1**

Quick Reference Summary   **QR 1**

Preface

The Shelly Cashman Series® offers the finest textbooks in computer education. We are proud that since Mircosoft Office 4.3, our series of Microsoft Office textbooks have been the most widely used books in education. With each new edition of our Office books, we make significant improvements based on the software and comments made by instructors and students. For this Microsoft Office 2010 text, the Shelly Cashman Series development team carefully reviewed our pedagogy and analyzed its effectiveness in teaching today's Office student. Students today read less, but need to retain more. They need not only to be able to perform skills, but to retain those skills and know how to apply them to different settings. Today's students need to be continually engaged and challenged to retain what they're learning.

With this Microsoft Office 2010 text, we continue our commitment to focusing on the user and how they learn best.

Objectives of This Textbook

Microsoft Office 2010: Essential is intended for a course that includes an essential introduction to Office 2010. No experience with a computer is assumed, and no mathematics beyond the high school freshman level is required. The objectives of this book are:

- To teach the fundamentals of, Microsoft Word 2010, Microsoft PowerPoint 2010, Microsoft Excel 2010, Microsoft Access 2010, and Microsoft Windows 7

- To expose students to practical examples of the computer as a useful tool

- To acquaint students with the proper procedures to create documents, worksheets, databases, and presentations suitable for coursework, professional purposes, and personal use

- To help students discover the underlying functionality of Office 2010 so they can become more productive

- To develop an exercise-oriented approach that allows learning by doing

New to This Edition

Microsoft Office 2010: Essential offers a number of new features and approaches, which improve student understanding, retention, transference, and skill in using Office 2010 programs. The following enhancements will enrich the learning experience:

- Office 2010 and Windows 7: Essential Concepts and Skills chapter prevents repetitive coverage of basic skills in the application chapters.

- Streamlined first chapters for each application allow the ability to cover more advanced skills earlier.

- Chapter topic redistribution offers concise chapters that ensure complete skill coverage.

- Expanded coverage of PowerPoint gives exposure to the numerous enhancements made to this application.

- New pedagogical elements enrich material creating an accessible and user-friendly approach.

  - Break Points, a new boxed element, identify logical stopping points and give students instructions regarding what they should do before taking a break.

  - Within step instructions, Tab | Group Identifiers, such as (Home tab | Bold button), help students more easily locate elements in the groups and on the tabs on the Ribbon.

  - Modified step-by-step instructions tell the student what to do and provide the generic reason why they are completing a specific task, which helps students easily transfer given skills to different settings.

The Shelly Cashman Approach

A Proven Pedagogy with an Emphasis on Project Planning

Each chapter presents a practical problem to be solved, within a project planning framework. The project orientation is strengthened by the use of Plan Ahead boxes, which encourage critical thinking about how to proceed at various points in the project. Step-by-step instructions with supporting screens guide students through the steps. Instructional steps are supported by the Q&A, Experimental Step, and BTW features.

A Visually Engaging Book that Maintains Student Interest

The step-by-step tasks, with supporting figures, provide a rich visual experience for the student. Call-outs on the screens that present both explanatory and navigational information provide students with information they need when they need to know it.

Supporting Reference Materials (Appendices, Quick Reference)

The appendices provide additional information about the Application at hand and include such topics and project planning guidelines and certification. With the Quick Reference, students can quickly look up information about a single task, such as keyboard shortcuts, and find page references of where in the book the task is illustrated.

Integration of the World Wide Web

The World Wide Web is integrated into the Office 2010 learning experience by (1) BTW annotations; (2) BTW, Q&A, and Quick Reference Summary Web pages; and (3) the Learn It Online section for each chapter.

End-of-Chapter Student Activities

Extensive end-of-chapter activities provide a variety of reinforcement opportunities for students where they can apply and expand their skills.

Instructor Resources

The Instructor Resources include both teaching and testing aids and can be accessed via CD-ROM or at www.cengage.com/login.

Instructor's Manual Includes lecture notes summarizing the chapter sections, figures and boxed elements found in every chapter, teacher tips, classroom activities, lab activities, and quick quizzes in Microsoft Word files.

Syllabus Easily customizable sample syllabi that cover policies, assignments, exams, and other course information.

Figure Files Illustrations for every figure in the textbook in electronic form.

PowerPoint Presentations A multimedia lecture presentation system that provides slides for each chapter. Presentations are based on chapter objectives.

Solutions to Exercises Includes solutions for all end-of-chapter and chapter reinforcement exercises.

Test Bank & Test Engine Test Banks include 112 questions for every chapter, featuring objective-based and critical thinking question types, and including page number references and figure references, when appropriate. Also included is the test engine, ExamView, the ultimate tool for your objective-based testing needs.

Data Files for Students Includes all the files that are required by students to complete the exercises.

Additional Activities for Students Consists of Chapter Reinforcement Exercises, which are true/false, multiple-choice, and short answer questions that help students gain confidence in the material learned.

SAM: Skills Assessment Manager

SAM 2010 is designed to help bring students from the classroom to the real world. It allows students to train on and test important computer skills in an active, hands-on environment.

SAM's easy-to-use system includes powerful interactive exams, training, and projects on the most commonly used Microsoft Office applications. SAM simulates the Microsoft Office 2010 application environment, allowing students to demonstrate their knowledge and think through the skills by performing real-world tasks such as bolding word text or setting up slide transitions. Add in live-in-the-application projects, and students are on their way to truly learning and applying skills to business-centric documents.

Designed to be used with the Shelly Cashman Series, SAM includes handy page references so that students can print helpful study guides that match the Shelly Cashman textbooks used in class. For instructors, SAM also includes robust scheduling and reporting features.

Content for Online Learning

Course Technology has partnered with the leading distance learning solution providers and class-management platforms today. To access this material, instructors will visit our password-protected instructor resources available at www.cengage.com/coursetechnology. Instructor resources include the following: additional case projects, sample syllabi, PowerPoint presentations per chapter, and more. For additional information or for an instructor user name and password, please contact your sales representative. For students to access this material, they must have purchased a WebTutor PIN-code specific to this title and your campus platform. The resources for students may include (based on instructor preferences), but are not limited to: topic review, review questions, and practice tests.

CourseNotes

Course Technology's CourseNotes are six-panel quick reference cards that reinforce the most important and widely used features of a software application in a visual and user-friendly format. CourseNotes serve as a great reference tool during and after the student completes the course. CourseNotes are available for software applications such as Microsoft Office 2010, Word 2010, PowerPoint 2010, Excel 2010, Access 2010, and Windows 7. Topic-based CourseNotes are available for Best Practices in Social Networking, Hot Topics in Technology, and Web 2.0. Visit www.cengage.com/ct/coursenotes to learn more!

A Guided Tour

Add excitement and interactivity to your classroom with "*A Guided Tour*" product line. Play one of the brief mini-movies to spice up your lecture and spark classroom discussion. Or, assign a movie for homework and ask students to complete the correlated assignment that accompanies each topic. "*A Guided Tour*" product line takes the prep work out of providing your students with information about new technologies and applications and helps keep students engaged with content relevant to their lives; all in under an hour!

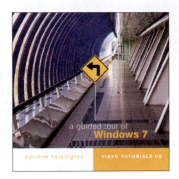

About Our Covers

The Shelly Cashman Series is continually updating our approach and content to reflect the way today's students learn and experience new technology. This focus on student success is reflected on our covers, which feature real students from Bentley University using the Shelly Cashman Series in their courses, and reflect the varied ages and backgrounds of the students learning with our books. When you use the Shelly Cashman Series, you can be assured that you are learning computer skills using the most effective courseware available.

Textbook Walk-Through

The Shelly Cashman Series Pedagogy: Project-Based — Step-by-Step — Variety of Assessments

Plan Ahead boxes prepare students to create successful projects by encouraging them to think strategically about what they are trying to accomplish before they begin working.

Step-by-step instructions now provide a context beyond the point-and-click. Each step provides information on why students are performing each task, or what will occur as a result.

Explanatory callouts summarize what is happening on screen.

Navigational callouts in red show students where to click.

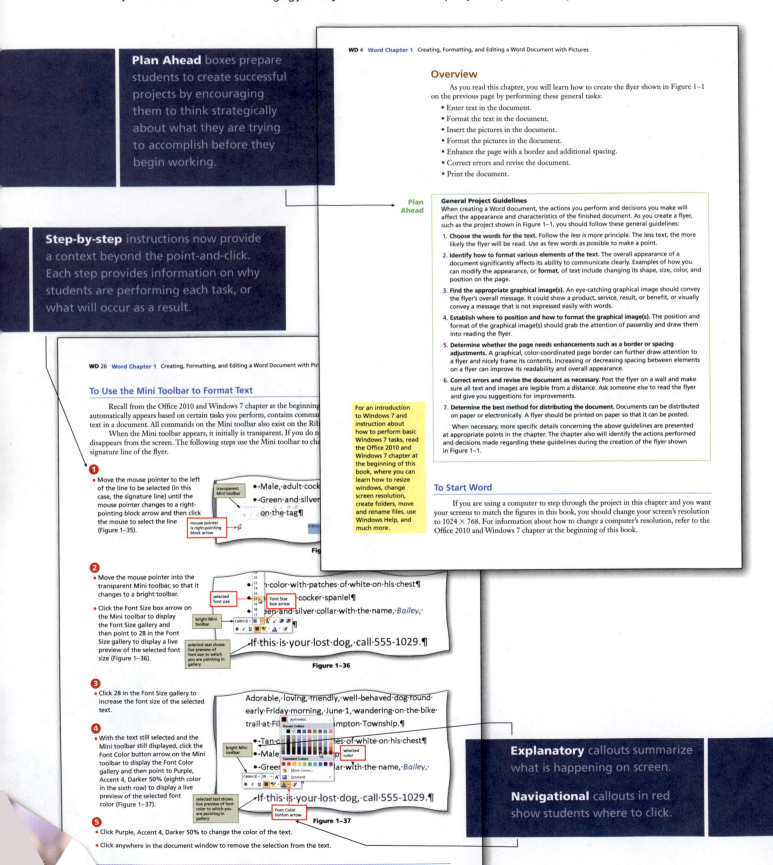

Overview

As you read this chapter, you will learn how to create the flyer shown in Figure 1–1 on the previous page by performing these general tasks:

- Enter text in the document.
- Format the text in the document.
- Insert the pictures in the document.
- Format the pictures in the document.
- Enhance the page with a border and additional spacing.
- Correct errors and revise the document.
- Print the document.

Plan Ahead

General Project Guidelines

When creating a Word document, the actions you perform and decisions you make will affect the appearance and characteristics of the finished document. As you create a flyer, such as the project shown in Figure 1–1, you should follow these general guidelines:

1. **Choose the words for the text.** Follow the *less is more* principle. The less text, the more likely the flyer will be read. Use as few words as possible to make a point.

2. **Identify how to format various elements of the text.** The overall appearance of a document significantly affects its ability to communicate clearly. Examples of how you can modify the appearance, or **format**, of text include changing its shape, size, color, and position on the page.

3. **Find the appropriate graphical image(s).** An eye-catching graphical image should convey the flyer's overall message. It could show a product, service, result, or benefit, or visually convey a message that is not expressed easily with words.

4. **Establish where to position and how to format the graphical image(s).** The position and format of the graphical image(s) should grab the attention of passersby and draw them into reading the flyer.

5. **Determine whether the page needs enhancements such as a border or spacing adjustments.** A graphical, color-coordinated page border can further draw attention to a flyer and nicely frame its contents. Increasing or decreasing spacing between elements on a flyer can improve its readability and overall appearance.

6. **Correct errors and revise the document as necessary.** Post the flyer on a wall and make sure all text and images are legible from a distance. Ask someone else to read the flyer and give you suggestions for improvements.

7. **Determine the best method for distributing the document.** Documents can be distributed on paper or electronically. A flyer should be printed on paper so that it can be posted.

When necessary, more specific details concerning the above guidelines are presented at appropriate points in the chapter. The chapter also will identify the actions performed and decisions made regarding these guidelines during the creation of the flyer shown in Figure 1–1.

For an introduction to Windows 7 and instruction about how to perform basic Windows 7 tasks, read the Office 2010 and Windows 7 chapter at the beginning of this book, where you can learn how to resize windows, change screen resolution, create folders, move and rename files, use Windows Help, and much more.

To Start Word

If you are using a computer to step through the project in this chapter and you want your screens to match the figures in this book, you should change your screen's resolution to 1024 × 768. For information about how to change a computer's resolution, refer to the Office 2010 and Windows 7 chapter at the beginning of this book.

To Use the Mini Toolbar to Format Text

Recall from the Office 2010 and Windows 7 chapter at the beginning automatically appears based on certain tasks you perform, contains comman text in a document. All commands on the Mini toolbar also exist on the Rib

When the Mini toolbar appears, it initially is transparent. If you do n disappears from the screen. The following steps use the Mini toolbar to cha signature line of the flyer.

1
- Move the mouse pointer to the left of the line to be selected (in this case, the signature line) until the mouse pointer changes to a right-pointing block arrow and then click the mouse to select the line (Figure 1–35).

transparent Mini toolbar

• Male, adult cock

• Green and silver

on the tag ¶

mouse pointer is right-pointing block arrow

2
- Move the mouse pointer into the transparent Mini toolbar, so that it changes to a bright toolbar.
- Click the Font Size box arrow on the Mini toolbar to display the Font Size gallery and then point to 28 in the Font Size gallery to display a live preview of the selected font size (Figure 1–36).

selected font size

Font Size box arrow

bright Mini toolbar

selected text shows live preview of font size to which you are pointing in gallery

...n color with patches of white on his chest ¶

...cocker spaniel ¶

...een and silver collar with the name, *Bailey,*

If this is your lost dog, call 555-1029. ¶

Figure 1–36

3
- Click 28 in the Font Size gallery to increase the font size of the selected text.

4
- With the text still selected and the Mini toolbar still displayed, click the Font Color button arrow on the Mini toolbar to display the Font Color gallery and then point to Purple, Accent 4, Darker 50% (eighth color in the sixth row) to display a live preview of the selected font color (Figure 1–37).

Adorable, loving, friendly, well-behaved dog found early Friday morning, June 1, wandering on the bike trail at Fil...mpton Township. ¶

• Tan c...es of white on his chest ¶

• Male...

• Green...ar with the name, *Bailey,*

If this is your lost dog, call 555-1029. ¶

bright Mini toolbar

selected color

selected text shows live preview of font color to which you are pointing in gallery

Font Color button arrow

Figure 1–37

5
- Click Purple, Accent 4, Darker 50% to change the color of the text.
- Click anywhere in the document window to remove the selection from the text.

Q&A boxes offer questions students may have when working through the steps and provide additional information about what they are doing right where they need it.

Experiment Steps within our step-by-step instructions, encourage students to explore, experiment, and take advantage of the features of the Office 2010 user interface. These steps are not necessary to complete the projects, but are designed to increase the confidence with the software and build problem-solving skills.

1
• With the shape still selected, click the More button (shown in Figure 3–6) in the Shape Styles gallery (Drawing Tools Format tab | Shape Styles group) to expand the gallery.

Q&A
What if my shape is no longer selected?
Click the shape to select it.

• Point to Intense Effect - Brown, Accent 4 in the Shape Styles gallery to display a live preview of that style applied to the shape in the document (Figure 3–7).

Experiment
• Point to various styles in the Shape Styles gallery and watch the style of the shape change in the document.

2
• Click Intense Effect - Brown, Accent 4 in the Shape Styles gallery to apply the selected style to the shape.

Figure 3–7

Other Ways

1. Click Format Shape Dialog Box Launcher (Drawing Tools Format tab | Shape Styles group), click Picture Color in left pane
2. Right-click shape, click Format Shape on

(Format Shape dialog box), select desired colors, click Close button

shortcut menu, click Picture Color in left pane (Format Shape dialog box), select desired colors, click Close button

...on name to the shape. The following steps add text to a shape.

Figure 3–8

WD 30   Word Chapter 1   Creating, Formatting, and Editing a Word Document with Pictures

Selecting Text

In many of the previous steps, you have selected text. Table 1–3 summarizes the techniques used to select various items.

Table 1–3 Techniques for Selecting Text

Item to Select	Mouse	Keyboard (where applicable)
Block of text	Click at beginning of selection, scroll to end of selection, position mouse pointer at end of selection, hold down SHIFT key and then click; or drag through the text.	
Character(s)	Drag through character(s).	SHIFT+RIGHT ARROW or SHIFT+LEFT ARROW
Document	Move mouse to left of text until mouse pointer changes to a right-pointing block arrow and then triple-click.	CTRL+A
Graphic	Click the graphic.	
Line	Move mouse to left of line until mouse pointer changes to a right-pointing block arrow and then click.	HOME, then SHIFT+END or END, then SHIFT+HOME
Lines	Move mouse to left of first line until mouse pointer changes to a right-pointing block arrow and then drag up or down.	HOME, then SHIFT+DOWN ARROW or END, then SHIFT+UP AROW
Paragraph	Triple-click paragraph; or move mouse to left of paragraph until mouse pointer changes to a right-pointing block arrow and then double-click.	CTRL+SHIFT+DOWN ARROW or CTRL+SHIFT+UP ARROW
Paragraphs	Move mouse to left of paragraph until mouse pointer changes to a right-pointing block arrow, double-click, and then drag up or down.	CTRL+SHIFT+DOWN ARROW or CTRL+SHIFT+UP ARROW repeatedly
Sentence	Press and hold down CTRL key and then click sentence.	
Word	Double-click the word.	CTRL+SHIFT+RIGHT ARROW or CTRL+SHIFT+LEFT ARROW
Words	Drag through words.	CTRL+SHIFT+RIGHT ARROW or CTRL+SHIFT+LEFT ARROW repeatedly

To Save an Existing Document with the Same File Name

You have made several modifications to the document since you last saved it. Thus, you should save it again. The following step saves the document again. For an example of the step listed below, refer to the Office 2010 and Windows 7 chapter at the beginning of this book.

1 Click the Save button on the Quick Access Toolbar to overwrite the previously saved file.

Break Point: If you wish to take a break, this is a good place to do so. You can quit Word now (refer to page WD 44 for instructions). To resume at a later time, start Word (refer to pages WD 4 and WD 5 for instructions), open the file called Found Dog Flyer (refer to page WD 45 for instructions), and continue following the steps from this location forward.

Inserting and Formatting Pictures in a Word Document

With the text formatted in the flyer, the next step is to insert digital pictures in the flyer and format the pictures. Flyers usually contain graphical images, such as a picture, to attract the attention of passersby. In the following pages, you will perform these tasks:

1. Insert the first digital picture into the flyer and then reduce its size.
2. Insert the second digital picture into the flyer and then reduce its size.
3. Change the look of the first picture and then the second picture.

Break Points identify logical breaks in the chapter if students need to stop before completing the project.

Textbook Walk-Through

Chapter Summary A concluding paragraph, followed by a listing of the tasks completed within a chapter together with the pages on which the step-by-step, screen-by-screen explanations appear.

To Quit Word

The project now is complete. Thus, the following steps quit Word. For an example of the step listed below, refer to the Office 2010 and Windows 7 chapter at the beginning of this book.

1 If you have one Word document open, click the Close button on the right side of the title bar to close the document and quit Word; or if you have multiple Word documents open, click File on the Ribbon to open the Backstage view and then click Exit in the Backstage view to close all open documents and quit Word.

2 If a Microsoft Word dialog box appears, click the Save button to save any changes made to the document since the last save.

BTW

Printed Borders
If one or more of your borders do not print, click the Page Borders button (Page Layout tab | Page Background group), click the Options button (Borders and Shading dialog box), click the Measure from box arrow and click Text, change the four text boxes to 15 pt, and then click the OK button in each dialog box. Try printing the document again. If the borders still do not print, adjust the text boxes in the dialog box to a number smaller than 15 point.

Chapter Summary

In this chapter, you have learned how to enter text in a document, format text, insert a picture, format a picture, add a page border, and print a document. The items listed below include all the new Word skills you have learned in this chapter.

1. Start Word (WD 4)
2. Type Text (WD 6)
3. Display Formatting Marks (WD 7)
4. Insert a Blank Line (WD 7)
5. Wordwrap Text as You Type (WD 8)
6. Check Spelling and Grammar as You Type (WD 9)
7. Save a Document (WD 12)
8. Center a Paragraph (WD 14)
9. Select a Line (WD 15)
10. Change the Font Size of Selected Text (WD 16)
11. Change the Font of Selected Text (WD 17)
12. Change the Case of Selected Text (WD 18)
13. Apply a Text Effect to Selected Text (WD 19)
23. Bold Text (WD 28)
24. Change Theme Colors (WD 28)
25. Save an Existing Document with the Same File Name (WD 30)
26. Insert a Picture (WD 31)
27. Zoom the Document (WD 33)
28. Resize a Graphic (WD 34)
29. Resize a Graphic by Entering Exact Measurements (WD 36)
30. Apply a Picture Style (WD 37)
31. Apply Picture Effects (WD 38)
32. View One Page (WD 40)
33. Add a Page Border (WD 41)
34. Change Spacing before and after a Paragraph (WD 44)
35. Quit Word (WD 44)
36. Open a Document from Word (WD 45)
37. Insert Text in an Existing Document (WD 46)
38. Delete Text (WD 47)
39. Move Text (WD 47)
40. Change Document Properties (WD 49)
41. Print a Document (WD 51)

profile, your instructor may have assigned an autogradable so, log into the SAM 2010 Web site at www.cengage.com/sam2010 and start files.

BTW

Quick Reference
For a table that lists how to complete the tasks covered in this book using the mouse, Ribbon, shortcut menu, and keyboard, see the Quick Reference Summary at the back of this book, or visit the Word 2010 Quick Reference Web page (scsite.com/wd2010/qr).

STUDENT ASSIGNMENTS

Learn It Online

Test your knowledge of chapter content and key terms.

Instructions: To complete the Learn It Online exercises, start your browser, click the Address bar, and then enter the Web address **scsite.com/wd2010/learn**. When the Word 2010 Learn It Online page is displayed, click the link for the exercise you want to complete and then read the instructions.

Chapter Reinforcement TF, MC, and SA
A series of true/false, multiple choice, and short answer questions that test your knowledge of the chapter content.

Flash Cards
An interactive learning environment where you identify chapter key terms associated with displayed definitions.

Practice Test
A series of multiple choice questions that test your knowledge of chapter content and key terms.

Who Wants To Be a Computer Genius?
An interactive game that challenges your knowledge of chapter content in the style of a television quiz show.

Wheel of Terms
An interactive game that challenges your knowledge of chapter key terms in the style of the television show *Wheel of Fortune*.

Crossword Puzzle Challenge
A crossword puzzle that challenges your knowledge of key terms presented in the chapter.

Apply Your Knowledge

Reinforce the skills and apply the concepts you learned in this chapter.

Modifying Text and Formatting a Document
Note: To complete this assignment, you will be required to use the Data Files for Students. See the inside back cover of this book for instructions on downloading the Data Files for Students, or contact your instructor for information about accessing the required files.

Instructions: Start Word. Open the document, Apply 1-1 Buffalo Photo Shoot Flyer Unformatted, from the Data Files for Students. The document you open is an unformatted flyer. You are to modify text, format paragraphs and characters, and insert a picture in the flyer.

Perform the following tasks:
1. Delete the word, single, in the sentence of body copy below the headline.
2. Insert the word, Creeks, between the words, Twin Buffalo, in the sentence of body copy below the headline.
3. At the end of the signature line, change the period to an exclamation point.
4. Center the headline and the signature line.
5. Change the theme colors to the Aspect color scheme.
6. Change the font and font size of the headline to 48-point Impact, or a similar font. Change the case of the headline text to all capital letters. Apply the text effect called Gradient Fill – Orange, Accent 1, Outline – White to the headline.
7. Change the font size of body copy between the headline and the signature line to 20 point.
8. Use the Mini toolbar to change the font size of the signature line to 26 point.
9. Select the words, hundreds of buffalo, in the paragraph below the headline and underline them.

Learn It Online Every chapter features a Learn It Online section that is comprised of six exercises. These exercises include True/False, Multiple Choice, Short Answer, Flash Cards, Practice Test, and Learning Games.

Apply Your Knowledge This exercise usually requires students to open and manipulate a file from the Data Files that parallels the activities learned in the chapter. To obtain a copy of the Data Files for Students, follow the instructions on the inside back cover of this text.

Extend Your Knowledge

Extend the skills you learned in this chapter and experiment with new skills. You may need to use Help to complete the assignment.

Modifying Text and Picture Formats and Adding Page Borders

Note: To complete this assignment, you will be required to use the Data Files for Students. See the inside back cover of this book for instructions on downloading the Data Files for Students, or contact your instructor for information about accessing the required files.

Instructions: Start Word. Open the document, Extend 1-1 TVC Cruises Flyer, from the Data Files for Students. You will enhance the look of the flyer shown in Figure 1–76. *Hint:* Remember, if you make a mistake while formatting the picture, you can reset it by clicking the Reset Picture button or Reset Picture button arrow (Picture Tools Format tab | Adjust group).

Perform the following tasks:
1. Use Help to learn about the following formats: remove bullets, grow font, shrink font, art page borders, decorative underline(s), picture bullets, picture border shading, shadow picture effects, and color saturation and tone.
2. Remove the bullet from the paragraph below the picture.

3. Select the text, 10 percent, and use the Grow Font button to increase its font size.
4. Add an art page border to the flyer. If the border is not in color, add color to it.
5. Change the solid underline below the word, cruises, to a decorative underline. Change

change border color and add shadow effect; change color saturation and color tone

add art page border

remove bullet

use Grow Font button to increase font size

change to picture bullets

Figure 1–76

Make It Right

Analyze a document and correct all errors and/or improve the design.

Correcting Spelling and Grammar Errors

Note: To complete this assignment, you will be required to use the Data Files for Students. See the inside back cover of this book for instructions on downloading the Data Files for Students, or contact your instructor for information about accessing the required files.

Instructions: Start Word. Open the document, Make It Right 1-1 Karate Academy Flyer Unchecked, from the Data Files for Students. The document is a flyer that contains spelling and grammar errors, as shown in Figure 1–77. You are to correct each spelling (red wavy underline) and grammar error (green and blue wavy underlines) by right-clicking the flagged text and then clicking the appropriate correction on the shortcut menu.

If your screen does not display the wavy underlines, click File on the Ribbon and then click Options in the Backstage view. When the Word Options dialog box is displayed, click Proofing in the left pane, be sure the 'Hide spelling errors in this document only' and 'Hide grammar errors in this document only' check boxes do not contain check marks, and then click the OK button. If your screen still does not display the wavy underlines, redisplay the Word Options dialog box, click Proofing, and then click the Recheck Document button.

Change the document properties, including keywords, as specified by your instructor. Save the revised document with the name, Make It Right 1-1 Karate Academy Flyer, and then submit it in the format specified by your instructor.

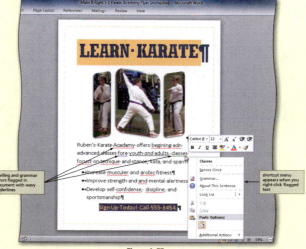

spelling and grammar errors flagged in document with wavy underlines

shortcut menu appears when you right-click flagged text

Figure 1–77

Textbook Walk-Through

In the Lab

Design and/or create a document using the guidelines, concepts, and skills presented in this chapter. Labs are listed in order of increasing difficulty.

Lab 1: Creating a Flyer with a Picture

Problem: As a part-time employee in the Student Services Center at school, you have been asked to prepare a flyer that advertises study habits classes. First, you prepare the unformatted flyer shown in Figure 1–78a, and then you format it so that it looks like Figure 1–78b. *Hint:* Remember, if you make a mistake while formatting the flyer, you can click the Undo button on the Quick Access Toolbar to undo your last action.

Note: To complete this assignment, you will be required to use the Data Files for Students. See the inside back cover of this book for instructions on downloading the Data Files for Students, or contact your instructor for information about accessing the required files.

Instructions: Perform the following tasks:
1. Start Word. Display formatting marks on the screen.
2. Type the flyer text, unformatted, as shown in Figure 1–78a, inserting a blank line between the headline and the body copy. If Word flags any misspelled words as you type, check their spelling and correct them.
3. Save the document using the file name, Lab 1-1 Study Habits Flyer.
4. Center the headline and the signature line.
5. Change the theme colors to Concourse.
6. Change the font size of the headline to 36 point and the font to Ravie, or a similar font. Apply the text effect called Gradient Fill – Dark Red, Accent 6, Inner Shadow.
7. Change the font size of body copy between the headline and the signature line to 20 point.
8. Change the font size of the signature line to 22 point. Bold the text in the signature line.

Studying All Night?

| blank line |

Let us help you! Our expert instructors teach effective stud
energy-building techniques.

Classes are $15.00 per session

Sessions last four weeks

Classes meet in the Student Services Center twice a week

Call 555-2838 or stop by to sign up today!

Figure 1–78 (a) Unforma

In the Lab Three all new in-depth assignments per chapter require students to utilize the chapter concepts and techniques to solve problems on a computer.

create a building block for Fair Grove Elementary School and insert the building block whenever you have to enter the school name. Resize table columns to fit contents. Check the spelling of the letter. Change the document properties, as specified by your instructor. Save the letter with Lab 3-3 Education Board Letter as the file name.

Cases and Places

Apply your creative thinking and problem solving skills to design and implement a solution.

Note: To complete these assignments, you may be required to use the Data Files for Students. See the inside back cover of this book for instructions on downloading the Data Files for Students, or contact your instructor for information about accessing the required files.

1: Create a Letter to a Potential Employer

Academic
As a student about to graduate, you are actively seeking employment in your field and have located an advertisement for a job in which you are interested. You decide to write a letter to the potential employer: Ms. Janice Tremont at Home Health Associates, 554 Mountain View Lane, Blue Dust, MO 64319.

The draft wording for the letter is as follows: I am responding to your advertisement for the nursing position in the *Blue Dust Press*. I have tailored my activities and education for a career in geriatric medicine. This month, I will graduate with concentrations in Geriatric Medicine (24 hours), Osteopathic Medicine (12 hours), and Holistic Nursing (9 hours). In addition to receiving my bachelor degree in nursing, I have enhanced my education by participating in the following activities: volunteered at Blue Dust's free health care clinic; attended several continuing education and career-specific seminars, including An Aging Populace, Care of the Homebound, and Special Needs of the Elderly; completed one-semester internship at Blue Dust Community Hospital in spring semester of 2012; completed Certified Nursing Assistant (CNA) program at Blue Dust Community College; and worked as nurse's aide for two years during college. I look forward to an interview so that we can discuss the position you offer and my qualifications. With my background and education, I am confident that I will make a positive contribution to Home Health Associates.

The letter should contain a letterhead that uses a shape and clip art, a table (use a table to present the areas of concentration), and a bulleted list (use a bulleted list to present the activities). Insert nonbreaking spaces in the newspaper name. Use the concepts and techniques presented in this chapter to create and format a letter according to the modified block style, creating appropriate paragraph breaks and rewording the draft as necessary. Use your personal information for contact information in the letter. Be sure to check the spelling and grammar of the finished letter. Submit your assignment in the format specified by your instructor.

2: Create a Letter Requesting Donations

Personal
As an alumnus of your historic high school, you are concerned that the building is being considered for demolition. You decide to write a letter to another graduate: Mr. Jim Lemon, 87 Travis Parkway, Vigil, CT 06802.

The draft wording for the letter is as follows: As a member of the class of 1988, you, like many others, probably have many fond memories of our alma mater, Vigil East High School. I recently learned that the building is being considered for demolition because of its age and structural integrity.

Continued >

Cases & Places exercises call on students to create open-ended projects that reflect academic, personal, and business settings.

Office 2010 and Windows 7: Essential Concepts and Skills

Objectives

You will have mastered the material in this chapter when you can:

- Perform basic mouse operations
- Start Windows and log on to the computer
- Identify the objects on the Windows 7 desktop
- Identify the programs in and versions of Microsoft Office
- Start a program
- Identify the components of the Microsoft Office Ribbon

- Create folders
- Save files
- Change screen resolution
- Perform basic tasks in Microsoft Office programs
- Manage files
- Use Microsoft Office Help and Windows Help

Office 2010 and Windows 7: Essential Concepts and Skills

Office 2010 and Windows 7

This introductory chapter covers features and functions common to Office 2010 programs, as well as the basics of Windows 7.

Overview

As you read this chapter, you will learn how to perform basic tasks in Windows and Office programs by performing these general activities:

- Start programs using Windows.
- Use features common across Office programs.
- Organize files and folders.
- Change screen resolution.
- Quit Office programs.

Introduction to the Windows 7 Operating System

Windows 7 is the newest version of Microsoft Windows, which is the most popular and widely used operating system. An **operating system** is a computer program (set of computer instructions) that coordinates all the activities of computer hardware such as memory, storage devices, and printers, and provides the capability for you to communicate with the computer.

The Windows 7 operating system simplifies the process of working with documents and programs by organizing the manner in which you interact with the computer. Windows 7 is used to run **application software**, which consists of programs designed to make users more productive and/or assist them with personal tasks, such as word processing.

Windows 7 has two interface variations, Windows 7 Basic and Windows 7 Aero. Computers with up to 1 GB of RAM display the Windows 7 Basic interface (Figure 1a). Computers with more than 1 GB of RAM also can display the Windows Aero interface (Figure 1b), which provides an enhanced visual appearance. The Windows 7 Professional, Windows 7 Enterprise, Windows 7 Home Premium, and Windows 7 Ultimate editions have the capability to use Windows Aero.

Using a Mouse

Windows users work with a mouse that has at least two buttons. For a right-handed user, the left button usually is the primary mouse button, and the right mouse button is the secondary mouse button. Left-handed people, however, can reverse the function of these buttons.

Figure 1 (a) Windows 7 Basic interface

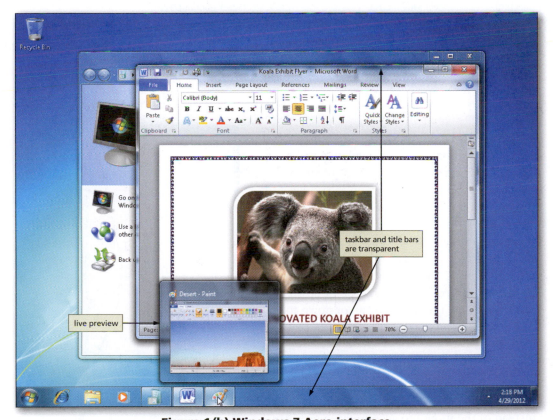

Figure 1 (b) Windows 7 Aero interface

Table 1 explains how to perform a variety of mouse operations. Some programs also use keys in combination with the mouse to perform certain actions. For example, when you hold down the CTRL key while rolling the mouse wheel, text on the screen becomes larger or smaller based on the direction you roll the wheel. The function of the mouse buttons and the wheel varies depending on the program.

Table 1 Mouse Operations		
Operation	**Mouse Action**	**Example***
Point	Move the mouse until the pointer on the desktop is positioned on the item of choice.	Position the pointer on the screen.
Click	Press and release the primary mouse button, which usually is the left mouse button.	Select or deselect items on the screen or start a program or program feature.
Right-click	Press and release the secondary mouse button, which usually is the right mouse button.	Display a shortcut menu.
Double-click	Quickly press and release the left mouse button twice without moving the mouse.	Start a program or program feature.
Triple-click	Quickly press and release the left mouse button three times without moving the mouse.	Select a paragraph.
Drag	Point to an item, hold down the left mouse button, move the item to the desired location on the screen, and then release the left mouse button.	Move an object from one location to another or draw pictures.
Right-drag	Point to an item, hold down the right mouse button, move the item to the desired location on the screen, and then release the right mouse button.	Display a shortcut menu after moving an object from one location to another.
Rotate wheel	Roll the wheel forward or backward.	Scroll vertically (up and down).
Free-spin wheel	Whirl the wheel forward or backward so that it spins freely on its own.	Scroll through many pages in seconds.
Press wheel	Press the wheel button while moving the mouse.	Scroll continuously.
Tilt wheel	Press the wheel toward the right or left.	Scroll horizontally (left and right).
Press thumb button	Press the button on the side of the mouse with your thumb.	Move forward or backward through Web pages and/or control media, games, etc.

*Note: the examples presented in this column are discussed as they are demonstrated in this chapter.

BTW

Minimize Wrist Injury
Computer users frequently switch between the keyboard and the mouse during a word processing session; such switching strains the wrist. To help prevent wrist injury, minimize switching. For instance, if your fingers already are on the keyboard, use keyboard keys to scroll. If your hand already is on the mouse, use the mouse to scroll.

Scrolling

A **scroll bar** is a horizontal or vertical bar that appears when the contents of an area may not be visible completely on the screen (Figure 2). A scroll bar contains **scroll arrows** and a **scroll box** that enable you to view areas that currently cannot be seen. Clicking the up and down scroll arrows moves the screen content up or down one line. You also can click above or below the scroll box to move up or down a section, or drag the scroll box up or down to move up or down to move to a specific location.

Shortcut Keys

In many cases, you can use the keyboard instead of the mouse to accomplish a task. To perform tasks using the keyboard, you press one or more keyboard keys, sometimes identified as

Figure 2

a **shortcut key** or **keyboard shortcut**. Some shortcut keys consist of a single key, such as the F1 key. For example, to obtain help about Windows 7, you can press the F1 key. Other shortcut keys consist of multiple keys, in which case a plus sign separates the key names, such as CTRL+ESC. This notation means to press and hold down the first key listed, press one or more additional keys, and then release all keys. For example, to display the Start menu, press CTRL+ESC, that is, hold down the CTRL key, press the ESC key, and then release both keys.

Starting Windows 7

It is not unusual for multiple people to use the same computer in a work, educational, recreational, or home setting. Windows 7 enables each user to establish a **user account**, which identifies to Windows 7 the resources, such as programs and storage locations, a user can access when working with a computer.

Each user account has a user name and may have a password and an icon, as well. A **user name** is a unique combination of letters or numbers that identifies a specific user to Windows 7. A **password** is a private combination of letters, numbers, and special characters associated with the user name that allows access to a user's account resources. A **user icon** is a picture associated with a user name.

When you turn on a computer, an introductory screen consisting of the Windows logo and copyright messages is displayed. The Windows logo is animated and glows as the Windows 7 operating system is loaded. After the Windows logo appears, depending on your computer's settings, you may or may not be required to log on to the computer. **Logging on** to a computer opens your user account and makes the computer available for use. If you are required to log on to the computer, the **Welcome screen** is displayed, which shows the user names of users on the computer (Figure 3). Clicking the user name or picture begins the process of logging on to the computer.

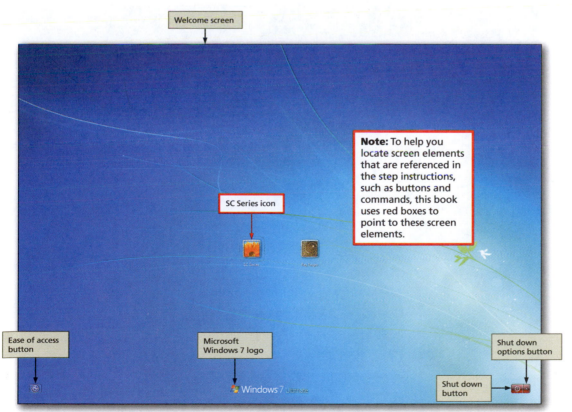

Figure 3

At the bottom of the Welcome screen is the 'Ease of access' button, Windows 7 logo, a Shut down button, and a 'Shut down options' button. The following list identifies the functions of the buttons and commands that typically appear on the Welcome screen:

- Clicking the 'Ease of access' button displays the Ease of Access Center, which provides tools to optimize your computer to accommodate the needs of the mobility, hearing, and vision impaired users.
- Clicking the Shut down button shuts down Windows 7 and the computer.
- Clicking the 'Shut down options' button, located to the right of the Shut down button, provides access to a menu containing commands that perform actions such as restarting the computer, putting the computer in a low-powered state, and shutting down the computer. The commands available on your computer may differ.
  - The **Restart command** closes open programs, shuts down Windows 7, and then restarts Windows 7 and displays the Welcome screen.
  - The **Sleep command** waits for Windows 7 to save your work and then turns off the computer fans and hard disk. To wake the computer from the Sleep state, press the power button or lift a notebook computer's cover, and log on to the computer.
  - The **Shut down command** shuts down and turns off the computer.

To Log On to the Computer

After starting Windows 7, you might need to log on to the computer. The following steps log on to the computer based on a typical installation. You may need to ask your instructor how to log on to your computer. This set of steps uses SC Series as the user name. The list of user names on your computer will be different.

- Click the user icon (SC Series, in this case) on the Welcome screen (shown in Figure 3 on the previous page); depending on settings, this either will display a password text box (Figure 4) or will log on to the computer and display the Windows 7 desktop.

Q&A Why do I not see a user icon?

Your computer may require you to type a user name instead of clicking an icon.

Q&A What is a text box?

A text box is a rectangular box in which you type text.

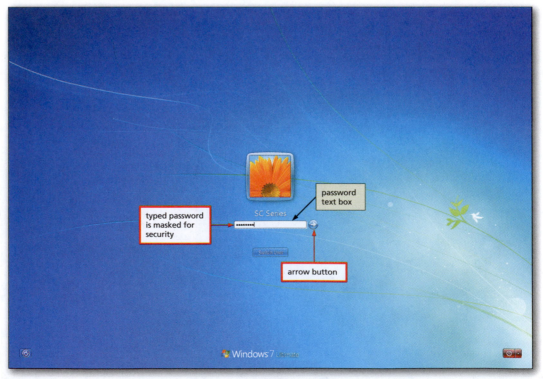

Figure 4

Q&A Why does my screen not show a password text box?

Your account does not require a password.

2

• If Windows 7 displays a password text box, type your password in the text box and then click the arrow button to log on to the computer and display the Windows 7 desktop (Figure 5).

Q&A

Why does my desktop look different from the one in Figure 5?

The Windows 7 desktop is customizable, and your school or employer may have modified the desktop to meet its needs. Also, your screen resolution, which affects the size of the elements on the screen, may differ from the screen resolution used in this book. Later in this chapter, you learn how to change screen resolution.

Figure 5

The Windows 7 Desktop

The Windows 7 desktop (Figure 5) and the objects on the desktop emulate a work area in an office. Think of the Windows desktop as an electronic version of the top of your desk. You can perform tasks such as placing objects on the desktop, moving the objects around the desktop, and removing items from the desktop.

When you start a program in Windows 7, it appears on the desktop. Some icons also may be displayed on the desktop. For instance, the icon for the **Recycle Bin**, the location of files that have been deleted, appears on the desktop by default. A **file** is a named unit of storage. Files can contain text, images, audio, and video. You can customize your desktop so that icons representing programs and files you use often appear on your desktop.

Introduction to Microsoft Office 2010

Microsoft Office 2010 is the newest version of Microsoft Office, offering features that provide users with better functionality and easier ways to work with the various files they create. These features include enhanced design tools, such as improved picture formatting tools and new themes, shared notebooks for working in groups, mobile versions of Office programs, broadcast presentation for the Web, and a digital notebook for managing and sharing multimedia information.

Microsoft Office 2010 Programs

Microsoft Office 2010 includes a wide variety of programs such as Word, PowerPoint, Excel, Access, Outlook, Publisher, OneNote, InfoPath, SharePoint Workspace, Communicator, and Web Apps:

- **Microsoft Word 2010**, or Word, is a full-featured word processing program that allows you to create professional-looking documents and revise them easily.
- **Microsoft PowerPoint 2010**, or PowerPoint, is a complete presentation program that allows you to produce professional-looking presentations.
- **Microsoft Excel 2010**, or Excel, is a powerful spreadsheet program that allows you to organize data, complete calculations, make decisions, graph data, develop professional-looking reports, publish organized data to the Web, and access real-time data from Web sites.
- **Microsoft Access 2010**, or Access, is a database management system that allows you to create a database; add, change, and delete data in the database; ask questions concerning the data in the database; and create forms and reports using the data in the database.
- **Microsoft Outlook 2010**, or Outlook, is a communications and scheduling program that allows you to manage e-mail accounts, calendars, contacts, and access to other Internet content.
- **Microsoft Publisher 2010**, or Publisher, is a desktop publishing program that helps you create professional-quality publications and marketing materials that can be shared easily.
- **Microsoft OneNote 2010**, or OneNote, is a note taking program that allows you to store and share information in notebooks with other people.
- **Microsoft InfoPath 2010**, or InfoPath, is a form development program that helps you create forms for use on the Web and gather data from these forms.
- **Microsoft SharePoint Workspace 2010**, or SharePoint, is collaboration software that allows you access and revise files stored on your computer from other locations.
- **Microsoft Communicator** is communications software that allows you to use different modes of communications such as instant messaging, video conferencing, and sharing files and programs.
- **Microsoft Web Apps** is a Web application that allows you to edit and share files on the Web using the familiar Office interface.

Microsoft Office 2010 Suites

A **suite** is a collection of individual programs available together as a unit. Microsoft offers a variety of Office suites. Table 2 lists the Office 2010 suites and their components.

Programs in a suite, such as Microsoft Office, typically use a similar interface and share features. In addition, Microsoft Office programs use **common dialog boxes** for performing actions such as opening and saving files. Once you are comfortable working with these elements and this interface and performing tasks in one program, the similarity can help you apply the knowledge and skills you have learned to another Office program(s). For example, the process for saving a file in Word is the same in PowerPoint, Excel, and the other Office programs. While briefly showing how to use several Office programs, this chapter illustrates some of the common functions across the programs and also identifies the characteristics unique to these programs.

Table 2 Microsoft Office 2010 Suites

	Microsoft Office Professional Plus 2010	Microsoft Office Professional 2010	Microsoft Office Home and Business 2010	Microsoft Office Standard 2010	Microsoft Office Home and Student 2010
Microsoft Word 2010	✔	✔	✔	✔	✔
Microsoft PowerPoint 2010	✔	✔	✔	✔	✔
Microsoft Excel 2010	✔	✔	✔	✔	✔
Microsoft Access 2010	✔	✔	✘	✘	✘
Microsoft Outlook 2010	✔	✔	✔	✔	✘
Microsoft Publisher 2010	✔	✔	✘	✔	✘
Microsoft OneNote 2010	✔	✔	✔	✔	✔
Microsoft InfoPath 2010	✔	✘	✘	✘	✘
Microsoft SharePoint Workspace 2010	✔	✘	✘	✘	✘
Microsoft Communicator	✔	✘	✘	✘	✘

Starting and Using a Program

To use a program, you must instruct the operating system to start the program. Windows 7 provides many different ways to start a program, one of which is presented in this section (other ways to start a program are presented throughout this chapter). After starting a program, you can use it to perform a variety of tasks. The following pages use Word to discuss some elements of the Office interface and to perform tasks that are common to other Office programs.

Word

Word is a full-featured word processing program that allows you to create many types of personal and business documents, including flyers, letters, memos, resumes, reports, fax cover sheets, mailing labels, and newsletters. Word also provides tools that enable you to create Web pages and save these Web pages directly on a Web server. Word has many features designed to simplify the production of documents and add visual appeal. Using Word, you easily can change the shape, size, and color of text. You also can include borders, shading, tables, images, pictures, charts, and Web addresses in documents.

To Start a Program Using the Start Menu

Across the bottom of the Windows 7 desktop is the taskbar. The taskbar contains the **Start button**, which you use to access programs, files, folders, and settings on a computer. A **folder** is a named location on a storage medium that usually contains related documents. The taskbar also displays a button for each program currently running on a computer.

Clicking the Start button displays the Start menu. The **Start menu** allows you to access programs, folders, and files on the computer and contains commands that allow you to start programs, store and search for documents, customize the computer, and obtain help about thousands of topics. A **menu** is a list of related items, including folders, programs, and commands. Each **command** on a menu performs a specific action, such as saving a file or obtaining help.

The following steps, which assume Windows 7 is running, use the Start menu to start an Office program based on a typical installation. You may need to ask your instructor how to start Office programs for your computer. Although the steps illustrate starting the Word program, the steps to start any Office program are similar.

1

- Click the Start button on the Windows 7 taskbar to display the Start menu (Figure 6).

Q&A Why does my Start menu look different?

It may look different depending on your computer's configuration. The Start menu may be customized for several reasons, such as usage requirements or security restrictions.

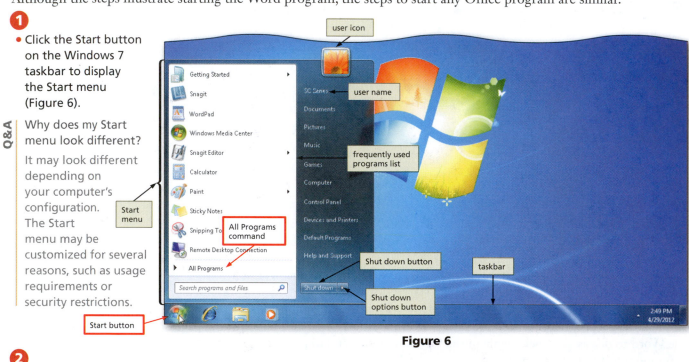

Figure 6

2

- Click All Programs at the bottom of the left pane on the Start menu to display the All Programs list (Figure 7).

Q&A What is a pane?

A **pane** is an area of a window that displays related content. For example, the left pane on the Start menu contains a list of frequently used programs, as well as the All Programs command.

Q&A Why might my All Programs list look different?

Most likely, the programs installed on your computer will differ from those shown in Figure 7. Your All Programs list will show the programs that are installed on your computer.

Figure 7

3

- If the program you wish to start is located in a folder, click or scroll to and then click the folder (Microsoft Office, in this case) in the All Programs list to display a list of the folder's contents (Figure 8).

Q&A

Why is the Microsoft Office folder on my computer?

During installation of Microsoft Office 2010, the Microsoft Office folder was added to the All Programs list.

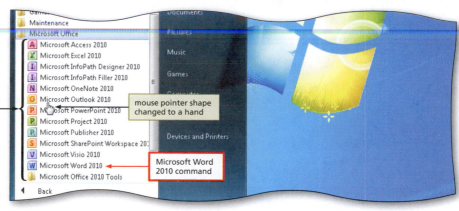

Microsoft Office list

mouse pointer shape changed to a hand

Microsoft Word 2010 command

Figure 8

4

- Click, or scroll to and then click, the program name (Microsoft Word 2010, in this case) in the list to start the selected program (Figure 9).

Q&A

What happens when you start a program?

Many programs initially display a blank document in a program window, as shown in the Word window in Figure 9; others provide a means for you to create a blank document. A **window** is a rectangular area that displays data and information. The top of a window has a **title bar**, which is a horizontal space that contains the window's name.

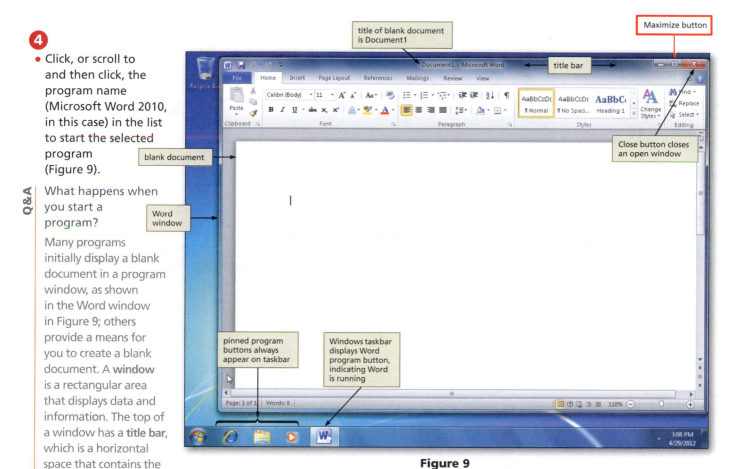

title of blank document is Document1

Maximize button

title bar

Close button closes an open window

blank document

Word window

pinned program buttons always appear on taskbar

Windows taskbar displays Word program button, indicating Word is running

Figure 9

Q&A

Why is my program window a different size?

The Word window shown in Figure 9 is not maximized. Your Word window already may be maximized. The next steps maximize a window.

Other Ways	
1. Double-click program icon on desktop, if one is present	3. Display Start menu, type program name in search box, click program name
2. Click program name in left pane of Start menu, if present	4. Double-click file created using program you want to start

To Maximize a Window

Sometimes content is not visible completely in a window. One method of displaying the entire contents of a window is to **maximize** it, or enlarge the window so that it fills the entire screen. The following step maximizes the Word window; however, any Office program's window can be maximized using this step.

- If the program window is not maximized already, click the Maximize button (shown in Figure 9 on the previous page) next to the Close button on the window's title bar (the Word window title bar, in this case) to maximize the window (Figure 10).

Q&A What happened to the Maximize button?

It changed to a Restore Down button, which you can use to return a window to its size and location before you maximized it.

Q&A How do I know whether a window is maximized?

A window is maximized if it fills the entire display area and the Restore Down button is displayed on the title bar.

Figure 10

Other Ways

1. Double-click title bar
2. Drag title bar to top of screen

The Word Document Window, Ribbon, and Elements Common to Office Programs

The Word window consists of a variety of components to make your work more efficient and documents more professional. These include the document window, Ribbon, Mini toolbar, shortcut menus, and Quick Access Toolbar. Most of these components are common to other Microsoft Office 2010 programs; others are unique to Word.

You view a portion of a document on the screen through a **document window** (Figure 11). The default (preset) view is **Print Layout view**, which shows the document on a mock sheet of paper in the document window.

Scroll Bars You use a scroll bar to display different portions of a document in the document window. At the right edge of the document window is a vertical scroll bar. If a document is too wide to fit in the document window, a horizontal scroll bar also appears at the bottom of the document window. On a scroll bar, the position of the scroll box reflects the location of the portion of the document that is displayed in the document window.

Figure 11

Status Bar The **status bar**, located at the bottom of the document window above the Windows 7 taskbar, presents information about the document, the progress of current tasks, and the status of certain commands and keys; it also provides controls for viewing the document. As you type text or perform certain tasks, various indicators and buttons may appear on the status bar.

The left side of the status bar in Figure 11 shows the current page followed by the total number of pages in the document, the number of words in the document, and an icon to check spelling and grammar. The right side of the status bar includes buttons and controls you can use to change the view of a document and adjust the size of the displayed document.

Ribbon   The Ribbon, located near the top of the window below the title bar, is the control center in Word and other Office programs (Figure 12). The Ribbon provides easy, central access to the tasks you perform while creating a document. The Ribbon consists of tabs, groups, and commands. Each **tab** contains a collection of groups, and each **group** contains related functions. When you start an Office program, such as Word, it initially displays several main tabs, also called default tabs. All Office programs have a **Home tab**, which contains the more frequently used commands.

In addition to the main tabs, Office programs display **tool tabs**, also called contextual tabs (Figure 13), when you perform certain tasks or work with objects such as pictures or tables. If you insert a picture in a Word document, for example, the Picture Tools tab and its related subordinate Format tab appear, collectively referred to as the Picture Tools Format tab. When you are finished working with the picture, the Picture Tools Format tab disappears from the Ribbon. Word and other Office programs determine when tool tabs should appear and disappear based on tasks you perform. Some tool tabs, such as the Table Tools tab, have more than one related subordinate tab.

Items on the Ribbon include buttons, boxes (text boxes, check boxes, etc.), and galleries (Figure 12). A **gallery** is a set of choices, often graphical, arranged in a grid or in a list. You can scroll through choices in an in-Ribbon gallery by clicking the gallery's scroll arrows. Or, you can click a gallery's More button to view more gallery options on the screen at a time.

Figure 12

Some buttons and boxes have arrows that, when clicked, also display a gallery; others always cause a gallery to be displayed when clicked. Most galleries support **live preview**, which is a feature that allows you to point to a gallery choice and see its effect in the document — without actually selecting the choice (Figure 13).

Figure 13

Some commands on the Ribbon display an image to help you remember their function. When you point to a command on the Ribbon, all or part of the command glows in shades of yellow and orange, and an Enhanced ScreenTip appears on the screen. An **Enhanced ScreenTip** is an on-screen note that provides the name of the command, available keyboard shortcut(s), a description of the command, and sometimes instructions for how to obtain help about the command (Figure 14). Enhanced ScreenTips are more detailed than a typical ScreenTip, which usually displays only the name of the command.

Some groups on the Ribbon have a small arrow in the lower-right corner, called a **Dialog Box Launcher**, that when clicked, displays a dialog box or a task pane with additional options for the group (Figure 15). When presented with a dialog box, you make selections and must close the dialog box before returning to the document. A **task pane**, in contrast to a dialog box, is a window that can remain open and visible while you work in the document.

Figure 14

Mini Toolbar   The **Mini toolbar**, which appears automatically based on tasks you perform, contains commands related to changing the appearance of text in a document. All commands on the Mini toolbar also exist on the Ribbon. The purpose of the Mini toolbar is to minimize mouse movement.

When the Mini toolbar appears, it initially is transparent (Figure 16a). If you do not use the transparent Mini toolbar, it disappears from the screen. To use the Mini toolbar, move the mouse pointer into the toolbar, which causes the Mini toolbar to change

Figure 15

from a transparent to bright appearance (Figure 16b). If you right-click an item in the document window, Word displays both the Mini toolbar and a shortcut menu, which is discussed in a later section in this chapter.

(a) transparent Mini toolbar

(b) bright Mini toolbar

Figure 16

Quick Access Toolbar   The **Quick Access Toolbar**, located initially (by default) above the Ribbon at the left edge of the title bar, provides convenient, one-click access to frequently used commands (Figure 14 on the previous page). The commands on the Quick Access Toolbar always are available, regardless of the task you are performing. The Quick Access Toolbar is discussed in more depth later in the chapter.

KeyTips   If you prefer using the keyboard instead of the mouse, you can press the ALT key on the keyboard to display **KeyTips**, or keyboard code icons, for certain commands (Figure 17). To select a command using the keyboard, press the letter or number displayed in the KeyTip, which may cause additional KeyTips related to the selected command to appear. To remove KeyTips from the screen, press the ALT key or the ESC key until all KeyTips disappear, or click the mouse anywhere in the program window.

Figure 17

To Display a Different Tab on the Ribbon

When you start Word, the Ribbon displays eight main tabs: File, Home, Insert, Page Layout, References, Mailings, Review, and View. The tab currently displayed is called the **active tab**.

The following step displays the Insert tab, that is, makes it the active tab.

1

• Click Insert on the Ribbon to display the Insert tab (Figure 18).

 Experiment

• Click the other tabs on the Ribbon to view their contents. When you are finished, click the Insert tab to redisplay the Insert tab.

Q&A
If I am working in a different Office program, such as PowerPoint or Access, how do I display a different tab on the Ribbon?

Follow this same procedure; that is, click the desired tab on the Ribbon.

Figure 18

To Minimize, Display, and Restore the Ribbon

To display more of a document or other item in the window of an Office program, some users prefer to minimize the Ribbon, which hides the groups on the Ribbon and displays only the main tabs. Each time you start an Office program, the Ribbon appears the same way it did the last time you used that Office program. The chapters in this book, however, begin with the Ribbon appearing as it did at the initial installation of the software.

The following steps minimize, display, and restore the Ribbon in an Office program.

- Click the Minimize the Ribbon button on the Ribbon (shown in Figure 18) to minimize the Ribbon (Figure 19).

Q&A
What happened to the groups on the Ribbon?

When you minimize the Ribbon, the groups disappear so that the Ribbon does not take up as much space on the screen.

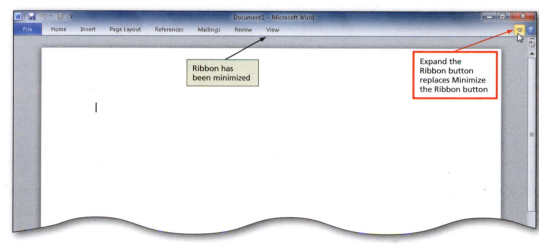

Figure 19

Q&A
What happened to the Minimize the Ribbon button?

The Expand the Ribbon button replaces the Minimize the Ribbon button when the Ribbon is minimized.

- Click Home on the Ribbon to display the Home tab (Figure 20).

Q&A
Why would I click the Home tab?

If you want to use a command on a minimized Ribbon, click the main tab to display the groups for that tab. After you select a command on the Ribbon, the groups will be hidden once again. If you decide not to use a command on the Ribbon, you can hide the groups by clicking the same main tab or clicking in the program window.

Figure 20

- Click Home on the Ribbon to hide the groups again (shown in Figure 19).
- Click the Expand the Ribbon button on the Ribbon (shown in Figure 19) to restore the Ribbon.

Other Ways
1. Double-click Home on the Ribbon
2. Press CTRL+F1

To Display and Use a Shortcut Menu

When you right-click certain areas of the Word and other program windows, a shortcut menu will appear. A **shortcut menu** is a list of frequently used commands that relate to the right-clicked object. When you right-click a scroll bar, for example, a shortcut menu appears with commands related to the scroll bar. When you right-click the Quick Access Toolbar, a shortcut menu appears with commands related to the Quick Access Toolbar. You can use shortcut menus to access common commands quickly. The following steps use a shortcut menu to move the Quick Access Toolbar, which by default is located on the title bar.

- Right-click the Quick Access Toolbar to display a shortcut menu that presents a list of commands related to the Quick Access Toolbar (Figure 21).

Figure 21

- Click Show Quick Access Toolbar Below the Ribbon on the shortcut menu to display the Quick Access Toolbar below the Ribbon (Figure 22).

Figure 22

- Right-click the Quick Access Toolbar to display a shortcut menu (Figure 23).

- Click Show Quick Access Toolbar Above the Ribbon on the shortcut menu to return the Quick Access Toolbar to its original position (shown in Figure 21).

Figure 23

To Customize the Quick Access Toolbar

The Quick Access Toolbar provides easy access to some of the more frequently used commands in Office programs. By default, the Quick Access Toolbar contains buttons for the Save, Undo, and Redo commands. You can customize the Quick Access Toolbar by changing its location in the window, as shown in the previous steps, and by adding more buttons to reflect commands you would like to access easily. The following steps add the Quick Print button to the Quick Access Toolbar.

1

- Click the Customize Quick Access Toolbar button to display the Customize Quick Access Toolbar menu (Figure 24).

Q&A Which commands are listed on the Customize Quick Access Toolbar menu?

It lists commands that commonly are added to the Quick Access Toolbar.

Q&A What do the check marks next to some commands signify?

Check marks appear next to commands that already are on the Quick Access Toolbar. When you add a button to the Quick Access Toolbar, a check mark will be displayed next to its command name.

Figure 24

2

- Click Quick Print on the Customize Quick Access Toolbar menu to add the Quick Print button to the Quick Access Toolbar (Figure 25).

Q&A How would I remove a button from the Quick Access Toolbar?

You would right-click the button you wish to remove and then click Remove from Quick Access Toolbar on the shortcut menu.

Figure 25

To Enter Text in a Document

The first step in creating a document is to enter its text by typing on the keyboard. By default, Word positions text at the left margin as you type. To begin creating a flyer, for example, you type the headline in the document window. The following steps type this first line of text, a headline, in a document.

1

• Type **SEE THE RENOVATED KOALA EXHIBIT** as the text (Figure 26).

Q&A

What is the blinking vertical bar to the right of the text?

The insertion point. It indicates where text, graphics, and other items will be inserted in the document. As you type, the insertion point moves to the right, and when you reach the end of a line, it moves downward to the beginning of the next line.

Q&A

What if I make an error while typing?

You can press the BACKSPACE key until you have deleted the text in error and then retype the text correctly.

Figure 26

2

• Press the ENTER key to move the insertion point to the beginning of the next line (Figure 27).

Q&A

Why did blank space appear between the entered text and the insertion point?

Each time you press the ENTER key, Word creates a new paragraph and inserts blank space between the two paragraphs.

Figure 27

Saving and Organizing Files

While you are creating a document, the computer stores it in memory. When you save a document, the computer places it on a storage medium such as a hard disk, USB flash drive, or optical disc. A saved document is referred to as a file. A **file name** is the name assigned to a file when it is saved. It is important to save a document frequently for the following reasons:

- The document in memory might be lost if the computer is turned off or you lose electrical power while a program is running.
- If you run out of time before completing a project, you may finish it at a future time without starting over.

When saving files, you should organize them so that you easily can find them later. Windows 7 provides tools to help you organize files.

BTW

File Type
Depending on your Windows 7 settings, the file type .docx may be displayed immediately to the right of the file name after you save the file. The file type .docx is a Word 2010 document.

Organizing Files and Folders

A file contains data. This data can range from a research paper to an accounting spreadsheet to an electronic math quiz. You should organize and store these files in folders to avoid misplacing a file and to help you find a file quickly.

If you are a freshman taking an introductory computer class (CIS 101, for example), you may want to design a series of folders for the different subjects covered in the class. To accomplish this, you can arrange the folders in a hierarchy for the class, as shown in Figure 28.

REMOVABLE (E:)

CIS 101

Word PowerPoint Excel Access Outlook Publisher OneNote

Figure 28

The hierarchy contains three levels. The first level contains the storage device, in this case a USB flash drive. Windows 7 identifies the storage device with a letter, and, in some cases, a name. In Figure 28, the USB flash drive is identified as REMOVABLE (E:). The second level contains the class folder (CIS 101, in this case), and the third level contains seven folders, one each for a different Office program that will be covered in the class (Word, PowerPoint, Excel, Access, Outlook, Publisher, and OneNote).

When the hierarchy in Figure 28 is created, the USB flash drive is said to contain the CIS 101 folder, and the CIS 101 folder is said to contain the separate Office folders (i.e., Word, PowerPoint, Excel, etc.). In addition, this hierarchy easily can be expanded to include folders from other classes taken during additional semesters.

The vertical and horizontal lines in Figure 28 form a pathway that allows you to navigate to a drive or folder on a computer or network. A **path** consists of a drive letter (preceded by a drive name when necessary) and colon, to identify the storage device, and one or more folder names. Each drive or folder in the hierarchy has a corresponding path.

BTW

Saving Online
Instead of saving files on a USB flash drive, some people prefer to save them online so that they can access the files from any computer with an Internet connection. For more information, read Appendix C.

Table 3 shows examples of paths and their corresponding drives and folders.

Table 3 Paths and Corresponding Drives and Folders	
Path	**Drive and Folder**
Computer ▶ REMOVABLE (E:)	Drive E (REMOVABLE (E:))
Computer ▶ REMOVABLE (E:) ▶ CIS 101	CIS 101 folder on drive E
Computer ▶ REMOVABLE (E:) ▶ CIS 101 ▶ Word	Word folder in CIS 101 folder on drive E

The following pages illustrate the steps to organize the folders for this class and save a file in one of those folders:

1. Create the folder identifying your class.
2. Create the Word folder in the folder identifying your class.
3. Create the remaining folders in the folder identifying your class (one each for PowerPoint, Excel, Access, Outlook, Publisher, and OneNote).
4. Save a file in the Word folder.
5. Verify the location of the saved file.

To Create a Folder

When you create a folder, such as the CIS 101 folder shown in Figure 28 on the previous page, you must name the folder. A folder name should describe the folder and its contents. A folder name can contain spaces and any uppercase or lowercase characters, except a backslash (\), slash (/), colon (:), asterisk (*), question mark (?), quotation marks ("), less than symbol (<), greater than symbol (>), or vertical bar (|). Folder names cannot be CON, AUX, COM1, COM2, COM3, COM4, LPT1, LPT2, LPT3, PRN, or NUL. The same rules for naming folders also apply to naming files.

To store files and folders on a USB flash drive, you must connect the USB flash drive to an available USB port on a computer. The following steps create your class folder (CIS 101, in this case) on a USB flash drive.

1

• Connect the USB flash drive to an available USB port on the computer to open the AutoPlay window (Figure 29).

Q&A Why does the AutoPlay window not open?

Some computers are not configured to open an AutoPlay window. Instead, they might display the contents of the USB flash drive automatically, or you might need to access contents of the USB flash drive using the Computer window. To use the Computer window to display the USB flash drive's contents, click the Start button, click Computer on the Start menu, and then click the icon representing the USB flash drive.

Figure 29

Q&A Why does the AutoPlay window look different from the one in Figure 29?

The AutoPlay window that opens on your computer might display different options. The type of USB flash drive, its contents, and the next available drive letter on your computer all will determine which options are displayed in the AutoPlay window.

2

- Click the 'Open folder to view files' link in the AutoPlay window to open the USB flash drive window (Figure 30).

Why does Figure 30 show REMOVABLE (E:) for the USB flash drive?

REMOVABLE is the name of the USB flash drive used to illustrate these steps. The (E:) refers to the drive letter assigned by Windows 7 to the USB flash drive. The name and drive letter of your USB flash drive probably will be different.

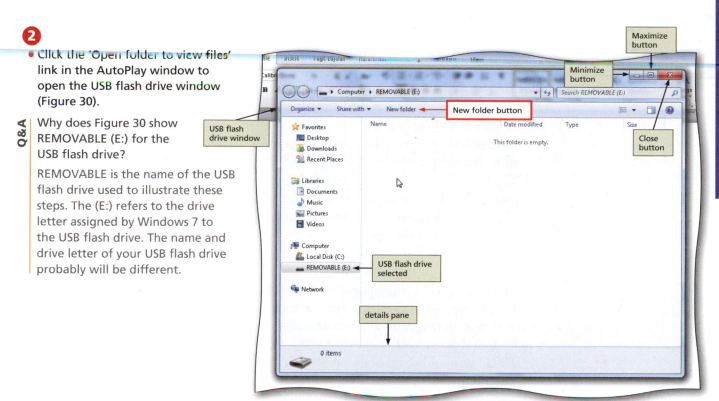

Figure 30

3

- Click the New folder button on the toolbar to display a new folder icon with the name, New folder, selected in a text box.

- Type **CIS 101** (or your class code) in the text box to name the folder.

- Press the ENTER key to create a folder identifying your class on the selected drive (Figure 31). If the CIS 101 folder does not appear in the navigation pane, double-click REMOVABLE (E:) in the navigation pane to display the folder just added.

What happens when I press the ENTER key?

The class folder (CIS 101, in this case) is displayed in the File list, which contains the folder name, date modified, type, and size.

Why is the folder icon displayed differently on my computer?

Windows might be configured to display contents differently on your computer.

Figure 31

Folder Windows

The USB flash drive window (shown in Figure 31 on the previous page) is called a folder window. Recall that a folder is a specific named location on a storage medium that contains related files. Most users rely on **folder windows** for finding, viewing, and managing information on their computer. Folder windows have common design elements, including the following (Figure 31).

- The **Address bar** provides quick navigation options. The arrows on the Address bar allow you to visit different locations on the computer.
- The buttons to the left of the Address bar allow you to navigate the contents of the left pane and view recent pages. Other buttons allow you to specify the size of the window.
- The **Previous Locations button** saves the locations you have visited and displays the locations when clicked.
- The **Refresh button** on the right side of the Address bar refreshes the contents of the right pane of the folder window.
- The **search box** to the right of the Address bar contains the dimmed word, Search. You can type a term in the search box for a list of files, folders, shortcuts, and elements containing that term within the location you are searching. A **shortcut** is an icon on the desktop that provides a user with immediate access to a program or file.
- The **Command bar** contains five buttons used to accomplish various tasks on the computer related to organizing and managing the contents of the open window.
- The **navigation pane** on the left contains the Favorites area, Libraries area, Computer area, and Network area.
- The **Favorites area** contains links to your favorite locations. By default, this list contains only links to your Desktop, Downloads, and Recent Places.
- The **Libraries area** shows links to files and folders that have been included in a library.

A **library** helps you manage multiple folders and files stored in various locations on a computer. It does not store the files and folders; rather, it displays links to them so that you can access them quickly. For example, you can save pictures from a digital camera in any folder on any storage location on a computer. Normally, this would make organizing the different folders difficult; however, if you add the folders to a library, you can access all the pictures from one location regardless of where they are stored.

To Create a Folder within a Folder

With the class folder created, you can create folders that will store the files you create using each Office program. The following steps create a Word folder in the CIS 101 folder (or the folder identifying your class).

- Double-click the icon or folder name for the CIS 101 folder (or the folder identifying your class) in the File list to open the folder (Figure 32).

Figure 32

- Click the New folder button on the toolbar to display a new folder icon and text box for the folder.

- Type **Word** in the text box to name the folder.

- Press the ENTER key to create the folder (Figure 33).

Figure 33

To Create the Remaining Folders

The following steps create the remaining folders in the folder identifying your class (in this case, CIS 101).

1 Click the New folder button on the toolbar to display a new folder icon and text box.

2 Type **PowerPoint** in the text box to name the folder.

3 Repeat Steps 1 and 2 to create each of the remaining folders, using the names Excel, Access, Outlook, Publisher, and OneNote as the folder names (Figure 34).

Figure 34

To Expand a Folder, Scroll through Folder Contents, and Collapse a Folder

Folder windows display the hierarchy of items and the contents of drives and folders in the right pane. You might want to expand a drive in the navigation pane to view its contents, scroll through its contents, and collapse it when you are finished viewing its contents. When a folder is expanded, it lists all the folders it contains. By contrast, a collapsed folder does not list the folders it contains. The following steps expand, scroll through, and then collapse the folder identifying your class (CIS 101, in this case).

1

- Double-click the folder identifying your class (CIS 101, in this case), which expands the folder to display its contents and displays a black arrow to the left of the folder icon (Figure 35).

Q&A Why are the subject folders indented below the CIS 101 folder in the navigation pane?

It shows that the folders are contained within the CIS 101 folder.

Q&A Why did a scroll bar appear in the navigation pane?

When all contents cannot fit in a window or pane, a scroll bar appears. As described earlier, you can view areas currently not visible by (1) clicking the scroll arrows, (2) clicking above or below the scroll bar, and (3) dragging the scroll box.

Figure 35

 Experiment

- Click the down scroll arrow on the vertical scroll bar to display additional folders at the bottom of the navigation pane.

- Click the scroll bar above the scroll box to move the scroll box to the top of the navigation pane.

- Drag the scroll box down the scroll bar until the scroll box is halfway down the scroll bar.

2

- Double-click the folder identifying your class (CIS 101, in this case) to collapse the folder (Figure 36).

Figure 36

Other Ways

1. Point in navigation pane to display arrows, click white arrow to expand or click black arrow to collapse

2. Select folder to expand or collapse using arrow keys, press RIGHT ARROW to expand; press LEFT ARROW to collapse.

To Switch from One Program to Another

The next step is to save the Word file containing the headline you typed earlier. Word, however, currently is not the active window. You can use the program button on the taskbar and live preview to switch to Word and then save the document in the Word document window.

If Windows Aero is active on your computer, Windows displays a live preview window whenever you move your mouse on a button or click a button on the taskbar. If Aero is not supported or enabled on your computer, you will see a window title instead of a live preview. The steps below use the Word program; however, the steps are the same for any active Office program currently displayed as a program button on the taskbar.

The following steps switch to the Word window.

 1

- Point to the Word program button on the taskbar to see a live preview of the open document(s) or the window title(s) of the open document(s), depending on your computer's configuration (Figure 37).

2

- Click the program button or the live preview to make the program associated with the program button the active window (shown in Figure 27 on page OFF 20).

Figure 37

Q&A

What if multiple documents are open in a program?

If Aero is enabled on your computer, click the desired live preview. If Aero is not supported or not enabled, click the window title.

To Save a File in a Folder

Now that you have created the folders for storing files, you can save the Word document. The following steps save a file on a USB flash drive in the Word folder contained in your class folder (CIS 101, in this case) using the file name, Koala Exhibit.

1

- With a USB flash drive connected to one of the computer's USB ports, click the Save button on the Quick Access Toolbar to display the Save As dialog box (Figure 38).

Q&A

Why does a file name already appear in the File name text box?

Word automatically suggests a file name the first time you save a document. The file name normally consists of the first few words contained in the document. Because the suggested file name is selected, you do not need to delete it; as soon as you begin typing, the new file name replaces the selected text.

Figure 38

2

● Type **Koala Exhibit** in the File name text box (Save As dialog box) to change the file name. Do not press the ENTER key after typing the file name because you do not want to close the dialog box at this time (Figure 39).

What characters can I use in a file name?

The only invalid characters are the backslash (\), slash (/), colon (:), asterisk (*), question mark (?), quotation mark ("), less than symbol (<), greater than symbol (>), and vertical bar (|).

Figure 39

3

● Navigate to the desired save location (in this case, the Word folder in the CIS 101 folder [or your class folder] on the USB flash drive) by performing the tasks in Steps 3a, 3b, and 3c.

3a

● If the navigation pane is not displayed in the dialog box, click the Browse Folders button to expand the dialog box.

● If Computer is not displayed in the navigation pane, drag the navigation pane scroll bar until Computer appears.

● If Computer is not expanded in the navigation pane, double-click Computer to display a list of available storage devices in the navigation pane.

● If necessary, scroll through the dialog box until your USB flash drive appears in the list of available storage devices in the navigation pane (Figure 40).

Figure 40

3b

- If your USB flash drive is not expanded, double-click the USB flash drive in the list of available storage devices in the navigation pane to select that drive as the new save location and display its contents in the right pane.

3c

- If your class folder (CIS 101, in this case) is not expanded, double-click the CIS 101 folder to select the folder and display its contents in the right pane.

Q&A

What if I do not want to save in a folder?

Although storing files in folders is an effective technique for organizing files, some users prefer not to store files in folders. If you prefer not to save this file in a folder, skip all instructions in Step 3c and proceed to Step 4.

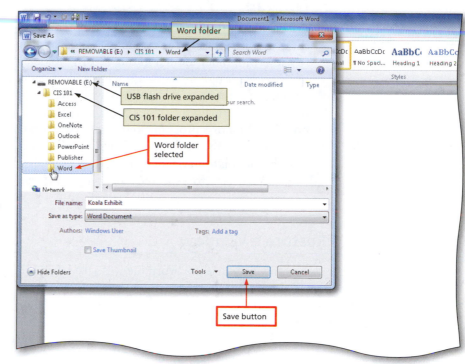

Figure 41

- Click the Word folder to select the folder and display its contents in the right pane (Figure 41).

4

- Click the Save button (Save As dialog box) to save the document in the selected folder on the selected drive with the entered file name (Figure 42).

Q&A

How do I know that the file is saved?

While an Office program is saving a file, it briefly displays a message on the status bar indicating the amount of the file saved. In addition, the USB flash drive may have a light that flashes during the save process.

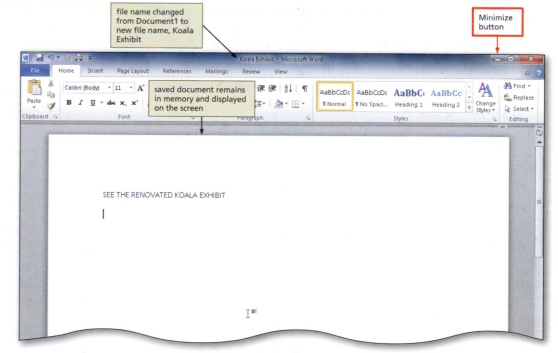

Figure 42

Other Ways
1. Click File on Ribbon, click Save, type file name, navigate to desired save location, click Save button 　　2. Press CTRL+S or press SHIFT+F12, type file name, navigate to desired save location, click Save button

Navigating in Dialog Boxes

Navigating is the process of finding a location on a storage device. While saving the Koala Exhibit file, for example, Steps 3a – 3c in the previous set of steps navigated to the Word folder located in the CIS 101 folder. When performing certain functions in Windows programs, such as saving a file, opening a file, or inserting a picture in an existing document, you most likely will have to navigate to the location where you want to save the file or to the folder containing the file you want to open or insert. Most dialog boxes in Windows programs requiring navigation follow a similar procedure; that is, the way you navigate to a folder in one dialog box, such as the Save As dialog box, is similar to how you might navigate in another dialog box, such as the Open dialog box. If you chose to navigate to a specific location in a dialog box, you would follow the instructions in Steps 3a – 3c on pages OFF 28 and OFF 29.

To Minimize and Restore a Window

Before continuing, you can verify that the Word file was saved properly. To do this, you will minimize the Word window and then open the USB flash drive window so that you can verify the file is stored on the USB flash drive. A **minimized window** is an open window hidden from view but that can be displayed quickly by clicking the window's program button on the taskbar.

In the following example, Word is used to illustrate minimizing and restoring windows; however, you would follow the same steps regardless of the Office program you are using.

The following steps minimize the Word window, verify that the file is saved, and then restore the minimized window.

1
- Click the Minimize button on the program's title bar (shown in Figure 42 on the previous page) to minimize the window (Figure 43).

Q&A

Is the minimized window still available?

The minimized window, Word in this case, remains available but no longer is the active window. It is minimized as a program button on the taskbar.

- If necessary, click the Windows Explorer program button on the taskbar to open the USB flash drive window.

Figure 43

2

- Double-click the Word folder to select the folder and display its contents (Figure 44).

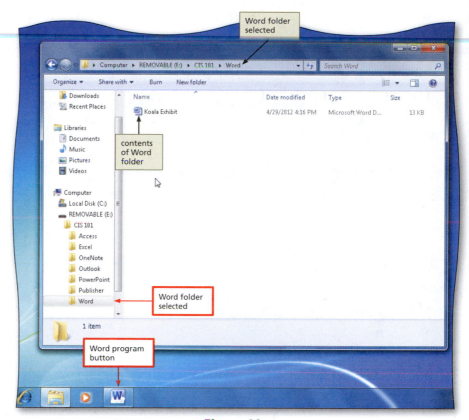

Figure 44

Q&A

Why does the Windows Explorer button on the taskbar change?

The button changes to reflect the status of the folder window (in this case, the USB flash drive window). A selected button indicates that the folder window is active on the screen. When the button is not selected, the window is open but not active.

3

- After viewing the contents of the selected folder, click the Word program button on the taskbar to restore the minimized window (as shown in Figure 42 on page OFF 29).

Other Ways	
1. Right-click title bar, click Minimize on shortcut menu, click taskbar button in taskbar button area	2. Press WINDOWS+M, press WINDOWS+SHIFT+M

Screen Resolution

Screen resolution indicates the number of pixels (dots) that the computer uses to display the letters, numbers, graphics, and background you see on the screen. When you increase the screen resolution, Windows displays more information on the screen, but the information decreases in size. The reverse also is true: as you decrease the screen resolution, Windows displays less information on the screen, but the information increases in size.

Screen resolution usually is stated as the product of two numbers, such as 1024 × 768 (pronounced "ten twenty-four by seven sixty-eight"). A 1024 × 768 screen resolution results in a display of 1,024 distinct pixels on each of 768 lines, or about

786,432 pixels. Changing the screen resolution affects how the Ribbon appears in Office programs. Figure 45 shows the Word Ribbon at screen resolutions of 1024×768 and 1280×800. All of the same commands are available regardless of screen resolution. Word, however, makes changes to the groups and the buttons within the groups to accommodate the various screen resolutions. The result is that certain commands may need to be accessed differently depending on the resolution chosen. A command that is visible on the Ribbon and available by clicking a button at one resolution may not be visible and may need to be accessed using its Dialog Box Launcher at a different resolution.

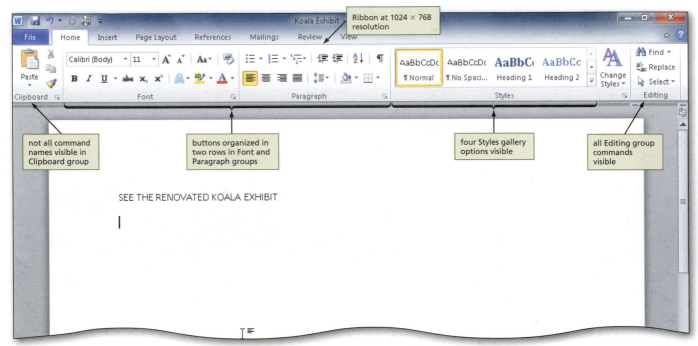

Figure 45 (a) Ribbon at Resolution of 1024 x 768

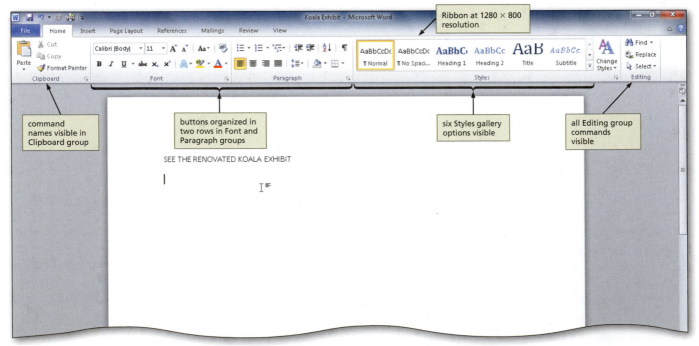

Figure 45 (b) Ribbon at Resolution of 1280 x 800

Comparing the two Ribbons in Figure 45, notice the changes in content and layout of the groups and galleries. In some cases, the content of a group is the same in each resolution, but the layout of the group differs. For example, the same gallery and buttons appear in the Styles groups in the two resolutions, but the layouts differ. In other cases, the content and layout are the same across the resolution, but the level of detail differs with the resolution. In the Clipboard group, when the resolution increases to 1280 × 800, the names of all the buttons in the group appear in addition to the buttons themselves. At the lower resolution, only the buttons appear.

To Change the Screen Resolution

If you are using a computer to step through the chapters in this book and you want your screen to match the figures, you may need to change your screen's resolution. The figures in this book use a screen resolution of 1024 × 768. The following steps change the screen resolution to 1024 × 768. Your computer already may be set to 1024 × 768 or some other resolution. Keep in mind that many computer labs prevent users from changing the screen resolution; in that case, read the following steps for illustration purposes.

1

- Click the Show desktop button on the taskbar to display the Windows 7 desktop.

- Right-click an empty area on the Windows 7 desktop to display a shortcut menu that displays a list of commands related to the desktop (Figure 46).

Q&A

Why does my shortcut menu display different commands?

Depending on your computer's hardware and configuration, different commands might appear on the shortcut menu.

Figure 46

2

- Click Screen resolution on the shortcut menu to open the Screen Resolution window (Figure 47).

Screen Resolution window

name of current display device

Resolution button shows current resolution

clicking link displays advanced settings

Figure 47

3

- Click the Resolution button in the Screen Resolution window to display the resolution slider.

Q&A What is a slider?

A **slider** is an object that allows users to choose from multiple predetermined options. In most cases, these options represent some type of numeric value. In most cases, one end of the slider (usually the left or bottom) represents the lowest of available values, and the opposite end (usually the right or top) represents the highest available value.

4

- If necessary, drag the resolution slider until the desired screen resolution (in this case, 1024 × 768) is selected (Figure 48).

Q&A What if my computer does not support the 1024 × 768 resolution?

Some computers do not support the 1024 × 768 resolution. In this case, select a resolution that is close to the 1024 × 768 resolution.

resolution slider dragged to 1024 × 768

OK button

Figure 48

- Click an empty area of the Screen Resolution window to close the resolution slider.

- Click the OK button to change the screen resolution and display the Display Settings dialog box (Figure 49).

- Click the Keep changes button (Display Settings dialog box) to accept the new screen resolution.

Q&A

Why does a message display stating that the image quality can be improved?

Some computer monitors are designed to display contents better at a certain screen resolution, sometimes referred to as an optimal resolution.

Figure 49

To Quit an Office Program with One Document Open

When you quit an Office program, such as Word, if you have made changes to a file since the last time the file was saved, the Office program displays a dialog box asking if you want save the changes you made to the file before it closes the program window. The dialog box contains three buttons with these resulting actions: the Save button saves the changes and then quits the Office program, the Don't Save button quits the Office program without saving changes, and the Cancel button closes the dialog box and redisplays the file without saving the changes.

If no changes have been made to an open document since the last time the file was saved, the Office program will close the window without displaying a dialog box.

The following steps quit an Office program. In the following example, Word is used to illustrate quitting an Office program; however, you would follow the same steps regardless of the Office program you were using.

1

- If necessary, click the Word program button on the taskbar to display the Word window on the desktop.

- Point to the Close button on the right side of the program's title bar, Word in this case (Figure 50).

Figure 50

2

- Click the Close button to close the document and quit Word.

Q&A

What if I have more than one document open in an Office program?

You would click the Close button for each open document. When you click the last open document's Close button, the Office program also quits. As an alternative, you could click File on the Ribbon to open the Backstage view and then click Exit in the Backstage view to close all open documents and quit the Office program.

Q&A

What is the Backstage view?

The **Backstage view** contains a set of commands that enable you to manage documents and data about the documents. The Backstage view is discussed in more depth later in this chapter.

3

- If a Microsoft Word dialog box appears, click the Save button to save any changes made to the document since the last save.

Other Ways
1. Right-click the Office program button on Windows 7 taskbar, click Close window or 'Close all windows' on shortcut menu
2. Press ALT + F4

Break Point: If you wish to take a break, this is a good place to do so. To resume at a later time, continue to follow the steps from this location forward.

Additional Microsoft Office Programs

The previous section used Word to illustrate common features of Office and some basic elements unique to Word. The following sections present elements unique to PowerPoint, Excel, and Access, as well as illustrate additional common features of Office.

In the following pages, you will learn how to do the following:

1. Start an Office program (PowerPoint) using the search box.
2. Create two small documents in the same Office program (PowerPoint).
3. Close one of the documents.
4. Reopen the document just closed.
5. Create a document in a different Office program (Excel).
6. Save the document with a new file name.
7. Create a file in a different Office program (Access).
8. Close the file and then open the file.

PowerPoint

PowerPoint is a complete presentation program that allows you to produce professional-looking presentations (Figure 51). A PowerPoint **presentation** also is called a **slide show**. PowerPoint contains several features to simplify creating a slide show. To make presentations more impressive, you can add diagrams, tables, pictures, video, sound, and animation effects. Additional PowerPoint features include the following:

- **Word processing** — Create bulleted lists, combine words and images, find and replace text, and use multiple fonts and font sizes.
- **Outlining** — Develop a presentation using an outline format. You also can import outlines from Microsoft Word or other word processing programs, including single-level and multilevel lists.
- **Charting** — Create and insert charts into presentations and then add effects and chart elements.
- **Drawing** — Create and modify diagrams using shapes such as arcs, arrows, cubes, rectangles, stars, and triangles. Then, customize and add effects to the diagrams, and arrange these objects by sizing, scaling, and rotating them.
- **Inserting multimedia** — Insert artwork and multimedia effects into a slide show. The Microsoft Clip Organizer, included with Office programs, contains hundreds of media files, including pictures, sounds, and movies.
- **Saving to the Web** — Save presentations or parts of a presentation so that they can be viewed in a Web browser. You can publish your slide show to the Internet or to an intranet.
- **E-mailing** — Send an entire slide show as an attachment to an e-mail message.
- **Collaborating** — Share a presentation with friends and coworkers. Ask them to review the slides and then insert comments that offer suggestions to enhance the presentation.
- **Preparing delivery** — Rehearse integrating PowerPoint slides into your speech by setting timings, using presentation tools, showing only selected slides in a presentation, and packaging the presentation for an optical disc.

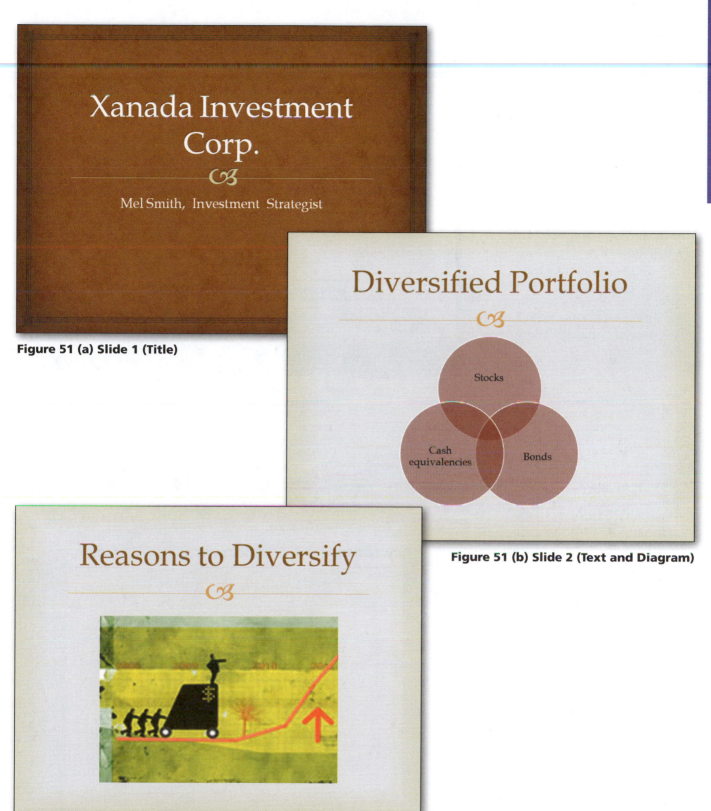

Figure 51 (a) Slide 1 (Title)

Figure 51 (b) Slide 2 (Text and Diagram)

Figure 51 (c) Slide 3 (Text and Picture)

To Start a Program Using the Search Box

The steps on the next page, which assume Windows 7 is running, use the search box to start the PowerPoint Office program based on a typical installation; however, you would follow similar steps to start any Office program. You may need to ask your instructor how to start programs for your computer.

1

- Click the Start button on the Windows 7 taskbar to display the Start menu.

2

- Type **Microsoft PowerPoint** as the search text in the 'Search programs and files' text box and watch the search results appear on the Start menu (Figure 52).

Q&A

Do I need to type the complete program name or correct capitalization?

No, just enough of it for the program name to appear on the Start menu. For example, you may be able to type PowerPoint or powerpoint, instead of Microsoft PowerPoint.

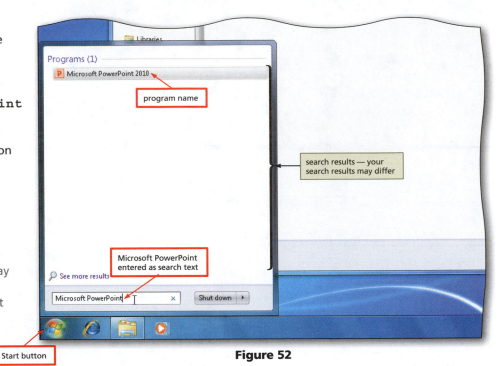

Figure 52

3

- Click the program name, Microsoft PowerPoint 2010 in this case, in the search results on the Start menu to start PowerPoint and display a new blank presentation in the PowerPoint window.

- If the program window is not maximized, click the Maximize button on its title bar to maximize the window (Figure 53).

Figure 53

The PowerPoint Window and Ribbon

The PowerPoint window consists of a variety of components to make your work more efficient and documents more professional: the window, Ribbon, Mini toolbar, shortcut menus, and Quick Access Toolbar. Many of these components are common to other Office programs and have been discussed earlier in this chapter. Other components, discussed in the following paragraphs and later in subsequent chapters, are unique to PowerPoint.

The basic unit of a PowerPoint presentation is a **slide**. A slide may contain text and objects, such as graphics, tables, charts, and drawings. **Layouts** are used to position this content on the slide. When you create a new presentation, the default **Title Slide** layout appears (Figure 54). The purpose of this layout is to introduce the presentation to the audience. PowerPoint includes eight other built-in standard layouts.

The default slide layouts are set up in **landscape orientation**, where the slide width is greater than its height. In landscape orientation, the slide size is preset to 10 inches wide and 7.5 inches high when printed on a standard sheet of paper measuring 11 inches wide and 8.5 inches high.

BTW

Portrait Orientation
If your slide content is dominantly vertical, such as a skyscraper or a person, consider changing the slide layout to a portrait orientation. To change the orientation to portrait, click the Slide Orientation button (Design tab | Page Setup group) and then click Portrait. You can use both landscape and portrait orientation in the same slide show.

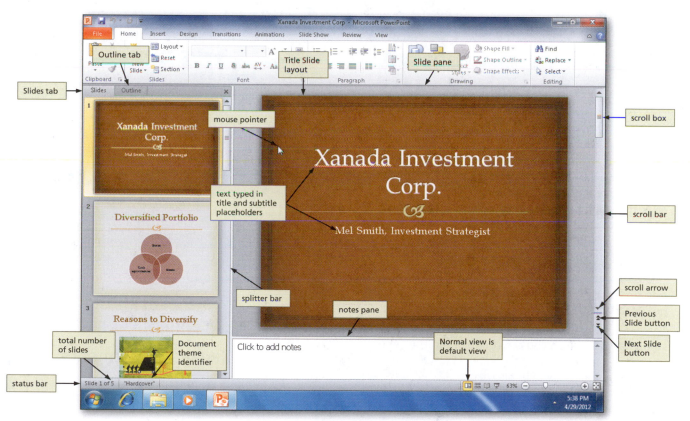

Figure 54

Placeholders **Placeholders** are boxes with dotted or hatch-marked borders that are displayed when you create a new slide. All layouts except the Blank slide layout contain placeholders. Depending on the particular slide layout selected, title and subtitle placeholders are displayed for the slide title and subtitle; a content text placeholder is displayed for text, art, or a table, chart, picture, graphic, or movie. The title slide in Figure 53 has two text placeholders for the main heading, or title, of a new slide and the subtitle.

Ribbon The Ribbon in PowerPoint is similar to the one in Word and the other Microsoft Office programs. When you start PowerPoint, the Ribbon displays nine main tabs: File, Home, Insert, Design, Transitions, Animations, Slide Show, Review, and View.

To Enter Content in a Title Slide

With the exception of a blank slide and a slide with a picture and caption, PowerPoint assumes every new slide has a title. Many of PowerPoint's layouts have both a title text placeholder and at least one content placeholder. To make creating a presentation easier, any text you type after a new slide appears becomes title text in the title text placeholder. As you begin typing text in the title text placeholder, the title text also is displayed in the Slide 1 thumbnail in the Slides tab. The presentation title for this presentation is Xanada Investments. The following steps enter a presentation title on the title slide.

1

• Click the label 'Click to add title' located inside the title text placeholder (shown in Figure 53 on page OFF 38) to select the placeholder (Figure 55).

Figure 55

2

• Type **Xanada Investments** in the title text placeholder. Do not press the ENTER key because you do not want to create a new line of text (Figure 56).

Q&A

What are the white squares and circles that appear around the title text placeholder as I type the presentation title?

The white squares and circles are sizing handles, which you can drag to change the size of the title text placeholder. Sizing handles also can be found around other placeholders and objects within a presentation.

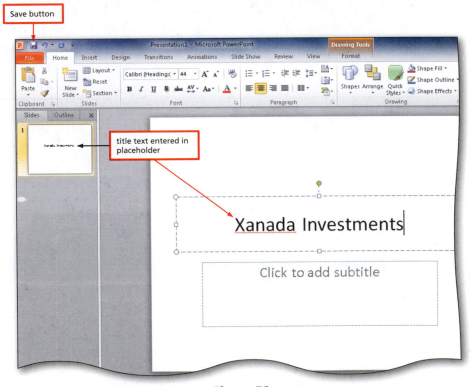

Figure 56

To Save a File in a Folder

The following steps save the presentation in the PowerPoint folder in the class folder (CIS 101, in this case) on a USB flash drive using the file name, Xanada Investments.

1 With a USB flash drive connected to one of the computer's USB ports, click the Save button on the Quick Access Toolbar to display the Save As dialog box.

2 If necessary, type `Xanada Investments` in the File name text box to change the file name. Do not press the ENTER key after typing the file name because you do not want to close the dialog box at this time.

3 Navigate to the desired save location (in this case, the PowerPoint folder in the CIS 101 folder [or your class folder] on the USB flash drive). For specific instructions, perform the tasks in Steps 3a through 3g.

3a If a navigation pane is not displayed in the Save As dialog box, click the Browse Folders button to expand the dialog box.

3b If Computer is not displayed in the navigation pane, drag the navigation pane scroll bar (Save As dialog box) until Computer appears.

3c If Computer is not expanded in the navigation pane, double-click Computer to display a list of available storage devices in the navigation pane.

3d If necessary, scroll through the Save As dialog box until your USB flash drive appears in the list of available storage devices in the navigation pane.

3e If your USB flash drive is not expanded, double-click the USB flash drive in the list of available storage devices in the navigation pane to select that drive as the new save location and display its contents in the right pane.

3f If your class folder (CIS 101, in this case) is not expanded, double-click the CIS 101 folder to select the folder and display its contents.

3g Click the PowerPoint folder to select it as the new save location and display its contents in the right pane.

4 Click the Save button (Save As dialog box) to save the presentation in the selected folder on the selected drive with the entered file name.

To Create a New Office Document from the Backstage View

As discussed earlier, the Backstage view contains a set of commands that enable you to manage documents and data about the documents. From the Backstage view in PowerPoint, for example, you can create, open, print, and save presentations. You also can share documents, manage versions, set permissions, and modify document properties. In other Office 2010 programs, the Backstage view may contain features specific to those programs. The steps on the following pages create a file, a blank presentation in this case, from the Backstage view.

1

- Click File on the Ribbon to open the Backstage view (Figure 57).

Q&A

What is the purpose of the File tab?

The **File** tab is used to display the Backstage view for each Office program.

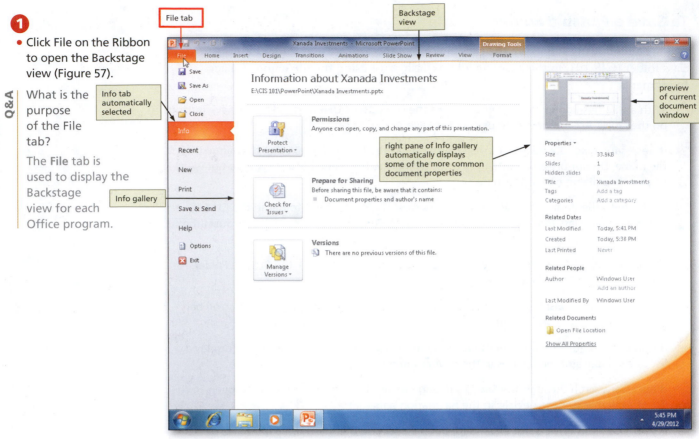

Figure 57

2

- Click the New tab in the Backstage view to display the New gallery (Figure 58).

Q&A

Can I create documents through the Backstage view in other Office programs?

Yes. If the Office program has a New tab in the Backstage view, the New gallery displays various options for creating a new file.

Figure 58

• Click the Create **button in the New** gallery to create a new presentation (Figure 59).

Figure 59

Other Ways
1. Press CTRL+N

To Enter Content in a Title Slide of a Second PowerPoint Presentation

The presentation title for this presentation is Koala Exhibit Gala. The following steps enter a presentation title on the title slide.

1 Click the title text placeholder (shown in Figure 59) to select it.

2 Type **Koala Exhibit Gala** in the title text placeholder. Do not press the ENTER key (Figure 60).

Figure 60

To Save a File in a Folder

The following steps save the second presentation in the PowerPoint folder in the class folder (CIS 101, in this case) on a USB flash drive using the file name, Koala Exhibit Gala.

1 With a USB flash drive connected to one of the computer's USB ports, click the Save button on the Quick Access Toolbar to display the Save As dialog box.

2 If necessary, type `Koala Exhibit Gala` in the File name text box to change the file name. Do not press the ENTER key after typing the file name because you do not want to close the dialog box at this time.

3 If necessary, navigate to the desired save location (in this case, the PowerPoint folder in the CIS 101 folder [or your class folder] on the USB flash drive).

4 Click the Save button (Save As dialog box) to save the presentation in the selected folder on the selected drive with the entered file name.

To Close an Office File Using the Backstage View

Sometimes, you may want to close an Office file, such as a PowerPoint presentation, entirely and start over with a new file. You also may want to close a file when you are finished working with it so that you can begin a new file. The following steps close the current active Office file, that is, the Koala Exhibit Gala presentation, without quitting the active program (PowerPoint in this case).

1
• Click File on the Ribbon to open the Backstage view (Figure 61).

2
• Click Close in the Backstage view to close the open file (Koala Exhibit Gala, in this case) without quitting the active program.

Q&A What if the Office program displays a dialog box about saving?

Click the Save button if you want to save the changes, click the Don't Save button if you want to ignore the changes since the last time you saved, and click the Cancel button if you do not want to close the document.

Q&A Can I use the Backstage view to close an open file in other Office programs, such as Word and Excel?

Yes.

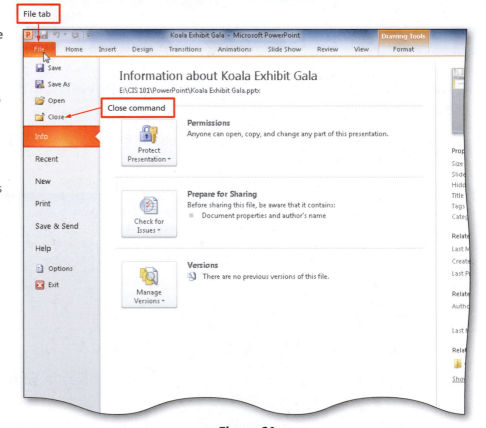

Figure 61

To Open a Recent Office File Using the Backstage View

You sometimes need to open a file that you recently modified. You may have more changes to make such as adding more content or correcting errors. The Backstage view allows you to access recent files easily. The following steps reopen the Koala Exhibit Gala file just closed.

1
- Click File on the Ribbon to open the Backstage view.

- Click the Recent tab in the Backstage view to display the Recent gallery (Figure 62).

2
- Click the desired file name in the Recent gallery, Koala Exhibit Gala in this case, to open the file (shown in Figure 60 on page OFF 43).

Q&A

Can I use the Backstage view to open a recent file in other Office programs, such as Word and Excel?

Yes, as long as the file name appears in the list of recent files in the Recent gallery.

Figure 62

Other Ways

1. Click Start button, point to program name, click file name on submenu
2. Click File on Ribbon, click Open in Backstage view, navigate to file (Open dialog box), click Open button

To Quit an Office Program

You are finished using PowerPoint. Thus, you should quit this Office program. The following steps quit PowerPoint.

1 If you have one Office document open, click the Close button on the right side of the title bar to close the document and quit the Office program; or if you have multiple Office documents open, click File on the Ribbon to open the Backstage view and then click Exit in the Backstage view to close all open documents and quit the Office program.

2 If a dialog box appears, click the Save button to save any changes made to the document since the last save.

Excel

Excel is a powerful spreadsheet program that allows users to organize data, complete calculations, make decisions, graph data, develop professional-looking reports (Figure 63), publish organized data to the Web, and access real-time data from Web sites. The four major parts of Excel are:

- **Workbooks and Worksheets** - A **workbook** is like a notebook. Inside the workbook are sheets, each of which is called a **worksheet**. In other words, a workbook is a collection of worksheets. Worksheets allow users to enter, calculate, manipulate, and analyze data such as numbers and text. The terms worksheet and spreadsheet are interchangeable.

- **Charts** - Excel can draw a variety of charts.

- **Tables** - Tables organize and store data within worksheets. For example, once a user enters data into a worksheet, an Excel table can sort the data, search for specific data, and select data that satisfies defined criteria.

- **Web Support –** Web support allows users to save Excel worksheets or parts of a worksheet in HTML format, so that a user can view and manipulate the worksheet using a browser. Excel Web support also provides access to real-time data, such as stock quotes, using Web queries.

Figure 63

To Create a New Blank Office Document from Windows Explorer

Windows Explorer provides a means to create a blank Office document without ever starting an Office program. The following steps use Windows Explorer to create a blank Excel document.

1

- If necessary, click the Windows Explorer program button on the taskbar to make the folder window the active window in Windows Explorer.

- Double-click your class folder (CIS 101, in this case) in the navigation pane to display the contents of the selected folder.

- Double-click the Excel folder to display its contents in the right pane.

- With the Excel folder selected, right-click an open area in the right pane to display a shortcut menu.

- Point to New on the shortcut menu to display the New submenu (Figure 64).

Figure 64

2

- Click Microsoft Excel Worksheet on the New submenu to display an icon and text box for a new file in the current folder window (Figure 65).

Figure 65

3

- Type **Brain Busters** in the text box and then press the ENTER key to assign a name to the new file in the current folder (Figure 66).

Figure 66

To Start a Program from Windows Explorer and Open a File

Previously, you learned how to start an Office program using the Start menu and the search box. Another way start an Office program is to open an existing file from Windows Explorer, which causes the program in which the file was created to start and then open the selected file. The following steps, which assume Windows 7 is running, use Windows Explorer to start the Excel Office program based on a typical installation. You may need to ask your instructor how to start Office programs for your computer.

 1

- If necessary, display the file to open in the folder window in Windows Explorer (shown in Figure 66 on the previous page).

- Right-click the file icon or file name (Brain Busters, in this case) to display a shortcut menu (Figure 67).

Figure 67

2

- Click Open on the shortcut menu to open the selected file in the program used to create the file, Microsoft Excel in this case (Figure 68).

- If the program window is not maximized, click the Maximize button on the title bar to maximize the window.

- For Excel users, if the worksheet window in Excel is not maximized, click the worksheet window Maximize button to maximize the worksheet window within Excel.

Figure 68

Q&A

Instead of using Windows Explorer, can I start Excel using the same method shown previously for Word and PowerPoint?

Yes, you can use any method of starting an Office program to start Excel.

Unique Features of Excel

The Excel window consists of a variety of components to make your work more efficient and worksheets more professional. These include the document window, Ribbon, Mini toolbar and shortcut menus, Quick Access Toolbar, and the Backstage view. Some of these components are common to other Microsoft Office 2010 programs; others are unique to Excel.

Excel opens a new workbook with three worksheets. If necessary, you can add additional worksheets as long as your computer has enough memory to accommodate them.

Each worksheet has a sheet name that appears on a **sheet tab** at the bottom of the workbook. For example, Sheet1 is the name of the active worksheet displayed in the Brain Busters workbook. If you click the sheet tab labeled Sheet2, Excel displays the Sheet2 worksheet.

The Worksheet   The worksheet is organized into a rectangular grid containing vertical columns and horizontal rows. A column letter above the grid, also called the **column heading**, identifies each column. A row number on the left side of the grid, also called the **row heading**, identifies each row. With the screen resolution set to 1024 × 768 and the Excel window maximized, Excel displays 15 columns (A through O) and 25 rows (1 through 25) of the worksheet on the screen, as shown in Figure 68.

The intersection of each column and row is a cell. A **cell** is the basic unit of a worksheet into which you enter data. Each worksheet in a workbook has 16,384 columns and 1,048,576 rows for a total of 17,179,869,180 cells. Only a small fraction of the active worksheet appears on the screen at one time.

A cell is referred to by its unique address, or **cell reference**, which is the coordinates of the intersection of a column and a row. To identify a cell, specify the column letter first, followed by the row number. For example, cell reference E2 refers to the cell located at the intersection of column E and row 2 (Figure 68).

One cell on the worksheet, designated the **active cell**, is the one into which you can enter data. The active cell in Figure 68 is A1. The active cell is identified in three ways. First, a heavy border surrounds the cell; second, the active cell reference shows immediately above column A in the Name box; and third, the column heading A and row heading 1 are highlighted so it is easy to see which cell is active (Figure 68).

The horizontal and vertical lines on the worksheet itself are called **gridlines**. Gridlines make it easier to see and identify each cell in the worksheet. If desired, you can turn the gridlines off so that they do not show on the worksheet, but it is recommended that you leave them on for now.

The mouse pointer in Figure 68 has the shape of a block plus sign. The mouse pointer appears as a block plus sign whenever it is located in a cell on the worksheet. Another common shape of the mouse pointer is the block arrow. The mouse pointer turns into the block arrow when you move it outside the worksheet or when you drag cell contents between rows or columns. The other mouse pointer shapes are described when they appear on the screen.

Ribbon   When you start Excel, the Ribbon displays eight main tabs: File, Home, Insert, Page Layout, Formulas, Data, Review, and View. The Formulas and Data tabs are specific to Excel. The Formulas tab allows you to work with Excel formulas, and the Data tab allows you to work with data processing features such as importing and sorting data.

BTW

The Worksheet Size and Window
The 16,384 columns and 1,048,576 rows in Excel make for a huge worksheet that – if you could imagine – takes up the entire side of a building to display in its entirety. Your computer screen, by comparison, is a small window that allows you to view only a minute area of the worksheet at one time. While you cannot see the entire worksheet, you can move the window over the worksheet to view any part of it.

BTW

Customizing the Ribbon
In addition to customizing the Quick Access Toolbar, you can add items to and remove items from the Ribbon. To customize the Ribbon, click File on the Ribbon to open the Backstage view, click Options in the Backstage view, and then click Customize Ribbon in the left pane of the Options dialog box. More information about customizing the Ribbon is presented in a later chapter.

Formula Bar   The formula bar appears below the Ribbon (Figure 69). As you type, Excel displays the entry in the **formula bar**. You can make the formula bar larger by dragging the sizing handle at the bottom of the formula bar or clicking the expand button to the right of the formula bar. Excel also displays the active cell reference in the **Name box** on the left side of the formula bar.

Figure 69

To Enter a Worksheet Title

To enter data into a cell, you first must select it. The easiest way to select a cell (make it active) is to use the mouse to move the block plus sign mouse pointer to the cell and then click. An alternative method is to use the arrow keys that are located just to the right of the typewriter keys on the keyboard. An arrow key selects the cell adjacent to the active cell in the direction of the arrow on the key.

In Excel, any set of characters containing a letter, hyphen (as in a telephone number), or space is considered text. **Text** is used to place titles, such as worksheet titles, column titles, and row titles, on the worksheet. The following steps enter the worksheet title in cell A1.

- If it is not already the active cell, click cell A1 to make it the active cell (Figure 70).

Figure 70

2

- Type **Brain Buster Book Rentals** in cell A1 (Figure 71).

Q&A Why did the appearance of the formula bar change?

Excel displays the title in the formula bar and in cell A1. When you begin typing a cell entry, Excel displays two additional boxes in the formula bar: the Cancel box and the Enter box. Clicking the Enter box completes an entry. Clicking the Cancel box cancels an entry.

Figure 71

3

- Click the Enter box to complete the entry and enter the worksheet title in cell A1 (Figure 72).

Figure 72

Other Ways		
1. To complete entry, click any cell other than active cell	2. To complete entry, press ENTER, HOME, PAGE UP, PAGE DOWN, END,	UP, DOWN, LEFT ARROW, or RIGHT ARROW

To Save an Existing Office Document with the Same File Name

Saving frequently cannot be overemphasized. You have made modifications to the file (spreadsheet) since you created it. Thus, you should save again. Similarly, you should continue saving files frequently so that you do not lose your changes since the time you last saved the file. You can use the same file name, such as Brain Busters, to save the changes made to the document. The following step saves a file again.

1

- Click the Save button on the Quick Access Toolbar to overwrite the previously saved file (Brain Busters, in this case) on the USB flash drive (Figure 73).

Q&A Why did the Save As dialog box not appear?

Office programs, including Excel, overwrite the document using the setting specified the first time you saved the document.

Figure 73

Other Ways
1. Press CTRL+S or press SHIFT+F12

To Use Save As to Change the Name of a File

You might want to save a file with a different name and even to a different location. For example, you might start a homework assignment with a data file and then save it with a final file name for submitting to your instructor, saving it to a location designated by your instructor. The following steps save a file with a different file name.

1 With your USB flash drive connected to one of the computer's USB ports, click File on the Ribbon to open the Backstage view.

2 Click Save As in the Backstage view to display the Save As dialog box.

3 Type **Brain Busters Rental Summary** in the File name text box (Save As dialog box) to change the file name. Do not press the ENTER key after typing the file name because you do not want to close the dialog box at this time.

4 Navigate to the desired save location (the Excel folder in the CIS 101 folder [or your class folder] on the USB flash drive, in this case). For specific instructions, perform the tasks in steps 4a through 4g.

4a If a navigation pane is not displayed in the Save As dialog box, click the Browse Folders button to expand the dialog box.

4b If Computer is not displayed in the navigation pane, drag the navigation pane scroll bar (Save As dialog box) until Computer appears.

4c If Computer is not expanded in the navigation pane, double-click Computer to display a list of available storage devices in the navigation pane.

4d If necessary, scroll through the Save As dialog box until your USB flash drive appears in the list of available storage devices in the navigation pane.

4e If your USB flash drive is not expanded, double-click the USB flash drive in the list of available storage devices in the navigation pane to select that drive as the new save location and display its contents in the right pane.

4f If your class folder (CIS 101, in this case) is not expanded, double-click the CIS 101 folder to select the folder and display its contents.

4g Double-click the Excel folder to select it and display its contents in the right pane.

5 Click the Save button (Save As dialog box) to save the file in the selected folder on the selected drive with the new file name.

To Quit an Office Program

You are finished using Excel. The following steps quit Excel.

1 If you have one Office document open, click the Close button on the right side of the title bar to close the document and quit the Office program; or if you have multiple Office documents open, click File on the Ribbon to open the Backstage view and then click Exit in the Backstage view to close all open documents and quit the Office program.

2 If a dialog box appears, click the Save button to save any changes made to the file since the last save.

Access

The term **database** describes a collection of data organized in a manner that allows access, retrieval, and use of that data. **Microsoft Access 2010**, usually referred to as simply **Access,** is a database management system. A **database management system** is software that allows you to use a computer to create a database; add, change, and delete data in the database; create queries that allow you to ask questions concerning the data in the database; and create forms and reports using the data in the database.

To Start a Program

The following steps, which assume Windows 7 is running, start the Access program based on a typical installation. You may need to ask your instructor how to start programs for your computer.

1 Click the Start button on the Windows 7 taskbar to display the Start menu.

2 Type the name of the program, `Microsoft Access` in this case, as the search text in the 'Search programs and files' text box and watch the search results appear on the Start menu.

3 Click the name of the program, Microsoft Access 2010 in this case, in the search results on the Start menu to start Access.

4 If the program window is not maximized, click the Maximize button on its title bar to maximize the window (Figure 74).

Q&A Do I have to start Access using these steps?

No. You can use any previously discussed method of starting an Office program to start Access.

Figure 74

Unique Elements in Access

You work on objects such as tables, forms, and reports in the **Access work area**. In Figure 74, the Access window contains no open objects. Figure 75 shows a work area with multiple objects open. **Object tabs** for the open objects appear at the top of the work area. You select an open object by clicking its tab. In the figure, the Suppliers Split Form is the selected object. To the left of the work area is the Navigation Pane, which contains a list of all the objects in the database. You use this pane to open an object. You also can customize the way objects are displayed in the Navigation Pane.

Because the Navigation Pane can take up space in the window, you may not have as much open space for working as you would with Word or Excel. You can use the Shutter Bar Open/Close button to minimize the Navigation Pane when you are not using it, which allows more space to work with tables, forms, reports, and other database elements.

Figure 75

Ribbon When you start Access, the Ribbon displays five main tabs: File, Home, Create, External Data, and Database Tools. Access has unique groupings such as Sort & Filter and Records that are designed specifically for working with databases. Many of the formatting options are reserved for the tool tabs that appear when you are working with forms and reports.

To Create an Access Database

Unlike the other Office programs, Access saves a database when you first create it. When working in Access, you will add data to an Access database. As you add data to a database, Access automatically saves your changes rather than waiting until you manually save the database or quit Access. Recall that in Word and Excel, you entered the data first and then saved it.

Because Access automatically saves the database as you add and change data, you do not have to always click the Save button. In fact, the Save button in Access is used for saving the objects (including tables, queries, forms, reports, and other database objects) a database contains. You can use either the Blank Database option or a template to create a new database. If you already know the organization of your database, you would use the Blank Database option. If not, you can use a template. Templates can guide you by suggesting some commonly used database organizations.

The following steps use the Blank Database option to create a database named Charmed Excursions in the Access folder in the class folder (CIS 101, in this case) on a USB flash drive.

1

- If necessary, click the Blank database button in the New gallery (shown in Figure 74 on page OFF 53) in the Backstage view to select the template type.

- Click the File Name text box to select the default database name.

- Type **Charmed Excursions** in the File Name text box to enter the new file name. Do not press the ENTER key after typing the file name because you do not want to create the database at this time (Figure 76).

Figure 76

Q&A

Why is the Backstage view automatically open when you start Access?

Unlike other Office programs, you first must save a database before adding any data. For this reason, the Backstage view opens automatically when you start Access.

2

- Click the 'Browse for a location to put your database' button to display the File New Database dialog box.

- Navigate to the location for the database, that is, the USB flash drive, then to the folder identifying your class (CIS 101, in this case), and then to the Access folder (Figure 77). For detailed steps about navigating, see Steps 3a – 3c on pages OFF 28 and OFF 29.

Q&A

Why does the 'Save as type' box say Microsoft Access 2007 Databases?

Microsoft Access database formats change with some new versions of Microsoft Access. The most recent format is the Microsoft Access 2007 Databases format, which was released with Access 2007.

Figure 77

3

- Click the OK button (File New Database dialog box) to select the Access folder as the location for the database and close the dialog box (Figure 78).

Figure 78

4

- Click the Create button in the Backstage view to create the database on the selected drive in the selected folder with the file name, Charmed Excursions. If necessary, click the Enable Content button (Figure 79).

Q&A How do I know that the Charmed Excursions database is created?

The name of the database appears on the title bar.

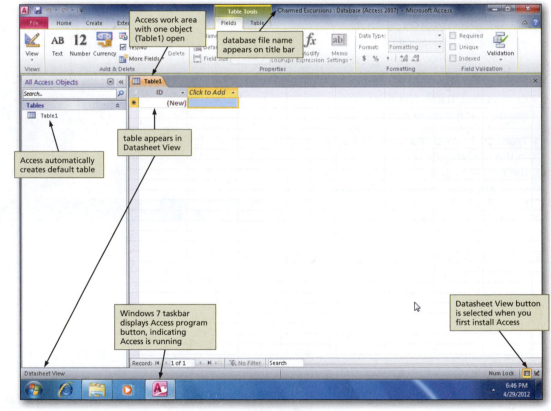

Figure 79

To Close an Office File

Assume you need to close the Access database and return to it later. The following step closes an Office file.

1 Click File on the Ribbon to open the Backstage view and then click Close Database in the Backstage view to close the open file (Charmed Excursions, in this case) without quitting the active program.

Q&A Why is Access still on the screen?

When you close a database, the program remains open.

To Open an Existing Office File

Assume you wish to continue working on an existing file, that is, a file you previously saved. Earlier in this chapter, you learned how to open a recently used file through the Backstage view. The following steps open a database, specifically the Charmed Excursions database, from the USB flash drive.

- With your USB flash drive connected to one of the computer's USB ports, if necessary, click File on the Ribbon to open the Backstage view.

- Click Open in the Backstage view to display the Open dialog box (Figure 80).

- Navigate to the location of the file to be opened (in this case, the USB flash drive, then to the CIS 101 folder [or your class folder], and then to the Access folder). For detailed steps about navigating, see Steps 3a – 3c on pages OFF 28 and OFF 29.

Q&A

What if I did not save my file in a folder?

If you did not save your file in a folder, the file you wish to open should be displayed in the Open dialog box before navigating to any folders.

Figure 80

❸

- Click the file to be opened, Charmed Excursions in this case, to select the file (Figure 81).

❹

- Click the Open button (Open dialog box) to open the selected file and display the opened file in the current program window (shown in Figure 79).

Other Ways

1. Click File on the Ribbon, click Recent in Backstage view, double-click file
2. Press CTRL+O
3. Navigate to file in Windows Explorer, double-click file

Figure 81

To Quit an Office Program

You are finished using Access. The following step quits Access.

1 Click the Close button on the right side of the title bar to close the file and quit the Office program.

Other Office Programs

In addition to the Office programs discussed thus far, three other programs are useful when collaborating and communicating with others: Outlook, Publisher, and OneNote.

Outlook

Outlook is a powerful communications and scheduling program that helps you communicate with others, keep track of contacts, and organize your calendar. Personal information manager (PIM) programs such as Outlook provide a way for individuals and workgroups to organize, find, view, and share information easily. Outlook allows you to send and receive electronic mail (e-mail) and permits you to engage in real-time messaging with family, friends, or coworkers using instant messaging. Outlook also provides a means to organize contacts. Users can track e-mail messages, meetings, and notes related to a particular contact. Outlook's Calendar, Contacts, Tasks, and Notes components aid in this organization. Contact information readily is available from the Outlook Calendar, Mail, Contacts, and Task components by accessing the Find a Contact feature.

Electronic mail (e-mail) is the transmission of messages and files over a computer network. E-mail has become an important means of exchanging information and files between business associates, classmates and instructors, friends, and family. Businesses find that using e-mail to send documents electronically saves both time and money. Parents with students away at college or relatives who live across the country find that communicating by e-mail is an inexpensive and easy way to stay in touch with their family members. Exchanging e-mail messages is one of the more widely used features of the Internet.

The Outlook Window   Figure 82 shows an Outlook window, which is divided into six panes: the Favorites folder pane, Mail folder pane, and Navigation Pane on the left side of the window, the Inbox message pane to the left of center, the Reading Pane to the right of center, and the People Pane just below the Reading Pane.

When an e-mail message is open in Outlook, it is displayed in a Message window (Figure 83). When you open a message, the Message window Ribbon displays the Message tab, which contains the more frequently used commands.

Inbox – Microsoft Outlook window

title bar

number of unread messages in blue

Favorites folder pane

Inbox folder

closed envelope icon indicates unread message

Mail folder pane

opened envelope icon indicates message that has been opened

To-Do Bar

Reading Pane

People Pane

Mail button

Navigation Pane

Inbox message pane

Figure 82

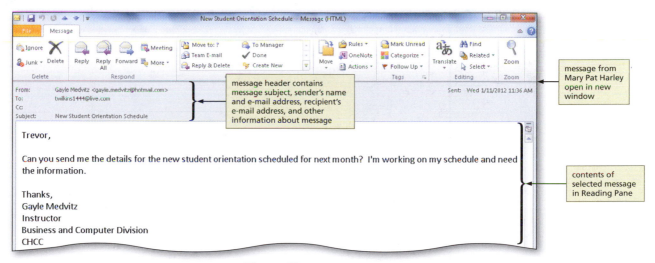

message header contains message subject, sender's name and e-mail address, recipient's e-mail address, and other information about message

message from Mary Pat Harley open in new window

contents of selected message in Reading Pane

Figure 83

Publisher

Publisher is a powerful desktop publishing (DTP) program that assists you in designing and producing professional-quality documents that combine text, graphics, illustrations, and photos. DTP software provides additional tools beyond those typically found in word processing programs, including design templates, graphic manipulation tools, color schemes or libraries, advanced layout and printing tools, and Web components. For large jobs, businesses use DTP software to design publications that are camera ready, which means the files are suitable for outside commercial printing. In addition, DTP software can be used to create Web pages and interactive Web forms.

Publisher is used by people who regularly produce high-quality color publications, such as newsletters, brochures, flyers, logos, signs, catalogs, cards, and business forms. Saving publications as Web pages or complete Web sites is a powerful component of Publisher. All publications can be saved in a format that easily is viewed and manipulated using a browser.

Publisher has many features designed to simplify production and make publications visually appealing. Using Publisher, you easily can change the shape, size, and color of text and graphics. You can include many kinds of graphical objects, including mastheads, borders, tables, images, pictures, charts, and Web objects in publications, as well as integrate spreadsheets and databases.

BTW

Starting Publisher
When you first start Publisher, the New templates gallery usually is displayed in the Backstage view. If it is not displayed, click File on the Ribbon, click Options in the Backstage view, click General (Options dialog box), and then click Show the New template gallery when starting Publisher to select the check box in the General panel.

The Publisher Window On the right side of the Backstage view, Publisher displays the New template gallery, which includes a list of publication types. **Publication types** are typical publications used by desktop publishers. The more popular types are displayed in the center of the window. Each publication type is a link to display various templates and blank publications from which you may choose.

Once you select a publication type, the window changes to allow you to select a specific template (Figure 84). Some templates are installed with Publisher, and others are available online. Clicking a publication type causes template previews to be displayed in the center of the window. The templates are organized by purpose (for example, Sales) and then alphabetically by design type. On the right, Publisher will display a larger preview of the selected template, along with some customization options if the template is installed or a download option if the template is online. In Figure 84, the installed Arrows template is selected so that the customize options appear.

Figure 84

When you click the Create button, Publisher creates the document and sets it up for you to edit. Figure 85 shows the Arrows document that Publisher creates when default options are selected.

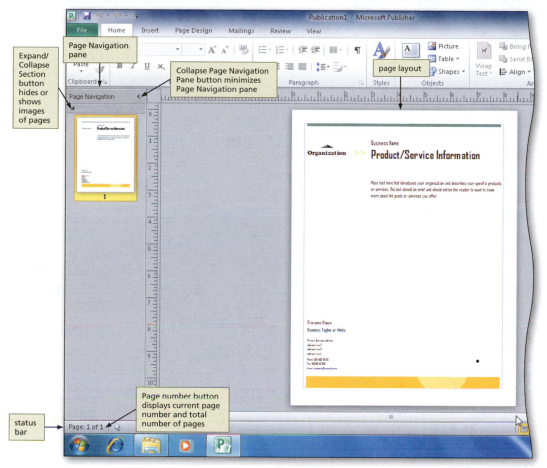

Figure 85

OneNote

OneNote is a note taking program that assists you in entering, saving, organizing, searching, and using notes. It enables you to create pages, which are organized in sections, just as in a physical notebook. In OneNote, you can type notes anywhere on a page and then easily move the notes around on the page. You can create lists and outlines, use handwriting to enter notes, and create drawings. If you use a Tablet PC to add handwritten notes to a document, OneNote can convert the handwriting to text. It also can perform searches on the handwritten entries. Pictures and data from other programs easily are incorporated in your notes.

In addition to typing and handwriting, you can take audio notes. For example, you could record conversations during a meeting or lecture. As you record, you can take additional notes. When you play back the audio notes, you can synchronize the additional notes you took; that is, OneNote will show you during playback the exact points at which you added the notes. A variety of note flags, which are symbols that call your attention to notes on a page, enable you to flag notes as being important. You then can use the Note Flags summary to view the flagged notes, which can be sorted in a variety of ways.

OneNote includes tools to assist you with organizing a notebook and navigating its contents. It also includes a search facility, making it easy to find the specific notes in which you are interested. For short notes that you always want to have available readily, you can use Side Notes, which are used much like the sticky notes that you might use in a physical notebook.

OneNote Window   All activity in OneNote takes place in the **notebook** (Figure 86). Like a physical notebook, the OneNote notebook consists of notes that are placed on **pages**. The pages are grouped into **sections**, which can be further grouped into **folders**. (No folders are shown in the notebook in the figure.) You can use the Search All Notebooks box to search for specific text in your notes.

You can add pages to the notebook using the New Page button in the Page Tabs pane. If Page Tabs are displayed, then you can switch to a page by clicking its tab. Figure 86 shows the Top Uses page being displayed for the General notebook.

Figure 86

Break Point: If you wish to take a break, this is a good place to do so. To resume at a later time, continue to follow the steps from this location forward.

Moving, Renaming, and Deleting Files

Earlier in this chapter, you learned how to organize files in folders, which is part of a process known as **file management**. The following sections cover additional file management topics including renaming, moving, and deleting files.

To Rename a File

In some circumstances, you may want to change the name of, or rename, a file or a folder. For example, you may want to distinguish a file in one folder or drive from a copy of a similar file, or you may decide to rename a file to better identify its contents. The Word folder shown in Figure 87 contains the Word document, Koala Exhibit. The following steps change the name of the Koala Exhibit file in the Word folder to Koala Exhibit Flyer.

1
- If necessary, click the Windows Explorer program button on the taskbar to display the folder window in Windows Explorer.

- Navigate to the location of the file to be renamed (in this case, the Word folder in the CIS 101 [or your class folder] folder on the USB flash drive) to display the file(s) it contains in the right pane.

- Right-click the Koala Exhibit icon or file name in the right pane to select the Koala Exhibit file and display a shortcut menu that presents a list of commands related to files (Figure 87).

Figure 87

2
- Click Rename on the shortcut menu to place the current file name in a text box.

- Type **Koala Exhibit Flyer** in the text box and then press the ENTER key (Figure 88).

Q&A
Are any risks involved in renaming files that are located on a hard disk?

If you inadvertently rename a file that is associated with certain programs, the programs may not be able to find the file and, therefore, may not execute properly. Always use caution when renaming files.

Q&A
Can I rename a file when it is open?

No, a file must be closed to change the file name.

Figure 88

Other Ways

1. Select file, press F2, type new file name, press ENTER

To Move a File

At some time, you may want to move a file from one folder, called the source folder, to another, called the destination. When you move a file, it no longer appears in the original folder. If the destination and the source folders are on the same disk drive, you can move a file by dragging it. If the folders are on different disk drives, then you will need to right-drag the file. The following step moves the Brain Busters Rental Summary file from the Excel folder to the OneNote folder.

- In Windows Explorer, navigate to the location of the file to be moved (in this case, the Excel folder in the CIS 101 folder [or your class folder] on the USB flash drive).

- Click the Excel folder in the navigation pane to display the files it contains in the right pane (Figure 89).

- Drag the Brain Busters Rental Summary file in the right pane to the OneNote folder in the navigation pane.

Figure 89

Other Ways

1. Right-click file, drag file to destination folder, click Move here

2. Right-click file to copy, click Cut on shortcut menu, right-click destination folder, click Paste on shortcut menu

3. Select file to copy, press CTRL+X, select destination folder, press CTRL+V

To Delete a File

A final task you may want to perform is to delete a file. Exercise extreme caution when deleting a file or files. When you delete a file from a hard disk, the deleted file is stored in the Recycle Bin where you can recover it until you empty the Recycle Bin. If you delete a file from removable media, such as a USB flash drive, the file is deleted permanently. The next steps delete the Koala Exhibit Gala file from the PowerPoint folder.

1

- In Windows Explorer, navigate to the location of the file to be deleted (in this case, the PowerPoint folder in the CIS 101 folder [or your class folder] on the USB flash drive).

- Click the PowerPoint folder in the navigation pane to display the files it contains in the right pane.

- Right-click the Koala Exhibit Gala icon or file name in the right pane to select the file and display a shortcut menu (Figure 90).

Figure 90

2

- Click Delete on the shortcut menu to display the Delete File dialog box (Figure 91).

- Click the Yes button (Delete File dialog box) to delete the selected file.

Q&A

Can I use this same technique to delete a folder?

Yes. Right-click the folder and then click Delete on the shortcut menu. When you delete a folder, all of the files and folders contained in the folder you are deleting, together with any files and folders on lower hierarchical levels, are deleted as well.

Figure 91

Other Ways

1. Select icon, press DELETE

Microsoft Office and Windows Help

At any time while you are using one of the Microsoft Office 2010 programs, you can use Office Help to display information about all topics associated with the program. To illustrate the use of Office Help, this section uses Word. Help in other Office 2010 programs operates in a similar fashion.

In Office 2010, Help is presented in a window that has Web-browser-style navigation buttons. Each Office 2010 program has its own Help home page, which is the starting Help page that is displayed in the Help window. If your computer is connected to the Internet, the contents of the Help page reflect both the local help files installed on the computer and material from Microsoft's Web site.

To Open the Help Window in an Office Program

The following step opens the Word Help window.

- Start an Office program, in this case Word.

- Click the Office program's Help button near the upper-right corner of the program window (the Microsoft Word Help button, in this case) to open the program's Help window (Figure 92).

Figure 92

Other Ways
1. Press F1

Moving and Resizing Windows

Up to this point, this chapter has used minimized and maximized windows. At times, however, it is useful, or even necessary, to have more than one window open and visible on the screen at the same time. You can resize and move these open windows so that you can view different areas of and elements in the window. In the case of the Help window, for example, it could be covering document text in the Word window that you need to see.

To Move a Window by Dragging

You can move any open window that is not maximized to another location on the desktop by dragging the title bar of the window. The following step drags the Word Help window to the top left of the desktop.

1

- Drag the window title bar (the Word Help window title bar, in this case) so that the window moves to the top left of the desktop, as shown in Figure 93.

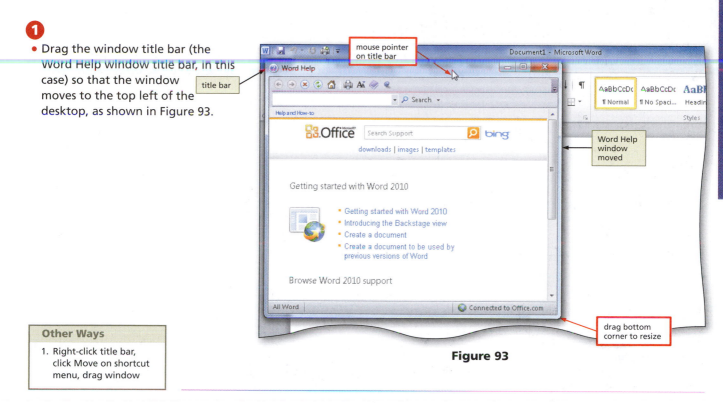

Figure 93

Other Ways

1. Right-click title bar, click Move on shortcut menu, drag window

To Resize a Window by Dragging

Sometimes, information is not visible completely in a window. A method used to change the size of the window is to drag the window borders. The following step changes the size of the Word Help window by dragging its borders.

1

- Point to the lower-right corner of the window (the Word Help window, in this case) until the mouse pointer changes to a two-headed arrow.

- Drag the bottom border downward to display more of the active window (Figure 94).

Q&A Can I drag other borders on the window to enlarge or shrink the window?

Yes, you can drag the left, right, and top borders and any window corner to resize a window.

Q&A Will Windows 7 remember the new size of the window after I close it?

Yes. When you reopen the window, Windows 7 will display it at the same size it was when you closed it.

Figure 94

Using Office Help

Once an Office program's Help window is open, several methods exist for navigating Help. You can search for help by using any of the three following methods from the Help window:

1. Enter search text in the 'Type words to search for' text box
2. Click the links in the Help window
3. Use the Table of Contents

To Obtain Help Using the 'Type words to search for' Text Box

Assume for the following example that you want to know more about the Backstage view. The following steps use the 'Type words to search for' text box to obtain useful information about the Backstage view by entering the word, Backstage, as search text.

1

- Type **Backstage** in the 'Type words to search for' text box at the top of the Word Help window to enter the search text.

- Click the Search button arrow to display the Search menu (Figure 95).

- If it is not selected already, click All Word on the Search menu, so that Help performs the most complete search of the current program (Word, in this case). If All Word already is selected, click the Search button arrow again to close the Search menu.

Figure 95

Why select All Word on the Search menu?

Selecting All Word on the Search menu ensures that Word Help will search all possible sources for information about your search term. It will produce the most complete search results.

2

- Click the Search button to display the search results (Figure 96).

Q&A Why do my search results differ?

If you do not have an Internet connection, your results will reflect only the content of the Help files on your computer. When searching for help online, results also can change as material is added, deleted, and updated on the online Help Web pages maintained by Microsoft.

Q&A Why were my search results not very helpful?

When initiating a search, be sure to check the spelling of the search text; also, keep your search specific, with fewer than seven words, to return the most accurate results.

Figure 96

3

- Click the Introducing Backstage link to open the Help document associated with the selected topic (Figure 97).

Figure 97

4

- Click the Home button on the toolbar to clear the search results and redisplay the Help home page (Figure 98).

Figure 98

To Obtain Help Using the Help Links

If your topic of interest is listed in the Browse area of the Help window, you can click the link to begin browsing the Help categories instead of entering search text. You browse Help just as you would browse a Web site. If you know which category contains your Help information, you may wish to use these links. The following step finds the Formatting Help information using the category links from the Word Help home page.

1

- Click the Formatting link on the Help home page (shown in Figure 98) to display the Formatting page (Figure 99).

Figure 99

To Obtain Help Using the Help Table of Contents

A third way to find Help in Office programs is through the Help Table of Contents. You can browse through the Table of Contents to display information about a particular topic or to familiarize yourself with an Office program. The following steps access the Help information about themes by browsing through the Table of Contents.

1
- Click the Home button on the toolbar to display the Help home page.

- Click the Show Table of Contents button on the toolbar to display the Table of Contents pane on the left side of the Help window. If necessary, click the Maximize button on the Help title bar to maximize the window (Figure 100).

Q&A Why does the appearance of the Show Table of Contents button change?

When the Table of Contents is displayed in the Help window, the Hide Table of Contents button replaces the Show Table of Contents button.

Figure 100

2
- Click the Creating documents link in the Table of Contents pane to view a list of Help subtopics.

- Click the Apply themes to Word documents link in the Table of Contents pane to view the selected Help document in the right pane (Figure 101).

- After reviewing the page, click the Close button to quit Help.

- Click the Office program's Close button (Word, in this case) to quit the Office program.

Figure 101

Q&A How do I remove the Table of Contents pane when I am finished with it?

The Show Table of Contents button acts as a toggle. When the Table of Contents pane is visible, the button changes to Hide Table of Contents. Clicking it hides the Table of Contents pane and changes the button to Show Table of Contents.

Obtaining Help while Working in an Office Program

Help in the Office programs provides you with the ability to obtain help directly, without the need to open the Help window and initiate a search. For example, you may be unsure about how a particular command works, or you may be presented with a dialog box that you are not sure how to use.

Figure 102 shows one option for obtaining help while working in Word. If you want to learn more about a command, point to the command button and wait for the Enhanced ScreenTip to appear. If the Help icon appears in the Enhanced ScreenTip, press the F1 key while pointing to the command to open the Help window associated with that command.

Figure 102

Figure 103 shows a dialog box that contains a Help button. Pressing the F1 key while the dialog box is displayed opens a Help window. The Help window contains help about that dialog box, if available. If no help file is available for that particular dialog box, then the main Help window opens.

Figure 103

Using Windows Help and Support

One of the more powerful Windows 7 features is Windows Help and Support. **Windows Help and Support** is available when using Windows 7 or when using any Microsoft program running under Windows 7. This feature is designed to assist you in using Windows 7 or the various programs. Table 4 describes the content found in the Help and Support Center. The same methods used for searching Microsoft Office Help can be used in Windows Help and Support. The difference is that Windows Help and Support displays help for Windows 7, instead of for Microsoft Office.

Table 4 Windows Help and Support Center Content Areas	
Area	**Function**
Find an answer quickly	This area contains instructions about how to do a quick search using the search box.
Not sure where to start?	This area displays three topics to help guide a user: How to get started with your computer, Learn about Windows Basics, and Browse Help topics. Clicking one of the options navigates to corresponding Help and Support pages.
More on the Windows Website	This area contains links to online content from the Windows Web site. Clicking the links navigates to the corresponding Web pages on the Web site.

To Start Windows Help and Support

The following steps start Windows Help and Support and display the Windows Help and Support window, containing links to more information about Windows 7.

1

- Click the Start button on the taskbar to display the Start menu (Figure 104).

Why are the programs that are displayed on the Start menu different?

Windows adds the programs you have used recently to the left pane on the Start menu. You have started several programs while performing the steps in this chapter, so those programs now are displayed on the Start menu.

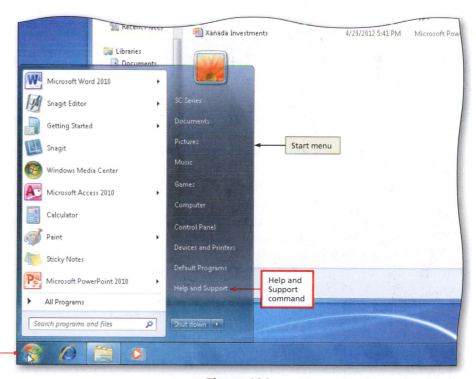

Figure 104

2

- Click Help and Support on the Start menu to open the Windows Help and Support window (Figure 105).

- After reviewing the Windows Help and Support window, click the Close button to quit Windows Help and Support.

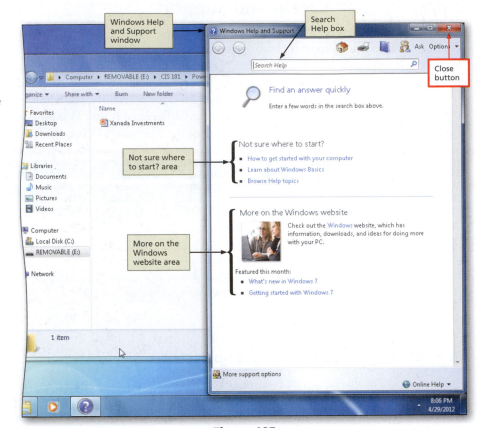

Figure 105

Other Ways

1. Press CTRL+ESC, press RIGHT ARROW, press UP ARROW, press ENTER
2. Press WINDOWS+F1

Chapter Summary

In this chapter, you learned about the Windows 7 interface. You started Windows 7, were introduced to the components of the desktop, and learned several mouse operations. You opened, closed, moved, resized, minimized, maximized, and scrolled a window. You used folder windows to expand and collapse drives and folders, display drive and folder contents, create folders, and rename and then delete a file.

You also learned some basic features of some Microsoft Office 2010 programs, including Word, PowerPoint, Excel, and Access. As part of this learning process, you discovered the common elements that exist among these different Office programs. You now can save basic document, presentation, spreadsheet, and database files. Additional Office programs, including Outlook, Publisher, and OneNote also were discussed.

Microsoft Office Help was demonstrated, and you learned how to use the Office Help window. You were introduced to the Windows 7 Help and Support Center and learned how to use it to obtain more information about Windows 7.

The items listed below include all of the new Windows 7 and Office 2010 skills you have learned in this chapter.

1. Log On to the Computer (OFF 6)
2. Start a Program Using the Start Menu (OFF 10)
3. Maximize a Window (OFF 12)
4. Display a Different Tab on the Ribbon (OFF 16)
5. Minimize, Display, and Restore the Ribbon (OFF 17)
6. Display and Use a Shortcut Menu (OFF 18)
7. Customize the Quick Access Toolbar (OFF 19)
8. Enter Text in a Document (OFF 20)
9. Create a Folder (OFF 22)
10. Create a Folder within a Folder (OFF 24)
11. Expand a Folder, Scroll through Folder Contents, and Collapse a Folder (OFF 26)
12. Switch from One Program to Another (OFF 27)
13. Save a File in a Folder (OFF 27)
14. Minimize and Restore a Window (OFF 30)
15. Change the Screen Resolution (OFF 33)

16. Quit an Office Program with One Document Open (OFF 35)
17. Start a Program Using the Search Box (OFF 37)
18. Enter Content in a Title Slide (OFF 40)
19. Create a New Office Document from the Backstage View (OFF 41)
20. Close an Office File Using the Backstage View (OFF 44)
21. Open a Recent Office File Using the Backstage View (OFF 45)
22. Create a New Blank Office Document from Windows Explorer (OFF 47)
23. Start a Program from Windows Explorer and Open a File (OFF 48)
24. Enter a Worksheet Title (OFF 50)
25. Save an Existing Document with the Same File Name (OFF 51)
26. Create an Access Database (OFF 55)
27. Open an Existing Office File (OFF 57)
28. Rename a File (OFF 63)
29. Move a File (OFF 64)
30. Delete a File (OFF 64)
31. Open the Help Window in an Office Program (OFF 66)
32. Move a Window by Dragging (OFF 66)
33. Resize a Window by Dragging (OFF 67)
34. Obtain Help Using the 'Type words to search for' Text Box (OFF 68)
35. Obtain Help Using the Help Links (OFF 70)
36. Obtain Help Using the Help Table of Contents (OFF 71)
37. Start Windows Help and Support (OFF 73)

If you have a SAM 2010 user profile, your instructor may have assigned an autogradable version of this assignment. If so, log into the SAM 2010 Web site at www.cengage.com/sam2010 to download the instruction and start files.

Learn It Online

Test your knowledge of chapter content and key terms.

Instructions: To complete the Learn It Online exercises, start your browser, click the Address bar, and then enter the Web address **scsite.com/office2010/learn**. When the Office 2010 Learn It Online page is displayed, click the link for the exercise you want to complete and then read the instructions.

Chapter Reinforcement TF, MC, and SA

A series of true/false, multiple choice, and short answer questions that test your knowledge of the chapter content.

Flash Cards

An interactive learning environment where you identify chapter key terms associated with displayed definitions.

Practice Test

A series of multiple choice questions that test your knowledge of chapter content and key terms.

Who Wants To Be a Computer Genius?

An interactive game that challenges your knowledge of chapter content in the style of a television quiz show.

Wheel of Terms

An interactive game that challenges your knowledge of chapter key terms in the style of the television show *Wheel of Fortune*.

Crossword Puzzle Challenge

A crossword puzzle that challenges your knowledge of key terms presented in the chapter.

Apply Your Knowledge

Reinforce the skills and apply the concepts you learned in this chapter.

Creating a Folder and a Document

Instructions: You will create a Word folder and then create a Word document and save it in the folder.

Perform the following tasks:

1. Connect a USB flash drive to an available USB port and then open the USB flash drive window.

2. Click the New folder button on the toolbar to display a new folder icon and text box for the folder name.

3. Type **Word** in the text box to name the folder. Press the ENTER key to create the folder on the USB flash drive.

4. Start Word.

5. Enter the text shown in Figure 106.

6. Click the Save button on the Quick Access Toolbar. Navigate to the Word folder on the USB flash drive and then save the document using the file name, Apply 1 Class List.

7. If your Quick Access Toolbar does not show the Quick Print button, add the Quick Print button to the Quick Access Toolbar. Print the document using the Quick Print button on the Quick Access Toolbar. When you are finished printing, remove the Quick Print button from the Quick Access Toolbar.

8. Submit the printout to your instructor.

9. Quit Word.

Good Study Habits

A schedule saves time

Make each minute count

Choose optimal study locations

Figure 106

Extend Your Knowledge

Extend the skills you learned in this chapter and experiment with new skills. You will use Help to complete the assignment.

Using Help

Instructions: Use Office Help to perform the following tasks.

Perform the following tasks:

1. Start Word.

2. Click the Microsoft Word Help button to open the Word Help window (Figure 107).

3. Search Word Help to answer the following questions.

   a. What are the steps to add a new group to the Ribbon?

   b. What are Quick Parts?

4. With the Word program still running, start PowerPoint.

Figure 107

5. Click the Microsoft PowerPoint Help button on the title bar to open the PowerPoint Help window.

6. Search PowerPoint Help to answer the following questions.

    a. What is a slide master?

    b. How do you copy slides from another presentation into the existing presentation?

7. Quit PowerPoint.

8. Start Excel.

9. Click the Microsoft Excel Help button to open the Excel Help window.

10. Search Excel Help to answer the following questions.

    a. What are three different functions available in Excel?

    b. What are sparklines?

11. Quit Excel.

12. Start Access.

13. Click the Microsoft Access Help button to open the Access Help window.

14. Search Access Help to answer the following questions.

    a. What is SQL?

    b. What is a data macro?

15. Quit Access.

16. Type the answers from your searches in the Word document. Save the document with a new file name and then submit it in the format specified by your instructor.

17. Quit Word.

Make It Right

Analyze a file structure and correct all errors and/or improve the design.

Organizing Vacation Photos

Instructions: See the inside back cover of this book for instructions on downloading the Data Files for Students, or contact your instructor for information on accessing the required files.

    Traditionally, you have stored photos from past vacations together in one folder. The photos are becoming difficult to manage, and you now want to store them in appropriate folders. You will create the folder structure shown in Figure 108. You then will move the photos to the folders so that they will be organized properly.

1. Connect a USB flash drive to an available USB port to open the USB flash drive window.

2. Using the techniques presented in the chapter, create the hierarchical folder structure shown in Figure 108.

3. Using the techniques presented in the chapter, move the vacation photos to their appropriate folders.

4. Submit your work in the format specified by your instructor.

Figure 108

In the Lab

Use the guidelines, concepts, and skills presented in this chapter to increase your knowledge of Windows 7 and Office 2010. Labs are listed in order of increasing difficulty.

Lab 1: Using Windows Help and Support

Problem: You have a few questions about using Windows 7 and would like to answer these questions using Windows Help and Support.

Instructions: Use Windows Help and Support to perform the following tasks:

1. Display the Start menu and then click Help and Support to start Windows Help and Support.

2. Use the Help and Support Content page to answer the following questions.

   a. How do you reduce computer screen flicker?

   b. Which dialog box do you use to change the appearance of the mouse pointer?

   c. How do you minimize all windows?

   d. What is a VPN?

3. Use the Search Help text box in Windows Help and Support to answer the following questions.

   a. How can you minimize all open windows on the desktop?

   b. How do you start a program using the Run command?

   c. What are the steps to add a toolbar to the taskbar?

   d. What wizard do you use to remove unwanted desktop icons?

4. The tools to solve a problem while using Windows 7 are called **troubleshooters**. Use Windows Help and Support to find the list of troubleshooters (Figure 109), and answer the following questions.

   a. What problems does the HomeGroup troubleshooter allow you to resolve?

   b. List five Windows 7 troubleshooters that are not listed in Figure 109.

5. Use Windows Help and Support to obtain information about software licensing and product activation, and answer the following questions.

   a. What is genuine Windows?

   b. What is activation?

   c. What steps are required to activate Windows?

   d. What steps are required to read the Microsoft Software License Terms?

   e. Can you legally make a second copy of Windows 7 for use at home, work, or on a mobile computer or device?

   f. What is registration?

6. Close the Windows Help and Support window.

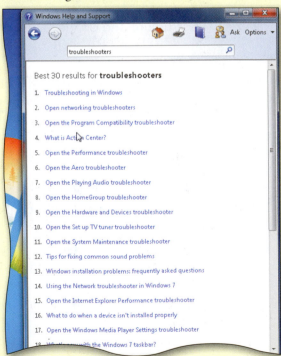

Figure 109

In the Lab

Lab 2: Creating Folders for a Pet Supply Store

Problem: Your friend works for Pete's Pet Supplies. He would like to organize his files in relation to the types of pets available in the store. He has five main categories: dogs, cats, fish, birds, and exotic. You are to create a folder structure similar to Figure 110.

Instructions: Perform the following tasks:

1. Connect a USB flash drive to an available USB port and then open the USB flash drive window.

2. Create the main folder for Pete's Pet Supplies.

3. Navigate to the Pete's Pet Supplies folder.

4. Within the Pete's Pet Supplies folder, create a folder for each of the following: Dogs, Cats, Fish, Birds, and Exotic.

5. Within the Exotic folder, create two additional folders, one for Primates and the second for Reptiles.

6. Submit the assignment in the format specified by your instructor.

Figure 110

In the Lab

Lab 3: Creating Office Documents

Problem: You are taking a class that requires you to create a Word, PowerPoint, Excel, and Access file. You will save these files to folders named for four different Office programs (Figure 111).

Instructions: Create the folders shown in Figure 111. Then, using the respective Office program, create a small file to save in each folder (i.e., create a Word document to save in the Word folder, a PowerPoint presentation to save in the PowerPoint folder, and so on).

Figure 111

1. Connect a USB flash drive to an available USB port and then open the USB flash drive window.

2. Create the folder structure shown in Figure 111.

3. Navigate to the Word folder.

4. Create a Word document containing the text, My First Word Document, and then save it in the Word folder.

5. Navigate to the PowerPoint folder.

6. Create a PowerPoint presentation containing the title text, My First PowerPoint Presentation, and then save it in the PowerPoint folder.

7. Navigate to the Excel folder.

Continued >

In the Lab *continued*

8. Create an Excel spreadsheet containing the text, My First Excel Spreadsheet, in cell A1 and then save it in the Excel folder.

9. Navigate to the Access folder.

10. Save an Access database named, My First Database, in the Access folder.

11. Close all open Office programs.

12. Submit the assignment in the format specified by your instructor.

Cases and Places

Apply your creative thinking and problem solving skills to design and implement a solution.

Note: To complete these assignments, you may be required to use the Data Files for Students. See the inside back cover of this book for instructions on downloading the Data Files for Students, or contact your instructor for information about accessing the required files.

1: Creating Beginning Files for Classes

Academic

You are taking the following classes: Introduction to Engineering, Beginning Psychology, Introduction to Biology, and Accounting. Create folders for each of the classes. Use the following folder names: Engineering, Psychology, Biology, and Accounting, when creating the folder structure. In the Engineering folder, use Word to create a Word document with the name of the class and the class meeting location and time (MW 10:30 – 11:45, Room 317). In the Psychology folder, use PowerPoint to create your first lab presentation. It should begin with a title slide containing the text, Behavioral Observations. In the Biology folder, save a database named Research in the Biology folder. In the Accounting folder, create an Excel spreadsheet with the text, Tax Information, in cell A1. Use the concepts and techniques presented in this chapter to create the folders and files.

2: Using Help

Personal

Your parents enjoy working and playing games on their home computers. Your mother uses a notebook computer downstairs, and your father uses a desktop computer upstairs. They expressed interest in sharing files between their computers and sharing a single printer, so you offered to research various home networking options. Start Windows Help and Support, and search Help using the keywords, home networking. Use the link for installing a printer on a home network. Start Word and then type the main steps for installing a printer. Use the link for setting up a HomeGroup and then type the main steps for creating a HomeGroup in the Word document. Use the concepts and techniques presented in this chapter to use Help and create the Word document.

3: Creating Folders

Professional

Your boss at the bookstore where you work part-time has asked for help with organizing her files. After looking through the files, you decided upon a file structure for her to use, including the following folders: books, magazines, tapes, DVDs, and general merchandise. Within the books folder, create folders for hardback and paperback books. Within magazines, create folders for special issues and periodicals. In the tapes folder, create folders for celebrity and major release. In the DVDs folder, create a folder for book to DVD. In the general merchandise folder, create folders for novelties, posters, and games. Use the concepts and techniques presented in this chapter to create the folders.

1 Creating, Formatting, and Editing a Word Document with Pictures

Objectives

You will have mastered the material in this chapter when you can:

- Enter text in a Word document
- Check spelling as you type
- Format paragraphs
- Format text
- Undo and redo commands or actions
- Change theme colors

- Insert digital pictures in a Word document
- Format pictures
- Add a page border
- Correct errors and revise a document
- Change document properties
- Print a document

1 | Creating, Formatting, and Editing a Word Document with Pictures

Introduction

To advertise a sale, promote a business, publicize an event, or convey a message to the community, you may want to create a flyer and hand it out in person or post it in a public location. Libraries, schools, religious organizations, grocery stores, coffee shops, and other places often provide bulletin boards or windows for flyers. These flyers announce personal items for sale or rent (car, boat, apartment); garage or block sales; services being offered (animal care, housecleaning, lessons); membership, sponsorship, or donation requests (club, religious organization, charity); and other messages such as a lost or found pet.

Project Planning Guidelines

> The process of developing a document that communicates specific information requires careful analysis and planning. As a starting point, establish why the document is needed. Once the purpose is determined, analyze the intended readers of the document and their unique needs. Then, gather information about the topic and decide what to include in the document. Finally, determine the document design and style that will be most successful at delivering the message. Details of these guidelines are provided in Appendix A. In addition, each project in this book provides practical applications of these planning considerations.

Project — Flyer with Pictures

Individuals and businesses create flyers to gain public attention. Flyers, which usually are a single page in length, are an inexpensive means of reaching the community. Many flyers, however, go unnoticed because they are designed poorly.

The project in this chapter follows general guidelines and uses Word to create the flyer shown in Figure 1–1. This colorful, eye-catching flyer announces that a dog has been found. The pictures of the dog, taken with a camera phone, entice passersby to stop and look at the flyer. The headline on the flyer is large and colorful to draw attention into the text. The body copy below the pictures briefly describes where and when the dog was found, along with a bulleted list that concisely highlights important identifying information. The signature line of the flyer calls attention to the contact phone number. The dog's name, Bailey, and signature line are in a different color so that they stand apart from the rest of the text on the flyer. Finally, the graphical page border nicely frames and complements the contents of the flyer.

Figure 1–1

Overview

As you read this chapter, you will learn how to create the flyer shown in Figure 1–1 on the previous page by performing these general tasks:

- Enter text in the document.
- Format the text in the document.
- Insert the pictures in the document.
- Format the pictures in the document.
- Enhance the page with a border and additional spacing.
- Correct errors and revise the document.
- Print the document.

Plan Ahead

General Project Guidelines

When creating a Word document, the actions you perform and decisions you make will affect the appearance and characteristics of the finished document. As you create a flyer, such as the project shown in Figure 1–1, you should follow these general guidelines:

1. **Choose the words for the text.** Follow the *less is more* principle. The less text, the more likely the flyer will be read. Use as few words as possible to make a point.

2. **Identify how to format various elements of the text.** The overall appearance of a document significantly affects its ability to communicate clearly. Examples of how you can modify the appearance, or **format**, of text include changing its shape, size, color, and position on the page.

3. **Find the appropriate graphical image(s).** An eye-catching graphical image should convey the flyer's overall message. It could show a product, service, result, or benefit, or visually convey a message that is not expressed easily with words.

4. **Establish where to position and how to format the graphical image(s).** The position and format of the graphical image(s) should grab the attention of passersby and draw them into reading the flyer.

5. **Determine whether the page needs enhancements such as a border or spacing adjustments.** A graphical, color-coordinated page border can further draw attention to a flyer and nicely frame its contents. Increasing or decreasing spacing between elements on a flyer can improve its readability and overall appearance.

6. **Correct errors and revise the document as necessary.** Post the flyer on a wall and make sure all text and images are legible from a distance. Ask someone else to read the flyer and give you suggestions for improvements.

7. **Determine the best method for distributing the document.** Documents can be distributed on paper or electronically. A flyer should be printed on paper so that it can be posted.

When necessary, more specific details concerning the above guidelines are presented at appropriate points in the chapter. The chapter also will identify the actions performed and decisions made regarding these guidelines during the creation of the flyer shown in Figure 1–1.

For an introduction to Windows 7 and instruction about how to perform basic Windows 7 tasks, read the Office 2010 and Windows 7 chapter at the beginning of this book, where you can learn how to resize windows, change screen resolution, create folders, move and rename files, use Windows Help, and much more.

To Start Word

If you are using a computer to step through the project in this chapter and you want your screens to match the figures in this book, you should change your screen's resolution to 1024×768. For information about how to change a computer's resolution, refer to the Office 2010 and Windows 7 chapter at the beginning of this book.

The following steps, which assume Windows 7 is running, start Word based on a typical installation. You may need to ask your instructor how to start Word for your computer. For a detailed example of the procedure summarized below, refer to the Office 2010 and Windows 7 chapter.

1 Click the Start button on the Windows 7 taskbar to display the Start menu.

2 Type `Microsoft Word` as the search text in the 'Search programs and files' text box and watch the search results appear on the Start menu.

3 Click Microsoft Word 2010 in the search results on the Start menu to start Word and display a new blank document in the Word window.

4 If the Word window is not maximized, click the Maximize button next to the Close button on its title bar to maximize the window.

5 If the Print Layout button on the status bar is not selected (shown in Figure 1–2 on the next page), click it so that your screen is in Print Layout view.

Q&A What is Print Layout view?

The default (preset) view in Word is **Print Layout view**, which shows the document on a mock sheet of paper in the document window.

6 If Normal (Home tab | Styles group) is not selected in the Quick Style gallery (shown in Figure 1–2), click it so that your document uses the Normal style.

Q&A What is the Normal style?

When you create a document, Word formats the text using a particular style. The default style in Word is called the **Normal style**, which is discussed later in this book.

Q&A What if rulers appear on my screen?

Click the View Ruler button above the vertical scroll bar to hide the rulers, or click View on the Ribbon to display the View tab and then place a check mark in the Ruler check box.

BTW

The Word Window
The chapters in this book begin with the Word window appearing as it did at the initial installation of the software. Your Word window may look different depending on your screen resolution and other Word settings.

Entering Text

The first step in creating a document is to enter its text. With the projects in this book, you enter text by typing on the keyboard. By default, Word positions text you type at the left margin. In a later section of this chapter, you will learn how to format, or change the appearance of, the entered text.

Choose the words for the text.
The text in a flyer is organized into three areas: headline, body copy, and signature line.

- The **headline** is the first line of text on the flyer. It conveys the product or service being offered, such as a car for sale or personal lessons, or the benefit that will be gained, such as a convenience, better performance, greater security, higher earnings, or more comfort; or it can contain a message such as a lost or found pet.

- The **body copy** consists of all text between the headline and the signature line. This text highlights the key points of the message in as few words as possible. It should be easy to read and follow. While emphasizing the positive, the body copy must be realistic, truthful, and believable.

- The **signature line**, which is the last line of text on the flyer, contains contact information or identifies a call to action.

Plan Ahead

BTW

Zooming
If text is too small for you to read on the screen, you can zoom the document by dragging the Zoom slider on the status bar or clicking the Zoom Out or Zoom In buttons on the status bar. Changing the zoom has no effect on the printed document.

To Type Text

To begin creating the flyer in this chapter, type the headline in the document window. The following steps type this first line of text in the document.

1

• Type **Found Dog** as the headline (Figure 1–2).

Q&A What if I make an error while typing?

You can press the BACKSPACE key until you have deleted the text in error and then retype the text correctly.

Q&A Why did the Spelling and Grammar Check icon appear on the status bar?

When you begin typing text, the **Spelling and Grammar Check icon** appears on the status bar with an animated pencil writing on paper to indicate that Word is checking for spelling and grammar errors. When you stop typing, the pencil changes to a blue check mark (no errors) or a red X (potential errors found). Word flags potential errors in the document with a red, green, or blue wavy underline. Later in this chapter, you will learn how to fix flagged errors.

Figure 1–2

2

• Press the ENTER key to move the insertion point to the beginning of the next line (Figure 1–3).

Q&A Why did blank space appear between the headline and the insertion point?

Each time you press the ENTER key, Word creates a new paragraph and inserts blank space between the two paragraphs. Later in this chapter, you will learn how to adjust the spacing between paragraphs.

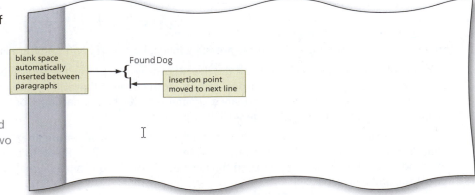

Figure 1–3

To Display Formatting Marks

To indicate where in a document you press the ENTER key or SPACEBAR, you may find it helpful to display formatting marks. A **formatting mark**, sometimes called a **nonprinting character**, is a character that Word displays on the screen but is not visible on a printed document. For example, the paragraph mark (¶) is a formatting mark that indicates where you press the ENTER key. A raised dot (·) shows where you press the SPACEBAR. Other formatting marks are discussed as they appear on the screen.

Depending on settings made during previous Word sessions, your Word screen already may display formatting marks (Figure 1–4). The following step displays formatting marks, if they do not show already on the screen.

1
- If the Home tab is not the active tab, click Home on the Ribbon to display the Home tab.

- If it is not selected already, click the Show/Hide ¶ button (Home tab | Paragraph group) to display formatting marks on the screen (Figure 1–4).

Q&A

What if I do not want formatting marks to show on the screen?

You can hide them by clicking the Show/Hide ¶ button (Home tab | Paragraph group) again. It is recommended that you display formatting marks so that you visually can identify when you press the ENTER key, SPACEBAR, and other keys associated with nonprinting characters; therefore, most of the document windows presented in this book show formatting marks.

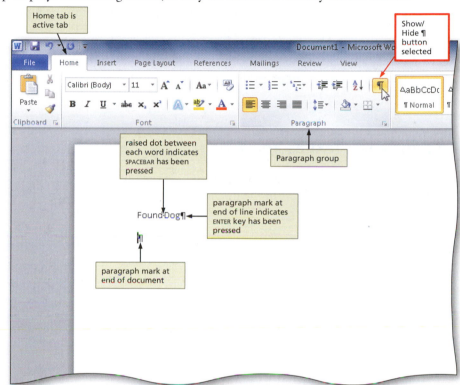

Figure 1–4

Other Ways

1. Press CTRL+SHIFT+*

To Insert a Blank Line

In the flyer, the digital pictures of the dog appear between the headline and body copy. You will not insert these pictures, however, until after you enter and format all text. Thus, you leave a blank line in the document as a placeholder for the pictures. To enter a blank line in a document, press the ENTER key without typing any text on the line. The following step inserts one blank line below the headline.

- Press the ENTER key to insert a blank line in the document (Figure 1–5).

Figure 1–5

Wordwrap

Wordwrap allows you to type words in a paragraph continually without pressing the ENTER key at the end of each line. As you type, if a word extends beyond the right margin, Word also automatically positions that word on the next line along with the insertion point.

Word creates a new paragraph each time you press the ENTER key. Thus, as you type text in the document window, do not press the ENTER key when the insertion point reaches the right margin. Instead, press the ENTER key only in these circumstances:

1. To insert a blank line(s) in a document (as shown in the steps on the previous page)

2. To begin a new paragraph

3. To terminate a short line of text and advance to the next line

4. To respond to questions or prompts in Word dialog boxes, task panes, and other on-screen objects

To Wordwrap Text as You Type

The next step in creating the flyer is to type the body copy. The following step illustrates how the body copy text wordwraps as you enter it in the document.

1

• Type the first sentence of the body copy: `Adorable, loving, friendly, well-behaved dog found early Friday morning, June 1, wandering on the bike trail at Filcher Park in Hampton Township.`

Q&A

Why does my document wrap on different words?

The printer connected to a computer is one factor that can control where wordwrap occurs for each line in a document. Thus, it is possible that the same document could wordwrap differently if printed on different printers.

• Press the ENTER key to position the insertion point on the next line in the document (Figure 1–6).

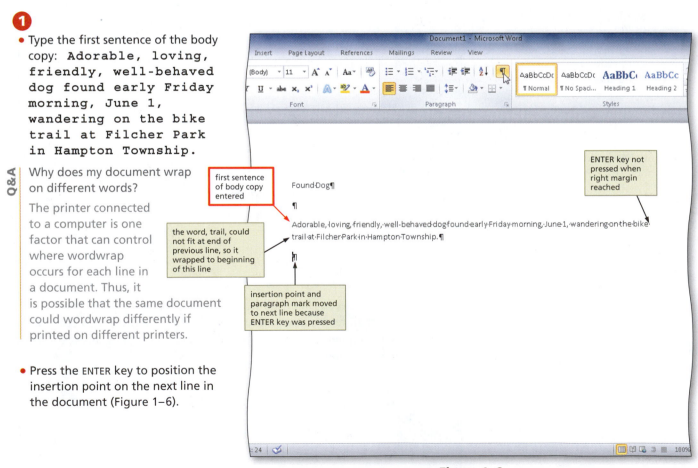

Figure 1–6

Spelling and Grammar Check

As you type text in a document, Word checks your typing for possible spelling and grammar errors. If all of the words you have typed are in Word's dictionary and your grammar is correct, as mentioned earlier, the Spelling and Grammar Check icon on the status bar displays a blue check mark. Otherwise, the icon shows a red X. In this case, Word flags the potential error in the document window with a red, green, or blue wavy underline. A red wavy underline means the flagged text is not in Word's dictionary (because it is a proper name or misspelled). A green wavy underline indicates the text may be incorrect grammatically. A blue wavy underline indicates the text may contain a contextual spelling error such as the misuse of homophones (words that are pronounced the same but that have different spellings or meanings, such as one and won). Although you can check the entire document for spelling and grammar errors at once, you also can check flagged errors as they appear on the screen.

A flagged word is not necessarily misspelled. For example, many names, abbreviations, and specialized terms are not in Word's main dictionary. In these cases, you can instruct Word to ignore the flagged word. As you type, Word also detects duplicate words while checking for spelling errors. For example, if your document contains the phrase, to the the store, Word places a red wavy underline below the second occurrence of the word, the.

BTW

Automatic Spelling Correction

As you type, Word automatically corrects some misspelled words. For example, if you type recieve, Word automatically corrects the misspelling and displays the word, receive, when you press the SPACEBAR or type a punctuation mark. To see a complete list of automatically corrected words, click File on the Ribbon to open the Backstage view, click Options in the Backstage view, click Proofing in the left pane (Word Options dialog box), click the AutoCorrect Options button, and then scroll through the list near the bottom of the dialog box.

To Check Spelling and Grammar as You Type

In the following steps, the word, patches, has been misspelled intentionally as paches to illustrate Word's check spelling as you type feature. If you are doing this project on a computer, your flyer may contain different misspelled words, depending on the accuracy of your typing.

1

- Type **Tan color with paches** and then press the SPACEBAR so that a red wavy line appears below the misspelled word (Figure 1–7).

Q&A

What if Word does not flag my spelling and grammar errors with wavy underlines?

To verify that the check spelling and grammar as you type features are enabled, click File on the Ribbon to open the Backstage view and then click Options in the Backstage view. When the Word Options dialog box is displayed, click Proofing in the left pane, and then ensure the 'Check spelling as you type' and 'Mark grammar errors as you type' check boxes contain check marks. Also ensure the 'Hide spelling errors in this document only' and 'Hide grammar errors in this document only' check boxes do not have check marks. Click the OK button.

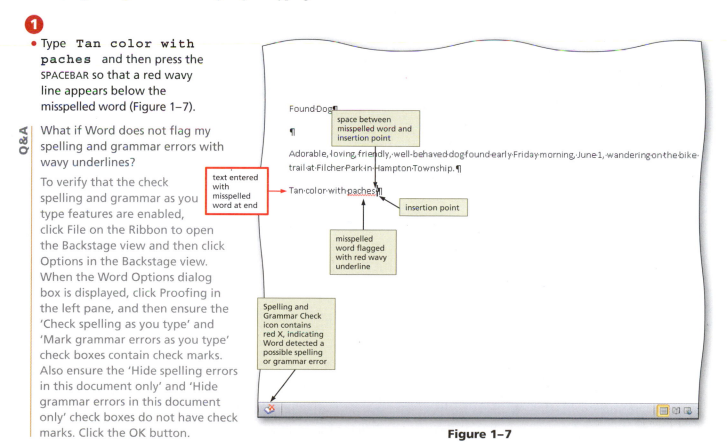

Figure 1–7

2

- Right-click the flagged word (paches, in this case) to display a shortcut menu that presents a list of suggested spelling corrections for the flagged word (Figure 1–8).

Q&A
What if, when I right-click the misspelled word, my desired correction is not in the list on the shortcut menu?

You can click outside the shortcut menu to close the shortcut menu and then retype the correct word, or you can click Spelling on the shortcut menu to display the Spelling dialog box. Chapter 2 discusses the Spelling dialog box.

Q&A
What if a flagged word actually is, for example, a proper name and spelled correctly?

Right-click it and then click Ignore All on the shortcut menu to instruct Word not to flag future occurrences of the same word in this document.

Figure 1–8

3

- Click patches on the shortcut menu to replace the misspelled word in the document with a correctly spelled word (Figure 1–9).

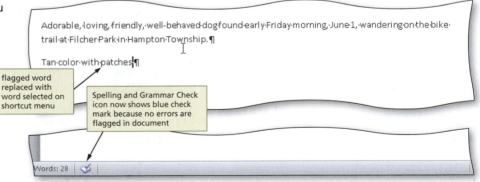

Figure 1–9

Other Ways

1. Click Spelling and Grammar Check icon on status bar, click desired word on shortcut menu

BTW

Character Widths
Many word processing documents use variable character fonts, where some characters are wider than others; for example, the letter w is wider than the letter i.

To Enter More Text

In the flyer, the text yet to be entered includes the remainder of the body copy, which will be formatted as a bulleted list, and the signature line. The next steps enter the remainder of text in the flyer.

1 Press the END key to move the insertion point to the end of the current line.

2 Type `of white on his chest` and then press the ENTER key.

3 Type `Male, adult cocker spaniel` and then press the ENTER key.

4 Type `Green and silver collar with the name, Bailey, on the tag` and then press the ENTER key.

5 Type the signature line in the flyer (Figure 1–10): `If this is your lost dog, call 555-1029.`

three paragraphs of body copy entered, which will be formatted as a bulleted list

Tan·color·with·patches·of·white·on·his·chest¶

Male,·adult·cocker·spaniel¶

Green·and·silver·collar·with·the·name,·Bailey,·on·the·tag¶

signature line entered

If·this·is·your·lost·dog,·call·555-1029.¶

Figure 1–10

Navigating a Document

You view only a portion of a document on the screen through the document window. At some point when you type text or insert graphics, Word probably will **scroll** the top or bottom portion of the document off the screen. Although you cannot see the text and graphics once they scroll off the screen, they remain in the document.

You can use either the keyboard or the mouse to scroll to a different location in a document and/or move the insertion point around a document. When you use the keyboard, the insertion point automatically moves when you press the desired keys. For example, the previous steps used the END key to move the insertion point to the end of the current line. Table 1–1 outlines various techniques to navigate a document using the keyboard.

With the mouse, you can use the scroll arrows or the scroll box on the scroll bar to display a different portion of the document in the document window and then click the mouse to move the insertion point to that location. Table 1–2 explains various techniques for using the scroll bar to scroll vertically with the mouse.

BTW

Minimize Wrist Injury
Computer users frequently switch between the keyboard and the mouse during a word processing session; such switching strains the wrist. To help prevent wrist injury, minimize switching. For instance, if your fingers already are on the keyboard, use keyboard keys to scroll. If your hand already is on the mouse, use the mouse to scroll.

Table 1–1 Moving the Insertion Point with the Keyboard			
Insertion Point Direction	**Key(s) to Press**	**Insertion Point Direction**	**Key(s) to Press**
Left one character	LEFT ARROW	Up one paragraph	CTRL+UP ARROW
Right one character	RIGHT ARROW	Down one paragraph	CTRL+DOWN ARROW
Left one word	CTRL+LEFT ARROW	Up one screen	PAGE UP
Right one word	CTRL+RIGHT ARROW	Down one screen	PAGE DOWN
Up one line	UP ARROW	To top of document window	ALT+CTRL+PAGE UP
Down one line	DOWN ARROW	To bottom of document window	ALT+CTRL+PAGE DOWN
To end of line	END	To beginning of document	CTRL+HOME
To beginning of line	HOME	To end of document	CTRL+END

Table 1–2 Using the Scroll Bar to Scroll Vertically with the Mouse			
Scroll Direction	**Mouse Action**	**Scroll Direction**	**Mouse Action**
Up	Drag the scroll box upward.	Down one screen	Click anywhere below the scroll box on the vertical scroll bar.
Down	Drag the scroll box downward.	Up one line	Click the scroll arrow at the top of the vertical scroll bar.
Up one screen	Click anywhere above the scroll box on the vertical scroll bar.	Down one line	Click the scroll arrow at the bottom of the vertical scroll bar.

Organizing Files and Folders

You should organize and store files in folders so that you easily can find the files later. For example, if you are taking an introductory computer class called CIS 101, a good practice would be to save all Word files in a Word folder in a CIS 101 folder. For a discussion of folders and detailed examples of creating folders, refer to the Office 2010 and Windows 7 chapter at the beginning of this book.

To Save a Document

You have performed many tasks while creating this flyer and do not want to risk losing work completed thus far. Accordingly, you should save the document.

The following steps assume you already have created folders for storing your files, for example, a CIS 101 folder (for your class) that contains a Word folder (for your assignments). Thus, these steps save the document in the Word folder in the CIS 101 folder on a USB flash drive using the file name, Found Dog Flyer. For a detailed example of the procedure summarized below, refer to the Office 2010 and Windows 7 chapter at the beginning of this book.

1 With a USB flash drive connected to one of the computer's USB ports, click the Save button on the Quick Access Toolbar to display the Save As dialog box.

2 Type `Found Dog Flyer` in the File name text box to change the file name. Do not press the ENTER key after typing the file name because you do not want to close the dialog box at this time.

3 Navigate to the desired save location (in this case, the Word folder in the CIS 101 folder [or your class folder] on the USB flash drive).

4 Click the Save button (Save As dialog box) to save the document in the selected folder on the selected drive with the entered file name.

Formatting Paragraphs and Characters

With the text for the flyer entered, the next step is to **format**, or change the appearance of, its text. A paragraph encompasses the text from the first character in the paragraph up to and including its paragraph mark (¶). **Paragraph formatting** is the process of changing the appearance of a paragraph. For example, you can center or add bullets to a paragraph. Characters include letters, numbers, punctuation marks, and symbols. **Character formatting** is the process of changing the way characters appear on the screen and in print. You use character formatting to emphasize certain words and improve readability of a document. For example, you can color or underline characters. Often, you apply both paragraph and character formatting to the same text. For example, you may center a paragraph (paragraph formatting) and underline some of the characters in the same paragraph (character formatting).

Although you can format paragraphs and characters before you type, many Word users enter text first and then format the existing text. Figure 1–11a shows the flyer in this chapter before formatting its paragraphs and characters. Figure 1–11b shows the flyer after formatting. As you can see from the two figures, a document that is formatted is easier to read and looks more professional. The following pages discuss how to format the flyer so that it looks like Figure 1–11b.

Characters that appear on the screen are a specific shape and size. The **font**, or typeface, defines the appearance and shape of the letters, numbers, and special characters. In Word, the default font usually is Calibri (shown in Figure 1–12 on page WD 14). You can leave characters in the default font or change them to a different font. **Font size** specifies the size of the characters and is determined by a measurement system called points. A single **point** is about 1/72 of one inch in height. The default font size in Word typically is 11 (Figure 1–12). Thus, a character with a font size of 11 is about 11/72 or a little less than 1/6 of one inch in height. You can increase or decrease the font size of characters in a document.

A document **theme** is a set of unified formats for fonts, colors, and graphics. Word includes a variety of document themes to assist you with coordinating these visual elements in a document. The default theme fonts are Cambria for headings and Calibri for body text. By changing the document theme, you quickly can give your document a new look. You also can define your own document themes.

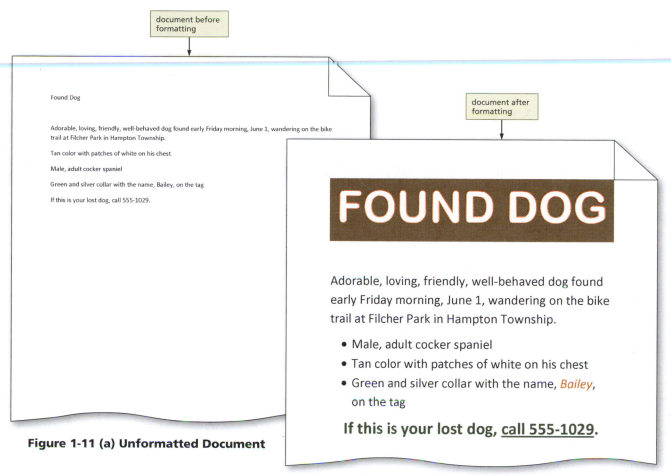

Figure 1-11 (a) Unformatted Document

Figure 1-11 (b) Formatted Document

Identify how to format various elements of the text.
By formatting the characters and paragraphs in a document, you can improve its overall appearance. In a flyer, consider the following formatting suggestions.

- **Increase the font size of characters.** Flyers usually are posted on a bulletin board or in a window. Thus, the font size should be as large as possible so that passersby easily can read the flyer. To give the headline more impact, its font size should be larger than the font size of the text in the body copy. If possible, make the font size of the signature line larger than the body copy but smaller than the headline.

- **Change the font of characters.** Use fonts that are easy to read. Try to use only two different fonts in a flyer, for example, one for the headline and the other for all other text. Too many fonts can make the flyer visually confusing.

- **Change paragraph alignment.** The default alignment for paragraphs in a document is **left-aligned**, that is, flush at the left margin of the document with uneven right edges. Consider changing the alignment of some of the paragraphs to add interest and variety to the flyer.

- **Highlight key paragraphs with bullets.** A bulleted paragraph is a paragraph that begins with a dot or other symbol. Use bulleted paragraphs to highlight important points in a flyer.

- **Emphasize important words.** To call attention to certain words or lines, you can underline them, italicize them, or bold them. Use these formats sparingly, however, because overuse will minimize their effect and make the flyer look too busy.

- **Use color.** Use colors that complement each other and convey the meaning of the flyer. Vary colors in terms of hue and brightness. Headline colors, for example, can be bold and bright. Signature lines should stand out more than body copy but less than headlines. Keep in mind that too many colors can detract from the flyer and make it difficult to read.

Plan Ahead

To Center a Paragraph

The headline in the flyer currently is left-aligned (Figure 1–12). You want the headline to be **centered**, that is, positioned horizontally between the left and right margins on the page. Recall that Word considers a single short line of text, such as the two-word headline, a paragraph. Thus, you will center the paragraph containing the headline. The following steps center a paragraph.

- Click somewhere in the paragraph to be centered (in this case, the headline) to position the insertion point in the paragraph to be formatted (Figure 1–12).

Figure 1–12

- Click the Center button (Home tab | Paragraph group) to center the paragraph containing the insertion point (Figure 1–13).

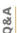

What if I want to return the paragraph to left-aligned?

You would click the Center button again or click the Align Text Left button (Home tab | Paragraph group).

Figure 1–13

Other Ways

1. Right-click paragraph, click Center button on Mini toolbar
2. Right-click paragraph, click Paragraph on shortcut menu, click Indents and Spacing tab
3. Click Paragraph Dialog Box Launcher (Home tab or Page Layout tab | Paragraph group), click Indents and Spacing tab (Paragraph dialog box), click Alignment box arrow, click Centered, click OK button
   (Paragraph dialog box), click Alignment box arrow, click Centered, click OK button
4. Press CTRL+E

BTW

File Type
Depending on your Windows settings, the file type .docx may be displayed on the title bar immediately to the right of the file name after you save the file. The file type .docx is a Word 2010 document.

To Center Another Paragraph

In the flyer, the signature line is to be centered to match the paragraph alignment of the headline. The following steps center the signature line.

1. Click somewhere in the paragraph to be centered (in this case, the signature line) to position the insertion point in the paragraph to be formatted.

2. Click the Center button (Home tab | Paragraph group) to center the paragraph containing the insertion point (shown in Figure 1–14).

Formatting Single versus Multiple Paragraphs and Characters

As shown on the previous pages, to format a single paragraph, simply move the insertion point in the paragraph, to make it the current paragraph, and then format the paragraph. Similarly, to format a single word, position the insertion point in the word, to make it the current word, and then format the word.

To format multiple paragraphs or words, however, you first must select the paragraphs or words you want to format and then format the selection. If your screen normally displays dark letters on a light background, which is the default setting in Word, then selected text displays light letters on a dark background.

To Select a Line

The default font size of 11 point is too small for a headline in a flyer. To increase the font size of the characters in the headline, you first must select the line of text containing the headline. The following steps select a line.

1
- Move the mouse pointer to the left of the line to be selected (in this case, the headline) until the mouse pointer changes to a right-pointing block arrow (Figure 1–14).

Figure 1–14

2
- While the mouse pointer is a right-pointing block arrow, click the mouse to select the entire line to the right of the mouse pointer (Figure 1–15).

Figure 1–15

Other Ways	
1. Drag mouse through line	2. With insertion point at beginning of desired line, press SHIFT+DOWN ARROW

To Change the Font Size of Selected Text

The next step is to increase the font size of the characters in the selected headline. You would like the headline to be as large as possible and still fit on a single line, which in this case is 72 point. The following steps increase the font size of the headline from 11 to 72 point.

1

- With the text selected, click the Font Size box arrow (Home tab | Font group) to display the Font Size gallery (Figure 1–16).

Q&A Why are the font sizes in my Font Size gallery different from those in Figure 1–16?

Font sizes may vary depending on the current font and your printer driver.

Q&A What happened to the Mini toolbar?

The Mini toolbar disappears if you do not use it. These steps use the Font Size box arrow on the Home tab instead of the Font Size box arrow on the Mini toolbar.

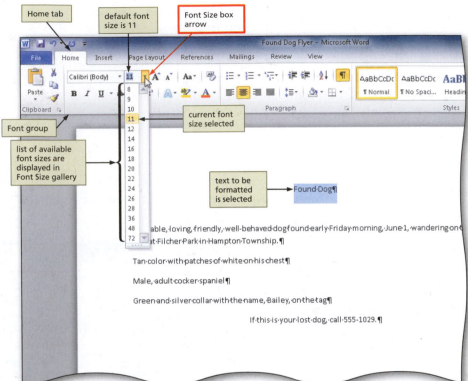

Figure 1–16

2

- Point to 72 in the Font Size gallery to display a live preview of the selected text at the selected point size (Figure 1–17).

⚲ Experiment

- Point to various font sizes in the Font Size gallery and watch the font size of the selected text change in the document window.

3

- Click 72 in the Font Size gallery to increase the font size of the selected text.

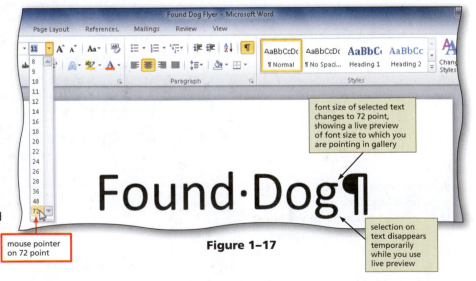

Figure 1–17

Other Ways

1. Click Font Size box arrow on Mini toolbar, click desired font size in Font Size gallery

2. Right-click selected text, click Font on shortcut menu, click Font tab (Font

dialog box), select desired font size in Size list, click OK button

3. Click Font Dialog Box Launcher, click Font tab (Font dialog box), select

desired font size in Size list, click OK button

4. Press CTRL+D, click Font tab (Font dialog box), select desired font size in Size list, click OK button

To Change the Font of Selected Text

The default theme font for headings is Cambria and for all other text, called body text in Word, is Calibri. Many other fonts are available, however, so that you can add variety to documents.

To draw more attention to the headline, you change its font so that it differs from the font of other text in the flyer. The following steps change the font of the headline from Calibri to Arial Rounded MT Bold.

1
• With the text selected, click the Font box arrow (Home tab | Font group) to display the Font gallery (Figure 1–18).

Q&A
Will the fonts in my Font gallery be the same as those in Figure 1–18?

Your list of available fonts may differ, depending on the type of printer you are using and other settings.

Q&A
What if the text is no longer selected?

Follow the steps on page WD 15 to select a line.

Figure 1–18

2
• Scroll through the Font gallery, if necessary, and then point to Arial Rounded MT Bold (or a similar font) to display a live preview of the selected text in the selected font (Figure 1–19).

 Experiment
• Point to various fonts in the Font gallery and watch the font of the selected text change in the document window.

3
• Click Arial Rounded MT Bold (or a similar font) to change the font of the selected text.

Figure 1–19

Other Ways
1. Click Font box arrow on Mini toolbar, click desired font in Font gallery 2. Right-click selected text, click Font on shortcut menu, click Font tab (Font dialog box), select desired font in Font list, click OK button 3. Click Font Dialog Box Launcher (Home tab | Font group), click Font tab (Font dialog box), select desired font in Font list, click OK button 4. Press CTRL+D, click Font tab (Font dialog box), select desired font in the Font list, click OK button

To Change the Case of Selected Text

The headline currently shows the first letter in each word capitalized, which sometimes is referred to as initial cap. To draw more attention to the headline, you would like the entire line of text to be capitalized, or in uppercase letters. The following steps change the headline to uppercase.

1
- With the text selected, click the Change Case button (Home tab | Font group) to display the Change Case gallery (Figure 1–20).

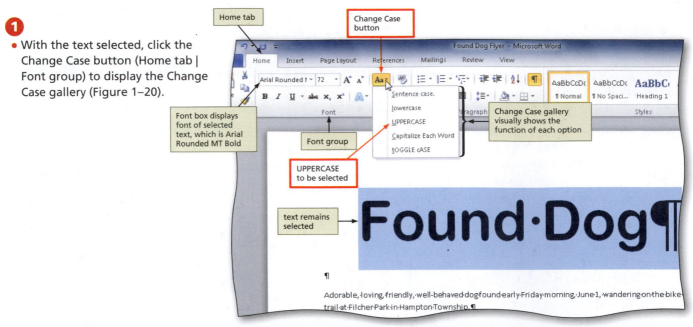

Figure 1–20

2
- Click UPPERCASE in the Change Case gallery to change the case of the selected text (Figure 1–21).

Q&A

What if a ruler appears on the screen or the mouse pointer shape changes?

Depending on the position of your mouse pointer and locations you click on the screen, a ruler may automatically appear or the mouse pointer shape may change. Simply move the mouse and the ruler should disappear and/or the mouse pointer shape will change.

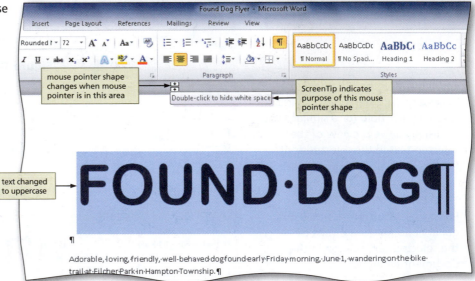

Figure 1–21

Other Ways

1. Right-click selected text, click Font on shortcut menu, click Font tab (Font dialog box), select All caps in Effects area, click OK button

2. Click Font Dialog Box Launcher (Home tab | Font group), click Font tab (Font dialog box), select All caps in Effects area, click OK button

3. Press SHIFT+F3 repeatedly until text is desired case

To Apply a Text Effect to Selected Text

You would like the text in the headline to be even more noticeable. Word provides many text effects to add interest and variety to text. The following steps apply a text effect to the headline.

1

- With the text selected, click the Text Effects button (Home tab | Font group) to display the Text Effects gallery (Figure 1–22).

Figure 1–22

2

- Point to Fill – White, Gradient Outline – Accent 1 (first text effect in third row) to display a live preview of the selected text in the selected text effect (Figure 1–23).

 Experiment

- Point to various text effects in the Text Effects gallery and watch the text effects of the selected text change in the document window.

3

- Click Fill – White, Gradient Outline – Accent 1 to change the text effect of the selected text.

4

- Click anywhere in the document window to remove the selection from the selected text.

Figure 1–23

Other Ways
1. Right-click selected text, click Font on shortcut menu, click Font tab (Font dialog box), click Text Effects button, select desired text effects	(Format Text Effects dialog box), click Close button, click OK button 2. Click Font Dialog Box Launcher (Home tab | Font group), click Font	tab (Font dialog box), click Text Effects button, select desired text effects (Format Text Effects dialog box), click Close button, click OK button

To Shade a Paragraph

To make the headline of the flyer more eye-catching, you would like to shade it. When you **shade** text, Word colors the rectangular area behind any text or graphics. If the text to shade is a paragraph, Word shades the area from the left margin to the right margin of the current paragraph. To shade a paragraph, place the insertion point in the paragraph. To shade any other text, you must first select the text to be shaded. This flyer uses brown as the shading color for the headline. The following steps shade a paragraph.

1

- Click somewhere in the paragraph to be shaded (in this case, the headline) to position the insertion point in the paragraph to be formatted.

- Click the Shading button arrow (Home tab | Paragraph group) to display the Shading gallery (Figure 1–24).

Q&A What if I click the Shading button by mistake?

Click the Shading button arrow and proceed with Step 2.

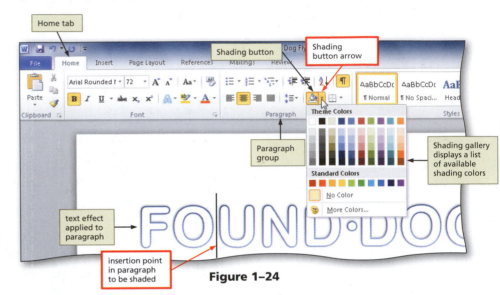

Figure 1–24

2

- Point to Orange, Accent 6, Darker 50% (rightmost color in the sixth row) to display a live preview of the selected shading color (Figure 1–25).

Experiment

- Point to various colors in the Shading gallery and watch the shading color of the current paragraph change.

Figure 1–25

3

- Click Orange, Accent 6, Darker 50% to shade the current paragraph.

Q&A What if I apply a dark shading color to dark text?

When the font color of text is Automatic, it usually is black. If you select a dark shading color, Word automatically may change the text color to white so that the shaded text is easier to read.

Other Ways

1. Click Border button arrow (Home tab | Paragraph group), click Borders and Shading, click Shading tab (Borders and Shading dialog box), click Fill box arrow, select desired color, click OK button

To Select Multiple Lines

The next formatting step for the flyer is to increase the font size of the characters between the headline and the signature line so that they are easier to read from a distance. To change the font size of the characters in multiple lines, you first must select all the lines to be formatted. The following steps select multiple lines.

1

- Move the mouse pointer to the left of the first paragraph to be selected until the mouse pointer changes to a right-pointing block arrow (Figure 1–26).

Figure 1–26

2

- Drag downward to select all lines that will be formatted (Figure 1–27).

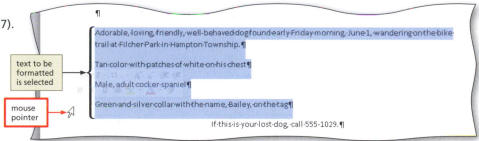

Figure 1–27

Other Ways

1. With insertion point at beginning of desired line, press SHIFT+DOWN ARROW repeatedly until all lines are selected

To Change the Font Size of Selected Text

The characters between the headline and the signature line in the flyer currently are 11 point. To make them easier to read from a distance, this flyer uses 22 point for these characters. The steps on the next page change the font size of the selected text.

1 With the text selected, click the Font Size box arrow (Home tab | Font group) to display the Font Size gallery.

2 Click 22 in the Font Size gallery to increase the font size of the selected text.

3 Click anywhere in the document window to remove the selection from the text.

4 If necessary, scroll so that you can see all the text on the screen (Figure 1–28).

Formatting Marks
With some fonts, formatting marks do not display properly on the screen. For example, the raised dot that signifies a blank space between words may be displayed behind a character instead of in the blank space, causing the characters to look incorrect.

Figure 1–28

To Bullet a List of Paragraphs

The next step is to format as a bulleted list the three paragraphs of identifying information that are above the signature line in the flyer. A **bulleted list** is a series of paragraphs, each beginning with a bullet character.

To format a list of paragraphs with bullets, you first must select all the lines in the paragraphs. The following steps bullet a list of paragraphs.

1

- Move the mouse pointer to the left of the first paragraph to be selected until the mouse pointer changes to a right-pointing block arrow.

- Drag downward until all paragraphs that will be formatted with a bullet character are selected (Figure 1–29).

Figure 1–29

• Click the Bullets button (Home tab | Paragraph group) to place a bullet character at the beginning of each selected paragraph (Figure 1–30).

Q&A How do I remove bullets from a list or paragraph?

Select the list or paragraph and then click the Bullets button again.

Q&A What if I accidentally click the Bullets button arrow?

Press the ESCAPE key to remove the Bullets gallery from the screen and then repeat Step 2.

Figure 1–30

Other Ways

1. Right-click selected paragraphs, point to Bullets on shortcut menu, click desired bullet style

To Undo and Redo an Action

Word provides a means of canceling your recent command(s) or action(s). For example, if you format text incorrectly, you can undo the format and try it again. When you point to the Undo button, Word displays the action you can undo as part of a ScreenTip.

If, after you undo an action, you decide you did not want to perform the undo, you can redo the undone action. Word does not allow you to undo or redo some actions, such as saving or printing a document. The next steps undo the bullet format just applied and then redo the bullet format.

1

• Click the Undo button on the Quick Access Toolbar to reverse your most recent action (in this case, remove the bullets from the paragraphs) (Figure 1–31).

2

• Click the Redo button on the Quick Access Toolbar to reverse your most recent undo (in this case, place a bullet character on the paragraphs again) (shown in Figure 1–30).

Figure 1–31

Other Ways

1. Press CTRL+Z to undo; press CTRL+Y to redo

To Italicize Text

The next step is to italicize the dog's name, Bailey, in the flyer to further emphasize it. **Italicized** text has a slanted appearance. As with a single paragraph, if you want to format a single word, you do not need to select it. Simply position the insertion point somewhere in the word and apply the desired format. The following step formats a word in italics.

- Click somewhere in the word to be italicized (Bailey, in this case) to position the insertion point in the word to be formatted.

- Click the Italic button (Home tab | Font group) to italicize the word containing the insertion point (Figure 1–32).

Q&A How would I remove an italic format?

You would click the Italic button a second time, or you immediately could click the Undo button on the Quick Access Toolbar or press CTRL+Z.

Q&A How can I tell what formatting has been applied to text?

The selected buttons and boxes on the Home tab show formatting characteristics of the location of the insertion point. With the insertion point in the word, Bailey, the Home tab shows these formats: 22-point Calibri italic font, bulleted paragraph.

Figure 1–32

Other Ways
1. Click Italic button on Mini toolbar 2. Right-click selected text, click Font on shortcut menu, click Font tab   (Font dialog box), click Italic in Font style list, click OK button 3. Click Font Dialog Box Launcher (Home tab | Font group), click Font tab (Font dialog box), click Italic in Font style list, click OK button 4. Press CTRL+I

Plan Ahead

Use color.
When choosing color, associate the meaning of color to your message:

- Red expresses danger, power, or energy, and often is associated with sports or physical exertion.

- Brown represents simplicity, honesty, and dependability.

- Orange denotes success, victory, creativity, and enthusiasm.

- Yellow suggests sunshine, happiness, hope, liveliness, and intelligence.

- Green symbolizes growth, healthiness, harmony, blooming, and healing, and often is associated with safety or money.

- Blue indicates integrity, trust, importance, confidence, and stability.

- Purple represents wealth, power, comfort, extravagance, magic, mystery, and spirituality.

- White stands for purity, goodness, cleanliness, precision, and perfection.

- Black suggests authority, strength, elegance, power, and prestige.

- Gray conveys neutrality and thus often is found in backgrounds and other effects.

BTW

Q&As
For a complete list of the Q&As found in many of the step-by-step sequences in this book, visit the Word 2010 Q&A Web page (scsite.com/wd2010/qa).

To Color Text

To emphasize the dog's name even more, its color is changed to a shade of blue. The following steps change the color of the word, Bailey.

- With the insertion point in the word to format, click the Font Color button arrow (Home tab | Font group) to display the Font Color gallery (Figure 1–33).

Q&A What if I click the Font Color button by mistake?

Click the Font Color button arrow and then proceed with Step 2.

- Point to Blue, Accent 1, Darker 25% (fifth color in the fifth row) to display a live preview of the selected font color.

 Experiment

- Point to various colors in the Font Color gallery and watch the color of the current word change.

Figure 1–33

- Click Blue, Accent 1, Darker 25% to change the color of the text (Figure 1–34).

Q&A How would I change the text color back to black?

You would position the insertion point in the word or select the text, click the Font Color button arrow (Home tab | Font group) again, and then click Automatic in the Font Color gallery.

Figure 1–34

Other Ways

1. Click Font Color button arrow on Mini toolbar, click desired color

2. Right-click selected text, click Font on shortcut menu, click Font tab

   (Font dialog box), click Font color box arrow, click desired color, click OK button

3. Click Font Dialog Box Launcher (Home tab |

   Font group), click Font tab (Font dialog box), click Font color box arrow, click desired color, click OK button

To Use the Mini Toolbar to Format Text

Recall from the Office 2010 and Windows 7 chapter at the beginning of this book that the Mini toolbar, which automatically appears based on certain tasks you perform, contains commands related to changing the appearance of text in a document. All commands on the Mini toolbar also exist on the Ribbon.

When the Mini toolbar appears, it initially is transparent. If you do not use the transparent Mini toolbar, it disappears from the screen. The following steps use the Mini toolbar to change the color and font size of text in the signature line of the flyer.

- Move the mouse pointer to the left of the line to be selected (in this case, the signature line) until the mouse pointer changes to a right-pointing block arrow and then click the mouse to select the line (Figure 1–35).

Figure 1–35

- Move the mouse pointer into the transparent Mini toolbar, so that it changes to a bright toolbar.

- Click the Font Size box arrow on the Mini toolbar to display the Font Size gallery and then point to 28 in the Font Size gallery to display a live preview of the selected font size (Figure 1–36).

Figure 1–36

- Click 28 in the Font Size gallery to increase the font size of the selected text.

- With the text still selected and the Mini toolbar still displayed, click the Font Color button arrow on the Mini toolbar to display the Font Color gallery and then point to Purple, Accent 4, Darker 50% (eighth color in the sixth row) to display a live preview of the selected font color (Figure 1–37).

Figure 1–37

- Click Purple, Accent 4, Darker 50% to change the color of the text.

- Click anywhere in the document window to remove the selection from the text.

To Select a Group of Words

To emphasize the contact information (call 555-1029), these words are underlined in the flyer. To format a group of words, you first must select them. The following steps select a group of words.

- Position the mouse pointer immediately to the left of the first character of the text to be selected, in this case, the c in call (Figure 1–38).

Q&A

Why did the shape of the mouse pointer change?

The mouse pointer's shape is an I-beam when positioned in unselected text in the document window.

Figure 1–38

- Drag the mouse pointer through the last character of the text to be selected, in this case, the 9 in the phone number (Figure 1–39).

Q&A

Why did the mouse pointer shape change again?

When the mouse pointer is positioned in selected text, its shape is a left-pointing block arrow.

Figure 1–39

Other Ways
1. With insertion point at beginning of first word in group, press CTRL+SHIFT+RIGHT ARROW repeatedly until all words are selected

To Underline Text

Underlines are used to emphasize or draw attention to specific text. **Underlined** text prints with an underscore (_) below each character. In the flyer, the contact information, call 555-1029, in the signature line is emphasized with an underline. The following step formats selected text with an underline.

- With the text selected, click the Underline button (Home tab | Font group) to underline the selected text (Figure 1–40).

Q&A

How would I remove an underline?

You would click the Underline button a second time, or you immediately could click the Undo button on the Quick Access Toolbar.

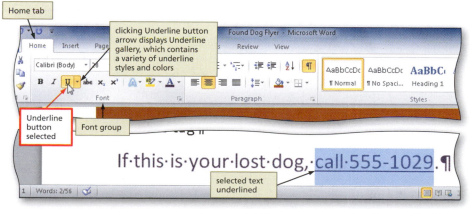

Figure 1–40

Other Ways
1. Right-click text, click Font on shortcut menu, click Font tab (Font dialog box), click Underline style box arrow, click desired underline style, click OK button
2. Click Font Dialog Box Launcher (Home tab | Font group), click Font tab (Font dialog box), click Underline style box arrow, click desired underline style, click OK button
3. Press CTRL+U

To Bold Text

Bold characters appear somewhat thicker and darker than those that are not bold. To further emphasize the signature line, it is bold in the flyer. To format the line, as you have learned previously, you select the line first. The following steps format the signature line bold.

- Move the mouse pointer to the left of the line to be selected (in this case, the signature line) until the mouse pointer changes to a right-pointing block arrow and then click the mouse to select the text to be formatted.

- With the text selected, click the Bold button (Home tab | Font group) to bold the selected text (Figure 1–41).

Q&A

How would I remove a bold format?

You would click the Bold button a second time, or you immediately could click the Undo button on the Quick Access Toolbar.

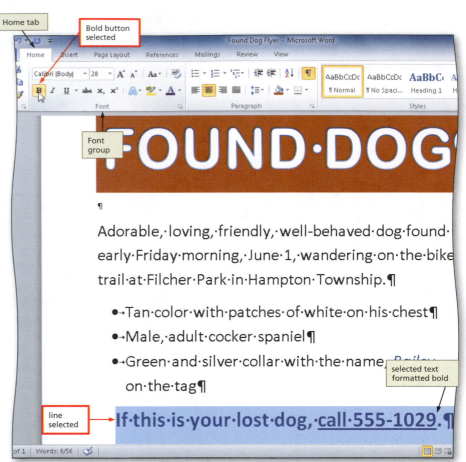

- Click anywhere in the document window to remove the selection from the screen.

Figure 1–41

Other Ways
1. Click Bold button on Mini toolbar
2. Right-click selected text, click Font on shortcut menu, click Font tab (Font dialog box), click Bold in Font style list, click OK button
3. Click Font Dialog Box Launcher (Home tab | Font group), click Font tab (Font dialog box), click Bold in Font style list, click OK button
4. Press CTRL+B

To Change Theme Colors

A **color scheme** in Word is a document theme that identifies 12 complementary colors for text, background, accents, and links in a document. With more than 20 predefined color schemes, Word provides a simple way to select colors that work well together.

In the flyer, you want all the colors to convey honesty, dependability, and healing, that is, shades of browns and greens. In Word, the Aspect color scheme uses these colors. Thus, you will change the color scheme from the default, Office, to Aspect. The next steps change theme colors.

1

● Click the Change Styles button (Home tab | Styles group) to display the Change Styles menu.

● Point to Colors on the Change Styles menu to display the Colors gallery (Figure 1–42).

Experiment

● Point to various color schemes in the Colors gallery and watch the colors change in the document window.

Figure 1–42

2

● Click Aspect in the Colors gallery to change the document theme colors (Figure 1–43).

Q&A

What if I want to return to the original color scheme?

You would click the Change Styles button again, click Colors on the Change Styles menu, and then click Office in the Colors gallery.

Figure 1–43

Other Ways

1. Click Theme Colors button (Page Layout tab | Themes group), select desired color scheme

Selecting Text

In many of the previous steps, you have selected text. Table 1–3 summarizes the techniques used to select various items.

Table 1–3 Techniques for Selecting Text		
Item to Select	**Mouse**	**Keyboard (where applicable)**
Block of text	Click at beginning of selection, scroll to end of selection, position mouse pointer at end of selection, hold down SHIFT key and then click; or drag through the text.	
Character(s)	Drag through character(s).	SHIFT+RIGHT ARROW or SHIFT+LEFT ARROW
Document	Move mouse to left of text until mouse pointer changes to a right-pointing block arrow and then triple-click.	CTRL+A
Graphic	Click the graphic.	
Line	Move mouse to left of line until mouse pointer changes to a right-pointing block arrow and then click.	HOME, then SHIFT+END or END, then SHIFT+HOME
Lines	Move mouse to left of first line until mouse pointer changes to a right-pointing block arrow and then drag up or down.	HOME, then SHIFT+DOWN ARROW or END, then SHIFT+UP AROW
Paragraph	Triple-click paragraph; or move mouse to left of paragraph until mouse pointer changes to a right-pointing block arrow and then double-click.	CTRL+SHIFT+DOWN ARROW or CTRL+SHIFT+UP ARROW
Paragraphs	Move mouse to left of paragraph until mouse pointer changes to a right-pointing block arrow, double-click, and then drag up or down.	CTRL+SHIFT+DOWN ARROW or CTRL+SHIFT+UP ARROW repeatedly
Sentence	Press and hold down CTRL key and then click sentence.	
Word	Double-click the word.	CTRL+SHIFT+RIGHT ARROW or CTRL+SHIFT+LEFT ARROW
Words	Drag through words.	CTRL+SHIFT+RIGHT ARROW or CTRL+SHIFT+LEFT ARROW repeatedly

To Save an Existing Document with the Same File Name

You have made several modifications to the document since you last saved it. Thus, you should save it again. The following step saves the document again. For an example of the step listed below, refer to the Office 2010 and Windows 7 chapter at the beginning of this book.

 Click the Save button on the Quick Access Toolbar to overwrite the previously saved file.

Break Point: If you wish to take a break, this is a good place to do so. You can quit Word now (refer to page WD 44 for instructions). To resume at a later time, start Word (refer to pages WD 4 and WD 5 for instructions), open the file called Found Dog Flyer (refer to page WD 45 for instructions), and continue following the steps from this location forward.

Inserting and Formatting Pictures in a Word Document

With the text formatted in the flyer, the next step is to insert digital pictures in the flyer and format the pictures. Flyers usually contain graphical images, such as a picture, to attract the attention of passersby. In the following pages, you will perform these tasks:

1. Insert the first digital picture into the flyer and then reduce its size.
2. Insert the second digital picture into the flyer and then reduce its size.
3. Change the look of the first picture and then the second picture.

<table>
<tr><td>

Find the appropriate graphical image.
To use a graphical image, also called a graphic, in a Word document, the image must be stored digitally in a file. Files containing graphical images are available from a variety of sources:

- Word includes a collection of predefined graphical images that you can insert in a document.

- Microsoft has free digital images on the Web for use in a document. Other Web sites also have images available, some of which are free, while others require a fee.

- You can take a picture with a digital camera or camera phone and **download** it, which is the process of copying the digital picture from the camera or phone to your computer.

- With a scanner, you can convert a printed picture, drawing, or diagram to a digital file.

    If you receive a picture from a source other than yourself, do not use the file until you are certain it does not contain a virus. A **virus** is a computer program that can damage files and programs on your computer. Use an antivirus program to verify that any files you use are virus free.

</td><td>

Plan Ahead

</td></tr>
</table>

<table>
<tr><td>

Establish where to position and how to format the graphical image.
The content, size, shape, position, and format of a graphic should capture the interest of passersby, enticing them to stop and read the flyer. Often, the graphic is the center of attraction and visually the largest element on a flyer. If you use colors in the graphical image, be sure they are part of the document's color scheme.

</td><td>

Plan Ahead

</td></tr>
</table>

To Insert a Picture

The next step in creating the flyer is to insert one of the digital pictures of the dog so that it is centered on the blank line below the headline. The picture, which was taken with a camera phone, is available on the Data Files for Students. See the inside back cover of this book for instructions on downloading the Data Files for Students, or contact your instructor for information about accessing the required files.

The following steps insert a centered picture, which, in this example, is located in the Chapter 01 folder in the Word folder in the Data Files for Students folder on a USB flash drive.

1

- Position the insertion point on the blank line below the headline, which is the location where you want to insert the picture.

- Click the Center button (Home tab | Paragraph group) to center the paragraph that will contain the picture.

- Click Insert on the Ribbon to display the Insert tab (Figure 1–44).

Figure 1–44

2

- With your USB flash drive connected to one of the computer's USB ports, click the Insert Picture from File button (Insert tab | Illustrations group) (shown in Figure 1-44) to display the Insert Picture dialog box (shown in Figure 1-45 on the next page).

3

- Navigate to the picture location (in this case, the Chapter 01 folder in the Word folder in the Data Files for Students folder on a USB flash drive). For a detailed example of this procedure, refer to Steps 3a – 3c in the To Save a File in a Folder section in the Office 2010 and Windows 7 chapter at the beginning of this book.

- Click Dog Picture 1 to select the file (Figure 1–45).

Q&A

What if the picture is not on a USB flash drive?

Use the same process, but select the storage location containing the picture.

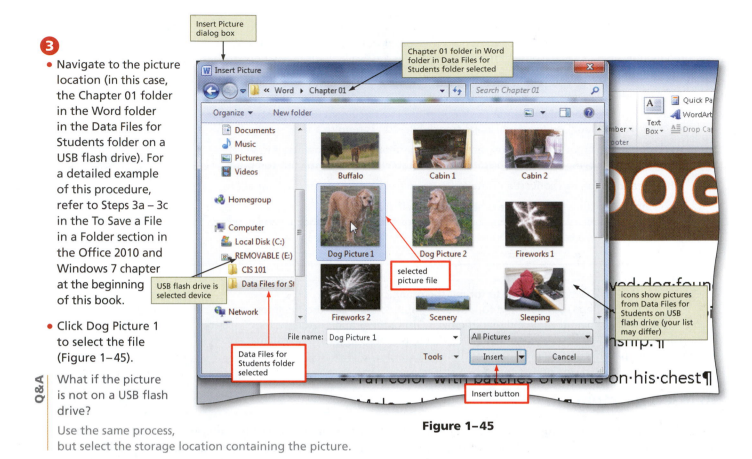

Insert Picture dialog box

Chapter 01 folder in Word folder in Data Files for Students folder selected

USB flash drive is selected device

Data Files for Students folder selected

selected picture file

icons show pictures from Data Files for Students on USB flash drive (your list may differ)

Insert button

Figure 1–45

4

- Click the Insert button (Insert Picture dialog box) to insert the picture at the location of the insertion point in the document (Figure 1–46).

Q&A

What are the symbols around the picture?

A selected graphic appears surrounded by a **selection rectangle**, which has small squares and circles, called **sizing handles**, at each corner and middle location.

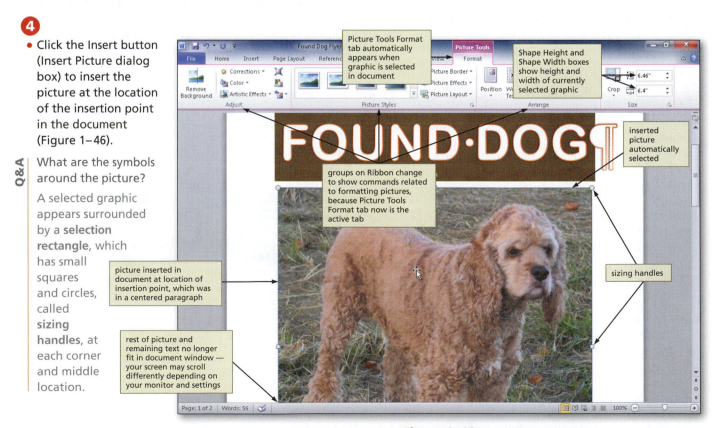

Picture Tools Format tab automatically appears when graphic is selected in document

Shape Height and Shape Width boxes show height and width of currently selected graphic

inserted picture automatically selected

groups on Ribbon change to show commands related to formatting pictures, because Picture Tools Format tab now is the active tab

picture inserted in document at location of insertion point, which was in a centered paragraph

sizing handles

rest of picture and remaining text no longer fit in document window — your screen may scroll differently depending on your monitor and settings

Figure 1–46

To Zoom the Document

The next step is to reduce the size of the picture so that both pictures will fit side-by-side on the same line. With the current picture size, the flyer now has expanded to two pages. The final flyer, however, should fit on a single page. In Word, you can change the zoom so that you can see the entire document (that is, both pages) on the screen at once. Seeing the entire document at once helps you determine the appropriate size for the picture. The following step zooms the document.

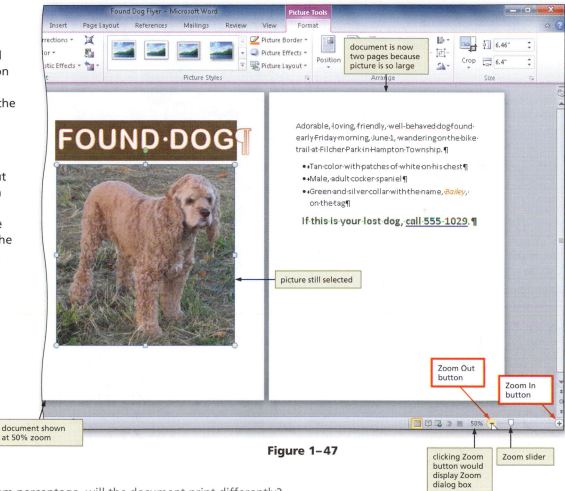

Experiment

- Repeatedly click the Zoom Out and Zoom In buttons on the status bar and watch the size of the document change in the document window.

- Click the Zoom Out or Zoom In button as many times as necessary until the Zoom button on the status bar displays 50% on its face (Figure 1–47).

Figure 1–47

Q&A | If I change the zoom percentage, will the document print differently?

Changing the zoom has no effect on the printed document.

Q&A | Are there predefined zoom options?

Yes. Through the View tab | Zoom group or the Zoom dialog box, you can zoom to one page, two pages, many pages, page width, text width, and a variety of set percentages. Page width zoom places the edges of the page at the edges of the Word window, whereas Text width zoom places the contents of the page at the edges of the Word window.

Other Ways

1. Drag Zoom slider on status bar

2. Click Zoom button on status bar, select desired zoom percent or type (Zoom dialog box), click OK button

3. Click Zoom button (View tab | Zoom group), select desired zoom percent or type (Zoom dialog box), click OK button

To Resize a Graphic

The next step is to resize the picture so that both pictures will fit side-by-side on the same line below the headline. **Resizing** includes both enlarging and reducing the size of a graphic. In this flyer, you will reduce the size of the picture. With the entire document displayed in the document window, you will be able to see how the resized graphic will look on the entire page. The following steps resize a selected graphic.

- With the graphic still selected, point to the upper-right corner sizing handle on the picture so that the mouse pointer shape changes to a two-headed arrow (Figure 1–48).

Q&A What if my graphic (picture) is not selected?

To select a graphic, click it.

Figure 1–48

- Drag the sizing handle diagonally inward until the crosshair mouse pointer is positioned approximately as shown in Figure 1–49.

- Release the mouse button to resize the graphic, which in this case should have a height of about 2.74" and a width of about 2.73".

Q&A How can I see the height and width measurements?

Look in the Size group on the Picture Tools Format tab to see the height and width measurements of the currently selected graphic (shown in Figure 1–46 on page WD 32).

Q&A What if the graphic is the wrong size?

Repeat Steps 1, 2, and 3; or enter the desired height and width values in the Shape Height and Shape Width boxes (Picture Tools Format tab | Size group).

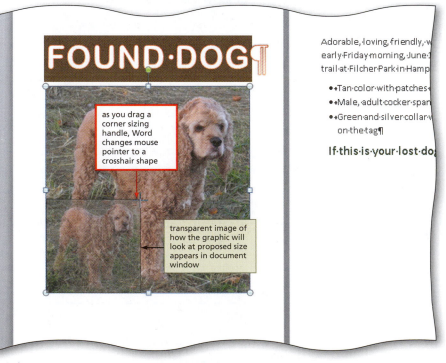

Figure 1–49

4
- Click to the right of the graphic to deselect it (Figure 1–50).

What happened to the Picture Tools Format tab?

When you click outside of a graphic or press a key to scroll through a document, Word deselects the graphic and removes the Picture Tools Format tab from the screen.

What if I want to return a graphic to its original size and start again?

With the graphic selected, click the Size Dialog Box Launcher (Picture Tools Format tab | Size group), click the Size tab (Layout dialog box), click the Reset button, and then click the OK button.

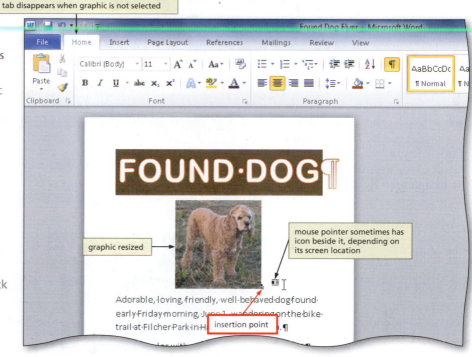

Figure 1–50

Other Ways

1. Enter height and width of graphic in Shape Height and Shape Width boxes (Picture Tools Format tab | Size group)

2. Click Size Dialog Box Launcher (Picture Tools Format tab | Size group), click Size tab (Layout dialog box), enter desired height and width values in boxes, click OK button

To Insert Another Picture

The next step is to insert the other digital picture of the dog immediately to the right of the current picture. This second picture also is available on the Data Files for Students. See the inside back cover of this book for instructions on downloading the Data Files for Students, or contact your instructor for information about accessing the required files.

The following steps insert another picture immediately to the right of the current picture.

1 With the insertion point positioned as shown in Figure 1–50, click Insert on the Ribbon to display the Insert tab.

2 With your USB flash drive connected to one of the computer's USB ports, click the Insert Picture from File button (Insert tab | Illustrations group) to display the Insert Picture dialog box.

3 If necessary, navigate to the picture location (in this case, the Word folder in the CIS 101 folder [or your class folder] on the USB flash drive). For a detailed example of this procedure, refer to Steps 3a – 3c in the To Save a File in a Folder section in the Office 2010 and Windows 7 chapter at the beginning of this book.

4 Click Dog Picture 2 to select the file.

5 Click the Insert button (Insert Picture dialog box) to insert the picture at the location of the insertion point in the document.

Word Help
At any time while using Word, you can find answers to questions and display information about various topics through Word Help. Used properly, this form of assistance can increase your productivity and reduce your frustrations by minimizing the time you spend learning how to use Word. For instruction about Word Help and exercises that will help you gain confidence in using it, read the Office 2010 and Windows 7 chapter at the beginning of this book.

To Resize a Graphic by Entering Exact Measurements

The next step is to resize the second picture so that it is the exact same size as the first picture. The height and width measurements of the first graphic are approximately 2.74" and 2.73", respectively. When a graphic is selected, its height and width measurements show in the Size group of the Picture Tools Format tab. The following steps resize a selected graphic by entering its desired exact measurements.

- With the second graphic still selected, click the Shape Height box (Picture Tools Format tab | Size group) to select the contents in the box and then type 2.74 as the height.

Q&A What if the Picture Tools Format tab no longer is displayed on my Ribbon?

Double-click the picture to display the Picture Tools Format tab.

Q&A What if the contents of the Shape Height box are not selected?

Triple-click the Shape Height box.

2

- Click the Shape Width box to select the contents in the box, type 2.73 as the width, and then click the picture to apply the settings.

- If necessary, scroll up to display the entire document in the window (Figure 1–51).

Q&A Why did my measurements change slightly?

Depending on relative measurements, the height and width values entered may change slightly.

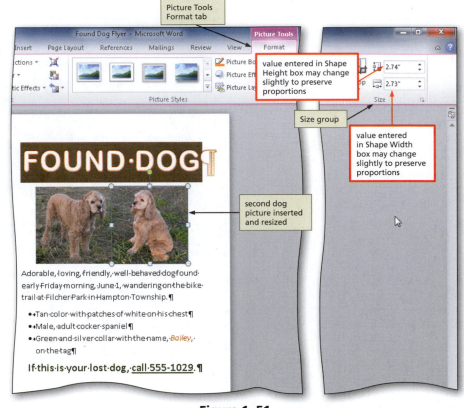

Figure 1–51

Other Ways		
1. Right-click picture, enter shape height and width values in boxes on shortcut menu	2. Right-click picture, click Size and Position on shortcut menu, click Size tab (Layout dialog box),	enter shape height and width values in boxes, click OK button

To Zoom the Document

You are finished resizing the graphics and no longer need to view the entire page in the document window. Thus, the following step changes the zoom back to 100 percent.

1 Click the Zoom In button on the status bar as many times as necessary until the Zoom button displays 100% on its face (shown in Figure 1–52).

To Apply a Picture Style

A **style** is a named group of formatting characteristics. Word provides more than 25 picture styles that enable you easily to change a picture's look to a more visually appealing style, including a variety of shapes, angles, borders, and reflections. The flyer in this chapter uses a style that applies soft edges to the picture. The following steps apply a picture style to a picture.

1

- Click the leftmost dog picture to select it (Figure 1–52).

Q&A

What is the green circle attached to the selected graphic?

It is called a rotate handle. When you drag a graphic's rotate handle, the graphic moves in either a clockwise or counterclockwise direction.

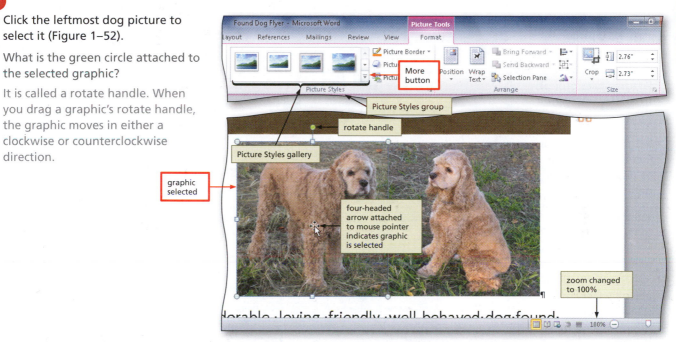

Figure 1–52

2

- Click the More button in the Picture Styles gallery (Picture Tools Format tab | Picture Styles group) (shown in Figure 1–52) to expand the gallery.

- Point to Soft Edge Rectangle in the Picture Styles gallery to display a live preview of that style applied to the picture in the document (Figure 1–53).

Experiment

- Point to various picture styles in the Picture Styles gallery and watch the style of the picture change in the document window.

3

- Click Soft Edge Rectangle in the Picture Styles gallery to apply the style to the selected picture.

Figure 1–53

To Apply Picture Effects

Word provides a variety of picture effects so that you can further customize a picture. Effects include shadows, reflections, glow, soft edges, bevel, and 3-D rotation. The difference between the effects and the styles is that each effect has several options, providing you with more control over the exact look of the image.

In this flyer, the leftmost dog picture has a slight tan glow effect and is turned inward toward the center of the page. The following steps apply picture effects to the selected picture.

1

- Click the Picture Effects button (Picture Tools Format tab | Picture Styles group) to display the Picture Effects menu.

- Point to Glow on the Picture Effects menu to display the Glow gallery.

- Point to Tan, 5 pt glow, Accent color 6 in the Glow Variations area (rightmost glow in first row) to display a live preview of the selected glow effect applied to the picture in the document window (Figure 1–54).

Figure 1–54

(P) **Experiment**

- Point to various glow effects in the Glow gallery and watch the picture change in the document window.

2

- Click Tan, 5 pt glow, Accent color 6 in the Glow gallery to apply the selected picture effect.

Q&A | What if I wanted to discard formatting applied to a picture?

You would click the Reset Picture button (Picture Tools Format tab | Adjust group). To reset formatting and size, you would click the Reset Picture button arrow (Picture Tools Format tab | Adjust group) and then click Reset Picture & Size on the Reset Picture menu.

3

- Click the Picture Effects button (Picture Tools Format tab | Picture Styles group) to display the Picture Effects menu again.

- Point to 3-D Rotation on the Picture Effects menu to display the 3-D Rotation gallery.

- Point to Off Axis 1 Right in the Parallel area (second rotation in second row) to display a live preview of the selected 3-D effect applied to the picture in the document window (Figure 1–55).

🔍 Experiment

- Point to various 3-D rotation effects in the 3-D Rotation gallery and watch the picture change in the document window.

4

- Click Off Axis 1 Right in the 3-D Rotation gallery to apply the selected picture effect.

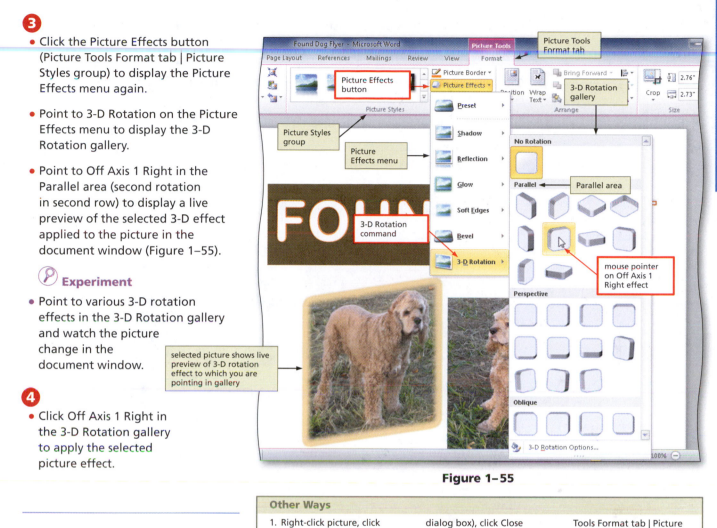

Figure 1–55

Other Ways

1. Right-click picture, click Format Picture on shortcut menu, select desired options (Format Picture dialog box), click Close button

2. Click Format Shape Dialog Box Launcher (Picture Tools Format tab | Picture Styles group), select desired options (Format Picture dialog box), click Close button

To Apply a Picture Style and Effects to Another Picture

In this flyer, the rightmost dog picture also uses the soft edge picture style, has a slight tan glow effect, and is turned inward toward the center of the page. The following steps apply the picture style and picture effects to the picture.

1 Click the rightmost dog picture to select it.

2 Click the More button in the Picture Styles gallery (Picture Tools Format tab | Picture Styles group) to expand the gallery and then click Soft Edge Rectangle in the Picture Styles gallery to apply the selected style to the picture.

3 Click the Picture Effects button (Picture Tools Format tab | Picture Styles group) to display the Picture Effects menu and then point to Glow on the Picture Effects menu to display the Glow gallery.

4 Click Tan, 5 pt glow, Accent color 6 (rightmost glow in first row) in the Glow gallery to apply the picture effect to the picture.

5 Click the Picture Effects button (Picture Tools Format tab | Picture Styles group) to display the Picture Effects menu again and then point to 3-D Rotation on the Picture Effects menu to display the 3-D Rotation gallery.

6 Click Off Axis 2 Left (rightmost rotation in second row) in the Parallel area in the 3-D Rotation gallery to apply the picture effect to the selected picture.

7 Click to the right of the picture to deselect it (Figure 1–56).

picture style and picture effects applied to picture

Figure 1–56

Enhancing the Page

With the text and graphics entered and formatted, the next step is to look at the page as a whole and determine if it looks finished in its current state. As you review the page, answer these questions:

- Does it need a page border to frame its contents, or would a page border make it look too busy?
- Is the spacing between paragraphs and graphics on the page adequate? Do any sections of text or graphics look as if they are positioned too closely to the items above or below them?

You determine that a graphical, color-coordinated border would enhance the flyer. You also notice that the flyer would look more proportionate if it had a little more space above and below the pictures. The following pages make these enhancements to the flyer.

To View One Page

Earlier in this chapter, you changed the zoom using the Zoom Out and Zoom In buttons on the status bar. If you want to display an entire page as large as possible in the document window, Word can compute the correct zoom percentage for you. The next steps display a single page in its entirety in the document window as large as possible.

1

- Click View on the Ribbon to display the View tab.

2

- Click the One Page button (View tab | Zoom group) to display the entire page in the document window as large as possible (Figure 1–57).

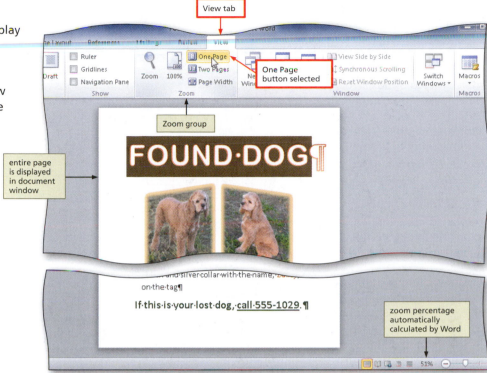

Figure 1–57

To Add a Page Border

In Word, you can add a border around the perimeter of an entire page. The flyer in this chapter has a light green dashed border. The following steps add a page border.

1

- Click Page Layout on the Ribbon to display the Page Layout tab.

- Click the Page Borders button (Page Layout tab | Page Background group) to display the Borders and Shading dialog box (Figure 1–58).

Figure 1–58

2

- Scroll through the Style list (Borders and Shading dialog box) and select the style shown in Figure 1–59.

- Click the Color box arrow to display a Color palette (Figure 1–59).

Figure 1–59

3

- Click Dark Green, Accent 4, Lighter 60% (eighth color in third row) in the Color palette to select the color for the page border.

- Click the Width box arrow and then click 3 pt to select the thickness of the page border (Figure 1–60).

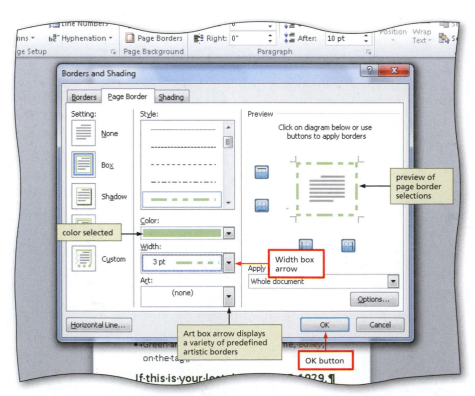

Figure 1–60

4

- Click the OK button to add the border to the page (Figure 1-61).

Q&A

What if I wanted to remove the border?

You would click None in the Setting list in the Borders and Shading dialog box.

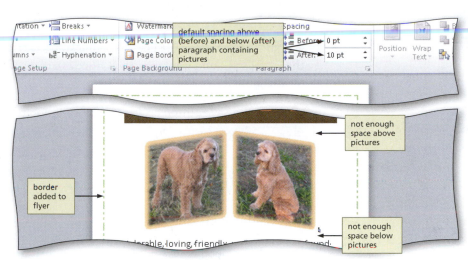

Figure 1-61

To Change Spacing before and after a Paragraph

The default spacing above (before) a paragraph in Word is 0 points and below (after) is 10 points. In the flyer, you want to increase the spacing above and below the paragraph containing the pictures. The following steps change the spacing above and below a paragraph.

1

- Position the insertion point in the paragraph to be adjusted, in this case, the paragraph containing the pictures.

- Click the Spacing Before box up arrow (Page Layout tab | Paragraph group) as many times as necessary until 24 pt is displayed in the Spacing Before box to increase the space above the current paragraph.

2

- Click the Spacing After box up arrow (Page Layout tab | Paragraph group) so that 12 pt is displayed in the Spacing After box to increase the space below the current paragraph (Figure 1-62).

- If the text flows to two pages, reduce the spacing above and below paragraphs as necessary.

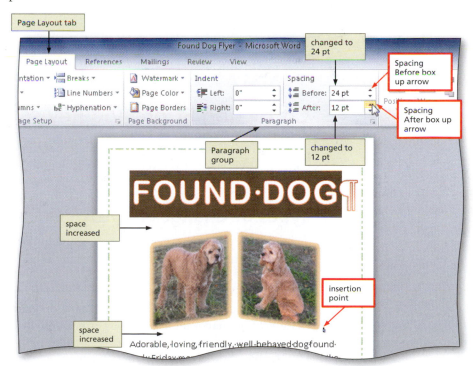

Figure 1-62

Other Ways

1. Right-click paragraph, click Paragraph on shortcut menu, click Indents and Spacing tab (Paragraph dialog box), enter spacing before and after values, click OK button

2. Click Paragraph Dialog Box Launcher (Home tab or Page Layout tab | Paragraph group), click Indents and Spacing tab (Paragraph dialog box), enter spacing before and after values, click OK button

To Save an Existing Document with the Same File Name

You have made several modifications to the document since you last saved it. Thus, you should save it again. The following step saves the document again. For an example of the step listed below, refer to the Office 2010 and Windows 7 chapter at the beginning of this book.

1 Click the Save button on the Quick Access Toolbar to overwrite the previously saved file.

To Quit Word

Although you still need to make some edits to this document, you want to quit Word and resume working on the project at a later time. Thus, the following steps quit Word. For a detailed example of the procedure summarized below, refer to the Office 2010 and Windows 7 chapter at the beginning of this book.

1 If you have one Word document open, click the Close button on the right side of the title bar to close the document and quit Word; or if you have multiple Word documents open, click File on the Ribbon to open the Backstage view and then click Exit in the Backstage view to close all open documents and quit Word.

2 If a Microsoft Word dialog box appears, click the Save button to save any changes made to the document since the last save.

BTW

Certification
The Microsoft Office Specialist (MOS) program provides an opportunity for you to obtain a valuable industry credential — proof that you have the Word 2010 skills required by employers. For more information, visit the Word 2010 Certification Web page (scsite.com/wd2010/cert).

Break Point: If you wish to take a break, this is a good place to do so. To resume at a later time, continue following the steps from this location forward.

Correcting Errors and Revising a Document

After creating a document, you may need to change it. For example, the document may contain an error, or new circumstances may require you to add text to the document.

Types of Changes Made to Documents

The types of changes made to documents normally fall into one of the three following categories: additions, deletions, or modifications.

Additions   Additional words, sentences, or paragraphs may be required in a document. Additions occur when you omit text from a document and want to insert it later. For example, you may want to add your e-mail address to the flyer.

Deletions   Sometimes, text in a document is incorrect or is no longer needed. For example, you may discover the dog's collar is just green. In this case, you would delete the words, and silver, from the flyer.

Modifications   If an error is made in a document or changes take place that affect the document, you might have to revise a word(s) in the text. For example, the dog may have been found in Hampton Village instead of Hampton Township.

To Start Word

Once you have created and saved a document, you may need to retrieve it from your storage medium. For example, you might want to revise the document or print it. The following steps, which assume Windows 7 is running, start Word so that you can open and modify the flyer. You may need to ask your instructor how to start Word for your computer. For a detailed example of the procedure summarized below, refer to the Office 2010 and Windows 7 chapter at the beginning of this book.

1 Click the Start button on the Windows 7 taskbar to display the Start menu.

2 Type `Microsoft Word` as the search text in the 'Search programs and files' text box and watch the search results appear on the Start menu.

3 Click Microsoft Word 2010 in the search results on the Start menu to start Word and display a new blank document in the Word window.

4 If the Word window is not maximized, click the Maximize button next to the Close button on its title bar to maximize the window.

To Open a Document from Word

Earlier in this chapter, you saved your project on a USB flash drive using the file name, Found Dog Flyer. The following steps open the Found Dog Flyer file from the Word folder in the CIS 101 folder on the USB flash drive. For a detailed example of the procedure summarized below, refer to the Office 2010 and Windows 7 chapter at the beginning of this book.

1 With your USB flash drive connected to one of the computer's USB ports, click File on the Ribbon to open the Backstage view.

2 Click Open in the Backstage view to display the Open dialog box.

3 Navigate to the location of the file to be opened (in this case, the Word folder in the CIS 101 folder [or your class folder] on the USB flash drive). For a detailed example of this procedure, refer to Steps 3a – 3c in the To Save a File in a Folder section in the Office 2010 and Windows 7 chapter at the beginning of this book.

4 Click Found Dog Flyer to select the file to be opened.

5 Click the Open button (Open dialog box) to open the selected file and display the opened document in the Word window.

Q&A Could I have clicked the Recent tab to open the file?

Yes. Because the file was recently closed, it should appear in the Recent Documents list.

To Zoom the Document

While modifying the document, you prefer the document at 100 percent so that it is easier to read. Thus, the following step changes the zoom back to 100 percent.

1 If necessary, click the Zoom In button on the status bar as many times as necessary until the Zoom button displays 100% on its face (shown in Figure 1–63 on the next page).

To Insert Text in an Existing Document

Word inserts text to the left of the insertion point. The text to the right of the insertion point moves to the right and downward to fit the new text. The following steps insert the word, very, to the left of the word, early, in the flyer.

 1

• Scroll through the document and then click to the left of the location of text to be inserted (in this case, the e in early) to position the insertion point where text should be inserted (Figure 1–63).

Figure 1–63

 2

• Type `very` and then press the SPACEBAR to insert the word to the left of the insertion point (Figure 1–64).

Q&A

Why did the text move to the right as I typed?

In Word, the default typing mode is **insert mode**, which means as you type a character, Word moves all the characters to the right of the typed character one position to the right.

Figure 1–64

Deleting Text from a Document

It is not unusual to type incorrect characters or words in a document. As discussed earlier in this chapter, you can click the Undo button on the Quick Access Toolbar to undo a command or action immediately — this includes typing. Word also provides other methods of correcting typing errors.

To delete an incorrect character in a document, simply click next to the incorrect character and then press the BACKSPACE key to erase to the left of the insertion point, or press the DELETE key to erase to the right of the insertion point.

To Delete Text

To delete a word or phrase, you first must select the word or phrase. The following steps select the word, very, that was just added in the previous steps and then delete the selection.

- Position the mouse pointer somewhere in the word to be selected (in this case, very) and then double-click to select the word (Figure 1–65).

Adorable, loving, friendly, well-behaved dog found very early Friday morning, June 1, wandering on the bike trail at Filcher Park in Hampton Township.¶

text to be deleted is selected

mouse pointer

Figure 1–65

- With the text selected, press the DELETE key to delete the selected text (shown in Figure 1–63).

To Move Text

While proofreading the flyer, you realize that the body copy would read better if the first two bulleted paragraphs were reversed. An efficient way to move text a short distance, such as reversing two paragraphs, is drag-and-drop editing. With **drag-and-drop editing**, you select the text to be moved and then drag the selected item to the new location and then *drop*, or insert, it there. Another technique for moving text is the cut-and-paste technique, which is discussed in the next chapter. The following steps use drag-and-drop editing to move text.

- Position the mouse pointer in the paragraph to be moved (in this case, the second bulleted item) and then triple-click to select the paragraph.

- With the mouse pointer in the selected text, press and hold down the mouse button, which displays a dotted insertion point and a small dotted box with the mouse pointer (Figure 1–66).

- • Tan color with patches of white on his chest¶
- • Male, adult cocker spaniel¶
- • Green and silver collar with the name, *Bailey*,

text to be moved is selected

mouse pointer has small box below it when you begin to drag selected text

If ... ur lost dog, call 555-1029.¶

100%

Figure 1–66

2

- Drag the dotted insertion point to the location where the selected text is to be moved, as shown in Figure 1–67.

selected text to be dropped at location of dotted insertion point

Adorable,·loving,·friendly,·well-behaved·dog·found·early·Friday·morning,·June·1,·wandering·on·the·bike·trail·at·Filcher·Park·in·Hampton·Township.¶

- →Tan·color·with·patches·of·white·on·his·chest¶
- →Male,·adult·cocker·spaniel¶
- →Green·and·silver·collar·with·the·name,·*Bailey*,·on·the·tag¶

If·this·is·your·lost·dog,·call·555-1029.¶

Figure 1–67

3

- Release the mouse button to move the selected text to the location of the dotted insertion point (Figure 1–68).

Q&A What if I accidentally drag text to the wrong location?

Click the Undo button on the Quick Access Toolbar and try again.

Q&A Can I use drag-and-drop editing to move any selected item?

Yes, you can select words, sentences, phrases, and graphics and then use drag-and-drop editing to move them.

Q&A What is the purpose of the Paste Options button?

If you click the Paste Options button, a menu appears that allows you to change the format of the item that was moved. The next chapter discusses the Paste Options menu.

- Click anywhere in the document window to remove the selection from the bulleted item.

selected text moved

Paste Options button automatically appears when you drag and drop text or other objects

Figure 1–68

Other Ways

1. Click Cut button (Home tab | Clipboard group), click where text or object is to be pasted, click Paste button (Home tab | Clipboard group)

2. Right-click selected text, click Cut on shortcut menu, right-click where text or object is to be pasted, click Keep Source Formatting on shortcut menu

3. Press CTRL+X, position insertion point where text or object is to be pasted, press CTRL+V

Changing Document Properties

Word helps you organize and identify your files by using **document properties**, which are the details about a file. Document properties, also known as **metadata**, can include information such as the project author, title, subject, and keywords. A **keyword** is a word or phrase that further describes the document. For example, a class name or document topic can describe the file's purpose or content.

Document properties are valuable for a variety of reasons:

- Users can save time locating a particular file because they can view a document's properties without opening the document.

- By creating consistent properties for files having similar content, users can better organize their documents.

- Some organizations require Word users to add document properties so that other employees can view details about these files.

Five different types of document properties exist, but the more common ones used in this book are standard and automatically updated properties. **Standard properties** are associated with all Microsoft Office documents and include author, title, and subject. **Automatically updated properties** include file system properties, such as the date you create or change a file, and statistics, such as the file size.

BTW

Printing Document Properties
To print document properties, click File on the Ribbon to open the Backstage view, click the Print tab in the Backstage view to display the Print gallery, click the first button in the Settings area to display a list of options specifying what you can print, click Document Properties in the list to specify you want to print the document properties instead of the actual document, and then click the Print button in the Print gallery to print the document properties on the currently selected printer.

To Change Document Properties

The **Document Information Panel** contains areas where you can view and enter document properties. You can view and change information in this panel at any time while you are creating a document. Before saving the flyer again, you want to add your name and course information as document properties. The following steps use the Document Information Panel to change document properties.

1

- Click File on the Ribbon to open the Backstage view.

- If necessary, click the Info tab to display the Info gallery (Figure 1–69).

Q&A

How do I close the Backstage view?

Click File on the Ribbon or click the preview of the document in the Info gallery to return to the Word document window.

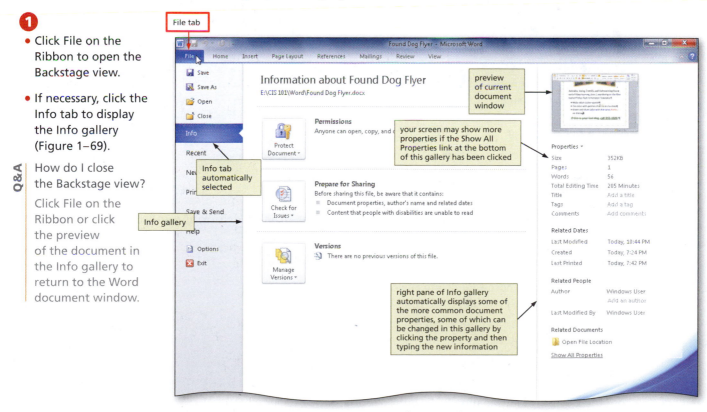

Figure 1–69

2

- Click the Properties button in the right pane of the Info gallery to display the Properties menu (Figure 1–70).

Figure 1–70

3

- Click Show Document Panel on the Properties menu to close the Backstage view and display the Document Information Panel in the Word document window (Figure 1–71).

Q&A Why are some of the document properties in my Document Information Panel already filled in?

The person who installed Microsoft Office 2010 on your computer or network may have set or customized the properties.

Figure 1–71

4

- Click the Author text box, if necessary, and then type your name as the Author property. If a name already is displayed in the Author text box, delete it before typing your name.

- Click the Subject text box, if necessary delete any existing text, and then type your course and section as the Subject property.

- If an AutoComplete dialog box appears, click its Yes button.

Figure 1–72

- Click the Keywords text box, if necessary delete any existing text, and then type **cocker spaniel** as the Keywords property (Figure 1–72).

Q&A What types of document properties does Word collect automatically?

Word records details such as time spent editing a document, the number of times a document has been revised, and the fonts and themes used in a document.

5

- Click the Close the Document Information Panel button so that the Document Information Panel no longer is displayed.

Other Ways

1. Click File on Ribbon, click Info in Backstage view, if necessary click Show All Properties link in Info gallery, click property to change and then type new information, close Backstage view

To Save an Existing Document with the Same File Name

You are finished editing the flyer. Thus, you should save it again. The following step saves the document again. For an example of the step listed below, refer to the Office 2010 and Windows 7 chapter at the beginning of this book.

 1 Click the Save button on the Quick Access Toolbar to overwrite the previously saved file.

Printing a Document

After creating a document, you may want to print it. Printing a document enables you to distribute the document to others in a form that can be read or viewed but typically not edited. It is a good practice to save a document before printing it, in the event you experience difficulties printing.

Determine the best method for distributing the document.

The traditional method of distributing a document uses a printer to produce a hard copy. A **hardcopy** or **printout** is information that exists on a physical medium such as paper. For users that can receive fax documents, you can elect to print a hard copy on a remote fax machine. Hard copies can be useful for the following reasons:

- Many people prefer proofreading a hard copy of a document rather than viewing it on the screen to check for errors and readability.
- Hard copies can serve as reference material if your storage medium is lost or becomes corrupted and you need to recreate the document.

    Instead of distributing a hard copy of a document, users can choose to distribute the document as an electronic image that mirrors the original document's appearance. The electronic image of the document can be e-mailed, posted on a Web site, or copied to a portable storage medium such as a USB flash drive. Two popular electronic image formats, sometimes called fixed formats, are PDF by Adobe Systems and XPS by Microsoft. In Word, you can create electronic image files through the Print tab in the Backstage view, the Send & Save tab in the Backstage view, and the Save As dialog box. Electronic images of documents, such as PDF and XPS, can be useful for the following reasons:

- Users can view electronic images of documents without the software that created the original document (e.g., Word). Specifically, to view a PDF file, you use a program called Acrobat Reader, which can be downloaded free from Adobe's Web site. Similarly, to view an XPS file, you use a program called an XPS Viewer, which is included in the latest versions of Windows and Internet Explorer.
- Sending electronic documents saves paper and printer supplies. Society encourages users to contribute to **green computing**, which involves reducing the environmental waste generated when using a computer.

Plan Ahead

BTW

Conserving Ink and Toner
If you want to conserve ink or toner, you can instruct Word to print draft quality documents by clicking File on the Ribbon to open the Backstage view, clicking Options in the Backstage view to display the Word Options dialog box, clicking Advanced in the left pane (Word Options dialog box), scrolling to the Print area in the right pane, placing a check mark in the 'Use draft quality' check box, and then clicking the OK button. Then, use the Backstage view to print the document as usual.

To Print a Document

With the completed document saved, you may want to print it. Because this flyer is being posted, you will print a hard copy on a printer. The steps on the next page print a hard copy of the contents of the saved Found Dog Flyer document.

• Click File on the Ribbon to open the Backstage view.

• Click the Print tab in the Backstage view to display the Print gallery (Figure 1–73).

Q&A How can I print multiple copies of my document?

Increase the number in the Copies box in the Print gallery.

Q&A What if I decide not to print the document at this time?

Click File on the Ribbon to close the Backstage view and return to the Word document window.

Figure 1–73

• Verify the printer name that appears on the Printer Status button will print a hard copy of the document. If necessary, click the Printer Status button to display a list of available printer options and then click the desired printer to change the currently selected printer.

• Click the Print button in the Print gallery to print the document on the currently selected printer.

• When the printer stops, retrieve the hard copy (Figure 1–74).

Q&A Do I have to wait until my document is complete to print it?

No, you can follow these steps to print a document at any time while you are creating it.

Q&A What if I want to print an electronic image of a document instead of a hard copy?

You would click the Printer Status button in the Print gallery and then select the desired electronic image option such as a Microsoft XPS Document Writer, which would create an XPS file.

Figure 1–74

Other Ways

1. Press CTRL+P, press ENTER

To Quit Word

The project now is complete. Thus, the following steps quit Word. For an example of the step listed below, refer to the Office 2010 and Windows 7 chapter at the beginning of this book.

1 If you have one Word document open, click the Close button on the right side of the title bar to close the document and quit Word; or if you have multiple Word documents open, click File on the Ribbon to open the Backstage view and then click Exit in the Backstage view to close all open documents and quit Word.

2 If a Microsoft Word dialog box appears, click the Save button to save any changes made to the document since the last save.

BTW

Printed Borders
If one or more of your borders do not print, click the Page Borders button (Page Layout tab | Page Background group), click the Options button (Borders and Shading dialog box), click the Measure from box arrow and click Text, change the four text boxes to 15 pt, and then click the OK button in each dialog box. Try printing the document again. If the borders still do not print, adjust the text boxes in the dialog box to a number smaller than 15 point.

Chapter Summary

In this chapter, you have learned how to enter text in a document, format text, insert a picture, format a picture, add a page border, and print a document. The items listed below include all the new Word skills you have learned in this chapter.

1. Start Word (WD 4)
2. Type Text (WD 6)
3. Display Formatting Marks (WD 7)
4. Insert a Blank Line (WD 7)
5. Wordwrap Text as You Type (WD 8)
6. Check Spelling and Grammar as You Type (WD 9)
7. Save a Document (WD 12)
8. Center a Paragraph (WD 14)
9. Select a Line (WD 15)
10. Change the Font Size of Selected Text (WD 16)
11. Change the Font of Selected Text (WD 17)
12. Change the Case of Selected Text (WD 18)
13. Apply a Text Effect to Selected Text (WD 19)
14. Shade a Paragraph (WD 20)
15. Select Multiple Lines (WD 21)
16. Bullet a List of Paragraphs (WD 22)
17. Undo and Redo an Action (WD 23)
18. Italicize Text (WD 24)
19. Color Text (WD 25)
20. Use the Mini Toolbar to Format Text (WD 26)
21. Select a Group of Words (WD 27)
22. Underline Text (WD 27)
23. Bold Text (WD 28)
24. Change Theme Colors (WD 28)
25. Save an Existing Document with the Same File Name (WD 30)
26. Insert a Picture (WD 31)
27. Zoom the Document (WD 33)
28. Resize a Graphic (WD 34)
29. Resize a Graphic by Entering Exact Measurements (WD 36)
30. Apply a Picture Style (WD 37)
31. Apply Picture Effects (WD 38)
32. View One Page (WD 40)
33. Add a Page Border (WD 41)
34. Change Spacing before and after a Paragraph (WD 44)
35. Quit Word (WD 44)
36. Open a Document from Word (WD 45)
37. Insert Text in an Existing Document (WD 46)
38. Delete Text (WD 47)
39. Move Text (WD 47)
40. Change Document Properties (WD 49)
41. Print a Document (WD 51)

If you have a SAM 2010 user profile, your instructor may have assigned an autogradable version of this assignment. If so, log into the SAM 2010 Web site at www.cengage.com/sam2010 to download the instruction and start files.

BTW

Quick Reference
For a table that lists how to complete the tasks covered in this book using the mouse, Ribbon, shortcut menu, and keyboard, see the Quick Reference Summary at the back of this book, or visit the Word 2010 Quick Reference Web page (scsite.com/wd2010/qr).

Learn It Online

Test your knowledge of chapter content and key terms.

Instructions: To complete the Learn It Online exercises, start your browser, click the Address bar, and then enter the Web address `scsite.com/wd2010/learn`. When the Word 2010 Learn It Online page is displayed, click the link for the exercise you want to complete and then read the instructions.

Chapter Reinforcement TF, MC, and SA
A series of true/false, multiple choice, and short answer questions that test your knowledge of the chapter content.

Flash Cards
An interactive learning environment where you identify chapter key terms associated with displayed definitions.

Practice Test
A series of multiple choice questions that test your knowledge of chapter content and key terms.

Who Wants To Be a Computer Genius?
An interactive game that challenges your knowledge of chapter content in the style of a television quiz show.

Wheel of Terms
An interactive game that challenges your knowledge of chapter key terms in the style of the television show *Wheel of Fortune*.

Crossword Puzzle Challenge
A crossword puzzle that challenges your knowledge of key terms presented in the chapter.

Apply Your Knowledge

Reinforce the skills and apply the concepts you learned in this chapter.

Modifying Text and Formatting a Document
Note: To complete this assignment, you will be required to use the Data Files for Students. See the inside back cover of this book for instructions on downloading the Data Files for Students, or contact your instructor for information about accessing the required files.

Instructions: Start Word. Open the document, Apply 1-1 Buffalo Photo Shoot Flyer Unformatted, from the Data Files for Students. The document you open is an unformatted flyer. You are to modify text, format paragraphs and characters, and insert a picture in the flyer.

Perform the following tasks:
1. Delete the word, single, in the sentence of body copy below the headline.
2. Insert the word, Creeks, between the words, Twin Buffalo, in the sentence of body copy below the headline.
3. At the end of the signature line, change the period to an exclamation point.
4. Center the headline and the signature line.
5. Change the theme colors to the Aspect color scheme.
6. Change the font and font size of the headline to 48-point Impact, or a similar font. Change the case of the headline text to all capital letters. Apply the text effect called Gradient Fill – Orange, Accent 1, Outline – White to the headline.
7. Change the font size of body copy between the headline and the signature line to 20 point.
8. Use the Mini toolbar to change the font size of the signature line to 26 point.
9. Select the words, hundreds of buffalo, in the paragraph below the headline and underline them.

10. Italicize the word, every, in the paragraph below the headline. Undo this change and then redo the change.

11. Select the three lines (paragraphs) of text above the signature line and add bullets to the selected paragraphs.

12. Switch the last two bulleted paragraphs. That is, select the Questions bullet and move it so that it is the last bulleted paragraph.

13. Bold the first word of each bulleted paragraph. Change the font color of these same three words to Dark Green, Accent 4, Darker 50%.

14. Bold the text in the signature line. Shade the signature line Dark Green, Accent 4, Darker 50%. If the font color does not automatically change to a lighter color, change it to a shade of white.

15. Change the zoom so that the entire page is visible in the document window.

16. Insert the picture of the buffalo centered on the blank line below the headline. The picture is called Buffalo and is available on the Data Files for Students. Apply the Snip Diagonal Corner, White picture style to the inserted picture. Apply the glow called Dark Green, 5 pt glow, Accent color 4 to the picture.

17. Change the spacing after the headline paragraph to 6 point.

18. The entire flyer now should fit on a single page. If it flows to two pages, resize the picture or decrease spacing before and after paragraphs until the entire flyer text fits on a single page.

19. Change the zoom to text width, then page width, then 100% and notice the differences.

20. Enter the text, Twin Creeks, as the keywords in the document properties. Change the other document properties, as specified by your instructor.

21. Click File on the Ribbon and then click Save As. Save the document using the file name, Apply 1-1 Buffalo Photo Shoot Flyer Formatted.

22. Print the document. Submit the revised document, shown in Figure 1–75, in the format specified by your instructor.

23. Quit Word.

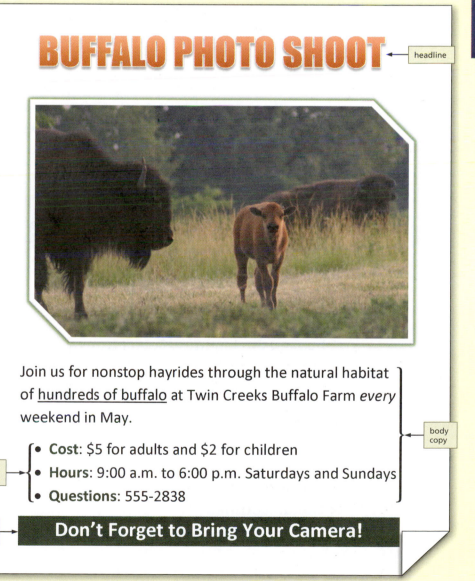

Figure 1–75

Extend Your Knowledge

Extend the skills you learned in this chapter and experiment with new skills. You may need to use Help to complete the assignment.

Modifying Text and Picture Formats and Adding Page Borders

Note: To complete this assignment, you will be required to use the Data Files for Students. See the inside back cover of this book for instructions on downloading the Data Files for Students, or contact your instructor for information about accessing the required files.

Instructions: Start Word. Open the document, Extend 1-1 TVC Cruises Flyer, from the Data Files for Students. You will enhance the look of the flyer shown in Figure 1–76. *Hint:* Remember, if you make a mistake while formatting the picture, you can reset it by clicking the Reset Picture button or Reset Picture button arrow (Picture Tools Format tab | Adjust group).

Perform the following tasks:
1. Use Help to learn about the following formats: remove bullets, grow font, shrink font, art page borders, decorative underline(s), picture bullets, picture border shading, shadow picture effects, and color saturation and tone.
2. Remove the bullet from the paragraph below the picture.

3. Select the text, 10 percent, and use the Grow Font button to increase its font size.

4. Add an art page border to the flyer. If the border is not in color, add color to it.

5. Change the solid underline below the word, cruises, to a decorative underline. Change the color of the underline.

6. Change the style of the bullets to picture bullet(s).

7. Change the color of the picture border. Add a shadow picture effect to the picture.

8. Change the color saturation and color tone of the picture.

9. Change the document properties, including keywords, as specified by your instructor. Save the revised document with a new file name and then submit it in the format specified by your instructor.

Figure 1–76

Make It Right

Analyze a document and correct all errors and/or improve the design.

Correcting Spelling and Grammar Errors

Note: To complete this assignment, you will be required to use the Data Files for Students. See the inside back cover of this book for instructions on downloading the Data Files for Students, or contact your instructor for information about accessing the required files.

Instructions: Start Word. Open the document, Make It Right 1-1 Karate Academy Flyer Unchecked, from the Data Files for Students. The document is a flyer that contains spelling and grammar errors, as shown in Figure 1–77. You are to correct each spelling (red wavy underline) and grammar error (green and blue wavy underlines) by right-clicking the flagged text and then clicking the appropriate correction on the shortcut menu.

If your screen does not display the wavy underlines, click File on the Ribbon and then click Options in the Backstage view. When the Word Options dialog box is displayed, click Proofing in the left pane, be sure the 'Hide spelling errors in this document only' and 'Hide grammar errors in this document only' check boxes do not contain check marks, and then click the OK button. If your screen still does not display the wavy underlines, redisplay the Word Options dialog box, click Proofing, and then click the Recheck Document button.

Change the document properties, including keywords, as specified by your instructor. Save the revised document with the name, Make It Right 1-1 Karate Academy Flyer, and then submit it in the format specified by your instructor.

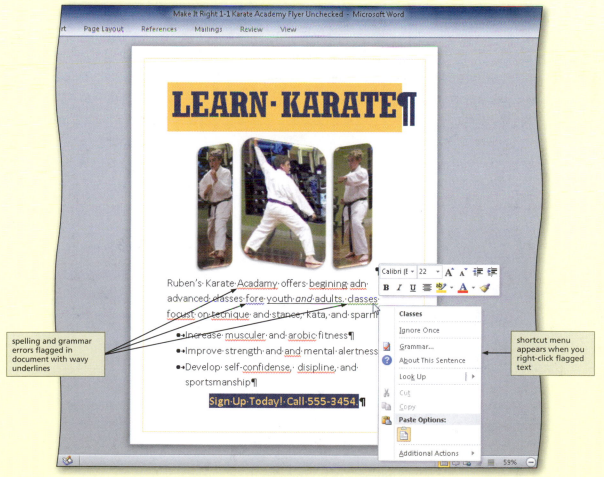

Figure 1–77

In the Lab

Design and/or create a document using the guidelines, concepts, and skills presented in this chapter. Labs are listed in order of increasing difficulty.

Lab 1: Creating a Flyer with a Picture

Problem: As a part-time employee in the Student Services Center at school, you have been asked to prepare a flyer that advertises study habits classes. First, you prepare the unformatted flyer shown in Figure 1–78a, and then you format it so that it looks like Figure 1–78b. *Hint:* Remember, if you make a mistake while formatting the flyer, you can click the Undo button on the Quick Access Toolbar to undo your last action.

Note: To complete this assignment, you will be required to use the Data Files for Students. See the inside back cover of this book for instructions on downloading the Data Files for Students, or contact your instructor for information about accessing the required files.

Instructions: Perform the following tasks:

1. Start Word. Display formatting marks on the screen.
2. Type the flyer text, unformatted, as shown in Figure 1–78a, inserting a blank line between the headline and the body copy. If Word flags any misspelled words as you type, check their spelling and correct them.
3. Save the document using the file name, Lab 1-1 Study Habits Flyer.
4. Center the headline and the signature line.
5. Change the theme colors to Concourse.
6. Change the font size of the headline to 36 point and the font to Ravie, or a similar font. Apply the text effect called Gradient Fill – Dark Red, Accent 6, Inner Shadow.
7. Change the font size of body copy between the headline and the signature line to 20 point.
8. Change the font size of the signature line to 22 point. Bold the text in the signature line.

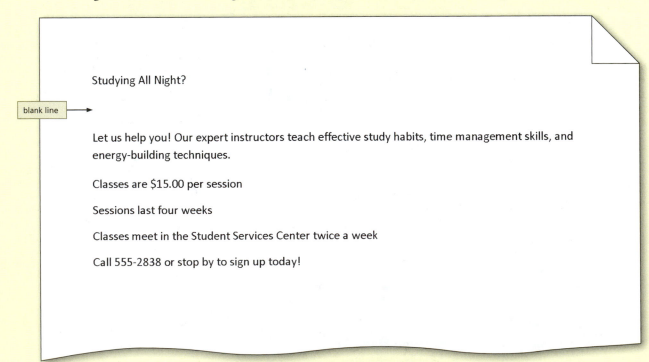

Studying All Night?

blank line

Let us help you! Our expert instructors teach effective study habits, time management skills, and energy-building techniques.

Classes are $15.00 per session

Sessions last four weeks

Classes meet in the Student Services Center twice a week

Call 555-2838 or stop by to sign up today!

Figure 1–78 (a) Unformatted Flyer

9. Change the font of the body copy and signature line to Rockwell, and change the color of the signature line to Dark Red, Accent 6.

10. Bullet the three lines (paragraphs) of text above the signature line.

11. Bold and capitalize the text, Let us help you!, and change its color to Dark Red, Accent 6.

12. Italicize the word, or, in the signature line.

13. Underline the text, Student Services Center, in the third bulleted paragraph.

14. Change the zoom so that the entire page is visible in the document window.

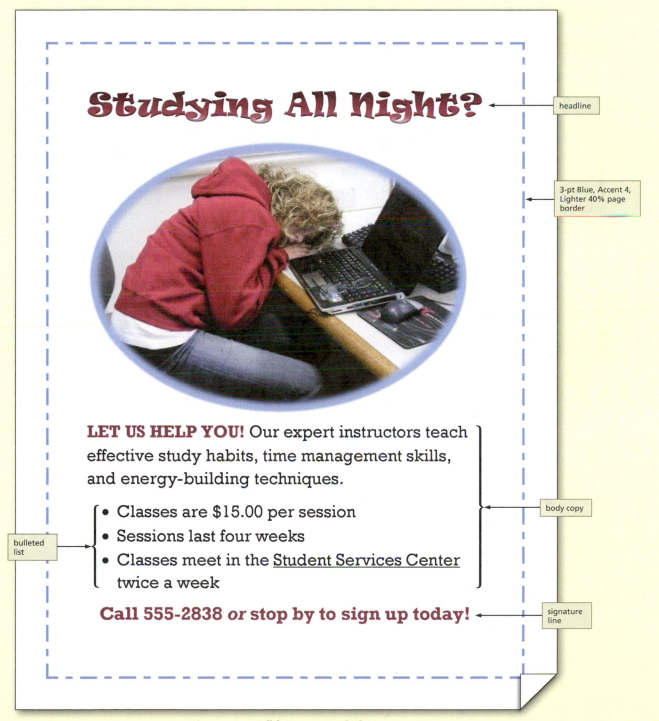

Figure 1–78 (b) Formatted Flyer

Continued >

In the Lab *continued*

15. Insert the picture centered on a blank line below the headline. The picture is called Sleeping and is available on the Data Files for Students.

16. Apply the Soft Edge Oval picture style to the inserted picture. Apply the glow effect called Blue, 5 pt glow, Accent color 4 to the picture.

17. The entire flyer should fit on a single page. If it flows to two pages, resize the picture or decrease spacing before and after paragraphs until the entire flyer text fits on a single page.

18. Add the page border shown in Figure 1–78b on the previous page.

19. Change the document properties, including keywords, as specified by your instructor. Save the flyer again with the same file name. Submit the document, shown in Figure 1–78b, in the format specified by your instructor.

In the Lab

Lab 2: Creating a Flyer with a Resized Picture

Problem: Your boss at Granger Camera House has asked you to prepare a flyer that announces the upcoming photography contest. You prepare the flyer shown in Figure 1–79. *Hint:* Remember, if you make a mistake while formatting the flyer, you can click the Undo button on the Quick Access Toolbar to undo your last action.

Note: To complete this assignment, you will be required to use the Data Files for Students. See the inside back cover of this book for instructions on downloading the Data Files for Students, or contact your instructor for information about accessing the required files.

Instructions: Perform the following tasks:

1. Start Word. Type the flyer text, unformatted. If Word flags any misspelled words as you type, check their spelling and correct them.

2. Save the document using the file name, Lab 1-2 Photography Contest Flyer.

3. Change the theme colors to the Apex color scheme.

4. Center the headline, the line that says RULES, and the signature line.

5. Change the font size of the headline to 36 point and the font to Stencil, or a similar font. Shade the headline paragraph Lavender, Background 2, Darker 50%. Apply the text effect called Fill – Lavender, Accent 6, Outline – Accent 6, Glow – Accent 6.

6. Change the font size of body copy between the headline and the signature line to 18 point.

7. Change the font size of the signature line to 24 point and the font to Stencil. Bold the text in the signature line. Change the font color of the text in the signature line to Gray-50%, Text 2.

8. Bullet the three paragraphs of text above the signature line.

9. Italicize the word, not.

10. Bold the word, landscape.

11. Underline the text, August 31.

12. Shade the line that says RULES to the Gray-50%, Text 2 color. If the font color does not automatically change to a lighter color, change it to White, Background 1.

13. Change the zoom so that the entire page is visible in the document window.

14. Insert the picture on a blank line below the headline. The picture is called Wind Power and is available on the Data Files for Students.

15. Resize the picture so that it is approximately 3.5" × 5.25". Apply the Rotated, White picture style to the inserted picture. Apply the glow effect called Lavender, 5 pt glow, Accent color 6 to the picture.

16. The entire flyer should fit on a single page. If it flows to two pages, resize the picture or decrease spacing before and after paragraphs until the entire flyer text fits on a single page.

17. Add the page border shown in Figure 1–79.

18. Change the document properties, including keywords, as specified by your instructor. Save the flyer again with the same file name. Submit the document, shown in Figure 1–79, in the format specified by your instructor.

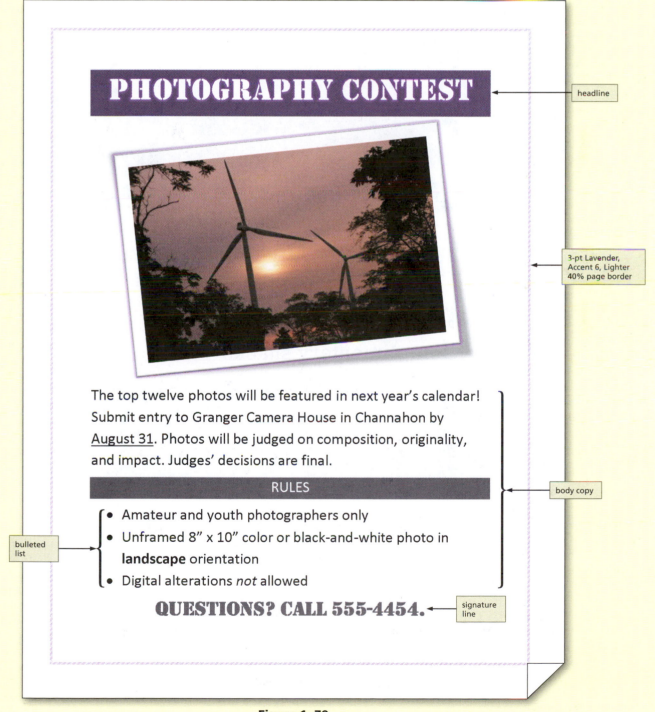

Figure 1–79

In the Lab

Lab 3: Creating a Flyer with Pictures

Problem: Your boss at Warner Depot has asked you to prepare a flyer that advertises its scenic train ride. You prepare the flyer shown in Figure 1–80.

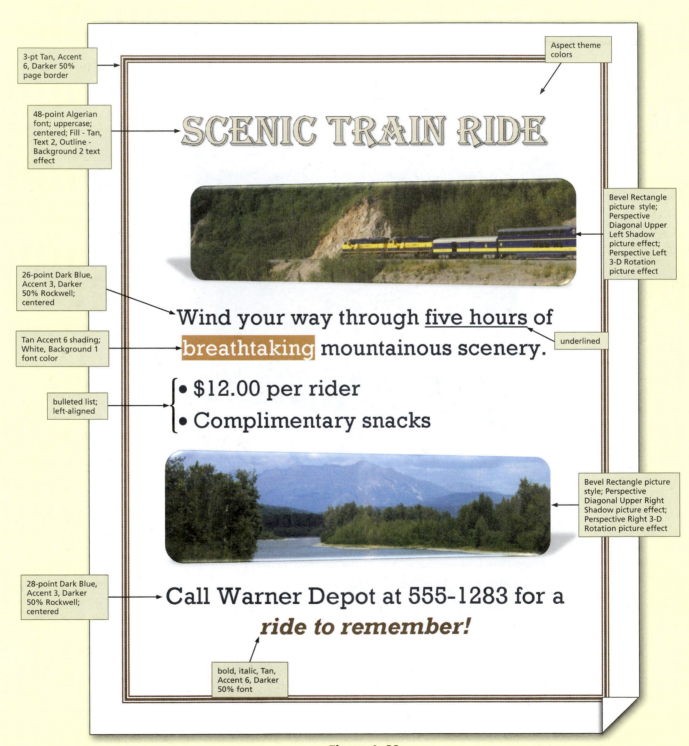

Figure 1–80

Note: To complete this assignment, you will be required to use the Data Files for Students. See the inside back cover of this book for instructions on downloading the Data Files for Students, or contact your instructor for information about accessing the required files.

Instructions: Start Word. Enter the text in the flyer, checking spelling as you type, and then format it as shown in Figure 1–80. The pictures to be inserted are called Train and Scenery and are available on the Data Files for Students. Adjust spacing before and after paragraphs and resize pictures as necessary so that the flyer fits on a single page.

Change the document properties, including keywords, as specified by your instructor. Save the document using the file name, Lab 1-3 Train Ride Flyer. Submit the document, shown in Figure 1–80, in the format specified by your instructor.

Cases and Places

Apply your creative thinking and problem solving skills to design and implement a solution.

Note: To complete these assignments, you may be required to use the Data Files for Students. See the inside back cover of this book for instructions on downloading the Data Files for Students, or contact your instructor for information about accessing the required files.

1: Design and Create a Spring Break Flyer

Academic

As secretary of your school's Student Government Association, you are responsible for creating and distributing flyers for spring break group outings. This year, you have planned a trip to Settlers Resort. The flyer should contain two digital pictures appropriately resized; the Data Files for Students contains two pictures called Cabin 1 and Cabin 2, or you can use your own digital pictures if they are appropriate for the topic of the flyer. The flyer should contain the headline, Feeling Adventurous?, and this signature line: Call Lyn at 555-9901 to sign up. The body copy consists of the following, in any order: Spring Break – Blast to the Past. Settlers Resort is like a page right out of a history textbook! Spend five days living in the 1800s. The bulleted list in the body copy is as follows: One-room cabins with potbelly stoves, Campfire dining with authentic meals, and Horseback riding and much more.

Use the concepts and techniques presented in this chapter to create and format this flyer. Be sure to check spelling and grammar. Submit your assignment in the format specified by your instructor.

2: Design and Create a Yard Sale Flyer

Personal

You are planning a yard sale and would like to create and post flyers around town advertising the upcoming sale. The flyer should contain two digital pictures appropriately resized; the Data Files for Students contains two pictures called Yard Sale 1 and Yard Sale 2, or you can use your own digital pictures if they are appropriate for the topic of the flyer. The flyer should contain the headline, Yard Sale!, and this signature line: Questions? Call 555-9820. The body copy consists of the following, in any order: Hundreds of items for sale. After 20 years, we are moving to a smaller house and are selling anything that won't fit. Everything for sale must go! The bulleted list in the body copy is as follows: When: August 7, 8, 9 from 9:00 a.m. to 7:00 p.m.; Where: 139 Ravel Boulevard; and What: something for everyone – from clothing to collectibles.

Use the concepts and techniques presented in this chapter to create and format this flyer. Be sure to check spelling and grammar. Submit your assignment in the format specified by your instructor.

Continued >

Cases and Places *continued*

3: Design and Create a Village Fireworks Flyer

Professional

As a part-time employee at the Village of Crestwood, your boss has asked you to create and distribute flyers for the upcoming fireworks extravaganza. The flyer should contain two digital pictures appropriately resized; the Data Files for Students contains two pictures called Fireworks 1 and Fireworks 2, or you can use your own digital pictures if they are appropriate for the topic of the flyer. The flyer should contain the headline, Light Up The Sky, and this signature line: Call 555-2983 with questions. The body copy consists of the following, in any order: Join Us! The Village of Crestwood will present its tenth annual Light Up The Sky fireworks extravaganza on August 8 at 9:00 p.m. during the end of summer celebration in Douglas Park. The bulleted list in the body copy is as follows: Pork chop dinners will be sold for $3.00 beginning at 6:00 p.m., Bring chairs and blankets, and Admission is free.

Use the concepts and techniques presented in this chapter to create and format this flyer. Be sure to check spelling and grammar. Submit your assignment in the format specified by your instructor.

1 Creating and Editing a Presentation with Clip Art

Objectives

You will have mastered the material in this chapter when you can:

- Select a document theme
- Create a title slide and a text slide with a multi-level bulleted list
- Add new slides and change slide layouts
- Insert clips and pictures into a slide with and without a content placeholder
- Move and size clip art

- Change font size and color
- Bold and italicize text
- Duplicate a slide
- Arrange slides
- Select slide transitions
- View a presentation in Slide Show view
- Print a presentation

1 | Creating and Editing a Presentation with Clip Art

Introduction

A PowerPoint **presentation,** also called a **slide show**, can help you deliver a dynamic, professional-looking message to an audience. PowerPoint allows you to produce slides to use in an academic, business, or other environment. One of the more common uses of these slides is to enhance an oral presentation. A speaker may desire to convey information, such as urging students to volunteer at a fund-raising event, explaining changes in employee compensation packages, or describing a new laboratory procedure. The PowerPoint slides should reinforce the speaker's message and help the audience retain the information presented. Custom slides can fit your specific needs and contain diagrams, charts, tables, pictures, shapes, video, sound, and animation effects to make your presentation more effective. An accompanying handout gives audience members reference notes and review material for your presentation.

Project Planning Guidelines

> The process of developing a presentation that communicates specific information requires careful analysis and planning. As a starting point, establish why the presentation is needed. Next, analyze the intended audience for the presentation and its unique needs. Then, gather information about the topic and decide what to include in the presentation. Finally, determine the presentation design and style that will be most successful at delivering the message. Details of these guidelines are provided in Appendix A. In addition, each project in this book provides practical applications of these planning considerations.

BTW

Energy-Saving Information
The U.S. Department of Energy's Web site has myriad information available on the topics of energy efficiency and renewable energy. These features can provide news and product research that you can share with audiences with the help of a PowerPoint presentation.

Project — Presentation with Bulleted Lists and Clip Art

In this chapter's project, you will follow proper design guidelines and learn to use PowerPoint to create, save, and print the slides shown in Figures 1–1a through 1–1e. The objective is to produce a presentation, called It Is Easy Being Green, to help consumers understand basic steps they can take to save energy in their homes. This slide show has a variety of clip art and visual elements to add interest and illustrate energy-cutting measures. Some of the text has formatting and color enhancements. Transitions help one slide flow gracefully into the next during a slide show. In addition, you will print a handout of your slides to distribute to audience members.

(a) Slide 1 (Title Slide with Clip Art)

(b) Slide 2 (Multi-Level Bulleted List with Clip Art)

(c) Slide 3 (Title and Photograph)

(d) Slide 4 (Comparison Layout and Clip Art)

(e) Slide 5 (Closing Slide)

Figure 1–1

Overview

BTWs
For a complete list of the BTWs found in the margins of this book, visit the PowerPoint 2010 BTW Web page (scsite.com/ppt2010/btw).

As you read this chapter, you will learn how to create the presentation shown in Figure 1–1 on the previous page by performing these general tasks:

- Select an appropriate document theme.
- Enter titles and text on slides.
- Change the size, color, and style of text.
- Insert clips and a photograph.
- Add a transition to each slide.
- View the presentation on your computer.
- Print your slides.

Plan Ahead

General Project Guidelines

When creating a PowerPoint document, the actions you perform and decisions you make will affect the appearance and characteristics of the finished document. As you create a presentation such as the project shown in Figure 1–1, you should follow these general guidelines:

1. **Find the appropriate theme.** The overall appearance of a presentation significantly affects its capability to communicate information clearly. The slides' graphical appearance should support the presentation's overall message. Colors, fonts, and layouts affect how audience members perceive and react to the slide content.

2. **Choose words for each slide.** Use the less is more principle. The less text, the more likely the slides will enhance your speech. Use the fewest words possible to make a point.

3. **Format specific elements of the text.** Examples of how you can modify the appearance, or **format**, of text include changing its shape, size, color, and position on the slide.

4. **Determine where to save the presentation.** You can store a document permanently, or **save** it, on a variety of storage media, including a hard disk, USB flash drive, or CD. You also can indicate a specific location on the storage media for saving the document.

5. **Determine the best method for distributing the presentation.** Presentations can be distributed on paper or electronically. You can print a hard copy of the presentation slides for proofing or reference, or you can distribute an electronic image in various formats.

When necessary, more specific details concerning the above guidelines are presented at appropriate points in the chapter. The chapter also will identify the actions performed and decisions made regarding these guidelines during the creation of the slides shown in Figure 1–1.

To Start PowerPoint

For an introduction to Windows 7 and instruction about how to perform basic Windows 7 tasks, read the Office 2010 and Windows 7 chapter at the beginning of this book, where you can learn how to resize windows, change screen resolution, create folders, move and rename files, use Windows Help, and much more.

If you are using a computer to step through the project in this chapter and you want your screens to match the figures in this book, you should change your screen's resolution to 1024 × 768. For information about how to change a computer's resolution, refer to the Office 2010 and Windows 7 chapter at the beginning of this book.

The following steps, which assume Windows 7 is running, start PowerPoint based on a typical installation. You may need to ask your instructor how to start PowerPoint for your computer. For a detailed example of the procedure summarized below, refer to the Office 2010 and Windows 7 chapter.

1 Click the Start button on the Windows 7 taskbar to display the Start menu.

2 Type `Microsoft PowerPoint` as the search text in the 'Search programs and files' text box and watch the search results appear on the Start menu.

3 Click Microsoft PowerPoint 2010 in the search results on the Start menu to start PowerPoint and display a new blank document in the PowerPoint window.

4 If the PowerPoint window is not maximized, click the Maximize button next to the Close button on its title bar to maximize the window.

Choosing a Document Theme

You can give a presentation a professional and integrated appearance easily by using a document theme. A **document theme** provides consistency in design and color throughout the entire presentation by setting the color scheme, font set, and layout of a presentation. This collection of formatting choices includes a set of colors (the Theme Colors group), a set of heading and content text fonts (the Theme Fonts group), and a set of lines and fill effects (the Theme Effects group). These groups allow you to choose and change the appearance of all the slides or individual slides in your presentation. The left edge of the status bar in Figure 1–2 shows the current slide number followed by the total number of slides in the document and a document theme identifier.

Find the appropriate theme.
In the initial steps of this project, you will select a document theme by locating a particular built-in theme in the Themes group. You could, however, apply a theme at any time while creating the presentation. Some PowerPoint slide show designers create presentations using the default Office Theme. This blank design allows them to concentrate on the words being used to convey the message and does not distract them with colors and various text attributes. Once the text is entered, the designers then select an appropriate document theme.

Plan Ahead

To Choose a Document Theme

The document theme identifier shows the theme currently used in the slide show. PowerPoint initially uses the **Office Theme** until you select a different theme. The following steps change the theme for this presentation from the Office Theme to the Oriel document theme.

1

• Click Design on the Ribbon to display the Design tab (Figure 1–2).

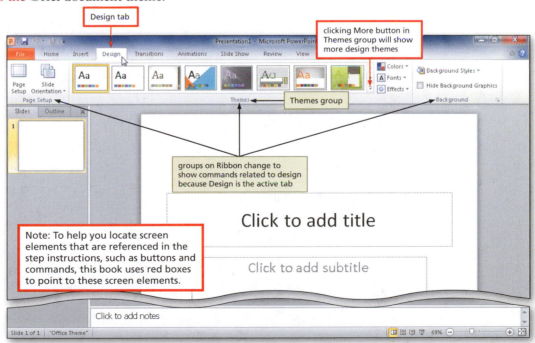

Design tab

clicking More button in Themes group will show more design themes

Themes group

groups on Ribbon change to show commands related to design because Design is the active tab

Note: To help you locate screen elements that are referenced in the step instructions, such as buttons and commands, this book uses red boxes to point to these screen elements.

Click to add title

Click to add subtitle

Click to add notes

Slide 1 of 1   "Office Theme"   69%

Figure 1–2

2

● Click the More button (Design tab | Themes group) to expand the gallery, which shows more Built-In theme gallery options (Figure 1–3).

Experiment

● Point to various document themes in the Themes gallery and watch the colors and fonts change on the title slide.

Q&A Are the themes displayed in a specific order?

Yes. They are arranged in alphabetical order running from left to right. If you point to a theme, a ScreenTip with the theme's name appears on the screen.

Figure 1–3

Q&A What if I change my mind and do not want to select a new theme?

Click anywhere outside the All Themes gallery to close the gallery.

3

● Click the Oriel theme to apply this theme to Slide 1 (Figure 1–4).

Q&A If I decide at some future time that this design does not fit the theme of my presentation, can I apply a different design?

Yes. You can repeat these steps at any time while creating your presentation.

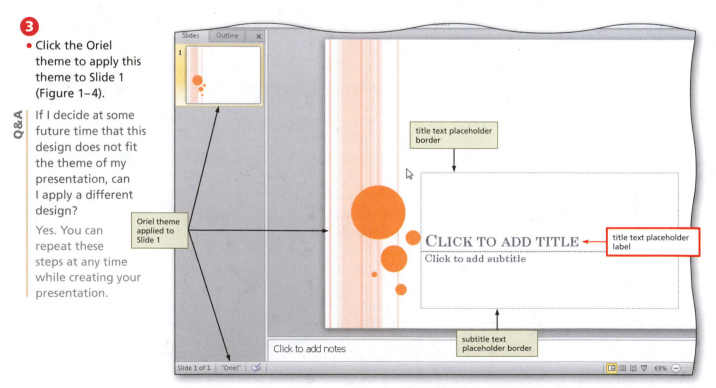

Figure 1–4

Creating a Title Slide

When you open a new presentation, the default **Title Slide** layout appears. The purpose of this layout is to introduce the presentation to the audience. PowerPoint includes eight other built-in standard layouts. The default (preset) slide layouts are set up in **landscape orientation**, where the slide width is greater than its height. In landscape orientation, the slide size is preset to 10 inches wide and 7.5 inches high when printed on a standard sheet of paper measuring 11 inches wide and 8.5 inches high.

Placeholders are boxes with dotted or hatch-marked borders that are displayed when you create a new slide. Most layouts have both a title text placeholder and at least one content placeholder. Depending on the particular slide layout selected, title and subtitle placeholders are displayed for the slide title and subtitle; a content text placeholder is displayed for text, art, or a table, chart, picture, graphic, or movie. The title slide has two text placeholders where you can type the main heading, or title, of a new slide and the subtitle.

With the exception of a blank slide, PowerPoint assumes every new slide has a title. To make creating a presentation easier, any text you type after a new slide appears becomes title text in the title text placeholder. The following steps create the title slide for this presentation.

**Plan
Ahead**

> **Choose the words for the slide.**
> No doubt you have heard the phrase, "You get only one chance to make a first impression." The same philosophy holds true for a PowerPoint presentation. The title slide gives your audience an initial sense of what they are about to see and hear. It is, therefore, extremely important to choose the text for this slide carefully. Avoid stating the obvious in the title. Instead, create interest and curiosity using key ideas from the presentation.
>
> Some PowerPoint users create the title slide as their last step in the design process so that it reflects the tone of the presentation. They begin by planning the final slide in the presentation so that they know where and how they want to end the slide show. All the slides in the presentation should work toward meeting this final slide.

To Enter the Presentation Title

The presentation title for Project 1 is It Is Easy Being Green. This title creates interest by introducing the concept of simple energy conservation tasks. The following step creates the slide show's title.

- Click the label, Click to add title, located inside the title text placeholder to select the placeholder (Figure 1–5).

Figure 1–5

- Type **It Is Easy Being Green** in the title text placeholder. Do not press the ENTER key (Figure 1–6).

Q&A

Why does the text display with capital letters despite the fact I am typing uppercase and lowercase letters?

The Oriel theme uses the Small Caps effect for the title text. This effect converts lowercase letters to uppercase and reduces their size.

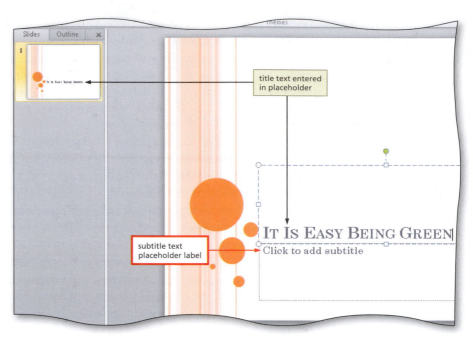

Figure 1–6

Correcting a Mistake When Typing

If you type the wrong letter, press the BACKSPACE key to erase all the characters back to and including the one that is incorrect. If you mistakenly press the ENTER key after typing the title and the insertion point is on the new line, simply press the BACKSPACE key to return the insertion point to the right of the letter n in the word, Green.

When you install PowerPoint, the default setting allows you to reverse up to the last 20 changes by clicking the Undo button on the Quick Access Toolbar. The ScreenTip that appears when you point to the Undo button changes to indicate the type of change just made. For example, if you type text in the title text placeholder and then point to the Undo button, the ScreenTip that appears is Undo Typing. For clarity, when referencing the Undo button in this project, the name displaying in the ScreenTip is referenced. You can reapply a change that you reversed with the Undo button by clicking the Redo button on the Quick Access Toolbar. Clicking the Redo button reverses the last undo action. The ScreenTip name reflects the type of reversal last performed.

Paragraphs

Text in the subtitle text placeholder supports the title text. It can appear on one or more lines in the placeholder. To create more than one subtitle line, you press the ENTER key after typing some words. PowerPoint creates a new line, which is the second paragraph in the placeholder. A **paragraph** is a segment of text with the same format that begins when you press the ENTER key and ends when you press the ENTER key again. This new paragraph is the same level as the previous paragraph. A **level** is a position within a structure, such as an outline, that indicates the magnitude of importance. PowerPoint allows for five paragraph levels.

For an introduction to Office 2010 and instruction about how to perform basic tasks in Office 2010 programs, read the Office 2010 and Windows 7 chapter at the beginning of this book, where you can learn how to start a program, use the Ribbon, save a file, open a file, quit a program, use Help, and much more.

To Enter the Presentation Subtitle Paragraph

The first subtitle paragraph links to the title by giving further detail that the presentation will focus on energy-saving measures at home. The following steps enter the presentation subtitle.

1
● Click the label, Click to add subtitle, located inside the subtitle text placeholder to select the placeholder (Figure 1–7).

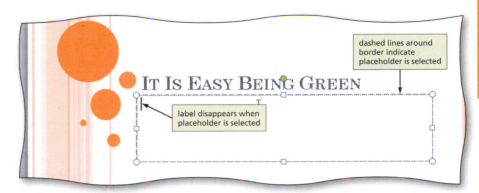

Figure 1–7

2
● Type `Saving Energy at Home` but do not press the ENTER key (Figure 1–8).

Figure 1–8

Identify how to format specific elements of the text.
Most of the time, you use the document theme's text attributes, color scheme, and layout. Occasionally, you may want to change the way a presentation looks, however, and still keep a particular document theme. PowerPoint gives you that flexibility.

Graphic designers use several rules when formatting text.

● Avoid all capital letters, if possible. Audiences have difficulty comprehending sentences typed in all capital letters, especially when the lines exceed seven words. All capital letters leaves no room for emphasis or inflection, so readers get confused about what material deserves particular attention. Some document themes, however, have a default title text style of all capital letters.

● Avoid text with a font size less than 30 point. Audience members generally will sit a maximum of 50 feet from a screen, and at this distance 30-point type is the smallest size text they can read comfortably without straining.

● Make careful color choices. Color evokes emotions, and a careless color choice may elicit the incorrect psychological response. PowerPoint provides a color gallery with hundreds of colors. The built-in document themes use complementary colors that work well together. If you stray from these themes and add your own color choices, without a good reason to make the changes, your presentation is apt to become ineffective.

Plan Ahead

Formatting Characters in a Presentation

Recall that each document theme determines the color scheme, font set, and layout of a presentation. You can use a specific document theme and then change the characters' formats any time before, during, or after you type the text.

BTW

Q&As
For a complete list of the Q&As found in many of the step-by-step sequences in this book, visit the PowerPoint 2010 Q&A Web page (scsite.com/ppt2010/qa).

Fonts and Font Styles

Characters that appear on the screen are a specific shape and size. Examples of how you can modify the appearance, or **format**, of these typed characters on the screen and in print include changing the font, style, size, and color. The **font**, or typeface, defines the appearance and shape of the letters, numbers, punctuation marks, and symbols. **Style** indicates how the characters are formatted. PowerPoint's text font styles include regular, italic, bold, and bold italic. **Size** specifies the height of the characters and is gauged by a measurement system that uses points. A **point** is 1/72 of an inch in height. Thus, a character with a font size of 36 is 36/72 (or 1/2) of an inch in height. **Color** defines the hue of the characters.

This presentation uses the Oriel document theme, which uses particular font styles and font sizes. The Oriel document theme default title text font is named Century Schoolbook. It has a bold style with no special effects, and its size is 30 point. The Oriel document theme default subtitle text font also is Century Schoolbook with a font size of 18 point.

To Select a Paragraph

You can use many techniques to format characters. When you want to apply the same formats to multiple words or paragraphs, it is efficient to select the desired text and then make the desired changes to all the characters simultaneously. The first formatting change you will make will apply to the title slide subtitle. The following step selects this paragraph.

- Triple-click the paragraph, Saving Energy at Home, in the subtitle text placeholder to select the paragraph (Figure 1–9).

Q&A

Can I select the paragraph using a technique other than triple-clicking?

Yes. You can move your mouse pointer to the left of the first paragraph and then drag to the end of the line.

Figure 1–9

To Italicize Text

Different font styles often are used on slides to make them more appealing to the reader and to emphasize particular text. **Italicized** text has a slanted appearance. Used sparingly, it draws the readers' eyes to these characters. The following step adds emphasis to the second line of the subtitle text by changing regular text to italic text.

1

- With the subtitle text still selected, click the Italic button on the Mini toolbar to italicize that text on the slide (Figure 1–10).

Q&A

If I change my mind and decide not to italicize the text, how can I remove this style?

Click the Italic button a second time or immediately click the Undo button on the Quick Access Toolbar or press CTRL+Z.

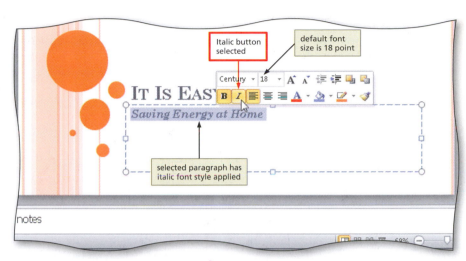

Figure 1–10

Other Ways		
1. Right-click selected text, click Font on shortcut menu, click Font tab (Font dialog box), click Italic in Font style list, click OK button	2. Select text, click Italic button (Home tab | Font group) 3. Click Font Dialog Box Launcher (Home tab | Font	group), click Font tab (Font dialog box), click Italic in Font style list, click OK button 4. Select text, press CTRL+I

To Increase Font Size

To add emphasis, you increase the font size for the subtitle text. The Increase Font Size button on the Mini toolbar increases the font size in preset increments. The following step uses this button to increase the font size.

1

- Click the Increase Font Size button on the Mini toolbar twice to increase the font size of the selected text from 18 to 24 point (Figure 1–11).

Figure 1–11

Other Ways		
1. Click Font Size box arrow on Mini toolbar, click desired font size in Font Size gallery	2. Click Increase Font Size button (Home tab | Font group) 3. Click Font Size box arrow (Home tab | Font group),	click desired font size in Font size gallery 4. Press CTRL+SHIFT+>

To Select a Word

PowerPoint designers use many techniques to emphasize words and characters on a slide. To add emphasis to the energy-saving concept of your slide show, you want to increase the font size and change the font color to green for the word, Green, in the title text. You could perform these actions separately, but it is more efficient to select the word and then change the font attributes. The following steps select a word.

● Position the mouse pointer somewhere in the word to be selected (in this case, in the word, Green) (Figure 1–12).

Figure 1–12

● Double-click the word to select it (Figure 1–13).

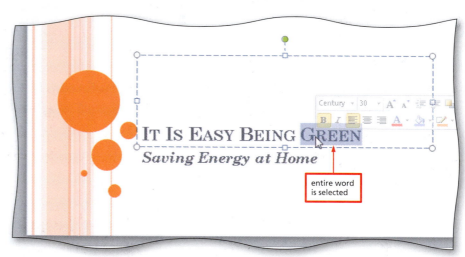

Figure 1–13

Other Ways

1. Position mouse pointer before first character, press CTRL+SHIFT+RIGHT ARROW

Plan Ahead

Format text colors.
When selecting text colors, try to limit using red. This color often is associated with dangerous or alarming situations. In addition, at least 15 percent of men have difficulty distinguishing varying shades of green or red. They also often see the color purple as blue and the color brown as green. This problem is more pronounced when the colors appear in small areas, such as slide paragraphs or line chart bars.

To Change the Text Color

PowerPoint allows you to use one or more text colors in a presentation. To add more emphasis to the word, Green, in the title slide text, you decide to change the color. The following steps add emphasis to this word by changing the font color from black to green.

- With the word, Green, selected, click the Font Color arrow on the Mini toolbar to display the gallery of Theme Colors and Standard Colors (Figure 1–14).

Q&A If the Mini toolbar disappears from the screen, how can I display it once again?

Right-click the text, and the Mini toolbar should appear.

Experiment

- Point to various colors in the gallery and watch the word's font color change.

Figure 1–14

- Click the Green button in the Standard Colors row on the Mini toolbar (sixth color) to change the font color to green (Figure 1–15).

Q&A Why did I select the color Green?

Green is one of the 10 standard colors associated with every document theme, and it is a universal color to represent respecting natural resources. The color will emphasize the fact that the presentation focuses on green conservation measures.

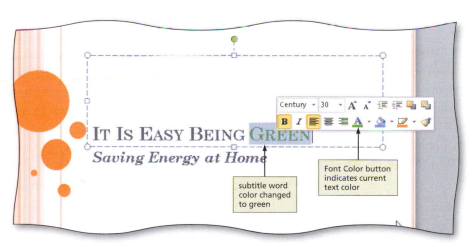

Figure 1–15

Q&A What is the difference between the colors shown in the Theme Colors area and the Standard Colors?

The 10 colors in the top row of the Theme Colors area are two text, two background, and six accent colors in the Oriel theme; the five colors in each column under the top row display different transparencies. These colors are available in every document theme.

3

- Click outside the selected area to deselect the word.

Other Ways
1. Right-click selected text, click Font on shortcut menu, click Font Color button, click Green in Standard Colors row   2. Click Font Color arrow (Home tab | Font group), click Green in Standard Colors row

To Save a Presentation

You have performed many tasks while creating this slide and do not want to risk losing work completed thus far. Accordingly, you should save the document.

The following steps assume you already have created folders for storing your files, for example, a CIS 101 folder (for your class) that contains a PowerPoint folder (for your assignments). Thus, these steps save the document in the PowerPoint folder in the CIS 101 folder on a USB flash drive using the file name, Saving Energy. For a detailed example of the procedure summarized below, refer to the Office 2010 and Windows 7 chapter at the beginning of this book.

1 With a USB flash drive connected to one of the computer's USB ports, click the Save button on the Quick Access Toolbar to display the Save As dialog box.

2 Type `Saving Energy` in the File name text box to change the file name. Do not press the ENTER key after typing the file name because you do not want to close the dialog box at this time.

3 Navigate to the desired save location (in this case, the PowerPoint folder in the CIS 101 folder [or your class folder] on the USB flash drive).

4 Click the Save button (Save As dialog box) to save the document in the selected folder on the selected drive with the entered file name.

Adding a New Slide to a Presentation

With the text for the title slide for the presentation created, the next step is to add the first text slide immediately after the title slide. Usually, when you create a presentation, you add slides with text, clip art, graphics, or charts. Some placeholders allow you to double-click the placeholder and then access other objects, such as media clips, charts, diagrams, and organization charts. You can change the layout for a slide at any time during the creation of a presentation.

To Add a New Text Slide with a Bulleted List

When you add a new slide, PowerPoint uses the Title and Content slide layout. This layout provides a title placeholder and a content area for text, art, charts, and other graphics. A vertical scroll bar appears in the Slide pane when you add the second slide so that you can move from slide to slide easily. A thumbnail of this slide also appears in the Slides tab. The following steps add a new slide with the Title and Content slide layout.

1

• Click Home on the Ribbon to display the Home tab (Figure 1–16).

Figure 1–16

2

- Click the New Slide button (Home tab | Slides group) to insert a new slide with the Title and Content layout (Figure 1–17).

Q&A Why does the bullet character display an orange circle?

The Oriel document theme determines the bullet characters. Each paragraph level has an associated bullet character.

Q&A I clicked the New Slide arrow instead of the New Slide button. What should I do?

Click the Title and Content slide thumbnail in the layout gallery.

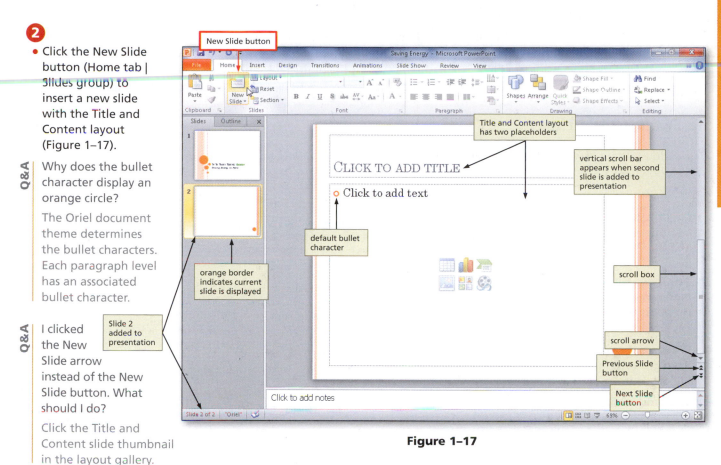

Figure 1–17

Other Ways

1. Press CTRL+M

Choose the words for the slide.

All presentations should follow the 7 × 7 rule, which states that each slide should have a maximum of seven lines, and each line should have a maximum of seven words. PowerPoint designers must choose their words carefully and, in turn, help viewers read the slides easily.

Avoid line wraps. Your audience's eyes want to stop at the end of a line. Thus, you must plan your words carefully or adjust the font size so that each point displays on only one line.

Plan Ahead

Creating a Text Slide with a Multi-Level Bulleted List

The information in the Slide 2 text placeholder is presented in a bulleted list with three levels. A **bulleted list** is a list of paragraphs, each of which is preceded by a bullet. A slide that consists of more than one level of bulleted text is called a **multi-level bulleted list slide**. In a multi-level bulleted list, a lower-level paragraph is a subset of a higher-level paragraph. It usually contains information that supports the topic in the paragraph immediately above it.

Two of the Slide 2 bullets appear at the same paragraph level, called the first level: Install low-flow faucets and shower heads, and Appliances count for 20 percent of electric bill. Beginning with the second level, each paragraph indents to the right of the preceding level and is pushed down to a lower level. For example, if you increase the indent of a first-level paragraph, it becomes a second-level paragraph. The second, fourth, and fifth paragraphs on Slide 2 are second-level paragraphs. The last paragraph, Wash clothes in cold water, is a third-level paragraph.

BTW

The Ribbon and Screen Resolution

PowerPoint may change how the groups and buttons within the groups appear on the Ribbon, depending on the computer's screen resolution. Thus, your Ribbon may look different from the ones in this book if you are using a screen resolution other than 1024 x 768.

Creating a text slide with a multi-level bulleted list requires several steps. Initially, you enter a slide title in the title text placeholder. Next, you select the content text placeholder. Then, you type the text for the multi-level bulleted list, increasing and decreasing the indents as needed. The next several sections add a slide with a multi-level bulleted list.

To Enter a Slide Title

PowerPoint assumes every new slide has a title. The title for Slide 2 is Make Small Changes to Cut Energy. The following step enters this title.

- Click the label, Click to add title, to select it and then type **Make Small Changes to Cut Energy** in the placeholder. Do not press the ENTER key (Figure 1–18).

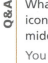

Q&A

What are those six icons grouped in the middle of the slide?

You can click one of the icons to insert a specific type of content: table, chart, SmartArt graphic, picture, clip art, or media clip.

Figure 1–18

To Select a Text Placeholder

Before you can type text into the text placeholder, you first must select it. The following step selects the text placeholder on Slide 2.

- Click the label, Click to add text, to select the text placeholder (Figure 1–19).

Q&A

Why does my mouse pointer have a different shape?

If you move the mouse pointer away from the bullet, it will change shape.

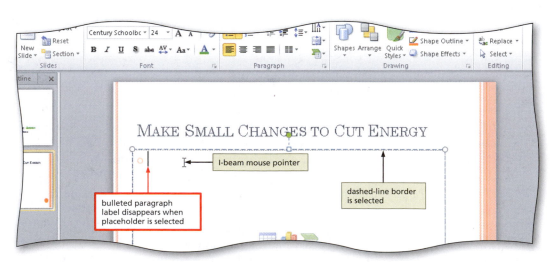

Figure 1–19

To Type a Multi-Level Bulleted List

The content placeholder provides an area for the text characters. When you click inside a placeholder, you then can type or paste text. As discussed previously, a bulleted list is a list of paragraphs, each of which is preceded by a bullet. A paragraph is a segment of text ended by pressing the ENTER key.

The content text placeholder is selected, so the next step is to type the multi-level bulleted list that consists of six paragraphs, as shown in Figure 1–1b on page PPT 3. Creating a lower-level paragraph is called **demoting** text; creating a higher-level paragraph is called **promoting** text. The following steps create a multi-level bulleted list consisting of three levels.

1
• Type `Install low-flow faucets and shower heads` and then press the ENTER key (Figure 1–20).

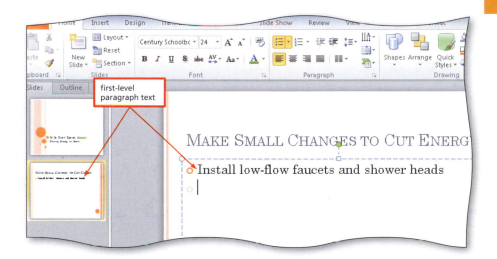

Figure 1–20

2
• Click the Increase List Level button (Home tab | Paragraph group) to indent the second paragraph below the first and create a second-level paragraph (Figure 1–21).

Q&A Why does the bullet for this paragraph have a different size and color?

A different bullet is assigned to each paragraph level.

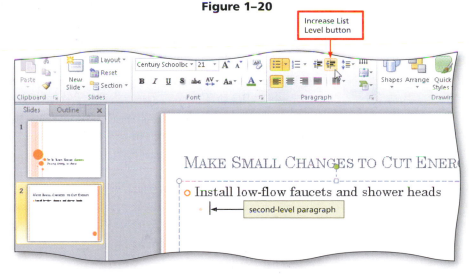

Figure 1–21

3
• Type `Cut water consumption in half` and then press the ENTER key (Figure 1–22).

Figure 1–22

4

- Click the Decrease List Level button (Home tab | Paragraph group) so that the second-level paragraph becomes a first-level paragraph (Figure 1–23).

Q&A

Can I delete bullets on a slide?

Yes. If you do not want bullets to display in a particular paragraph, click the Bullets button (Home tab | Paragraph group) or right-click the paragraph and then click the Bullets button on the shortcut menu.

Other Ways

1. Press TAB to promote paragraph; press SHIFT+TAB to demote paragraph

Figure 1–23

To Type the Remaining Text for Slide 2

The following steps complete the text for Slide 2.

1 Type `Appliances count for 20 percent of electric bill` and then press the ENTER key.

2 Click the Increase List Level button (Home tab | Paragraph group) to demote the paragraph to the second level.

3 Type `Buy ENERGY STAR qualified products` and then press the ENTER key to add a new paragraph at the same level as the previous paragraph.

4 Type `Run dishwasher, clothes washer with full loads` and then press the ENTER key.

5 Click the Increase List Level button (Home tab | Paragraph group) to demote the paragraph to the third level.

6 Type `Wash clothes in cold water` but do not press the ENTER key (Figure 1–24).

Q&A

I pressed the ENTER key in error, and now a new bullet appears after the last entry on this slide. How can I remove this extra bullet?

Press the BACKSPACE key twice.

Figure 1–24

To Select a Group of Words

PowerPoint designers use many techniques to emphasize words and characters on a slide. To add emphasis to your slide show's concept of saving natural resources, you want to bold and increase the font size of the words, in half, in the body text. You could perform these actions separately, but it is more efficient to select the words and then change the font attributes. The following steps select two words.

- Position the mouse pointer immediately to the left of the first character of the text to be selected (in this case, the i in the word, in) (Figure 1–25).

Figure 1–25

- Drag the mouse pointer through the last character of the text to be selected (in this case, the f in half) (Figure 1–26).

Figure 1–26

Other Ways
1. Press CTRL+SHIFT+RIGHT ARROW

To Bold Text

Bold characters display somewhat thicker and darker than those that display in a regular font style. Clicking the Bold button on the Mini toolbar is an efficient method of bolding text. To add more emphasis to the amount of water savings that can occur by installing low-flow faucets and shower heads, you want to bold the words, in half. The following step bolds this text.

1
• With the words, in half, selected, click the Bold button on the Mini toolbar to bold the two words (Figure 1–27).

Figure 1–27

To Increase Font Size

To add emphasis, you increase the font size for the words, in half. The following step increases the font size from 21 to 24 point.

1 With the words, in half, still selected, click the Increase Font Size button on the Mini toolbar once (Figure 1–28).

Figure 1–28

Adding New Slides and Changing the Slide Layouts

Slide 3 in Figure 1–1c on page PPT 3 contains a photograph and does not contain a bulleted list. When you add a new slide, PowerPoint applies the Title and Content layout. This layout along with the Title Slide layout for Slide 1 are the default styles. A **layout** specifies the arrangement of placeholders on a slide. These placeholders are arranged in various configurations and can contain text, such as the slide title or a bulleted list, or they can contain content, such as SmartArt graphics, pictures, charts, tables, shapes, and clip art. The placement of the text, in relationship to content, depends on the slide layout. You can specify a particular slide layout when you add a new slide to a presentation or after you have created the slide.

Using the **Layout gallery**, you can choose a slide layout. The nine layouts in this gallery have a variety of placeholders to define text and content positioning and formatting. Three layouts are for text: Title Slide, Section Header, and Title Only. Five are for text and content: Title and Content, Two Content, Comparison, Content with Caption, and Picture with Caption. The Blank layout has no placeholders. If none of these standard layouts meets your design needs, you can create a **custom layout**. A custom layout specifies the number, size, and location of placeholders, background content, and optional slide and placeholder-level properties.

When you change the layout of a slide, PowerPoint retains the text and objects and repositions them into the appropriate placeholders. Using slide layouts eliminates the need to resize objects and the font size because PowerPoint automatically sizes the objects and text to fit the placeholders.

To Add a Slide with the Title Only Layout

The following steps add Slide 3 to the presentation with the Title Only slide layout style.

1

- If necessary, click Home on the Ribbon to display the Home tab.

- Click the New Slide arrow (Home tab | Slides group) to display the Layout gallery (Figure 1–29).

Figure 1–29

2
• Click Title Only to add a new slide and apply that layout to Slide 3 (Figure 1–30).

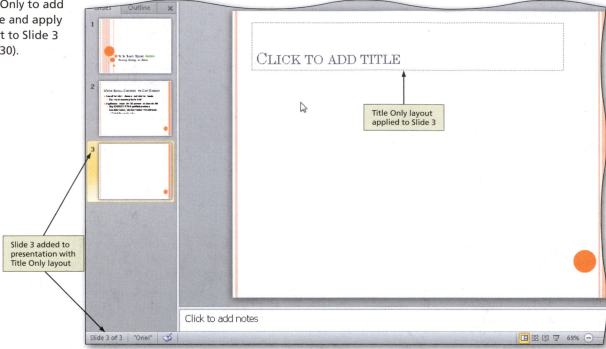

Figure 1–30

To Enter a Slide Title

The only text on Slide 3 is the title. The following step enters the title text for this slide.

BTW

Portrait Page Orientation
If your slide content is dominantly vertical, such as a skyscraper or a person, consider changing the slide layout to a portrait page orientation. To change the orientation, click the Slide Orientation button (Design tab | Page Setup group) and then click the desired orientation.

1 Type `Use Energy Efficient Lighting` as the title text but do not press the ENTER key (Figure 1–31).

Figure 1–31

To Add a New Slide and Enter a Slide Title and Headings

The text on Slide 4 in Figure 1–1d on page PPT 3 consists of a title and two headings. The appropriate layout for this slide is named Comparison. The following steps add Slide 4 to the presentation with the Comparison layout and then enter the title and heading text for this slide.

1
- Click the New Slide arrow in the Slides group to display the Layout gallery (Figure 1–32).

Figure 1–32

2
- Click Comparison to add Slide 4 and apply that layout.

- Type **Adjust Your Thermostats** in the title text placeholder but do not press the ENTER key.

- Click the left orange heading placeholder with the label, Click to add text, to select this placeholder (Figure 1–33).

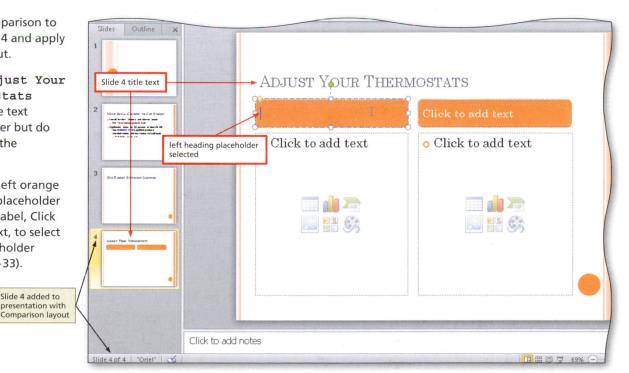

Figure 1–33

3

- Type **Furnace: 68 degrees** but do not press the ENTER key.

- Click the right orange heading placeholder and then type **Water heater: 120 degrees** but do not press the ENTER key (Figure 1–34).

Figure 1–34

Break Point: If you wish to take a break, this is a good place to do so. You can quit PowerPoint now (refer to page PPT 50 for instructions). To resume at a later time, start PowerPoint (refer to pages PPT 4 and PPT 5 for instructions), open the file called Saving Energy (refer to pages PPT 50 and PPT 51 for instructions), and continue following the steps from this location forward.

PowerPoint Views

The PowerPoint window display varies depending on the view. A **view** is the mode in which the presentation appears on the screen. PowerPoint has four main views: Normal, Slide Sorter, Reading, and Slide Show. It also has another view, called Notes Page view, used for entering information about a slide.

The default view is **Normal view**, which is composed of three working areas that allow you to work on various aspects of a presentation simultaneously. The left side of the screen has a Tabs pane that consists of a **Slides tab** and an **Outline tab**. These tabs alternate between views of the presentation in a thumbnail, or miniature, view of the slides and an outline of the slide text. You can type the text of the presentation on the Outline tab and easily rearrange bulleted lists, paragraphs, and individual slides. As you type, you can view this text in the **Slide pane**, which shows a large view of the current slide on the right side of the window. You also can enter text, graphics, animations, and hyperlinks directly in the Slide pane. The **Notes pane** at the bottom of the window is an area where you can type notes and additional information. This text can consist of notes to yourself or remarks to share with your audience. If you want to work with your notes in full page format, you can display them in **Notes Page view**.

In Normal view, you can adjust the width of the Slide pane by dragging the **splitter bar** and the height of the Notes pane by dragging the pane borders. After you have created at least two slides, a scroll bar containing **scroll arrows** and **scroll boxes** will appear on the right edge of the window.

To Move to Another Slide in Normal View

When creating or editing a presentation in Normal view (the view you are currently using), you often want to display a slide other than the current one. Before continuing with developing this project, you want to display the title slide by dragging the scroll box on the vertical scroll bar. When you drag the scroll box, the **slide indicator** shows the number and title of the slide you are about to display. Releasing the mouse button shows the slide. The following steps move from Slide 4 to Slide 1 using the scroll box on the Slide pane.

• Position the mouse pointer on the scroll box.

• Press and hold down the mouse button so that Slide: 4 of 4 Adjust Your Thermostats appears in the slide indicator (Figure 1–35).

Figure 1–35

2

• Drag the scroll box up the vertical scroll bar until Slide: 1 of 4 It Is Easy Being Green appears in the slide indicator (Figure 1–36).

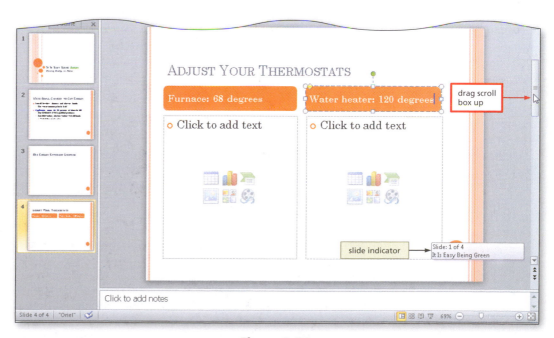

Figure 1–36

3

● Release the mouse button so that Slide 1 appears in the Slide pane and the Slide 1 thumbnail has an orange border in the Slides tab (Figure 1–37).

Figure 1–37

Other Ways

1. Click Next Slide button or Previous Slide button to move forward or back one slide
2. Click slide thumbnail on Slides tab
3. Press PAGE DOWN or PAGE UP to move forward or back one slide

BTW

Today's Clip
Each day, Microsoft features "today's clip," which reflects events or themes specific to this time. For example, the pictures, illustrations, and clip art have back-to-school images, winter scenes, and holiday characters.

Inserting Clip Art and Photographs into Slides

A **clip** is a single media file that can include art, sound, animation, or movies. Adding a clip can help increase the visual appeal of many slides and can offer a quick way to add professional-looking graphic images and sounds to a presentation without creating these files yourself. This art is contained in the **Microsoft Clip Organizer**, a collection of drawings, photographs, sounds, videos, and other media files shared among Microsoft Office applications. The **Office Collections** contains all these media files included with Microsoft Office.

You also can add your own clips to slides. You can insert these files directly from a storage medium, such as a USB flash drive. In addition, you can add them to the other files in the Clip Organizer so that you can search for and reuse these images, sounds, animations, and movies. When you create these media files, they are stored on your hard disk in **My Collections**. The Clip Organizer will find these files and create a new collection with these files. Two other locations for clips are Shared Collections and Web Collections. Files in the **Shared Collections** typically reside on a shared network file server and are accessible to multiple users. The **Web Collections** clips reside on the Microsoft Clip Art and Media Home page on the Microsoft Office Online Web site. They are available only if you have an active Internet connection.

The Clip Art Task Pane

You can add clips to your presentation in two ways. One way is by selecting one of the slide layouts that includes a content placeholder with a Clip Art button. A second method is by clicking the Clip Art button in the Images area on the Insert tab. Clicking the Clip Art button opens the Clip Art task pane. The **Clip Art task pane** allows you to search for clips by using descriptive keywords, file names, media file formats, and clip collections. Specific file formats could be for clip art, photographs, movies, and sounds.

Clips are organized in hierarchical **clip collections** that combine topic-related clips into categories, such as Academic, Business, and Technology.

Clips have one or more keywords associated with various entities, activities, labels, and emotions. In most instances, the keywords give the name of the clip and related categories. For example, an image of a cow in the Animals category has the keywords animals, cattle, cows, dairies, farms, and Holsteins. You can enter these keywords in the Search for text box to find clips when you know one of the words associated with the image. Otherwise, you might find it necessary to scroll through several categories to find an appropriate clip.

Depending on the installation of the Microsoft Clip Organizer on your computer, you might not have the clip art used in this chapter. Contact your instructor if you are missing clips used in the following steps. If you have an active connection to the Internet, clips from the Microsoft Office Online Web site will display automatically as the result of your search results.

Adhere to copyright regulations.
You have permission to use the clips from the Microsoft Clip Organizer. If you want to use a clip from another source, be certain you have the legal right to insert this file in your presentation. Read the copyright notices that may accompany the clip and may be posted on the Web site where you obtained the clip. The owners of these images and files often ask you to give them credit for using their work, which may be satisfied by stating where you obtained the images.

Plan Ahead

To Insert a Clip from the Clip Organizer into the Title Slide

Slide 1 uses the Title Slide layout, which has two placeholders for text but none for graphical content. You desire to place a graphic on Slide 1, so you will locate a clip art image of a green globe and flower and then insert it in this slide. Later in this chapter, you will size and position it in an appropriate location. The following steps add a clip to Slide 1.

1

- Click Insert on the Ribbon to display the Insert tab.

- Click the Clip Art button (Insert tab | Images group) to display the Clip Art task pane.

- Click the Search for text box in the Clip Art task pane, if necessary delete any letters that are present, and then type **green globe** in the Search for text box.

- If necessary, click the 'Include Office.com content' check box to select it (Figure 1–38).

Figure 1–38

2

- Click the Go button so that the Microsoft Clip Organizer will search for and display all clips having the keywords, green globe.

- If necessary, click the Yes button if a Microsoft Clip Organizer dialog box appears asking if you want to include additional clip art images from Office.com.

- If necessary, scroll down the list to display the globe clip shown in Figure 1–39.

- Click the clip to insert it into the slide (Figure 1–39).

Figure 1–39

Q&A | What if the globe image displayed in Figure 1–39 is not shown in my Clip Art task pane?

Select a similar clip. Your clips may be different depending on the clips installed on your computer and if you have an active connection to the Internet.

Q&A | What is the yellow star image that displays in the lower-right corner of some clips in the Clip Art task pane?

The star indicates the image is animated and will move when the slide containing this clip is displayed during a slide show.

Q&A | Why is this globe clip displayed in this location on the slide?

The slide layout does not have a content placeholder, so PowerPoint inserts the clip in the center of the slide.

To Insert a Clip from the Clip Organizer into a Slide without a Content Placeholder

The next step is to add two clips to Slide 2. Slide 2 has a bulleted list in the text placeholder, so the icon group does not display in the center of the placeholder. Later in this chapter, you will resize the inserted clips. The Clip Art task pane is displayed and will remain open until you close it. The following steps add one clip to Slide 2.

1 Click the Next Slide button to display Slide 2.

2 Click the Search for text box in the Clip Art task pane and then delete the letters in the Search for text box.

3 Type `faucets` and then click the Go button.

4 If necessary, scroll down the list to display the faucet clip shown in Figure 1–40 and then click the clip to insert it into Slide 2 (Figure 1–40).

Figure 1–40

To Insert a Second Clip from the Clip Organizer into a Slide without a Content Placeholder

The following steps add a second clip to Slide 2. PowerPoint inserts this clip on top of the faucet clip in the center of the slide. Both clips will be moved and resized later in this project.

1 Click the Search for text box in the Clip Art task pane and then delete the letters in the text box.

2 Type `dishwasher`, click the Go button, locate the clip shown in Figure 1–41, and then click the clip to insert it into Slide 2 (Figure 1–41).

BTW

Clip Properties
Each clip has properties that identify its characteristics. When you right-click a clip in the Microsoft Clip Organizer, you will see details of the clip's name, file type, size, dimensions, keywords, and creation date. You also can preview the clip and edit its assigned keywords.

Figure 1–41

To Insert a Clip from the Clip Organizer into a Content Placeholder

Slide 4 uses the Comparison layout, which has a content placeholder below each of the two headings. You desire to insert clip art into both content placeholders to reinforce the concept that consumers should adjust the heating temperatures of their furnace and water heater. The following steps insert clip art of a furnace into the left content placeholder and a water heater into the right content placeholder on Slide 4.

- Click the Close button in the Clip Art task pane so that it no longer is displayed.

- Click the Next Slide button twice to display Slide 4.

- Click the Clip Art button in the left content placeholder to select that placeholder and to open the Clip Art task pane (Figure 1–42).

Q&A

Do I need to close the Clip Art task pane when I am finished inserting the two clips into Slide 2?

No. You can leave the Clip Art task pane open and then display Slide 4. It is often more convenient, however, to open this pane when you are working with a layout that has a content placeholder so that the clip is inserted in the desired location.

Figure 1–42

- Click the Search for text box in the Clip Art task pane, delete any letters that are present, type **furnace** in the Search for text box, and then click the Go button to search for and display all pictures having the keyword, furnace.

- If necessary, scroll down the list to display the furnace clip shown in Figure 1–43.

- Click the clip to insert it into the left content placeholder (Figure 1–43).

Figure 1–43

3

• Click anywhere in the right placeholder except one of the six icons to select the placeholder.

Q&A

I clicked the Clip Art icon by mistake, which closed the Clip Art task pane. How do I open it?

Click the Clip Art icon.

4

• Click the Search for text box in the Clip Art task pane, delete any letters that are present, type **water heater** in the Search for text box, and then click the Go button.

• If necessary, scroll down the list to display the water heater clip shown in Figure 1–44 and then click the clip to insert it into the right content placeholder (Figure 1–44).

Figure 1–44

Photographs and the Clip Organizer

In addition to clip art, you can insert pictures into a presentation. These may include scanned photographs, line art, and artwork from storage media, such as USB flash drives, hard disks, optical discs, and memory cards. To insert a picture into a presentation, the picture must be saved in a format that PowerPoint can recognize. Table 1–1 identifies some of the formats PowerPoint recognizes.

Table 1–1 Primary File Formats PowerPoint Recognizes

Format	File Extension
Computer Graphics Metafile	.cgm
CorelDRAW	.cdr, .cdt, .cmx, and .pat
Encapsulated PostScript	.eps
Enhanced Metafile	.emf
FlashPix	.fpx
Graphics Interchange Format	.gif
Hanako	.jsh, .jah, and .jbh
Joint Photographic Experts Group (JPEG)	.jpg
Kodak PhotoCD	.pcd
Macintosh PICT	.pct
PC Paintbrush	.pcx
Portable Network Graphics	.png
Tagged Image File Format	.tif
Windows Bitmap	.bmp, .rle, .dib
Microsoft Windows Metafile	.wmf
WordPerfect Graphics	.wpg

BTW

Compressing File Size
When you add a picture to a presentation, PowerPoint automatically compresses this image. Even with this compression applied, a presentation that contains pictures usually has a large file size. To reduce this size, you can compress a picture further without affecting the quality of how it displays on the slide. To compress a picture, select the picture and then click the Compress Pictures button (Picture Tools Format tab | Adjust group). You can restore the picture's original settings by clicking the Reset Picture button (Picture Tools Format tab | Adjust group).

BTW

Wrapping Text around a Picture
PowerPoint 2010 does not allow you to wrap text around a picture or other graphics, such as tables, shapes, charts, or graphics. This feature, however, is available in Word 2010.

You can import files saved with the .emf, .gif, .jpg, .png, .bmp, .rle, .dib, and .wmf formats directly into PowerPoint presentations. All other file formats require separate filters that are shipped with the PowerPoint installation software and must be installed separately. You can download additional filters from the Microsoft Office Online Web site.

To Insert a Photograph from the Clip Organizer into a Slide without a Content Placeholder

Next, you will add a photograph to Slide 3. You will not insert this picture into a content placeholder, so it will display in the center of the slide. Later in this chapter, you will resize this picture. To start the process of locating this photograph, you do not need to click the Clip Art button in the content placeholder because the Clip Art task pane already is displayed. The following steps add a photograph to Slide 3.

1 Click the Previous Slide button to display Slide 3.

2 Click the Search for text box in the Clip Art task pane, delete the letters in the text box, type **CFL**, and then click the Go button.

3 If necessary, scroll down the list to display the picture of a light bulb shown in Figure 1–45, and then click the photograph to insert it into Slide 2 (Figure 1–45).

Q&A Why is my photograph a different size from the one shown in Figure 1–1c on page PPT 3?

The photograph was inserted into the slide and not into a content placeholder. You will resize the picture later in this chapter.

Figure 1–45

Break Point: If you wish to take a break, this is a good place to do so. You can quit PowerPoint now (refer to page PPT 50 for instructions). To resume at a later time, start PowerPoint (refer to pages PPT 4 and PPT 5 for instructions), open the file called Saving Energy (refer to pages PPT 50 and PPT 51 for instructions), and continue following the steps from this location forward.

Resizing Clip Art and Photographs

Sometimes it is necessary to change the size of clip art. **Resizing** includes enlarging or reducing the size of a clip art graphic. You can resize clip art using a variety of techniques. One method involves changing the size of a clip by specifying exact dimensions in a dialog box. Another method involves dragging one of the graphic's sizing handles to the desired location. A selected graphic appears surrounded by a **selection rectangle**, which has small squares and circles, called **sizing handles** or move handles, at each corner and middle location.

To Resize Clip Art

On Slides 1, 2, and 4, much space appears around the clips, so you can increase their sizes. Likewise, the photograph on Slide 3 can be enlarged to fill more of the space below the slide title. To change the size, drag the corner sizing handles to view how the clip will look on the slide. Using these corner handles maintains the graphic's original proportions. Dragging the square sizing handles alters the proportions so that the graphic's height and width become larger or smaller. The following steps increase the size of the Slide 1 clip using a corner sizing handle.

1
- Click the Close button in the Clip Art task pane so that it no longer is displayed.

- Click the Previous Slide button two times to display Slide 1.

- Click the globe clip to select it and display the selection rectangle.

- Point to the lower-left corner sizing handle on the clip so that the mouse pointer changes to a two-headed arrow (Figure 1–46).

Figure 1–46

2

- Drag the sizing handle diagonally toward the lower-left corner of the slide until the mouse pointer is positioned approximately as shown in Figure 1–47.

Q&A What if the clip is not the same size as the one shown in Figure 1–47?

Repeat Steps 1 and 2.

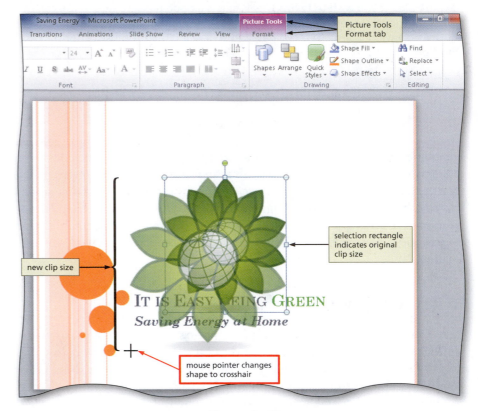

Figure 1–47

3

- Release the mouse button to resize the clip.
- Click outside the clip to deselect it (Figure 1–48).

Q&A What happened to the Picture Tools Format tab?

When you click outside the clip, PowerPoint deselects the clip and removes the Picture Tools Format tab from the screen.

Q&A What if I want to return the clip to its original size and start again?

With the graphic selected, click the Reset Picture button (Picture Tools Format tab | Adjust group).

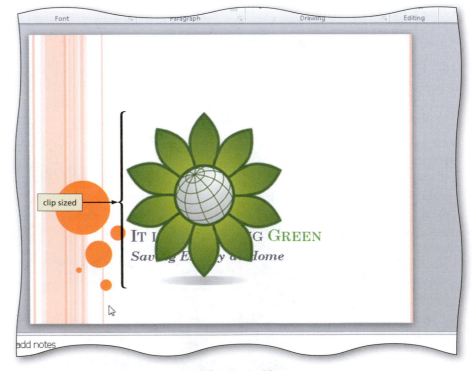

Figure 1–48

To Resize Clips on Slide 4

The two clip art images on Slide 4 also can be enlarged to fill much of the white space below the headings. You will reposition the clips in a later step. The following steps resize these clips using a sizing handle.

1 Click the Next Slide button three times to display Slide 4.

2 Click the furnace clip to select it.

3 Drag the lower-left corner sizing handle on the clip diagonally outward until the clip is resized approximately as shown in Figure 1–49.

4 Click the water heater clip to select it.

5 Drag the lower-right corner sizing handle on the clip diagonally outward until the clip is resized approximately as shown in Figure 1–49.

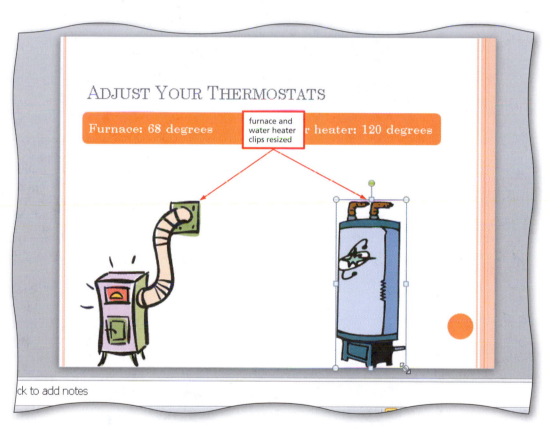

Figure 1–49

To Resize a Photograph

The light bulb picture in Slide 3 can be enlarged slightly to fill much of the space below the slide title. You resize a photograph in the same manner that you resize clip art. The following steps resize this photograph using a sizing handle.

1 Click the Previous Slide button to display Slide 3.

2 Click the light bulb photograph to select it.

BTW

Minimalist Design
Resist the urge to fill your slides with clips from the Microsoft Clip Organizer. Minimalist style reduces clutter and allows the slide content to display prominently. This simple, yet effective design helps audience members with short attention spans to focus on the message.

3 Drag the lower-left corner sizing handle on the photograph diagonally outward until the photograph is resized approximately as shown in Figure 1–50.

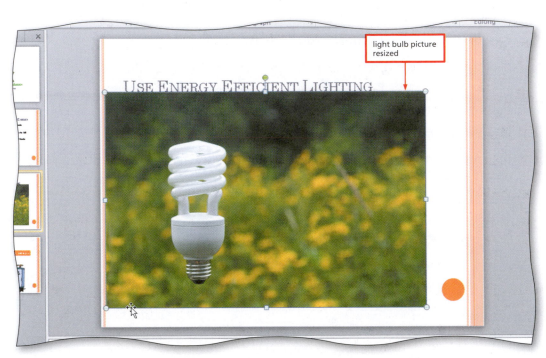

light bulb picture resized

Figure 1–50

To Move Clips

After you insert clip art or a photograph on a slide, you might want to reposition it. The light bulb photograph on Slide 3 could be centered in the space between the slide title and the left and right edges of the slide. The clip on Slide 1 could be positioned in the upper-right corner of the slide. On Slide 4, the furnace and water heater clips could be centered under each heading. The following steps move these graphics.

1

- If necessary, click the light bulb photograph on Slide 3 to select it.

- Press and hold down the mouse button and then drag the photograph diagonally downward below the title text (Figure 1–51).

- If necessary, select the photograph and then use the ARROW keys to position it precisely as shown in Figure 1–51.

Q&A

The photograph still is not located exactly where I want it to display. What can I do to align the photograph?

Press the CTRL key while you press the ARROW keys. This key combination moves the clip in smaller increments than when you press only an ARROW key.

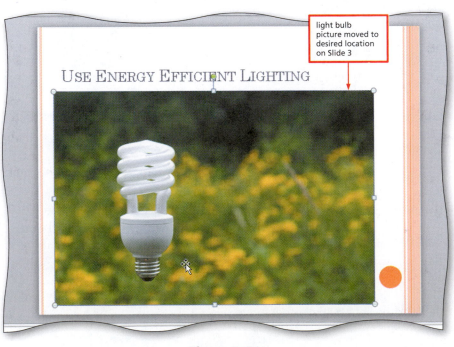

light bulb picture moved to desired location on Slide 3

Figure 1–51

2
- Click the Next Slide button to display Slide 4.

- Click the furnace clip to select it, press and hold down the mouse button, and then drag the clip to center it under the furnace heading.

- Click the water heater clip and then drag the clip to center it under the water heater heading (Figure 1–52).

Figure 1–52

3
- Click the Previous Slide button twice to display Slide 2.

- Click the dishwasher clip, which is on top of the faucet clip, and then drag the clip to center it under the last bulleted paragraph, Wash clothes in cold water.

- Click the faucet clip and then drag the clip so that the faucet handle is centered under the words, full loads.

- Drag a corner sizing handle on the faucet clip diagonally outward until the clip is resized approximately as shown in Figure 1–53. You may need to drag the clip to position it in the desired location.

Figure 1–53

- Select the dishwasher clip and then resize and move it so that the clip displays approximately as shown in Figure 1–53.

4
- Click the Previous Slide button to display Slide 1.

- Click the globe clip and then drag it to the upper-right corner of the slide. You may want to adjust its size by selecting it and then dragging the corner sizing handles.

- Click outside the clip to deselect it (Figure 1–54).

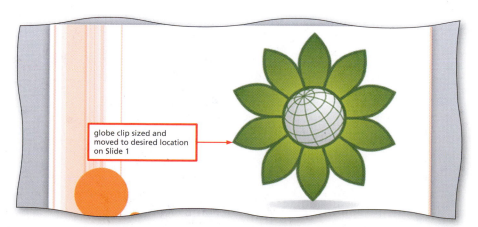

Figure 1–54

Plan Ahead

> **Choose a closing slide.**
> After the last slide appears during a slide show, the default PowerPoint setting is to end the presentation with a **black slide**. This black slide appears only when the slide show is running and concludes the slide show, so your audience never sees the PowerPoint window. It is a good idea, however, to end the presentation with a final closing slide to display at the end of the presentation. This slide ends the presentation gracefully and should be an exact copy, or a very similar copy, of your title slide. The audience will recognize that the presentation is drawing to a close when this slide appears. It can remain on the screen when the audience asks questions, approaches the speaker for further information, or exits the room.

Ending a Slide Show with a Closing Slide

All the text for the slides in the Saving Energy slide show has been entered. This presentation thus far consists of a title slide, one text slide with a multi-level bulleted list, a third slide for a photograph, and a fourth slide with a Comparison layout. A closing slide that resembles the title slide is the final slide to create.

To Duplicate a Slide

When two slides contain similar information and have the same format, duplicating one slide and then making minor modifications to the new slide saves time and increases consistency.

Slide 5 will have the same layout and design as Slide 1. The most expedient method of creating this slide is to copy Slide 1 and then make minor modifications to the new slide. The following steps duplicate the title slide.

1
- With Slide 1 selected, click the New Slide arrow (Home tab | Slides group) to display the Oriel layout gallery (Figure 1–55).

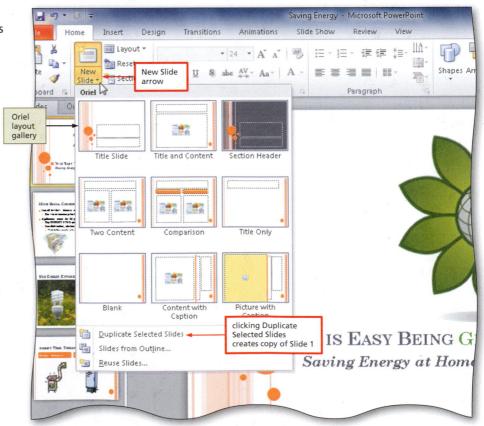

Figure 1–55

2

• Click Duplicate Selected Slides in the Oriel layout gallery to create a new Slide 2, which is a duplicate of Slide 1 (Figure 1–56).

Figure 1–56

Break Point: If you wish to take a break, this is a good place to do so. You can quit PowerPoint now (refer to page PPT 50 for instructions). To resume at a later time, start PowerPoint (refer to pages PPT 4 and PPT 5 for instructions), open the file called Saving Energy (refer to pages PPT 50 and PPT 51 for instructions), and continue following the steps from this location forward.

To Arrange a Slide

The new Slide 2 was inserted directly below Slide 1 because Slide 1 was the selected slide. This duplicate slide needs to display at the end of the presentation directly after the final title and content slide.

Changing slide order is an easy process and is best performed in the Slides pane. When you click the slide thumbnail and begin to drag it to a new location, a line indicates the new location of the selected slide. When you release the mouse button, the slide drops into the desired location. Hence, this process of dragging and then dropping the thumbnail in a new location is called **drag and drop**. You can use the drag-and-drop method to move any selected item, including text and graphics. The following step moves the new Slide 2 to the end of the presentation so that it becomes a closing slide.

1
- With Slide 2 selected, drag the Slide 2 slide thumbnail in the Slides pane below the last slide thumbnail (Figure 1–57).

Q&A

The Slide 2 thumbnail is not visible in the Slides pane when I am dragging the thumbnail downward. How do I know it will be positioned in the desired location?

A blue horizontal bar indicates where the slide will move.

Figure 1–57

Other Ways

1. Click slide icon on Outline tab, drag icon to new location
2. Click Slide Sorter (View tab | Presentation Views group), click slide thumbnail, drag thumbnail to new location

Making Changes to Slide Text Content

After creating slides in a presentation, you may find that you want to make changes to the text. Changes may be required because a slide contains an error, the scope of the presentation shifts, or the style is inconsistent. This section explains the types of changes that commonly occur when creating a presentation.

You generally make three types of changes to text in a presentation: additions, replacements, and deletions.

BTW

Checking Spelling
As you review your slides, you should examine the text for spelling errors. In Chapter 3, you will learn to use PowerPoint's built-in spelling checker to help you perform this task.

- Additions are necessary when you omit text from a slide and need to add it later. You may need to insert text in the form of a sentence, word, or single character. For example, you may want to add the presenter's middle name on the title slide.
- Replacements are needed when you want to revise the text in a presentation. For example, you may want to substitute the word *their* for the word *there*.
- Deletions are required when text on a slide is incorrect or no longer is relevant to the presentation. For example, a slide may look cluttered. Therefore, you may want to remove one of the bulleted paragraphs to add more space.

Editing text in PowerPoint basically is the same as editing text in a word processing program. The following sections illustrate the most common changes made to text in a presentation.

Replacing Text in an Existing Slide

When you need to correct a word or phrase, you can replace the text by selecting the text to be replaced and then typing the new text. As soon as you press any key on the keyboard, the selected text is deleted and the new text is displayed.

PowerPoint inserts text to the left of the insertion point. The text to the right of the insertion point moves to the right (and shifts downward if necessary) to accommodate the added text.

Deleting Text

You can delete text using one of three methods. One is to use the BACKSPACE key to remove text just typed. The second is to position the insertion point to the left of the text you want to delete and then press the DELETE key. The third method is to drag through the text you want to delete and then press the DELETE or BACKSPACE key. Use the third method when deleting large sections of text.

To Delete Text in a Placeholder

To keep the ending slide clean and simple, you want to delete a few words in the slide show title and subtitle text. The following steps change It Is Easy Being Green to Be Green and then change Saving Energy at Home to Save Energy.

1
- With Slide 5 selected, position the mouse pointer immediately to the left of the first character of the text to be selected (in this case, the I in the word, It).

- Drag the mouse pointer through the last character of the text to be selected (in this case, the space after the y in Easy) (Figure 1–58).

Figure 1–58

2
• Click the Cut button (Home tab | Clipboard group) to delete all the selected text (Figure 1–59).

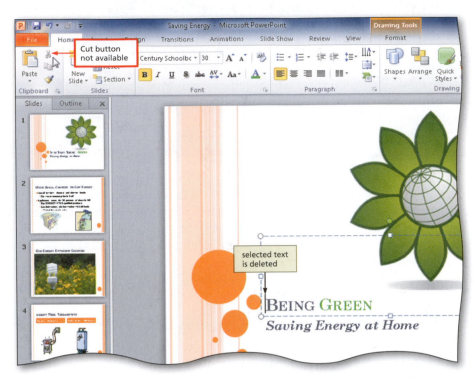

Figure 1–59

3
• Select the letters, ing, in the word, Being.

• Click the Cut button (Figure 1–60).

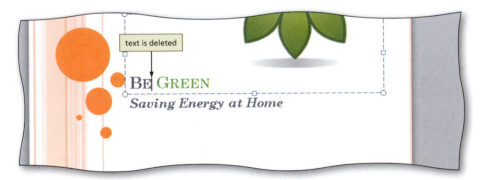

Figure 1–60

4
• Select the letters, ing, in the word, Saving, and then click the Cut button.

• Type e to change the word to Save (Figure 1–61).

Other Ways

1. Right-click selected text, click Cut on shortcut menu

2. Select text, press DELETE or BACKSPACE key

3. Select text, press CTRL+X

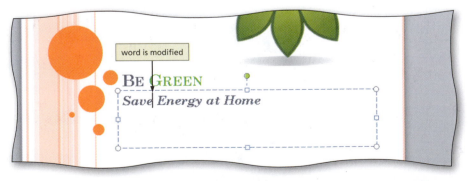

Figure 1–61

Adding a Transition

PowerPoint provides many animation effects to add interest and make a slide show presentation look professional. **Animation** includes special visual and sound effects applied to text or content. A **slide transition** is a special animation effect used to progress from one slide to the next in a slide show. You can control the speed of the transition effect and add a sound.

PowerPoint provides a variety of transitions arranged into three categories that describe the types of effects: Subtle, Exciting, and Dynamic Content.

To Add a Transition between Slides

In this presentation, you apply the Doors transition in the Exciting category to all slides and change the transition speed from 1.40 seconds to 2 seconds. The following steps apply this transition to the presentation.

1

- Click the Transitions tab on the Ribbon and then point to the More button (Transitions tab | Transition to This Slide group) (Figure 1–62).

Q&A Is a transition applied now?

No. The first slide icon in the Transitions group has an orange border, which indicates no transition has been applied.

Figure 1–62

2

- Click the More button to expand the Transitions gallery.

- Point to the Doors transition in the Exciting category in the Transitions gallery (Figure 1–63).

Q&A Can I add a sound to play during this transition?

Yes. Click the Sound arrow (Transitions tab | Timing group) to display the Sound list and then select a sound from this list. You also can use your own sound if you select Other Sound in the list, select the desired sound (Add Audio dialog box), and then click the OK button.

Figure 1–63

3
● Click Doors in the Exciting category in the Transitions gallery to apply this transition to the closing slide.

Q&A
Why does a star appear next to Slide 5 in the Slides tab?

The star indicates that a transition animation effect is applied to that slide.

● Click the Duration up arrow (Transitions tab | Timing group) three times to change the transition speed from 01.40 seconds to 02.00 seconds (Figure 1–64).

Q&A
Why did the time change?

Each transition has a default duration time. The Doors transition time is 1:40 seconds.

Figure 1–64

4
● Click the Preview Transitions button (Transitions tab | Preview area) to view the transition and the new transition time (Figure 1–65).

Q&A
Can I adjust the duration time I just set?

Yes. Click the Duration up or down arrows or type a speed in the Duration text box and preview the transition until you find the time that best fits your presentation.

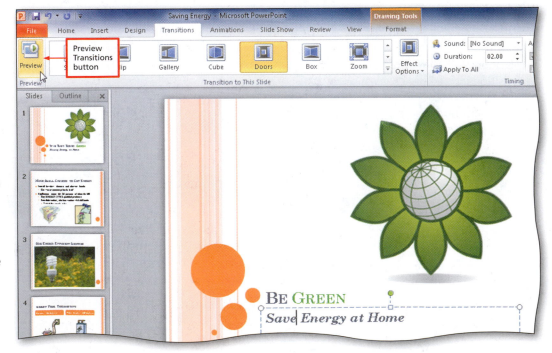

Figure 1–65

5
- Click the Apply To All button (Transitions tab | Timing group) to apply the Doors transition and the increased transition time to Slides 1 through 4 in the presentation (Figure 1–66).

Q&A

What if I want to apply a different transition and duration to each slide in the presentation?

Repeat Steps 2 and 3 for each slide individually.

Apply To All button

stars under slide numbers indicate transition is applied to all slides in presentation

Be Green

Save Energy at Home

Click to add notes

Figure 1–66

Changing Document Properties

PowerPoint helps you organize and identify your files by using **document properties**, which are the details about a file. Document properties, also known as **metadata**, can include information such as the project author, title, subject, and keywords. A **keyword** is a word or phrase that further describes the document. For example, a class name or document topic can describe the file's purpose or content.

Document properties are valuable for a variety of reasons:

- Users can save time locating a particular file because they can view a document's properties without opening the document.

- By creating consistent properties for files having similar content, users can better organize their documents.

- Some organizations require PowerPoint users to add document properties so that other employees can view details about these files.

Five different types of document properties exist, but the more common ones used in this book are standard and automatically updated properties. **Standard properties** are associated with all Microsoft Office documents and include author, title, and subject. **Automatically updated properties** include file system properties, such as the date you create or change a file, and statistics, such as the file size.

BTW

PowerPoint Help
At any time while using PowerPoint, you can find answers to questions and display information about various topics through PowerPoint Help. Used properly, this form of assistance can increase your productivity and reduce your frustrations by minimizing the time you spend learning how to use PowerPoint. For instruction about PowerPoint Help and exercises that will help you gain confidence in using it, read the Office 2010 and Windows 7 chapter at the beginning of this book.

To Change Document Properties

The **Document Information Panel** contains areas where you can view and enter document properties. You can view and change information in this panel at any time while you are creating a document. Before saving the presentation again, you want to add your name and course information as document properties. The following steps use the Document Information Panel to change document properties.

- Click File on the Ribbon to open the Backstage view.

- If necessary, click the Info tab in the Backstage view to display the Info gallery (Figure 1–67).

Q&A How do I close the Backstage view?

Click File on the Ribbon or click the preview of the document in the Info gallery to return to the PowerPoint document window.

Figure 1–67

- Click the Properties button in the right pane of the Info gallery to display the Properties menu (Figure 1–68).

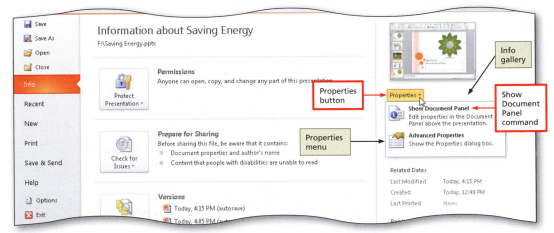

Figure 1–68

- Click Show Document Panel on the Properties menu to close the Backstage view and display the Document Information Panel in the PowerPoint document window (Figure 1–69).

Q&A Why are some of the document properties in my Document Information Panel already filled in?

The person who installed Microsoft Office 2010 on your computer or network may have set or customized the properties.

Figure 1–69

4

• Click the Author text box, if necessary, and then type your name as the Author property. If a name already is displayed in the Author text box, delete it before typing your name.

Figure 1–70

• Click the Subject text box, if necessary delete any existing text, and then type your course and section as the Subject property.

• If an AutoComplete dialog box appears, click its Yes button.

• Click the Keywords text box, if necessary delete any existing text, and then type `energy savings` as the Keywords property (Figure 1–70).

Q&A   What types of document properties does PowerPoint collect automatically?

PowerPoint records details such as time spent editing a document, the number of times a document has been revised, and the fonts and themes used in a document.

5

• Click the Close the Document Information Panel button so that the Document Information Panel no longer is displayed.

Other Ways

1. Click File on Ribbon, click Info in Backstage view, if necessary click Show All Properties link in Info gallery, click property to change and type new information, close Backstage view

To Save an Existing Presentation with the Same File Name

You have made several modifications to the presentation since you last saved it. Thus, you should save it again. The following step saves the document again. For an example of the step listed below, refer to the Office 2010 and Windows 7 chapter at the beginning of this book.

1   Click the Save button on the Quick Access Toolbar to overwrite the previously saved file.

Viewing the Presentation in Slide Show View

The Slide Show button, located in the lower-right corner of the PowerPoint window above the status bar, allows you to show a presentation using a computer. The computer acts like a slide projector, displaying each slide on a full screen. The full-screen slide hides the toolbars, menus, and other PowerPoint window elements.

To Start Slide Show View

When making a presentation, you use **Slide Show view**. You can start Slide Show view from Normal view or Slide Sorter view. Slide Show view begins when you click the Slide Show button on the lower-right corner of the status bar. PowerPoint then shows the current slide on the full screen without any of the PowerPoint window objects, such as the menu bar or toolbars. The following steps start Slide Show view.

1

- Click the Slide 1 thumbnail in the Slides pane to select and display Slide 1.

- Point to the Slide Show button in the lower-right corner of the PowerPoint window on the status bar (Figure 1–71).

 Why did I need to select Slide 1?

When you run a slide show, PowerPoint begins the show with the currently displayed slide. If you had not selected Slide 1, then only Slide 5 would have displayed in the slide show.

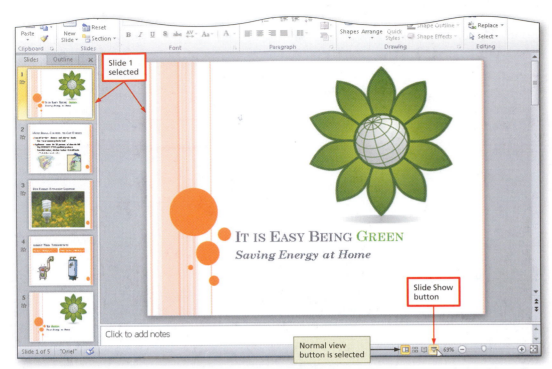

Figure 1–71

2

- Click the Slide Show button to display the title slide (Figure 1–72).

 Where is the PowerPoint window?

When you run a slide show, the PowerPoint window is hidden. It will reappear once you end your slide show.

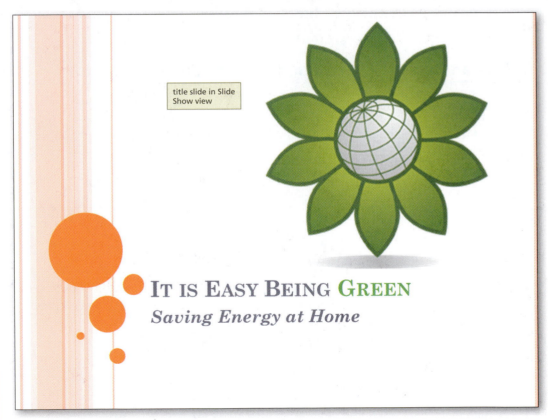

Figure 1–72

Other Ways

1. Click Slide Show From Beginning button (Slide Show tab | Start Slide Show group)

2. Press F5

To Move Manually through Slides in a Slide Show

After you begin Slide Show view, you can move forward or backward through the slides. PowerPoint allows you to advance through the slides manually or automatically. During a slide show, each slide in the presentation shows on the screen, one slide at a time. Each time you click the mouse button, the next slide appears. The following steps move manually through the slides.

1

• Click each slide until Slide 5 (Be Green) is displayed (Figure 1–73).

Q&A

I see a small toolbar in the lower-left corner of my slide. What is this toolbar?

The Slide Show toolbar appears when you begin running a slide show and then move the mouse pointer. The buttons on this toolbar allow you to navigate to the next slide, the previous slide, to mark up the current slide, or to change the current display.

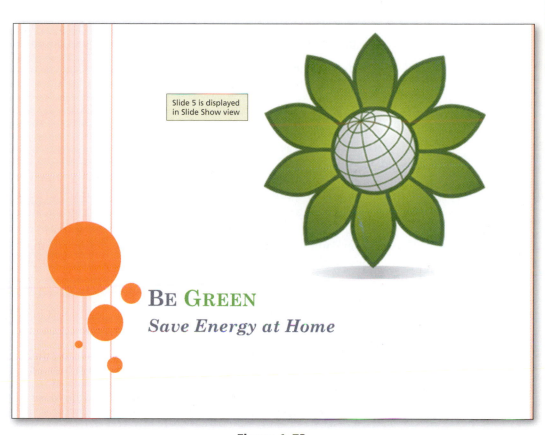

Slide 5 is displayed in Slide Show view

BE GREEN
Save Energy at Home

Figure 1–73

2

• Click Slide 5 so that the black slide appears with a message announcing the end of the slide show (Figure 1–74).

Q&A

How can I end the presentation at this point?

Click the black slide to return to Normal view in the PowerPoint window or press the ESC key.

End of slide show, click to exit.

message announces end of slide show

Figure 1–74

Other Ways		
1. Press PAGE DOWN to advance one slide at a time, or press PAGE UP to go back one slide at a time	2. Press RIGHT ARROW or DOWN ARROW to advance one slide at a time, or press LEFT ARROW or UP ARROW to go back one slide at a time	3. If Slide Show toolbar is displayed, click Next Slide or Previous Slide button on toolbar

BTW

Eliminating the Black Slide
By default, a black slide is displayed at the end of a slide show. If you do not want this slide to appear, click the File tab, click Options, and then click the Advanced link. In the Slide Show group, click 'End with black slide' to uncheck it.

To Quit PowerPoint

This project now is complete. The following steps quit PowerPoint. For a detailed example of the procedure summarized below, refer to the Office 2010 and Windows 7 chapter at the beginning of this book.

1 If you have one PowerPoint presentation open, click the Close button on the right side of the title bar to close the document and quit PowerPoint; or if you have multiple PowerPoint presentations open, click File on the Ribbon to open the Backstage view and then click Exit in the Backstage view to close all open documents and quit PowerPoint.

2 If a Microsoft PowerPoint dialog box appears, click the Save button to save any changes made to the document since the last save.

BTW

Certification
The Microsoft Office Specialist (MOS) program provides an opportunity for you to obtain a valuable industry credential — proof that you have the PowerPoint 2010 skills required by employers. For more information, visit the PowerPoint 2010 Certification Web page (scsite.com/ppt2010/cert).

To Start PowerPoint

Once you have created and saved a document, you may need to retrieve it from your storage medium. For example, you might want to revise the presentation or print it. The following steps, which assume Windows 7 is running, start PowerPoint so that you can open and modify the presentation. You may need to ask your instructor how to start PowerPoint for your computer. For a detailed example of the procedure summarized below, refer to the Office 2010 and Windows 7 chapter at the beginning of this book.

1 Click the Start button on the Windows 7 taskbar to display the Start menu.

2 Type **Microsoft PowerPoint** as the search text in the 'Search programs and files' text box and watch the search results appear on the Start menu.

3 Click Microsoft PowerPoint 2010 in the search results on the Start menu to start PowerPoint and display a new blank document in the PowerPoint window.

4 If the PowerPoint window is not maximized, click the Maximize button next to the Close button on its title bar to maximize the window.

To Open a Document from PowerPoint

Earlier in this chapter you saved your project on a USB flash drive using the file name, Saving Energy. The following steps open the Saving Energy file from the PowerPoint folder in the CIS 101 folder on the USB flash drive. For a detailed example of the procedure summarized below, refer to the Office 2010 and Windows 7 chapter at the beginning of this book.

1 With your USB flash drive connected to one of the computer's USB ports, click File on the Ribbon to open the Backstage view.

2 Click Open in the Backstage view to display the Open dialog box.

3 Navigate to the location of the file to be opened (in this case, the USB flash drive, then to the CIS 101 folder [or your class folder], and then to the PowerPoint folder).

4 Click Saving Energy to select the file to be opened.

5 Click the Open button (Open dialog box) to open the selected file and display the opened document in the PowerPoint window.

Printing a Presentation

After creating a presentation, you may want to print the slides. Printing a presentation enables you to distribute the document to others in a form that can be read or viewed but typically not edited. It is a good practice to save a presentation before printing it, in the event you experience difficulties printing.

Determine the best method for distributing the presentation.
The traditional method of distributing a presentation uses a printer to produce a hard copy. A **hardcopy** or **printout** is information that exists on a physical medium such as paper. For users who can receive fax documents, you can elect to print a hard copy on a remote fax machine. Hard copies can be useful for the following reasons:

- Many people prefer proofreading a hard copy of a document rather than viewing it on the screen to check for errors and readability.

- Hard copies can serve as reference material if your storage medium is lost or becomes corrupted and you need to recreate the document.

   Instead of distributing a hard copy of a presentation slides, users can choose to distribute the presentation as an electronic image that mirrors the original document's appearance. The electronic image of the document can be e-mailed, posted on a Web site, or copied to a portable storage medium such as a USB flash drive. Two popular electronic image formats, sometimes called fixed formats, are PDF by Adobe Systems and XPS by Microsoft. In PowerPoint, you can create electronic image files through the Print tab in the Backstage view, the Save & Send tab in the Backstage view, and the Save As dialog box. Electronic images of documents, such as PDF and XPS, can be useful for the following reasons.

- Users can view electronic images of documents without the software that created the original document (e.g., PowerPoint). Specifically, to view a PDF file, you use a program called Acrobat Reader, which can be downloaded free from Adobe's Web site. Similarly, to view an XPS file, you use a program called an XPS Viewer, which is included in the latest versions of Windows and Internet Explorer.

- Sending electronic documents saves paper and printer supplies. Society encourages users to contribute to **green computing**, which involves reducing the environmental waste generated when using a computer.

Plan Ahead

To Print a Presentation

   With the completed presentation saved, you may want to print it. If copies of the presentation are being distributed to audience members, you will print a hard copy of each individual slide on a printer. The following steps print a hard copy of the contents of the saved Saving Energy presentation.

1
- Click File on the Ribbon to open the Backstage view.
- Click the Print tab in the Backstage view to display the Print gallery (Figure 1–75).

Figure 1–75

How do I preview Slides 2 through 5?

Click the Next Page button in the Print gallery to scroll forward through pages in the document; similarly, click the Previous Page button to scroll backward through pages.

How can I print multiple copies of my slides?

Increase the number in the Copies box in the Print gallery.

What if I decide not to print the document at this time?

Click File on the Ribbon to close the Backstage view and return to the PowerPoint document window.

2
- Verify the printer name that appears on the Printer box Status button will print a hard copy of the document. If necessary, click the Printer Status button to display a list of available printer options and then click the desired printer to change the currently selected printer.

BTW

Quick Reference
For a table that lists how to complete the tasks covered in this book using the mouse, Ribbon, shortcut menu, and keyboard, see the Quick Reference Summary at the back of this book, or visit the PowerPoint 2010 Quick Reference Web page (scsite.com/ppt2010/qr).

3

- Click the Print button in the Print gallery to print the document on the currently selected printer.

- When the printer stops, retrieve the hard copy (Figure 1–76).

Q&A

Do I have to wait until my document is complete to print it?

No, you can follow these steps to print a document at any time while you are creating it.

Q&A

What if I want to print an electronic image of a document instead of a hard copy?

You would click the Printer Status button in the Print gallery and then select the desired electronic image option such as a Microsoft XPS Document Writer, which would create an XPS file.

(a) Slide 1

(b) Slide 2

(c) Slide 3

(d) Slide 4

(e) Slide 5

Figure 1–76

Other Ways
1. Press CTRL+P, press ENTER

To Quit PowerPoint

The project now is complete. The following steps quit PowerPoint. For a detailed example of the procedure summarized below, refer to the Office 2010 and Windows 7 chapter at the beginning of this book.

1 If you have one PowerPoint document open, click the Close button on the right side of the title bar to close the document and quit PowerPoint; or if you have multiple PowerPoint documents open, click File on the Ribbon to open the Backstage view and then click Exit in the Backstage view to close all open documents and quit PowerPoint.

2 If a Microsoft Office PowerPoint dialog box appears, click the Save button to save any changes made to the document since the last save.

Chapter Summary

In this chapter you have learned how to apply a document theme, create a title slide and text slides with a bulleted list, clip art, and a photograph, size and move clip art and a photograph, format and edit text, add a slide transition, view the presentation in Slide Show view, and print slides as handouts. The items listed below include all the new PowerPoint skills you have learned in this chapter.

1. Start PowerPoint (PPT 4)
2. Choose a Document Theme (PPT 5)
3. Enter the Presentation Title (PPT 7)
4. Enter the Presentation Subtitle Paragraph (PPT 9)
5. Select a Paragraph (PPT 10)
6. Italicize Text (PPT 11)
7. Increase Font Size (PPT 11)
8. Select a Word (PPT 12)
9. Change the Text Color (PPT 13)
10. Save a Presentation (PPT 14)
11. Add a New Text Slide with a Bulleted List (PPT 14)
12. Enter a Slide Title (PPT 16)
13. Select a Text Placeholder (PPT 16)
14. Type a Multi-Level Bulleted List (PPT 17)
15. Select a Group of Words (PPT 19)
16. Bold Text (PPT 19)
17. Add a Slide with the Title Only Layout (PPT 21)
18. Add a New Slide and Enter a Slide Title and Headings (PPT 23)
19. Move to Another Slide in Normal View (PPT 25)
20. Insert a Clip from the Clip Organizer into the Title Slide (PPT 27)
21. Insert a Clip from the Clip Organizer into a Content Placeholder (PPT 30)
22. Insert a Photograph from the Clip Organizer into a Slide without a Content Placeholder (PPT 32)
23. Resize Clip Art (PPT 33)
24. Move Clips (PPT 36)
25. Duplicate a Slide (PPT 38)
26. Arrange a Slide (PPT 39)
27. Delete Text in a Placeholder (PPT 41)
28. Add a Transition between Slides (PPT 43)
29. Change Document Properties (PPT 46)
30. Save an Existing Presentation with the Same File Name (PPT 47)
31. Start Slide Show View (PPT 47)
32. Move Manually through Slides in a Slide Show (PPT 49)
33. Quit PowerPoint (PPT 50)
34. Open a Document from PowerPoint (PPT 50)
35. Print a Presentation (PPT 51)

 If you have a SAM 2010 user profile, your instructor may have assigned an autogradable version of this assignment. If so, log into the SAM 2010 Web site at www.cengage.com/sam2010 to download the instruction and start files.

Learn It Online

Test your knowledge of chapter content and key terms.

Instructions: To complete the Learn It Online exercises, start your browser, click the Address bar, and then enter the Web address **scsite.com/ppt2010/learn**. When the PowerPoint 2010 Learn It Online page is displayed, click the link for the exercise you want to complete and then read the instructions.

Chapter Reinforcement TF, MC, and SA

A series of true/false, multiple choice, and short answer questions that test your knowledge of the chapter content.

Flash Cards

An interactive learning environment where you identify chapter key terms associated with displayed definitions.

Practice Test

A series of multiple choice questions that test your knowledge of chapter content and key terms.

Who Wants To Be a Computer Genius?

An interactive game that challenges your knowledge of chapter content in the style of a television quiz show.

Wheel of Terms

An interactive game that challenges your knowledge of chapter key terms in the style of the television show *Wheel of Fortune*.

Crossword Puzzle Challenge

A crossword puzzle that challenges your knowledge of key terms presented in the chapter.

Apply Your Knowledge

Reinforce the skills and apply the concepts you learned in this chapter.

Modifying Character Formats and Paragraph Levels and Moving a Clip

Note: To complete this assignment, you will be required to use the Data Files for Students. See the inside back cover of this book for instructions on downloading the Data Files for Students, or contact your instructor for information about accessing the required files.

Instructions: Start PowerPoint. Open the presentation, Apply 1-1 Flu Season, from the Data Files for Students.

The two slides in the presentation discuss ways to avoid getting or spreading the flu. The document you open is an unformatted presentation. You are to modify the document theme, indent the paragraphs, resize and move the clip art, and format the text so the slides look like Figure 1–77 on the next page.

Continued >

Apply Your Knowledge *continued*

Perform the following tasks:

1. Change the document theme to Urban. On the title slide, use your name in place of Student Name and bold and italicize your name. Increase the title text font size to 60 point. Resize and position the clip as shown in Figure 1–77a.

2. On Slide 2, increase the indent of the second, third, and fifth paragraphs (Cover mouth and nose with a tissue; No tissue? Use your elbow or sleeve; Use soap, warm water for 20 seconds) to second-level paragraphs. Then combine paragraphs six and seven (Drink fluids; Get plenty of rest) to read, Drink fluids and get plenty of rest, as shown in Figure 1–77b.

3. Change the document properties, as specified by your instructor. Save the presentation using the file name, Apply 1–1 Avoid the Flu. Submit the revised document in the format specified by your instructor.

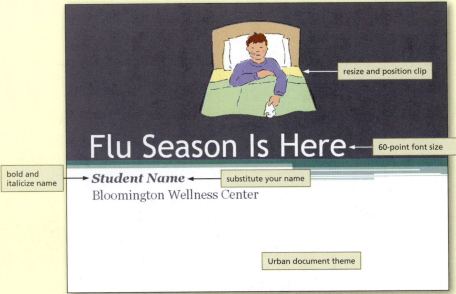

(a) Slide 1 (Title Slide with Clip Art)

(b) Slide 2 (Multi-Level Bulleted List)

Figure 1–77

Extend Your Knowledge

Extend the skills you learned in this chapter and experiment with new skills. You may need to use Help to complete the assignment.

Changing Slide Theme, Layout, and Text

Note: To complete this assignment, you will be required to use the Data Files for Students. See the inside back cover of this book for instructions on downloading the Data Files for Students, or contact your instructor for information about accessing the required files.

Instructions: Start PowerPoint. Open the presentation that you are going to prepare for your dental hygiene class, Extend 1–1 Winning Smile, from the Data Files for Students.

You will choose a theme, format slides, and create a closing slide.

Perform the following tasks:

1. Apply an appropriate document theme.
2. On Slide 1, use your name in place of Student Name. Format the text on this slide using techniques you learned in this chapter, such as changing the font size and color and also bolding and italicizing words.
3. On Slide 2, change the slide layout and adjust the paragraph levels so that the lines of text are arranged under two headings: Discount Dental and Dental Insurance (Figure 1–78).
4. On Slide 3, create paragraphs and adjust the paragraph levels to create a bulleted list. Edit the text so that the slide meets the 7 × 7 rule, which states that each line should have a maximum of seven words, and each slide should have a maximum of seven lines.
5. Create an appropriate closing slide using the title slide as a guide.
6. The slides contain a variety of clips downloaded from the Microsoft Clip Organizer. Size and move them when necessary.
7. Apply an appropriate transition to all slides.
8. Change the document properties, as specified by your instructor. Save the presentation using the file name, Extend 1–1 Dental Plans.
9. Submit the revised document in the format specified by your instructor.

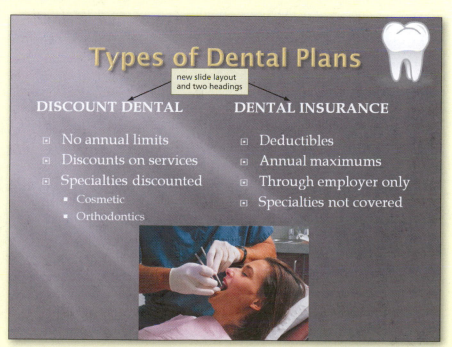

Figure 1–78

Make It Right

Analyze a presentation and correct all errors and/or improve the design.

Correcting Formatting and List Levels

Note: To complete this assignment, you will be required to use the Data Files for Students. See the inside back cover of this book for instructions on downloading the Data Files for Students, or contact your instructor for information about accessing the required files.

Instructions: Start PowerPoint. Open the presentation, Make It Right 1–1 Air Ducts, from the Data Files for Students.

Members of your homeowners' association are having their semiannual meeting, and each member of the board is required to give a short presentation on the subject of energy savings. You have decided to discuss the energy-saving benefits of maintaining the air ducts in your home. Correct the formatting problems and errors in the presentation while keeping in mind the guidelines presented in this chapter.

Perform the following tasks:

1. Change the document theme from Origin, shown in Figure 1–79, to Module.
2. On Slide 1, replace the words, Student Name, with your name. Format your name so that it displays prominently on the slide.
3. Increase the size of the clip on Slide 1 and move it to the upper-right corner.
4. Move Slide 2 to the end of the presentation so that it becomes the new Slide 3.
5. On Slide 2, correct the spelling errors and then increase the font size of the Slide 2 title text, Check Hidden Air Ducts, to 54 point. Increase the size of the clip and move it up to fill the white space on the right of the bulleted list.
6. On Slide 3, correct the spelling errors and then change the font size of the title text, Energy Savings, to 54 point. Increase the indent levels for paragraphs 2 and 4. Increase the size of the clips. Center the furnace clip at the bottom of the slide.
7. Change the document properties, as specified by your instructor. Save the presentation using the file name, Make It Right 1–1 Ducts Presentation.
8. Apply the same transition and duration to all slides.
9. Submit the revised document in the format specified by your instructor.

Figure 1–79

In the Lab

Design and/or create a presentation using the guidelines, concepts, and skills presented in this chapter. Labs 1, 2, and 3 are listed in order of increasing difficulty.

Lab1: Creating a Presentation with Bulleted Lists, a Closing Slide, and Clips

Problem: You are working with upper-level students to host a freshmen orientation seminar. When you attended this seminar, you received some helpful tips on studying for exams. Your contribution to this year's seminar is to prepare a short presentation on study skills. You develop the outline shown in Figure 1–80 and then prepare the PowerPoint presentation shown in Figures 1–81a through 1–81d.

Hit the Books
Studying for an Exam
Sarah Jones

Prepare in Advance
   Location
      Quiet, well-lit
   Timing
      15-minute breaks every hour
   Material
      Quiz yourself

Exam Time
   Day of Exam
      Rest properly
      Eat a good meal
      Wear comfy clothes
      Be early
      Be confident

Figure 1–80

Perform the following tasks:

1. Create a new presentation using the Aspect document theme.

2. Using the typed notes illustrated in Figure 1–80, create the title slide shown in Figure 1–81a, using your name in place of Sarah Jones. Italicize your name and increase the font size to 24 point. Increase the font size of the title text paragraph, Hit the Books, to 48 point. Increase the font size of the first paragraph of the subtitle text, Studying for an Exam, to 28 point.

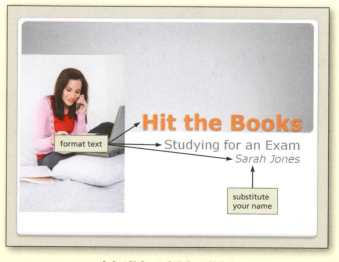

(a) Slide 1 (Title Slide)
Figure 1–81

Continued >

In the Lab *continued*

3. Using the typed notes in Figure 1–80, create the two text slides with bulleted lists and find and insert clips from the Microsoft Clip Organizer, as shown in Figures 1–81b and 1–81c.

4. Create a closing slide by duplicating Slide 1, deleting your name, replacing the photograph with the photograph shown in Figure 1–81d, and moving the slide to the end of the presentation.

5. On Slide 3, change the font color of the words, Be confident, to Yellow (fourth color in the Standard Colors row) and then bold this text.

6. Apply the Uncover transition in the Subtle category to all slides. Change the duration to 1.25 seconds.

7. Drag the scroll box to display Slide 1. Click the Slide Show button to start Slide Show view. Then click to display each slide.

8. Change the document properties, as specified by your instructor. Save the presentation using the file name, Lab 1–1 Study Skills.

9. Submit the document in the format specified by your instructor.

(b) Slide 2

(c) Slide 3

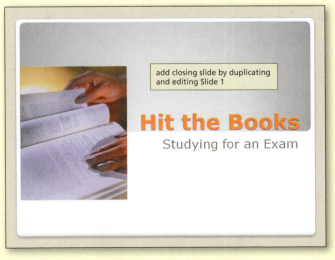

(d) Slide 4 (Closing Slide)
Figure 1–81 (continued)

In the Lab

Lab 2: Creating a Presentation with Bulleted Lists and Clips

Problem: Your health class instructor has assigned every student a different vitamin to research. She hands you the outline shown in Figure 1–82 and asks you to create the presentation about Vitamin D shown in Figures 1–83a through 1–83d on pages PPT 62 and PPT 63.

Vitamin D

The Sunshine Vitamin
Are You D-ficient?
Presented by Jim Warner

Why Is Vitamin D Important?
　We need Vitamin D
　　Vital to our bodies
　　　　Promotes absorption of calcium and magnesium
　　　　　For healthy teeth and bones
　　　　Maintains calcium and phosphorus in blood

　Daily Requirements
　　How much do we need?
　　　Child: 5 mcg (200 IU)
　　　Adult: 10-20 mcg (400-600 IU)

Vitamin D Sources
　Sunshine
　　Is our primary source
　　　　Vitamin manufactured by our body after exposure
　　　　　Three times a week
　　　　　For 10-15 minutes
　Foods and Supplements
　　Contained in few foods
　　　　Some fish liver oils
　　　　Flesh of fatty fish
　　Fortified products
　　　　Milk and cereals
　　Available as supplement

Vitamin D History
　Research began in 1924
　　Found to prevent rickets
　United States and Canada
　　Instituted policy of fortifying foods with Vitamin D
　　　　Milk – food of choice
　Other countries
　　Fortified cereal, bread, margarine

Figure 1–82

Continued >

In the Lab *continued*

Perform the following tasks:

1. Create a new presentation using the Solstice document theme.

2. Using the typed notes illustrated in Figure 1–82, create the title slide shown in Figure 1–83a, using your name in place of Jim Warner. Italicize the title, The Sunshine Vitamin, and increase the font size to 48 point. Change the font size of the first line of the subtitle text, Are You D-ficient?, to 36 point. Change the font color of the title text to Orange (third color in the Standard Colors row) and both lines of the subtitle text to Light Blue (seventh color in the Standard Colors row).

3. Using the typed notes in Figure 1–82, create the three text slides with bulleted lists shown in Figures 1–83b through 1–83d. Change the color of the title text on all slides and the text above the bulleted lists on Slides 2 and 3 to Orange.

4. Add the photographs and clip art shown in Figures 1–83a through 1–83d from the Microsoft Clip Organizer. Adjust the clip sizes when necessary.

5. Apply the Ripple transition in the Exciting category to all slides. Change the duration to 2.00 seconds.

6. Drag the scroll box to display Slide 1. Click the Slide Show button to start Slide Show view. Then click to display each slide.

(a) Slide 1 (Title Slide)

(b) Slide 2

Figure 1–83

7. Change the document properties, as specified by your instructor. Save the presentation using the file name, Lab 1–2 Vitamin D.

8. Submit the revised document in the format specified by your instructor.

(c) Slide 3

(d) Slide 4

Figure 1–83 (continued)

In the Lab

Lab 3: Creating and Updating Presentations with Clip Art

Problem: You are employed part time at your health club, and the Child Care Center director has asked you to put together a presentation for her to use at the next open house. The club has a large playroom that is perfect for children's parties.

Instructions Part 1: Using the outline in Figure 1–84, create the presentation shown in Figure 1–85. Use the Office Theme document theme. On the title slide shown in Figure 1–85a, increase the font size of the title paragraph, Make It a Party!, to 48, change the font color to Red, and change the text font style to italic. Decrease the font size of the entire subtitle paragraph to 28, and change the font color to Blue.

Make It a Party!
 Host Your Child's
 Next Birthday Party
 at the Oaks Health Club

We Do the Work
You Enjoy the Moment
 Two-hour party
 Two chaperones
 Lunch & cake provided
 Game or craft activity available
 Decorations

Two Party Packages
 Package No. 1 - $8/child
  Lunch
   Hot Dogs
   Pizza
 Package No. 2 - $12/child
  Lunch including beverage
   Hot Dogs
   Pizza
  Game
  Craft (age appropriate)

Reserve Your Party Date
 Reserve 2 weeks in advance
 Deposit required
 Party room can hold 20 children
 Sign up in the Child Care Center

Figure 1–84

Create the three text slides with multi-level bulleted lists, photographs, and clip art shown in Figures 1–85b through 1–85d on the next page. Adjust the clip sizes when necessary. Apply the Vortex transition in the Exciting category to all slides and decrease the duration to 3.00 seconds. Change the document properties, as specified by your instructor. Save the presentation using the file name, Lab 1–3 Part One Child Party.

(a) Slide 1 (Title Slide)

(b) Slide 2
Figure 1–85

Continued >

In the Lab *continued*

Two Party Packages

Package No. 1 - $8/child

- Lunch
  - Hot Dogs
  - Pizza

Package No. 2 - $12/child

- Lunch including beverage
  - Hot Dogs
  - Pizza
- Game
- Craft (age appropriate)

(c) Slide 3

Reserve Your Party Date

- Reserve 2 weeks in advance
- Deposit required
- Party room can hold 20 children
- Sign up in the Child Care Center

(d) Slide 4
Figure 1–85 (continued)

Instructions Part 2:   The children's parties have proved to be a great perk for members of the health club. A large group of older adults work out at the club and also meet socially once a month. These members have asked about renting the playroom to hold a retirement party for some of their friends. You decide to modify the children's party presentation to promote retirement parties. Use the outline in Figure 1–86 to modify the presentation created in Part 1 to create the presentation shown in Figure 1–87 on the next page. Required changes are indicated by a yellow highlight.

To begin, save the current presentation with the new file name, Lab 1–3 Part Two Retirement Party. Change the document theme to Flow. On Slide 3, change the pianist's name from Ms. Winn to your name. Apply the Fade transition in the Subtle category to all slides and change the duration speed to 2.25 seconds. View the slide show. Change the document properties, as specified by your instructor. Submit both Part One and Part Two documents in the format specified by your instructor.

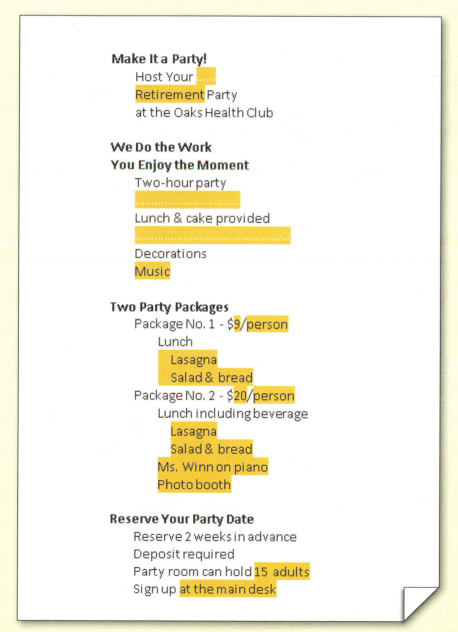

Figure 1–86

Continued >

In the Lab *continued*

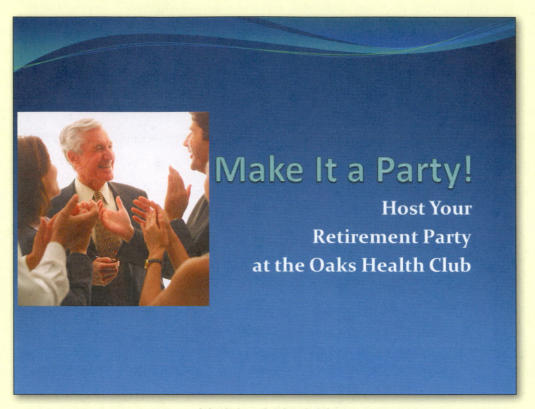

(a) Slide 1 (Title Slide)

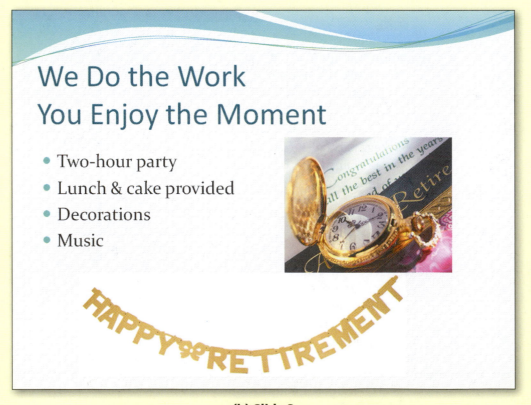

(b) Slide 2

Figure 1–87

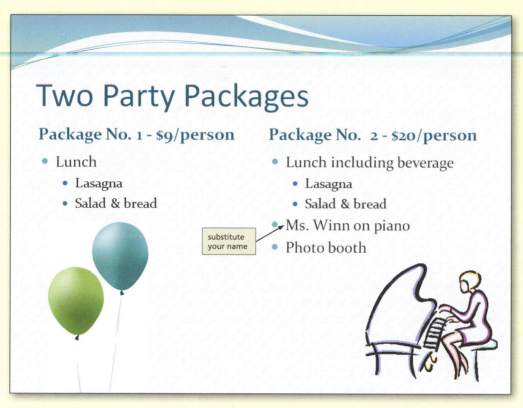

Two Party Packages

Package No. 1 - $9/person

- Lunch
  - Lasagna
  - Salad & bread

Package No. 2 - $20/person

- Lunch including beverage
  - Lasagna
  - Salad & bread
- Ms. Winn on piano
- Photo booth

substitute your name

(c) Slide 3

Reserve Your Party Date

- Reserve 2 weeks in advance
- Deposit required
- Party room can hold 15 adults
- Sign up at the main desk

(d) Slide 4
Figure 1–87 (continued)

Cases and Places

Apply your creative thinking and problem-solving skills to design and implement a solution.

Note: To complete these assignments, you may be required to use the Data Files for Students. See the inside back cover of this book for instructions on downloading the Data Files for Students, or contact your instructor for information about accessing the required files.

As you design the presentations, remember to use the 7 × 7 rule: a maximum of seven words on a line and a maximum of seven lines on one slide.

1: Design and Create a Presentation about Galileo

Academic

Italian-born Galileo is said to be the father of modern science. After the invention of the telescope by a Dutch eyeglass maker named Hans Lippershey, Galileo made his own telescope and made many discoveries. You decide to prepare a PowerPoint presentation to accompany a speech that is required in your Astronomy class. You create the outline shown in Figure 1–88 about Galileo. Use this outline, along with the concepts and techniques presented in this chapter, to develop and format a slide show with a title slide and three text slides with bulleted lists. Add photographs and clip art from the Microsoft Clip Organizer and apply a transition. Submit your assignment in the format specified by your instructor.

Galileo Galilei
- Father of Modern Science
- Astronomy 201
- Sandy Wendt

Major Role in Scientific Revolution
February 15, 1564 – January 8, 1642
- Physicist
- Mathematician
- Astronomer
- Philosopher

Galileo's Research Years
- 1581 – Studied medicine
- 1589-1592 – Studied math and physics
- 1592-1607 – Padua University
    - Developed Law of Inertia
- 1609 – Built telescope
    - Earth's moon
    - Jupiter's moons

Galileo's Later Years
- Dialogue – Two Chief World Systems
    - Controversy develops
- 1633 – Rome
    - Heresy trial
    - Imprisoned
- 1642 – Dies

Figure 1–88

2: Design and Create a Presentation Promoting Hiking for Family Fitness

Personal

A great way for the entire family to get exercise is by participating in a hiking adventure. Employees at the local forest preserve district near your home have remodeled the nature center, and you have volunteered to give a presentation at the open house to help families plan their hikes. Use the outline shown in Figure 1–89 and then create an accompanying PowerPoint presentation. Use the concepts and techniques presented in this chapter to develop and format this slide show with a title slide, three text slides with bulleted lists, and clip art. Add photographs and clip art from the Microsoft Clip Organizer and apply a transition. Submit your assignment in the format specified by your instructor.

Take a Hike
    An Adventure with Kids
    Presented by Joshua Lind
    Pines Nature Center

Planning the Adventure
    Trail length – varies by child's age
        Ages 2 to 4: 1 to 2 miles
        Ages 5 to 7: 3 to 4 miles
        Ages 8 to 12: 5 to 7 miles
    Backpack – limit to 20 percent of child's weight

Packing Supplies
    Snacks and Drinks
        Child's favorite healthy foods
            Fruit and nuts
        Water
    Miscellaneous
        Sunscreen
        Insect repellent
        First-aid kit

Wearing the Right Clothes
    Dress in layers
        Children get cold quicker than adults
    Wear long pants and long-sleeved shirt
        Protect against insects and cuts
    Wear a hat and comfortable shoes
        Keep body warm

Figure 1–89

Continued >

Cases and Places *continued*

3: Design and Create a Landscaping Service Presentation

Professional

The home and garden center where you work is hosting weekend clinics for customers. The owner asks you to give a presentation about the center's new landscaping division and hands you the outline shown in Figure 1–90. Use the concepts and techniques presented in this chapter to develop and format a PowerPoint presentation with a title slide, three text slides with bulleted lists, and clip art. Add photographs and clip art from the Microsoft Clip Organizer and apply a transition. Submit your assignment in the format specified by your instructor.

Barry's Landscaping Service
Bensenville, Indiana

Full-Service Landscaping
  Initial design
  Installation
  Maintenance

Scope of Services
  Landscape design
  Irrigation
  Lighting
  Lawn-care programs
  Tree/shrub maintenance
  Masonry, carpentry
  Water features

Our Promise to You
  Deliver on-time service
  Provide highest level of workmanship
  Give maximum value for your dollar
  Install high-quality plants and materials
  Respond quickly to your needs

Figure 1–90

1

Creating a Worksheet and an Embedded Chart

Objectives

You will have mastered the material in this chapter when you can:

- Describe the Excel worksheet

- Enter text and numbers

- Use the Sum button to sum a range of cells

- Copy the contents of a cell to a range of cells using the fill handle

- Apply cell styles

- Format cells in a worksheet

- Create a Clustered Cylinder chart

- Change a worksheet name and worksheet tab color

- Change document properties

- Preview and print a worksheet

- Use the AutoCalculate area to display statistics

- Correct errors on a worksheet

1 | Creating a Worksheet and an Embedded Chart

Introduction

Almost any organization collects vast amounts of data. Often, data is consolidated into a summary so that people in the organization better understand the meaning of the data. An Excel worksheet allows data easily to be summarized and charted. A chart conveys a visual representation of data. In this chapter, you will create a worksheet that includes a chart. The data in the worksheet and chart includes data for donations made to a not-for-profit organization that operates in several cities.

Project Planning Guidelines

> The process of developing a worksheet that communicates specific information requires careful analysis and planning. As a starting point, establish why the worksheet is needed. Once the purpose is determined, analyze the intended users of the worksheet and their unique needs. Then, gather information about the topic and decide what to include in the worksheet. Finally, determine the worksheet design and style that will be most successful at delivering the message. Details of these guidelines are provided in Appendix A. In addition, each project developed in this book provides practical applications of these planning considerations.

Project — Worksheet with an Embedded Chart

The project in this chapter follows proper design guidelines and uses Excel to create the worksheet shown in Figure 1–1. The worksheet contains fundraising data for the Save Sable River Foundation. The Save Sable River Foundation raises funds to care for the environment and preserve the usability of a river that flows through six cities. The foundation raises funds by using five different fundraising activities. Through a concentrated marketing campaign and providing visible results to the communities, the Save Sable River Foundation quickly became a popular local institution. After several years of successful fundraising, senior management requested an easy-to-read worksheet that shows lifetime fundraising amounts for each fundraising technique by city. In addition, they asked for a chart showing lifetime fundraising amounts because the president of the foundation likes to have a graphical representation that allows him quickly to identify stronger and weaker fundraising activities by city.

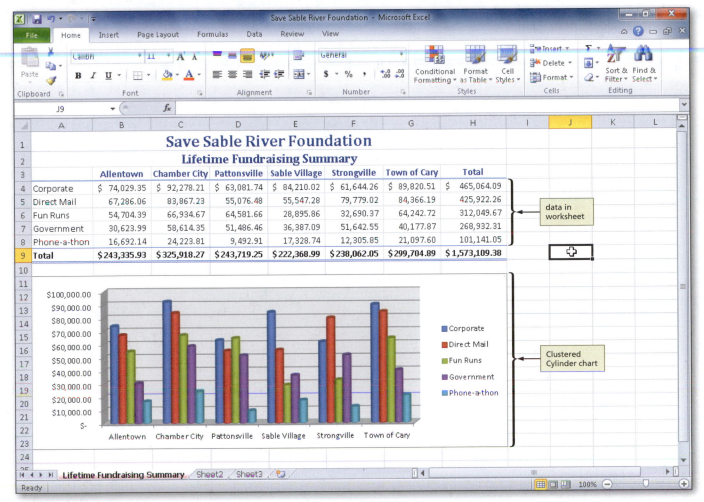

Figure 1–1

The first step in creating an effective worksheet is to make sure you understand what is required. The person or persons requesting the worksheet should supply their requirements in a requirements document. A **requirements document** includes a needs statement, a source of data, a summary of calculations, and any other special requirements for the worksheet, such as charting and Web support. Figure 1–2 on the following page shows the requirements document for the new workbook to be created in this chapter.

Excel 2010 Features
With its what-if analysis tools, research capabilities, collaboration tools, streamlined user interface, smart tags, charting features, Web capabilities, hundreds of functions, and enhanced formatting capabilities, Excel 2010 is one of the easier and more powerful spreadsheet programs available. Its dynamic analytical features make it possible to answer complicated what-if questions and its Web capabilities allow you to create, publish, view, share, and analyze data on an intranet or the World Wide Web.

requirements document →

Worksheet Development Cycle
Spreadsheet specialists do not sit down and start entering text, formulas, and data into a blank Excel worksheet as soon as they have a spreadsheet assignment. Instead, they follow an organized plan, or methodology, that breaks the development cycle into a series of tasks. The recommended methodology for creating worksheets includes: (1) analyze requirements (supplied in a requirements document); (2) design solution; (3) validate design; (4) implement design; (5) test solution; and (6) document solution.

REQUEST FOR NEW WORKBOOK

Date Submitted:	March 22, 2012
Submitted By:	Kevin Li
Worksheet Title:	Save Sable River Foundation Lifetime Fundraising Summary
Needs:	An easy-to-read worksheet that shows a summary of the Save Sable River Foundation's lifetime fundraising efforts for each city in which we operate (Allentown, Chamber City, Pattonsville, Sable Village, Strongville, and the Town of Cary). The worksheet also should include total funds raised for each city, total funds raised for each fundraising activity, and total lifetime funds raised.
Source of Data:	The data for the worksheet is available from the chief financial officer (CFO) of the Save Sable River Foundation.
Calculations:	The following calculations must be made for the worksheet: (a) total lifetime funds raised for each of the six cities; (b) total lifetime funds raised for each of the five fundraising activities; and (c) total lifetime funds raised for the organization.
Chart Requirements:	Below the data in the worksheet, construct a Clustered Cylinder chart that compares the total funds raised for each city within each type of fundraising activity.

Approvals

Approval Status:	X	Approved
		Rejected
Approved By:	Marsha Davis	
Date:	March 29, 2012	
Assigned To:	J. Quasney, Spreadsheet Specialist	

Figure 1–2

Overview

As you read this chapter, you will learn how to create the worksheet shown in Figure 1–1 on the previous page by performing these general tasks:

- Enter text in the worksheet
- Total data in the worksheet
- Format the text in the worksheet
- Insert a chart into the worksheet
- Identify the worksheet with a worksheet name
- Preview and print the worksheet

Plan Ahead

BTWs
For a complete list of the BTWs found in the margins of this book, visit the Excel 2010 BTW Web page (scsite.com/ex2010/btw).

General Project Guidelines

While creating an Excel worksheet, you need to make several decisions that will determine the appearance and characteristics of the finished worksheet. As you create the worksheet shown in Figure 1–1, you should follow these general guidelines:

1. **Select titles and subtitles for the worksheet.** Follow the *less is more* guideline. The less text in the titles and subtitles, the more impact the titles and subtitles will have. Use the fewest words possible to specify the information presented in the worksheet to the intended audience.

(continued)

(continued)

2. **Determine the contents for rows and columns.** Rows typically contain information that is analogous to items in a list, such as the fundraising techniques used by an organization. Columns typically contain descriptive information about items in rows or contain information that helps to group the data in the worksheet, such as the locations in which the organization operates. Row headings and column headings are usually placed in alphabetical sequence, unless an alternative order is recommended in the requirements document.

3. **Determine the calculations that are needed.** You can decide to total data in a variety of ways, such as across rows or in columns. You also can include a grand total.

4. **Determine where to save the workbook.** You can store a workbook permanently, or **save** it, on a variety of storage media including a hard disk, USB flash drive, CD, or DVD. You also can indicate a specific location on the storage media for saving the workbook.

5. **Identify how to format various elements of the worksheet.** The overall appearance of a worksheet significantly affects its ability to communicate clearly. Examples of how you can modify the appearance, or format, of text include changing its shape, size, color, and position on the worksheet.

6. **Decide on the type of chart needed.** Excel can create many different types of charts, such as cylinder charts and pie charts. Each type of chart relays a different message about the data in the worksheet. Choose a type of chart that relays the message that you want to convey.

7. **Establish where to position and how to format the chart.** The position and format of the chart should command the attention of the intended audience. If possible, position the chart so that it prints with the worksheet data on a single page.

8. **Choose a name for the worksheet.** Each worksheet in a workbook should be named to clarify its purpose. A good worksheet name is succinct, unique to the workbook, and meaningful to any user of the workbook.

9. **Determine the best method for distributing the workbook.** Workbooks and worksheets can be distributed on paper or electronically. The decision regarding how to distribute workbooks and worksheets greatly depends on your intended audience. For example, a worksheet may be printed for inclusion in a report, or a workbook may be distributed using e-mail if the recipient intends to update the workbook.

When necessary, more specific details concerning the above guidelines are presented at appropriate points in the chapter. The chapter also will identify the actions performed and decisions made regarding these guidelines during the creation of the worksheet shown in Figure 1–1 on page EX 3.

Plan Ahead

BTW

Worksheet Development
The key to developing a useful worksheet is careful planning. Careful planning can reduce your effort significantly and result in a worksheet that is accurate, easy to read, flexible, and useful. When analyzing a problem and designing a worksheet solution, you should follow these steps: (1) define the problem, including need, source of data, calculations, charting, and Web or special requirements; (2) design the worksheet; (3) enter the data and formulas; and (4) test the worksheet.

After carefully reviewing the requirements document (Figure 1–2) and making the necessary decisions, the next step is to design a solution or draw a sketch of the worksheet based on the requirements, including titles, column and row headings, the location of data values, and the Clustered Cylinder chart, as shown in Figure 1–3 on the following page. The dollar signs, 9s, and commas that you see in the sketch of the worksheet indicate formatted numeric values.

sketch of worksheet →

Save Sable River Foundation
Lifetime Fundraising Summary

	Allentown	Chamber City	Pattonsville	Sable Village	Strongville	Town of Cary	Total
Corporate Direct Mail Fun Runs Government Phone-a-thon	$99,999.99	$99,999.99	$99,999.99	$99,999.99	$99,999.99	$99,999.99	$99,999.99
Total	$999,999.99	$999,999.99	$999,999.99	$999,999.99	$999,999.99	$999,999.99	$9,999,999.99

Legend of Fundraising Types

	Allentown	Chamber City	Pattonsville	Sable Village	Strongville	Town of Cary

Figure 1–3

With a good understanding of the requirements document, an understanding of the necessary decisions, and a sketch of the worksheet, the next step is to use Excel to create the worksheet and chart.

To Start Excel

If you are using a computer to step through the project in this chapter and you want your screens to match the figures in this book, you should change your screen's resolution to 1024 × 768. For information about how to change a computer's resolution, refer to the Office 2010 and Windows 7 chapter at the beginning of this book.

The following steps, which assume Windows 7 is running, start Excel based on a typical installation. You may need to ask your instructor how to start Excel for your computer. For a detailed example of the procedure summarized below, refer to the Office 2010 and Windows 7 chapter.

1 Click the Start button on the Windows 7 taskbar to display the Start menu.

2 Type `Microsoft Excel` as the search text in the 'Search programs and files' text box and watch the search results appear on the Start menu.

3 Click Microsoft Excel 2010 in the search results on the Start menu to start Excel and display a new blank workbook in the Excel window.

4 If the Excel window is not maximized, click the Maximize button next to the Close button on its title bar to maximize the window.

BTW

The Ribbon and Screen Resolution
Excel may change how the groups and buttons within the groups appear on the Ribbon, depending on the computer's screen resolution. Thus, your Ribbon may look different from the ones in this book if you are using a screen resolution other than 1024 × 768.

Selecting a Cell

To enter data into a cell, you first must select it. The easiest way to select a cell (make it active) is to use the mouse to move the block plus sign mouse pointer to the cell and then click.

An alternative method is to use the arrow keys that are located just to the right of the alphanumeric keys on a standard keyboard. An arrow key selects the cell adjacent to the active cell in the direction of the arrow on the key.

You know a cell is selected, or active, when a heavy border surrounds the cell and the active cell reference appears in the Name box on the left side of the formula bar. Excel also changes the active cell's column heading and row heading to a gold color.

Entering Text

In Excel, any set of characters containing a letter, hyphen (as in a telephone number), or space is considered text. **Text** is used to place titles, such as worksheet titles, column titles, and row titles, on the worksheet.

BTW

Selecting a Cell
You can select any cell by entering its cell reference, such as B4, in the Name box on the left side of the formula bar.

For an introduction to Office 2010 and instruction about how to perform basic tasks in Office 2010 programs, read the Office 2010 and Windows 7 chapter at the beginning of this book, where you can learn how to start a program, use the Ribbon, save a file, open a file, quit a program, use Help, and much more.

Plan
Ahead

Select titles and subtitles for the worksheet.
Worksheet titles and subtitles should be as brief and meaningful as possible. A worksheet title could include the name of the organization, department, or a description of the content of the worksheet. A worksheet subtitle, if included, could include a more detailed description of the content of the worksheet. Examples of worksheet titles are December 2010 Payroll and Year 2011 Projected Budget, and examples of subtitles are Marketing Department and Rent and Utilities, respectively.

Plan
Ahead

Determine the contents of rows and columns.
As shown in Figure 1–4, data in a worksheet often is identified by row and column titles so that the user of a worksheet easily can identify the meaning of the data. Rows typically contain information that is similar to items in a list. Columns typically contain descriptive information about items in rows or contain information that helps to group the data in the worksheet. Examples of row titles are Product and Total, and examples of column titles are Name and Address.

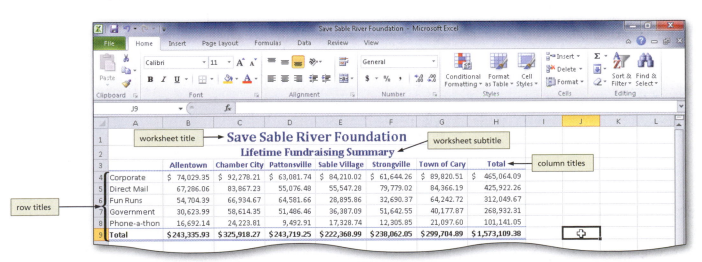

Figure 1–4

To Enter the Worksheet Titles

As shown in Figure 1–4 on the previous page, the worksheet title, Save Sable River Foundation, identifies the organization for which the worksheet is being created in Chapter 1. The worksheet subtitle, Lifetime Fundraising Summary, identifies the type of report.

The following steps enter the worksheet titles in cells A1 and A2. Later in this chapter, the worksheet titles will be formatted so they appear as shown in Figure 1–4.

1

• If necessary, click cell A1 to make cell A1 the active cell (Figure 1–5).

Q&A What if I make a mistake while typing?

If you type the wrong letter and notice the error before clicking the Enter box or pressing the ENTER key, use the BACKSPACE key to delete all the characters back to and including the incorrect letter. To cancel the entire entry before entering it into the

Figure 1–5

cell, click the Cancel box in the formula bar or press the ESC key. If you see an error in a cell after entering the text, select the cell and retype the entry.

2

• Type **Save Sable River Foundation** in cell A1 and then point to the Enter box in the formula bar to prepare to enter text in the active cell (Figure 1–6).

Q&A Why did the appearance of the formula bar change?

Excel displays the title in the formula bar and in cell A1. When you begin typing a cell entry, Excel displays two additional boxes in the formula bar:

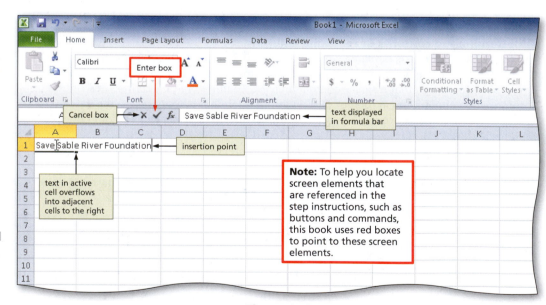

Note: To help you locate screen elements that are referenced in the step instructions, such as buttons and commands, this book uses red boxes to point to these screen elements.

Figure 1–6

the Cancel box and the Enter box. Clicking the **Enter box** completes an entry. Clicking the **Cancel box** cancels an entry.

Q&A What is the vertical line in cell A1?

The text in cell A1 is followed by the insertion point. The **insertion point** is a blinking vertical line that indicates where the next typed character will appear.

3
- Click the Enter box to complete the entry and enter a worksheet title (Figure 1–7).

 Why does the entered text appear in three cells?

When the text is longer than the width of a column, Excel displays the overflow characters in adjacent cells to the right as long as those adjacent cells contain no data. If the adjacent cells contain data, Excel would hide the overflow characters. Excel displays the overflow characters in the formula bar whenever that cell is the active cell.

Figure 1–7

4
- Click cell A2 to select it.

- Type **Lifetime Fundraising Summary** as the cell entry.

- Click the Enter box to complete the entry and enter a worksheet subtitle (Figure 1–8).

Q&A What happens when I click the Enter box?

When you complete an entry by clicking the Enter box, the insertion point disappears and the cell in which the text is entered remains the active cell.

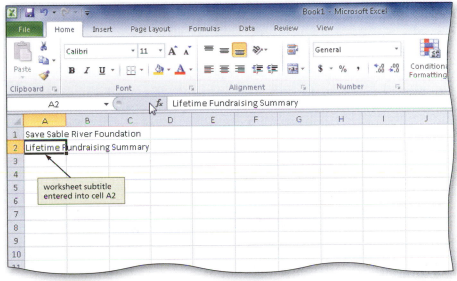

Figure 1–8

Other Ways
1. To complete entry, click any cell other than active cell 2. To complete entry, press ENTER	3. To complete entry, press HOME, PAGE UP, PAGE DOWN, or END 4. To complete entry, press UP ARROW, DOWN ARROW,	LEFT ARROW, or RIGHT ARROW.

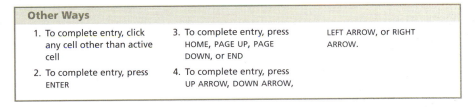

AutoCorrect

The **AutoCorrect feature** of Excel works behind the scenes, correcting common mistakes when you complete a text entry in a cell. AutoCorrect makes three types of corrections for you:

1. Corrects two initial capital letters by changing the second letter to lowercase.
2. Capitalizes the first letter in the names of days.
3. Replaces commonly misspelled words with their correct spelling. For example, it will change the misspelled word *recieve* to *receive* when you complete the entry. AutoCorrect will correct the spelling of hundreds of commonly misspelled words automatically.

BTW

Q&As
For a complete list of the Q&As found in many of the step-by-step sequences in this book, visit the Excel 2010 Q&A Web page (scsite.com/ex2010/qa).

To Enter Column Titles

The column titles in row 3 (Allentown, Chamber City, Pattonsville, Sable Village, Strongville, Town of Cary, and Total) identify the numbers in each column. In the case of the Save the Sable River Foundation data, the cities identify the funds raised using each fundraising type. The cities, therefore, are placed in columns. To enter the column titles in row 3, select the appropriate cell and then enter the text. The following steps enter the column titles in row 3.

1
• Click cell B3 to make it the active cell (Figure 1–9).

Figure 1–9

2
• Type **Allentown** to begin entry of a column title in the active cell (Figure 1–10).

Figure 1–10

3

● Press the RIGHT ARROW key to enter a column title and make the cell to the right the active cell (Figure 1–11).

Q&A

Why is the RIGHT ARROW key used to complete the entry in the cell?

If the next entry you want to enter is in an adjacent cell, use the arrow keys to complete the entry in a cell. When you press an arrow key to complete an entry, the adjacent cell in the direction of the arrow (up, down, left, or right) becomes the active cell. If the next entry is in a nonadjacent cell, complete the current entry by clicking the next cell in which you plan to enter data. You also can click the Enter box or press the ENTER key and then click the appropriate cell for the next entry.

Figure 1–11

4

● Repeat Steps 2 and 3 to enter the remaining column titles; that is, enter **Chamber City** in cell C3, **Pattonsville** in cell D3, **Sable Village** in cell E3, **Strongville** in cell F3, **Town of Cary** in cell G3, and **Total** in cell H3 (complete the last entry in cell H3 by clicking the Enter box in the formula bar) (Figure 1–12).

Figure 1–12

To Enter Row Titles

The next step in developing the worksheet for this project is to enter the row titles in column A. For the Save Sable River Foundation data, the list of fundraising activities meets the criterion that information that identifies columns be in a list. It is more likely that in the future, the organization will add more fundraising activities as opposed to more cities. Each fundraising activity, therefore, should be placed in its own row. The row titles in column A (Corporate, Direct Mail, Fun Runs, Government, Phone-a-thon, and Total) identify the numbers in each row.

This process for entering row titles is similar to the process for entering column titles. The following steps enter the row titles in the worksheet.

1
- Click cell A4 to select it.

- Type `Corporate` and then press the DOWN ARROW key to enter a row title and to make the cell below the current cell the active cell (Figure 1–13).

Figure 1–13

2
- Repeat Step 1 to enter the remaining row titles in column A; that is, enter `Direct Mail` in cell A5, `Fun Runs` in cell A6, `Government` in cell A7, `Phone-a-thon` in cell A8, and `Total` in cell A9 (Figure 1–14).

Q&A

Why is the text left-aligned in the cells?

When you enter text, Excel automatically left-aligns the text in the cell. Excel treats any combination of numbers, spaces, and nonnumeric characters as text. For example, Excel recognizes the following entries as text: 401AX21, 921–231, 619 321, 883XTY

You can change the text alignment in a cell by realigning it. Other alignment techniques are discussed later in this chapter.

Figure 1–14

Entering Numbers

In Excel, you can enter numbers into cells to represent amounts. A **number** can contain only the following characters:

0 1 2 3 4 5 6 7 8 9 + - ( ) , / . $ % E e

If a cell entry contains any other keyboard character (including spaces), Excel interprets the entry as text and treats it accordingly. The use of the special characters is explained when they are used in this book.

BTW

Numeric Limitations
In Excel, a number can be between approximately -1×10^{308} and 1×10^{308}. This means it can be between a negative 1 followed by 308 zeros and a positive 1 followed by 308 zeros. To enter a number such as 6,000,000,000,000,000, you can type 6,000,000,000,000,000, or you can type 6E15, which translates to 6×10^{15}.

To Enter Numbers

The Save Sable River Foundation Lifetime Fundraising Summary numbers used in Chapter 1 are summarized in Table 1–1. These numbers, which represent lifetime fundraising amounts for each of the fundraising activities and cities, must be entered in rows 4, 5, 6, 7, and 8.

Table 1–1 Save Sable River Foundation Lifetime Fundraising Summary						
	Allentown	**Chamber City**	**Pattonsville**	**Sable Village**	**Strongville**	**Town of Cary**
Corporate	74029.35	92278.21	63081.74	84210.02	61644.26	89820.51
Direct Mail	67286.06	83867.23	55076.48	55547.28	79779.02	84366.19
Fun Runs	54704.39	66934.67	64581.66	28895.86	32690.37	64242.72
Government	30623.99	58614.35	51486.46	36387.09	51642.55	40177.87
Phone-a-thon	16692.14	24223.81	9492.91	17328.74	12305.85	21097.60

The following steps enter the numbers in Table 1–1 one row at a time.

1

- Click cell B4 to select it.

- Type **74029.35** and then press the RIGHT ARROW key to enter the data in the selected cell and make the cell to the right the active cell (Figure 1–15).

Figure 1–15

Q&A

Do I need to enter dollar signs, commas, or trailing zeros for the fundraising summary amounts?

You are not required to type dollar signs, commas, or trailing zeros. When you enter a dollar value that has cents, however, you must add the decimal point and the numbers representing the cents. Later in this chapter, the numbers will be formatted to use dollar signs, commas, and trailing zeros to improve the appearance and readability of the numbers.

2

- Enter `92278.21` in cell C4, `63081.74` in cell D4, `84210.02` in cell E4, `61644.26` in cell F4, and `89820.51` in cell G4 to complete the first row of numbers in the worksheet (Figure 1–16).

Q&A

Why are the numbers right-aligned?

When you enter numeric data in a cell, Excel recognizes the values as numbers and right-aligns the values in order to properly vertically align decimal and integer values. For example, values entered below those entered in this step

Figure 1–16

automatically will be right-aligned as well so that the decimals of the values properly align.

3

- Click cell B5 to select it and complete the entry in the previously selected cell.

- Enter the remaining lifetime fundraising summary numbers provided in Table 1–1 on page EX 13 for each of the four remaining fundraising activities in rows 5, 6, 7, and 8 to finish entering numbers in the worksheet (Figure 1–17).

Q&A

Why did clicking cell B5 complete the entry in cell G4?

Selecting another cell completes the entry in the previously selected cell in the same way as pressing the ENTER key, pressing an arrow key, or clicking the Enter box on the formula bar. In the next set of steps, the entry of the number in cell G4 will be completed by selecting another cell.

Figure 1–17

Calculating a Sum

The next step in creating the worksheet is to perform any necessary calculations, such as calculating the column and row totals.

To Sum a Column of Numbers

As stated in the requirements document in Figure 1–2 on page EX 4, totals are required for each city, each fundraising activity, and the organization. The first calculation is to determine the fundraising total for the fundraising activities in the city of Allentown in column B. To calculate this value in cell B9, Excel must add, or sum, the numbers in cells B4, B5, B6, B7, and B8. Excel's **SUM function**, which adds all of the numbers in a range of cells, provides a convenient means to accomplish this task.

A **range** is a series of two or more adjacent cells in a column or row or a rectangular group of cells. For example, the group of adjacent cells B4, B5, B6, B7, and B8 is called a range. Many Excel operations, such as summing numbers, take place on a range of cells.

After the total lifetime fundraising amount for the fundraising activities in the city of Allentown in column B is determined, the totals for the remaining cities and totals for each fundraising activity will be determined. The following steps sum the numbers in column B.

1

- Click cell B9 to make it the active cell and complete the entry in the previously selected cell.

- Click the Sum button (Home tab | Editing group) to display a formula in the formula bar and in the active cell (Figure 1–18).

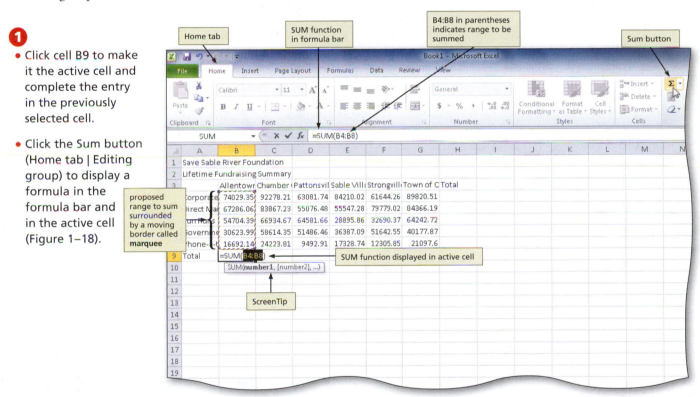

Figure 1–18

Q&A

How does Excel know which cells to sum?

When you enter the SUM function using the Sum button, Excel automatically selects what it considers to be your choice of the range to sum. When proposing the range to sum, Excel first looks for a range of cells with numbers above the active cell and then to the left. If Excel proposes the wrong range, you can correct it by dragging through the correct range before pressing the ENTER key. You also can enter the correct range by typing the beginning cell reference, a colon (:), and the ending cell reference.

BTW

Calculating Sums

Excel calculates sums for a variety of data types. For example, Boolean values, such as TRUE and FALSE, can be summed. Excel treats the value of TRUE as 1 and the value of FALSE as 0. Times also can be summed. For example, Excel treats the sum of 1:15 and 2:45 as 4:00.

2

- Click the Enter box in the formula bar to enter a sum in the active cell (Figure 1–19).

Q&A

What is the purpose of the Sum button arrow?

If you click the Sum button arrow on the right side of the Sum button (Home tab | Editing group) (Figure 1–19), Excel displays a list of often used functions from which you can choose. The list includes functions that allow you to determine the average, the number of items in the selected range, the maximum value, or the minimum value of a range of numbers.

Figure 1–19

Other Ways

1. Click Insert Function button in the formula bar, select SUM in Select a function list, click OK button, select range, click OK button

2. Click Sum button arrow (Home tab | Editing group), click More Functions, select SUM (Insert Function dialog box), click OK button, select range, click OK button

3. Type = s in cell, select SUM from list, select range

4. Press ALT + EQUAL SIGN (=) twice

BTW

Entering Numbers as Text
Sometimes, you will want Excel to treat numbers, such as postal codes and telephone numbers, as text. To enter a number as text, start the entry with an apostrophe (').

Using the Fill Handle to Copy a Cell to Adjacent Cells

Excel also must calculate the totals for Chamber City in cell C9, Pattonsville in cell D9, Sable Village in cell E9, Strongville in cell F9, and the Town of Cary in cell G9. Table 1–2 illustrates the similarities between the entry in cell B9 and the entries required to sum the totals in cells C9, D9, E9, F9 and G9.

Table 1–2 Sum Function Entries in Row 9		
Cell	**Sum Function Entries**	**Remark**
B9	=SUM(B4:B8)	Sums cells B4, B5, B6, B7, and B8
C9	=SUM(C4:C8)	Sums cells C4, C5, C6, C7, and C8
D9	=SUM(D4:D8)	Sums cells D4, D5, D6, D7, and D8
E9	=SUM(E4:E8)	Sums cells E4, E5, E6, E7, and E8
F9	=SUM(F4:F8)	Sums cells F4, F5, F6, F7, and F8
G9	=SUM(G4:G8)	Sums cells G4, G5, G6, G7, and G8

To place the SUM functions in cells C9, D9, E9, F9, and G9, you could follow the same steps shown previously in Figures 1–18 on page EX 15 and 1–19. A second, more efficient method, however, is to copy the SUM function from cell B9 to the range C9:G9. The cell being copied is called the **source area** or **copy area**. The range of cells receiving the copy is called the **destination area** or **paste area**.

Although the SUM function entries in Table 1–2 are similar, they are not exact copies. The range in each SUM function entry uses cell references that are one column to the right of the previous column. When you copy formulas that include cell references, Excel automatically adjusts them for each new position, resulting in the SUM function entries illustrated in Table 1–2. Each adjusted cell reference is called a **relative reference**.

To Copy a Cell to Adjacent Cells in a Row

The easiest way to copy the SUM formula from cell B9 to cells C9, D9, E9, F9, and G9 is to use the fill handle. The **fill handle** is the small black square located in the lower-right corner of the heavy border around the active cell. The following steps use the fill handle to copy cell B9 to the adjacent cells C9:G9.

1
- With cell B9 active, point to the fill handle to activate it (Figure 1–20).

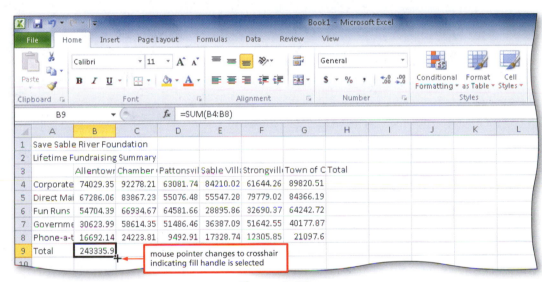

Figure 1–20

2
- Drag the fill handle to select the destination area, range C9:G9, to display a shaded border around the source area and the destination area (Figure 1–21). Do not release the mouse button.

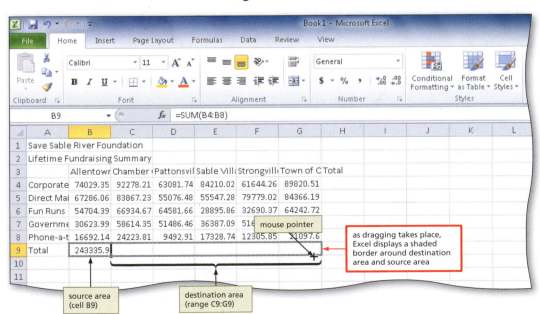

Figure 1–21

3

- Release the mouse button to copy the SUM function from the active cell to the destination area and calculate the sums (Figure 1–22).

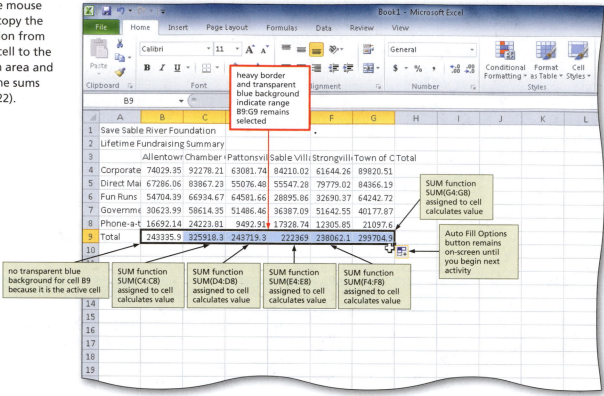

Figure 1–22

Q&A

What is the purpose of the Auto Fill Options button?

When you copy one range to another, Excel displays an Auto Fill Options button (Figure 1–22). The Auto Fill Options button allows you to choose whether you want to copy the values from the source area to the destination area with formatting, do so without formatting, or copy only the format. To view the available fill options, click the Auto Fill Options button. The Auto Fill Options button disappears when you begin another activity in Excel, such as typing data in another cell or applying formatting to a cell or range of cells.

Other Ways

1. Select source area, click Copy button (Home tab | Clipboard group), select destination area, click Paste button (Home tab | Clipboard group)

2. Right-click source area, click Copy on shortcut menu, right-click destination area, click Paste on shortcut menu

3. Select source area and then point to border of range; while holding down CTRL, drag source area to destination area

To Determine Multiple Totals at the Same Time

The next step in building the worksheet is to determine the lifetime fundraising totals for each fundraising activity and total lifetime fundraising for the organization in column H. To calculate these totals, you can use the SUM function much as it was used to total the lifetime fundraising amounts by city in row 9. In this example, however, Excel will determine totals for all of the rows at the same time. The following steps sum multiple totals at once.

1

- Click cell H4 to make it the active cell (Figure 1–23).

Figure 1–23

2

- With the mouse pointer in cell H4 and in the shape of a block plus sign, drag the mouse pointer down to cell H9 to highlight the range with a transparent view (Figure 1–24).

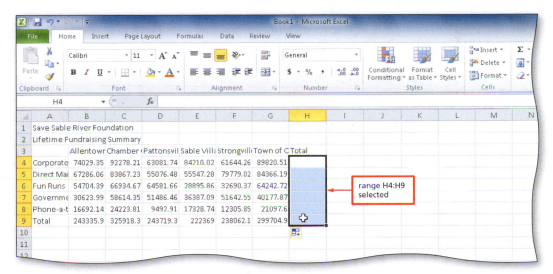

Figure 1–24

3

- Click the Sum button (Home tab | Editing group) to calculate and display the sums of the corresponding rows (Figure 1–25).

- Select cell A10 to deselect the selected range.

Q&A How does Excel create unique totals for each row?

If each cell in a selected range is next to a row of numbers, Excel assigns the SUM function to each cell when you click the Sum button.

Figure 1–25

Organizing Files and Folders
You should organize and store files in folders so that you easily can find the files later. For example, if you are taking an introductory computer class called CIS 101, a good practice would be to save all Excel files in an Excel folder in a CIS 101 folder. For a discussion of folders and detailed examples of creating folders, refer to the Office 2010 and Windows 7 chapter at the beginning of this book.

BTW

To Save a Workbook

You have performed many tasks while creating this workbook and do not want to risk losing work completed thus far. Accordingly, you should save the workbook.

The following steps assume you already have created folders for storing your files, for example, a CIS 101 folder (for your class) that contains an Excel folder (for your assignments). Thus, these steps save the workbook in the Excel folder in the CIS 101 folder on a USB flash drive using the file name, Save Sable River Foundation. For a detailed example of the procedure summarized below, refer to the Office 2010 and Windows 7 chapter at the beginning of this book.

1 With a USB flash drive connected to one of the computer's USB ports, click the Save button on the Quick Access Toolbar to display the Save As dialog box.

2 Type `Save Sable River Foundation` in the File name text box to change the file name. Do not press the ENTER key after typing the file name because you do not want to close the dialog box at this time.

3 Navigate to the desired save location (in this case, the Excel folder in the CIS 101 folder [or your class folder] on the USB flash drive).

4 Click the Save button (Save As dialog box) to save the document in the selected folder on the selected drive with the entered file name.

Break Point: If you wish to take a break, this is a good place to do so. You can quit Excel. To resume at a later time, start Excel, open the file called Save Sable River Foundation, and continue following the steps from this location forward.

BTW

AutoRecover
The AutoRecover feature of Excel, sometimes called AutoSave, allows you to specify how often and where Excel automatically saves workbooks. If your computer loses power, becomes unusable while you are interacting with a workbook, or you forget to save a workbook before closing it, Excel notifies you if there are workbooks that were automatically saved when one of these events occurred. You view and change AutoRecover options by clicking the Options button in the Backstage view and then clicking Save in the left panel of the Excel Options dialog box.

Formatting the Worksheet

The text, numeric entries, and functions for the worksheet now are complete. The next step is to format the worksheet. You **format** a worksheet to emphasize certain entries and make the worksheet easier to read and understand.

Figure 1–26a shows the worksheet before formatting. Figure 1–26b shows the worksheet after formatting. As you can see from the two figures, a worksheet that is formatted not only is easier to read but also looks more professional.

Plan Ahead

Identify how to format various elements of the worksheet.
By formatting the contents of the worksheet, you can improve its overall appearance. When formatting a worksheet, consider the following formatting suggestions:

- **Increase the font size of cells.** An increased font size gives more impact to the text in a cell. In order to indicate their relative importance, worksheet titles should have the largest font size, followed by worksheet subtitles, and then column and row headings.

- **Change the font color of cells.** Different cell colors help the reader of a worksheet quickly differentiate between the sections of a worksheet. Worksheet titles and subtitles easily should be identifiable from column and row headings. The overuse of too many colors, however, may be distracting to the reader of a worksheet.

- **Center the worksheet titles, subtitles, and column headings.** Centering text in worksheet titles and subtitles over the portion of the worksheet that they represent helps the reader of a worksheet quickly to identify the information that is of interest to them.

(continued)

(continued)

**Plan
Ahead**

- **Modify column widths to best fit text in cells.** Make certain that text in a cell does not overflow into another cell. A column's width should be adjusted to accommodate the largest amount of text used in a cell in the column. Columns that contain data that is similar in nature to other columns should share the same column width.

- **Change the font style of cells.** Use a bold font style to make worksheet titles, worksheet subtitles, column headings, row heading, and totals stand out. Use italics and underline font styles judiciously, as specific rules of grammar apply to their use.

Figure 1–26 (a) Before Formatting

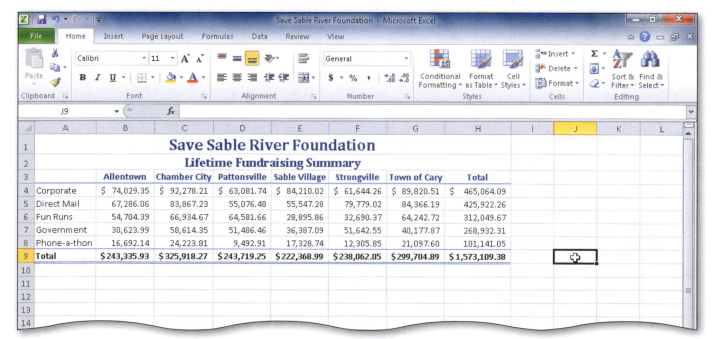

Figure 1–26 (b) After Formatting

To change the unformatted worksheet in Figure 1–26a on the previous page to the formatted worksheet in Figure 1–26b on the previous page, the following tasks must be completed:

1. Change the font, change the font style to bold, increase the font size, and change the font color of the worksheet titles in cells A1 and A2.

2. Center the worksheet titles in cells A1 and A2 across columns A through H.

3. Format the body of the worksheet. The body of the worksheet, range A3:H9, includes the column titles, row titles, and numbers. Formatting the body of the worksheet changes the numbers to use a dollars-and-cents format, with dollar signs in the first row (row 4) and the total row (row 9); adds underlining that emphasizes portions of the worksheet; and modifies the column widths to fit the text in the columns and make the text and numbers readable.

The remainder of this section explains the process required to format the worksheet. Although the formatting procedures are explained in the order described above, you should be aware that you could make these format changes in any order. Modifying the column widths, however, usually is done last because other formatting changes may affect the size of data in the cells in the column.

Font, Style, Size, and Color

The characters that Excel displays on the screen are a specific font, style, size, and color. The **font**, or font face, defines the appearance and shape of the letters, numbers, and special characters. Examples of fonts include Calibri, Cambria, Times New Roman, Arial, and Courier. **Font style** indicates how the characters are emphasized. Common font styles include regular, bold, underline, and italic. The **font size** specifies the size of the characters on the screen. Font size is gauged by a measurement system called points. A single point is about 1/72 of one inch in height. Thus, a character with a **point size** of 10 is about 10/72 of one inch in height. The **font color** defines the color of the characters. Excel can display characters in a wide variety of colors, including black, red, orange, and blue.

When Excel begins, the preset font for the entire workbook is Calibri, with a font size, font style, and font color of 11–point regular black. Excel allows you to change the font characteristics in a single cell, a range of cells, the entire worksheet, or the entire workbook.

To Change a Cell Style

Excel includes the capability of changing several characteristics of a cell, such the font, font size, and font color, all at once by assigning a predefined cell style to a cell. Using the predefined styles that Excel includes provides a consistent appearance to common portions of your worksheets, such as worksheet titles, worksheet subtitles, column headings, and total rows. The following steps assign the Title cell style to the worksheet title in cell A1.

1

• Click cell A1 to make cell A1 the active cell.

• Click the Cell Styles button (Home tab | Styles group) to display the Cell Styles gallery (Figure 1–27).

Figure 1–27

2

• Point to the Title cell style in the Titles and Headings area of the Cell Styles gallery to see a live preview of the cell style in the active cell (Figure 1–28).

Experiment

• Point to several other cell styles in the Cell Styles gallery to see a live preview of other cell styles in cell A1.

Figure 1–28

3

• Click the Title cell style to apply the cell style to the active cell (Figure 1–29).

Q&A

Why do several items in the Font group on the Ribbon change?

The changes to the Font box, Bold button, and Font Size box indicate the font changes applied to the active cell, cell A1, as a result of applying the Title cell style.

Figure 1–29

To Change the Font

Different fonts often are used in a worksheet to make it more appealing to the reader and to relate or distinguish data in the worksheet. The following steps change the worksheet subtitle's fonts from Calibri to Cambria.

1
● Click cell A2 to make it the active cell.

● Click the Font box arrow (Home tab | Font group) to display the Font gallery (Figure 1–30).

Q&A Which fonts are displayed in the Font gallery?

Because many programs supply additional fonts beyond what comes with the Windows 7 operating system, the number of fonts available on your computer will depend on the programs installed. This book uses only fonts that come with the Windows 7 operating system and Microsoft Office 2010.

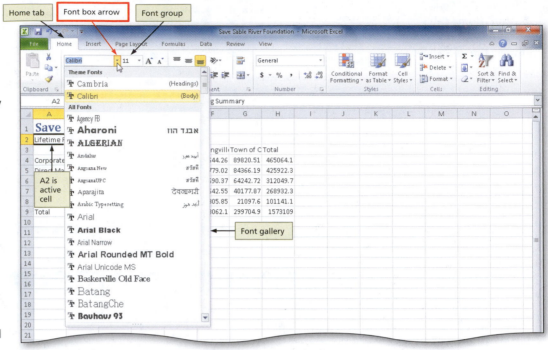

Figure 1–30

2
● Point to Cambria in the Theme Fonts area of the Font gallery to see a live preview of the selected font in the active cell (Figure 1–31).

🔍 **Experiment**

● Point to several other fonts in the Font gallery to see a live preview of other fonts in the selected cell.

Q&A What is the Theme Fonts area?

Excel applies the same default theme to any new workbook that you start. A **theme** is a collection of cell styles and other styles that have common characteristics, such as a color scheme and font. The default theme for an Excel workbook is the Office theme. The Theme Fonts area of the Font gallery includes the fonts included in the default Office theme. Cambria is recommended for headings and Calibri is recommended by Microsoft for cells in the body of the worksheet (Figure 1–31).

Figure 1–31

3

• Click Cambria in the Theme Fonts area to change the font of the worksheet subtitle to Cambria (Figure 1–32).

Figure 1–32

To Bold a Cell

You **bold** an entry in a cell to emphasize it or make it stand out from the rest of the worksheet. The following step bolds the worksheet subtitle in cell A2.

1

• With cell A2 active, click the Bold button (Home tab | Font group) to change the font style of the active cell to bold (Figure 1–33).

Q&A What if a cell already includes a bold style?

If the active cell is already bold, then Excel displays the Bold button with a transparent orange background.

Q&A How do I remove the bold style from a cell?

Clicking the Bold button (Home tab | Font group) a second time removes the bold font style.

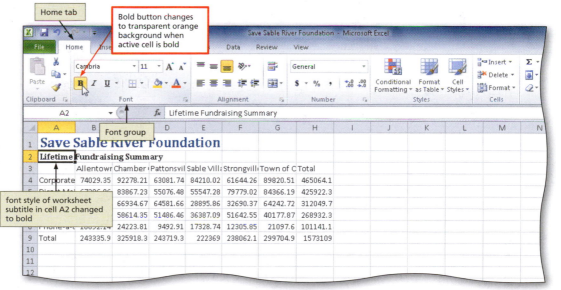

Figure 1–33

To Increase the Font Size of a Cell Entry

Increasing the font size is the next step in formatting the worksheet subtitle. You increase the font size of a cell so that the entry stands out and is easier to read. The following steps increase the font size of the worksheet subtitle in cell A2.

1

- With cell A2 selected, click the Font Size box arrow (Home tab | Font group) to display the Font Size list.

- Point to 14 in the Font Size list to see a live preview of the active cell with the selected font size (Figure 1–34).

 Experiment

- Point to several other font sizes in the Font Size list to see a live preview of other font sizes in the selected cell.

Figure 1–34

2

- Click 14 in the Font Size list to change the font size in the active cell (Figure 1–35).

Q&A

Can I assign a font size that is not in the Font Size list?

Yes. An alternative to clicking a font size in the Font Size list is to click the Font Size box (Home tab | Font group), type the font size, and then press the ENTER key. This procedure allows you to assign a font size not available in the Font Size list to a selected cell entry.

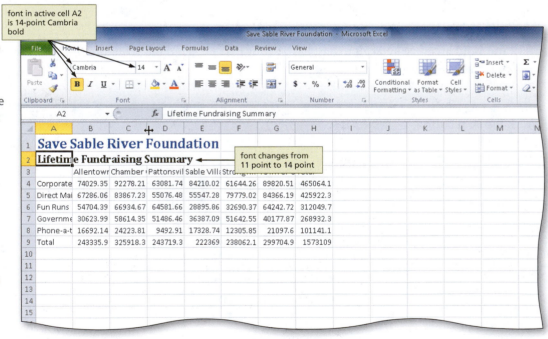

Figure 1–35

Other Ways

1. Click Increase Font Size button (Home tab | Font group) or Decrease Font Size button (Home tab | Font group)

2. Click Font Size box arrow on Mini toolbar, click desired font size in Font Size gallery

3. Right-click cell, click Format Cells on shortcut menu, click Font tab (Format Cells dialog box), select font size in Size box, click OK button

To Change the Font Color of a Cell Entry

The next step is to change the color of the font in cell A2 from black to dark blue. The following steps change the font color of a cell entry.

1

- With cell A2 selected, click the Font Color button arrow (Home tab | Font group) to display the Font Color gallery.

- Point to Dark Blue, Text 2 (dark blue color in column 4, row 1) in the Theme Colors area of the Font Color gallery to see a live preview of the font color in the active cell (Figure 1–36).

 Experiment

- Point to several other colors in the Font Color gallery to see a live preview of other font colors in the active cell.

Q&A Which colors does Excel make available on the Font Color gallery?

You can choose from more than 60 different font colors on the Font Color gallery (Figure 1–36). Your Font Color gallery may have more or fewer colors, depending on color settings of your operating system. The Theme Colors area includes colors that are included in the current workbook's theme.

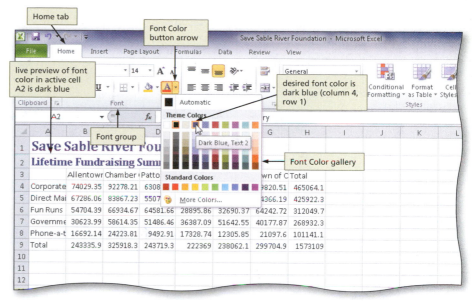

Figure 1–36

2

- Click Dark Blue, Text 2 (column 4, row 1) on the Font Color gallery to change the font of the worksheet subtitle in the active cell (Figure 1–37).

Q&A Why does the Font Color button change after I select the new font color?

When you choose a color on the Font Color gallery, Excel changes the Font Color button (Home tab | Font group) to the chosen color. Thus, to change the font color of the cell entry in another cell to the same color, you need only to select the cell and then click the Font Color button (Home tab | Font group).

Figure 1–37

Other Ways

1. Click Font Color box arrow on Mini toolbar, click desired font color in the Font Color gallery
2. Right-click cell, click Format Cells on shortcut menu, click Font tab (Format Cells dialog box), select color in Font Color gallery, click OK button

To Center Cell Entries Across Columns by Merging Cells

The final step in formatting the worksheet title and subtitle is to center them across columns A through H. Centering a title across the columns used in the body of the worksheet improves the worksheet's appearance. To do this, the eight cells in the range A1:H1 are combined, or merged, into a single cell that is the width of the columns in the body of the worksheet. The eight cells in the range A2:H2 are merged in a similar manner. **Merging cells** involves creating a single cell by combining two or more selected cells. The following steps center the worksheet title and subtitle across columns by merging cells.

1

- Select cell A1 and then drag to cell H1 to highlight the range to be merged and centered (Figure 1–38).

Q&A

What if a cell in the range B1:H1 contains data?

For the Merge & Center button (Home tab | Alignment group) to work properly, all the cells except the leftmost cell in the selected range must be empty.

Figure 1–38

2

- Click the Merge & Center button (Home tab | Alignment group) to merge cells A1 through H1 and center the contents of the leftmost cell across the selected columns (Figure 1–39).

Q&A

What happened to cells B1 through H1?

After the merge, cells B1 through H1 no longer exist. The new cell A1 now extends across columns A through H.

Figure 1–39

3

- Repeat Steps 1 and 2 to merge and center the worksheet subtitle across cells A2 through H2 (Figure 1–40).

Q&A

Are cells B1 through H1 and B2 through H2 lost forever?

No. The opposite of merging cells is **splitting a merged cell**. After you have merged multiple cells to create one merged cell, you can unmerge, or split, the merged cell to display the original cells on the worksheet. You split a merged cell by selecting it and clicking the Merge & Center button. For example, if you click the Merge & Center button a second time in Step 2, it will split the merged cell A1 into cells A1, B1, C1, D1, E1, F1, G1, and H1.

Figure 1–40

Other Ways

1. Right-click selection, click Merge & Center button on Mini toolbar
2. Right-click selection, click Format Cells on shortcut menu, click Alignment tab (Format Cells dialog box), select Center Across Selection in Horizontal list, click OK button

To Format Column Titles and the Total Row

The next step to format the worksheet is to format the column titles in row 3 and the total values in row 9. Column titles and the total row should be formatted so anyone who views the worksheet quickly can distinguish the column titles and total row from the data in the body of the worksheet. The following steps format the column titles and total row using cell styles in the default worksheet theme.

1

- Click cell A3 and then drag the mouse pointer to cell H3 to select a range (Figure 1–41).

Q&A

Why is cell A3 selected in the range for the column headings?

The style to be applied to the column headings includes an underline that will help to distinguish the column headings from the rest of the worksheet. Including cell A3 in the range ensures that the cell will include the underline, which is visually appealing and further helps to separate the data in the worksheet.

Figure 1–41

2

- Click the Cell Styles button (Home tab | Styles group) to display the Cell Styles gallery.

- Point to the Heading 3 cell style in the Titles and Headings area of the Cell Styles gallery to see a live preview of the cell style in the selected range (Figure 1–42).

Figure 1–42

🔍 **Experiment**

- Point to other cell styles in the Titles and Headings area of the Cell Styles gallery to see a live preview of other cell styles in the selected range, A3:H3.

3

- Click the Heading 3 cell style to apply the cell style to the selected range.

- Click the Center button (Home tab | Alignment group) to center the column headings in the selected range.

- Click cell A9 and then drag the mouse pointer to cell H9 to select a range (Figure 1–43).

Figure 1–43

Q&A Why should I choose Heading 3 instead of another heading cell style?

Excel includes many types of headings, such as Heading 1 and Heading 2, because worksheets often include many levels of headings above columns. In the case of the worksheet created for this project, the Heading 3 title includes formatting that makes the column titles' font size smaller than the title and subtitle and makes the column titles stand out from the data in the body of the worksheet.

4

- Click the Cell Styles button (Home tab | Styles group) to display the Cell Styles gallery and then click the Total cell style in the Titles and Headings area to apply the selected cell style to the cells in the selected range.

- Click cell A11 to select it (Figure 1–44).

Figure 1–44

To Format Numbers in the Worksheet

As previously noted, the numbers in the worksheet should be formatted to use a dollar-and-cents format, with dollar signs in the first row (row 4) and the total row (row 9). Excel allows you to format numbers in a variety of ways, and these methods are discussed in other chapters in this book. The following steps use buttons on the Ribbon to format the numbers in the worksheet.

1

- Select cell B4 and drag the mouse pointer to cell H4 to select a range (Figure 1–45).

Figure 1–45

2
- Click the Accounting Number Format button (Home tab | Number group) to apply the Accounting Number format to the cells in the selected range.

- Select the range B5:H8 (Figure 1–46).

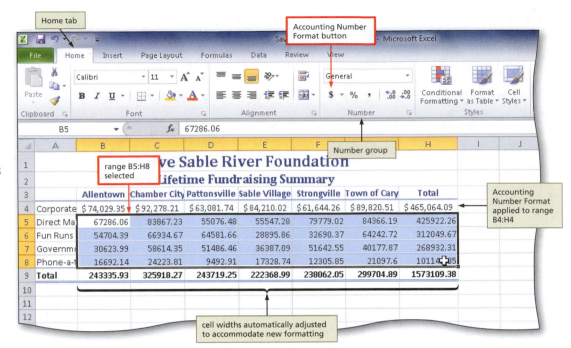

Figure 1–46

Q&A What effect does the Accounting Number format have on the selected cells?

The Accounting Number format causes the cells to be displayed with two decimal places so that decimal places in cells below the selected cells align vertically. Cell widths are adjusted automatically to accommodate the new formatting.

3
- Click the Comma Style button (Home tab | Number group) to apply the Comma Style format to the selected range.

- Select the range B9:H9 to make it the active range (Figure 1–47).

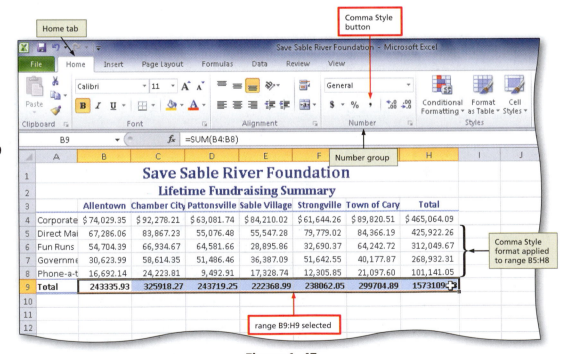

Figure 1–47

Q&A What effect does the Comma Style format have on the selected cells?

The Comma Style format causes the cells to be displayed with two decimal places and commas as thousands separators.

4

• Click the Accounting Number Format button (Home tab | Number group) to apply the Accounting Number format to the cells in the selected range.

• Select cell A11 (Figure 1–48).

Why did the column widths automatically adjust again?

Because the total row contains larger numbers, the Accounting Number format again causes the cell widths automatically to adjust to accommodate the new formatting just as occurred in Step 2.

Figure 1–48

Other Ways

1. Click Accounting Number Format or Comma Style button on Mini toolbar

2. Right-click selection, click Format Cells on the shortcut menu, click

Number tab (Format Cells dialog box), select Accounting in Category list or select Number and click Use 1000 Separator, click OK button

To Adjust the Column Width

The last step in formatting the worksheet is to adjust the width of column A so that the word Phone-a-thon in cell A8 is shown in its entirety in the cell. Excel includes several methods for adjusting cell widths and row heights, and these methods are discussed later in this book. The following steps adjust the width of column A so that the contents of cell A8 are displayed in the cell.

1

• Point to the boundary on the right side of the column A heading above row 1 to change the mouse pointer to a split double arrow (Figure 1–49).

Figure 1–49

2

- Double-click on the boundary to adjust the width of the column to the width of the largest item in the column (Figure 1–50).

Q&A

What if none of the items in column A extends through the entire width of the column?

If all of the items in column A were shorter in length than the width of the column when you double-click the right side of the column A heading, then Excel still would adjust the column width to the largest item in the column. That is, Excel would reduce the width of the column to the largest item.

Figure 1–50

Using the Name Box to Select a Cell

The next step is to chart the lifetime fundraising amounts for the five fundraising activities used by the organization. To create the chart, you first must select the cell in the upper-left corner of the range to chart (cell A3). Rather than clicking cell A3 to select it, the next section describes how to use the Name box to select the cell.

To Use the Name Box to Select a Cell

The Name box is located on the left side of the formula bar. To select any cell, click the Name box and enter the cell reference of the cell you want to select. The following steps select cell A3 using the Name box.

1

- Click the Name box in the formula bar and then type **a3** as the cell you wish to select (Figure 1–51).

Q&A

Why is cell A11 still selected?

Even though cell A11 is the active cell, Excel displays the typed cell reference a3 in the Name box until you press the ENTER key.

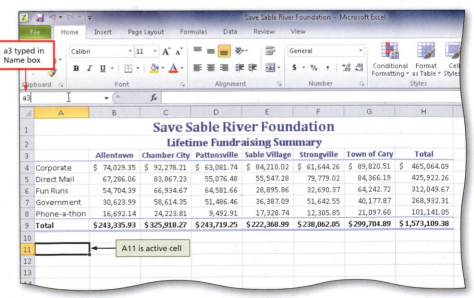

Figure 1–51

2

• Press the ENTER key to change the active cell in the Name box (Figure 1–52).

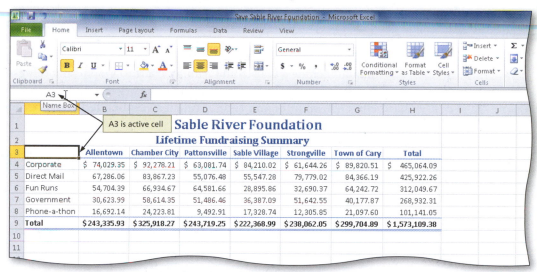

Figure 1–52

Other Ways to Select Cells

As you will see in later chapters, in addition to using the Name box to select any cell in a worksheet, you also can use it to assign names to a cell or range of cells. Excel supports several additional ways to select a cell, as summarized in Table 1–3.

Table 1–3 Selecting Cells in Excel	
Key, Box, or Command	**Function**
ALT+PAGE DOWN	Selects the cell one worksheet window to the right and moves the worksheet window accordingly.
ALT+PAGE UP	Selects the cell one worksheet window to the left and moves the worksheet window accordingly.
ARROW	Selects the adjacent cell in the direction of the arrow on the key.
CTRL+ARROW	Selects the border cell of the worksheet in combination with the arrow keys and moves the worksheet window accordingly. For example, to select the rightmost cell in the row that contains the active cell, press CTRL+RIGHT ARROW. You also can press the END key, release it, and then press the appropriate arrow key to accomplish the same task.
CTRL+HOME	Selects cell A1 or the cell one column and one row below and to the right of frozen titles and moves the worksheet window accordingly.
Find command on Find and Select menu or SHIFT+F5	Finds and selects a cell that contains specific contents that you enter in the Find and Replace dialog box. If necessary, Excel moves the worksheet window to display the cell. You also can press CTRL+F to display the Find dialog box.
Go To command on Find and Select menu or F5	Selects the cell that corresponds to the cell reference you enter in the Go To dialog box and moves the worksheet window accordingly. You also can press CTRL+G to display the Go To dialog box.
HOME	Selects the cell at the beginning of the row that contains the active cell and moves the worksheet window accordingly.
Name box	Selects the cell in the workbook that corresponds to the cell reference you enter in the Name box.
PAGE DOWN	Selects the cell down one worksheet window from the active cell and moves the worksheet window accordingly.
PAGE UP	Selects the cell up one worksheet window from the active cell and moves the worksheet window accordingly.

Break Point: If you wish to take a break, this is a good place to do so. Be sure to save the Save Sable River Foundation file again and then you can quit Excel. To resume at a later time, start Excel, open the file called Save Sable River Foundation, and continue following the steps from this location forward.

Adding a Clustered Cylinder Chart to the Worksheet

As outlined in the requirements document in Figure 1–2 on page EX 4, the worksheet should include a Clustered Cylinder chart to graphically represent the lifetime fundraising for each fundraising activity in which the organization engages. The Clustered Cylinder chart shown in Figure 1–53 is called an **embedded chart** because it is drawn on the same worksheet as the data.

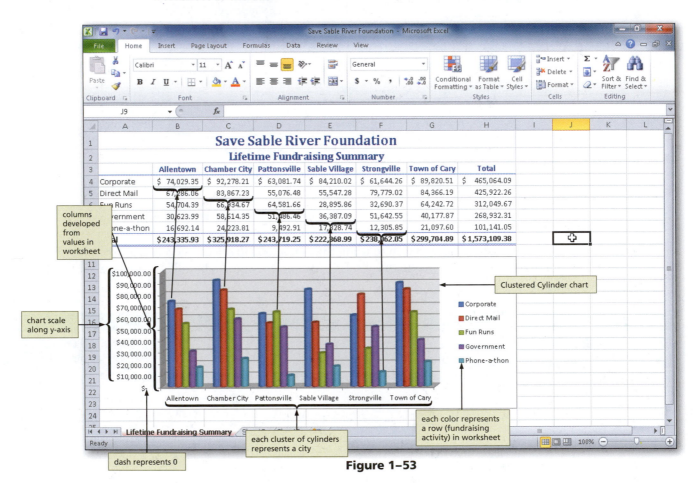

Figure 1–53

Plan Ahead

Decide on the type of chart needed.

Excel includes 11 chart types from which you can choose, including column, line, pie, bar, area, X Y (scatter), stock, surface, doughnut, bubble, and radar. The type of chart you choose depends on the type of data that you have, how much data you have, and the message you want to convey.

A line chart often is used to illustrate changes in data over time. Pie charts show the contribution of each piece of data to the whole, or total, of the data. Area charts, like line charts, illustrate changes over time, but often are used to compare more than one set of data and the area under the lines is filled in with a different color for each set of data. An X Y (scatter) chart is used much line a line chart, but each piece of data is represented by a dot and is not connected with a line. A stock chart provides a number of methods commonly

(continued)

(continued)

used in the financial industry to show stock market data. A surface chart compares data from three columns and/or rows in a three-dimensional manner. A doughnut chart is much like a pie chart, but a doughnut chart allows for comparing more than one set of data, resulting in a chart that looks like a doughnut, with each subsquent set of data surrounding the previous set. A bubble chart is much like an X Y (scatter) chart, but a third set of data results indicates how large each individual dot, or bubble, is on the chart. A radar chart can compare several sets of data in a manner that resembles a radar screen, with each set of data represented by a different color. A column or cylinder chart is a good way to compare values side by side. A Clustered Cylinder chart can go even further in comparing values across categories.

Establish where to position and how to format the chart.

- When possible, try to position charts so that both the data and chart appear on the screen on the worksheet together and so that the data and chart can be printed in the most readable manner possible.

- When choosing/selecting colors for a chart, consider the color scheme of the rest of the worksheet. The chart should not present colors that are in stark contrast to the rest of the worksheet. If the chart will be printed in color, minimize the amount of dark colors on the chart so that the chart both prints quickly and conserves ink.

In the case of the Save Sable River Foundation Lifetime Fundraising Summary, comparisons of fundraising activities within each city can be made side by side with a Clustered Cylinder chart. The chart uses differently colored cylinders to represent amounts raised for different fundraising activities. Each city uses the same color scheme for identifying fundraising activities, which allows for easy identification and comparison.

- For the city of Allentown, for example, the dark blue cylinder representing Corporate donations shows lifetime donations of $74,029.35

- For Chamber City, the maroon cylinder representing Direct Mail donations shows lifetime donations of $83,867.23

- For the city of Pattonsville, the lime green cylinder representing donations for Fun Runs shows lifetime donations of $64,581.66

- For Sable Village, the purple cylinder representing Government donations shows lifetime donations of $36,387.09

- For the city of Strongville, the light blue cylinder representing Phone-a-thon donations shows lifetime donations of $12,305.85

Because the same color scheme is used in each city to represent the five fundraising activities, you easily can compare funds raised by each fundraising activity among the cities. The totals from the worksheet are not represented, because the totals are not in the range specified for charting.

Excel derives the chart scale based on the values in the worksheet and then displays the scale along the vertical axis (also called the **y-axis** or **value axis**) of the chart. For example, no value in the range B4:G8 is less than 0 or greater than $100,000.00, so the scale ranges from 0 to $100,000.00. Excel also determines the $10,000.00 increments of the scale automatically. For the numbers along the y-axis, Excel uses a format that includes representing the 0 value with a dash (Figure 1–53).

Plan Ahead

BTW

Cell Values and Charting
When you change a cell value on which a chart is dependent, Excel redraws the chart instantaneously, unless automatic recalculation is disabled. If automatic recalculation is disabled, then you must press the F9 key to redraw the chart. To enable or disable automatic recalculation, click the Calculations Options button (Formulas tab | Calculation group).

BTW

Using Dual Axes on a Chart
Figure 1–53 shows a chart with a y-axis along the left side of the chart. If you have additional data to chart for each city, you can overlay a second chart with a different y-axis on top of the first chart. The second y-axis is displayed on the right side of the chart. In this case, the chart is said to have dual axes. Additionally, a different type of chart usually is laid over the first chart. For example, if a second y-axis were added to the chart shown in Figure 1–53, a good choice for the second chart would be a line chart. To add a second y-axis to a chart, click the data series to plot on the new axis, click Format Selection (Chart Tools Format tab | Current Selection group), click the Secondary Axis option button (Format Data Series dialog box), and then click the Close button.

To Add a Clustered Cylinder Chart to the Worksheet

The area on the worksheet where the chart appears is called the chart location. As shown in Figure 1–53 on page EX 36, the chart location in this worksheet is the range A11:G23; this range is immediately below the worksheet data. Placing the chart below the data on the Save Sable River Foundation Lifetime Fundraising Summary worksheet makes it easier to read the chart along with the data, and the chart and data easily can be printed on one sheet of paper.

The following steps draw a Clustered Cylinder chart that compares the funds raised by fundraising activity for the six cities.

1

• Click cell A3 and then drag the mouse pointer to cell G8 to select the range to be charted (Figure 1–54).

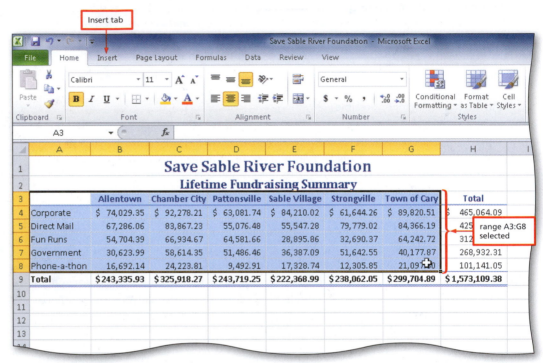

Figure 1–54

2

• Click Insert on the Ribbon to display the Insert tab (Figure 1–55).

Q&A

What tasks can I perform with the Insert tab?

The Insert tab includes commands that allow you to insert various objects, such as shapes, tables, illustrations, and charts, into a worksheet. These objects will be discussed as they are used throughout this book.

Figure 1–55

3
- Click the Column button (Insert tab | Charts group) to display the Column gallery (Figure 1–56).

Figure 1–56

4
- Click the Clustered Cylinder chart type in the Cylinder area of the Column gallery to add the selected chart type to the middle of the worksheet in a selection rectangle.

- Press and hold down the mouse button while pointing to the upper-right edge of the selection rectangle to change the mouse pointer to a double two-headed arrow (Figure 1–57).

Q&A

Why is a new tab displayed on the Ribbon?

When you select objects such as shapes or charts, Excel displays contextual tabs that include special commands that are used to work

Figure 1–57

with the type of object selected. Because a chart is selected, Excel displays the Chart Tools contextual tab. The three tabs below the Chart Tools contextual tab, Design, Layout, and Format, are tabs that include commands to work with charts.

5

- Drag the chart down and to the left to position the upper-left corner of the dotted line rectangle over the upper-left corner of cell A11.

- Press and hold down the mouse button while pointing to the middle sizing handle on the right edge of the chart (Figure 1–58).

Q&A

How does Excel know which data to use to create the chart?

Excel automatically selects the entries in the topmost row of the chart range (row 3) as the titles for the horizontal axis (also called the **x-axis** or **category axis**) and draws a column for each of the 30 cells in the range containing numbers.

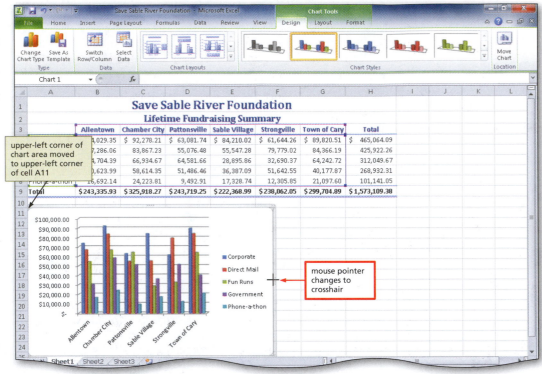

Figure 1–58

6

- While continuing to hold down the mouse button, press the ALT key and drag the right edge of the chart to the right edge of column H and then release the mouse button to resize the chart.

- Press and hold down the mouse button while pointing to the middle sizing handle on the bottom edge of the selection rectangle and do not release the mouse button (Figure 1–59).

Q&A

Why should I hold the ALT key down while I resize a chart?

Holding down the ALT key while you drag a chart **snaps** (aligns) the edge of the chart area to the worksheet gridlines. If you do not hold down the ALT key, then you can place an edge of a chart in the middle of a column or row.

Figure 1–59

❼
- While continuing to hold down the mouse button, press the ALT key and drag the bottom edge of the chart up to the bottom edge of row 23 and then release the mouse button to resize the chart.

- If necessary, scroll the worksheet so that row 1 displays at the top of the worksheet.

- Click the More button in the Chart Styles gallery (Chart Tools Design tab | Chart Styles group) to expand the gallery (Figure 1–60).

Figure 1–60

❽
- Click Style 34 in the Chart Styles gallery (column 2, row 5) to apply the chart style to the chart.

- Click cell J9 to deselect the chart and complete the worksheet (Figure 1–61).

Q&A

What is the purpose of the items on the right side of the chart?

The items to the right of the column chart in Figure 1–61 are the **legend**, which identifies the colors assigned to each bar in the chart. Excel automatically selects the entries in the leftmost column of the chart range (column A) as titles within the legend.

Figure 1–61

Changing the Worksheet Names

The sheet tabs at the bottom of the window allow you to view any worksheet in the workbook. You click the sheet tab of the worksheet you want to view in the Excel window. By default, Excel presets the names of the worksheets to Sheet1, Sheet2, and so on. The worksheet names become increasingly important as you move toward more sophisticated workbooks, especially workbooks in which you reference cells between worksheets.

Plan Ahead

> **Choose a name for the worksheet.**
> Use simple, meaningful names for each worksheet. Worksheet names often match the worksheet title. If a worksheet includes multiple titles in multiple sections of the worksheet, use a name that encompasses the meaning of all of the sections.

To Change the Worksheet Names

Lifetime Fundraising Summary is a meaningful name for the Save Sable River Foundation Lifetime Fundraising Summary worksheet. The following steps rename worksheets by double-clicking the sheet tabs.

1
- Double-click the sheet tab labeled Sheet1 in the lower-left corner of the window.

- Type **Lifetime Fundraising Summary** as the worksheet name and then press the ENTER key to display the new worksheet name on the sheet tab (Figure 1–62).

Q&A
What is the maximum length for a worksheet tab?

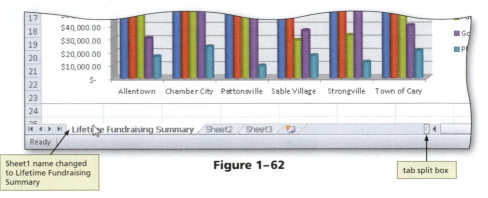

Figure 1–62

Worksheet names can be up to 31 characters (including spaces) in length. Longer worksheet names, however, mean that fewer sheet tabs will show. To view more sheet tabs, you can drag the tab split box (Figure 1–62) to the right. This will reduce the size of the scroll bar at the bottom of the screen. Double-click the tab split box to reset it to its normal position.

2
- Right-click the sheet tab labeled Lifetime Fundraising Summary in the lower-left corner of the window to display a shortcut menu.

- Point to Tab Color on the shortcut menu to display the color gallery (Figure 1–63).

Q&A
How can I quickly move between worksheet tabs?

You can use the tab scrolling buttons to the left of the sheet tabs (Figure 1–63) to move between worksheets. The leftmost and rightmost scroll buttons move to the first or last worksheet in the workbook. The two middle scroll buttons move one worksheet to the left or right.

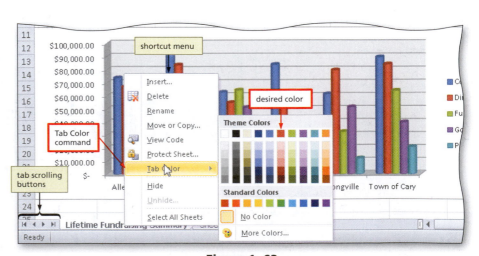

Figure 1–63

3
- Click Red, Accent 2 (column 6, row 1) in the Theme Colors area to change the color of the tab (Figure 1–64).

4
- If necessary, click Home on the Ribbon to display the Home tab.

Figure 1–64

Changing Document Properties

Excel helps you organize and identify your files by using **document properties**, which are the details about a file. Document properties, also known as **metadata**, can include information such as the project author, title, subject, and keywords. A **keyword** is a word or phrase that further describes the document. For example, a class name or document topic can describe the file's purpose or content.

Document properties are valuable for a variety of reasons:

- Users can save time locating a particular file because they can view a document's properties without opening the document.

- By creating consistent properties for files having similar content, users can better organize their documents.

- Some organizations require Excel users to add document properties so that other employees can view details about these files.

Five different types of document properties exist, but the more common ones used in this book are standard and automatically updated properties. **Standard properties** are associated with all Microsoft Office documents and include author, title, and subject. **Automatically updated properties** include file system properties, such as the date you create or change a file, and statistics, such as the file size.

To Change Document Properties

The **Document Information Panel** contains areas where you can view and enter document properties. You can view and change information in this panel at any time while you are creating a workbook. Before saving the workbook again, you want to add your name and course information as document properties. The following steps use the Document Information Panel to change document properties.

1
- Click File on the Ribbon to open the Backstage view. If necessary, click the Info tab in the Backstage view to display the Info gallery (Figure 1–65).

Q&A
How do I close the Backstage view?

Click File on the Ribbon or click the preview of the document in the Info gallery to return to the Excel document window.

Figure 1–65

2
- Click the Properties button in the right pane of the Info gallery to display the Properties menu (Figure 1–66).

Figure 1–66

3
- Click Show Document Panel on the Properties menu to close the Backstage view and display the Document Information Panel in the Excel workbook window (Figure 1–67).

Q&A Why are some of the document properties in my Document Information Panel already filled in?

The person who installed Microsoft Office 2010 on your computer or network may have set or customized the properties.

Figure 1–67

4
- Click the Author text box, if necessary, and then type your name as the Author property. If a name already is displayed in the Author text box, delete it before typing your name.

- Click the Subject text box, if necessary delete any existing text, and then type your course and section as the Subject property.

- If an AutoComplete dialog box appears, click its Yes button.

- Click the Keywords text box, if necessary delete any existing text, and then type `Lifetime Fundraising Summary` as the Keywords property (Figure 1–68).

Figure 1–68

Q&A What types of document properties does Excel collect automatically?

Excel records details such as time spent editing a workbook, the number of times a workbook has been revised, and the fonts and themes used in a workbook.

5
- Click the Close the Document Information Panel button so that the Document Information Panel no longer is displayed. If a dialog box is displayed, click the No button to close it.

Other Ways

1. Click File on Ribbon, click Info in the Backstage view, if necessary click Show All Properties link in Info gallery, click property to change and type new information, close the Backstage view

To Save an Existing Workbook with the Same File Name

You have made several modifications to the workbook since you last saved it. Thus, you should save it again. The following step saves the workbook again. For an example of the step listed below, refer to the Introduction to Office 2010 and Windows 7 chapter at the beginning of this book.

 Click the Save button on the Quick Access Toolbar to overwrite the previously saved file.

Previewing and Printing a Worksheet

After creating a worksheet, you may want to print it. Printing a worksheet enables you to distribute the worksheet to others in a form that can be read or viewed but typically not edited. It is a good practice to save a workbook before printing a worksheet, in the event you experience difficulties printing.

Determine the best method for distributing the worksheet.
The traditional method of distributing a worksheet uses a printer to produce a hard copy. A **hardcopy or printout** is information that exists on a physical medium such as paper. For users that can receive fax documents, you can elect to print a hard copy on a remote fax machine. Hard copies can be useful for the following reasons:

- Many people prefer proofreading a hard copy of a worksheet rather than viewing it on the screen to check for errors and readability.

- Hard copies can serve as reference material if your storage medium is lost or becomes corrupted and you need to re-create the worksheet.

Instead of distributing a hard copy of a worksheet, users can choose to distribute the worksheet as an electronic image that mirrors the original worksheet's appearance. The electronic image of the worksheet can be e-mailed, posted on a Web site, or copied to a portable storage medium such as a USB flash drive. Two popular electronic image formats, sometimes called fixed formats, are PDF by Adobe Systems and XPS by Microsoft. In Excel, you can create electronic image files through the Print tab in the Backstage view, the Save & Send tab in the Backstage view, and the Save As dialog box. Electronic images of worksheets, such as PDF and XPS, can be useful for the following reasons:

- Users can view electronic images of worksheets without the software that created the original worksheet (e.g., Excel). Specifically, to view a PDF file, you use a program called Acrobat Reader, which can be downloaded free from Adobe's Web site. Similarly, to view an XPS file, you use a program called an XPS Viewer, which is included in the latest versions of Windows and Internet Explorer.

- Sending electronic documents saves paper and printer supplies. Society encourages users to contribute to **green computing**, which involves reducing the environmental waste generated when using a computer.

To Preview and Print a Worksheet in Landscape Orientation

With the completed workbook saved, you may want to print it. Because the worksheet is included in a report, you will print a hard copy on a printer. The following steps print a hard copy of the contents of the Save Sable River Foundation Lifetime Fundraising Summary worksheet.

1

● Click File on the Ribbon to open the Backstage view.

● Click the Print tab in the Backstage view to display the Print gallery (Figure 1–69).

Q&A How can I print multiple copies of my worksheet?

Increase the number in the Copies box in the Print gallery.

Q&A What if I decide not to print the worksheet at this time?

Click File on the Ribbon to close the Backstage view and return to the Excel workbook window.

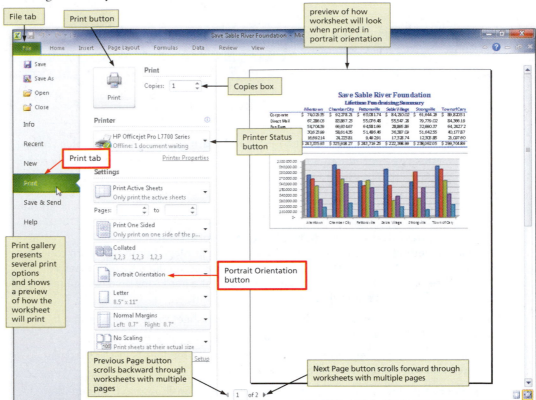

Figure 1–69

2

● Verify the printer name that appears on the Printer Status button will print a hard copy of the document. If necessary, click the Printer Status button to display a list of available printer options and then click the desired printer to change the currently selected printer.

3

● Click the Portrait Orientation button in the Settings area and then select Landscape Orientation to change the orientation of the page to landscape and view the entire worksheet on one page (Figure 1–70).

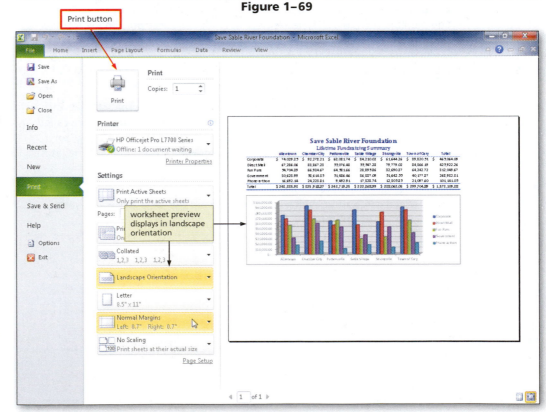

Figure 1–70

4

- Click the Print button in the Print gallery to print the worksheet in landscape orientation on the currently selected printer.

- When the printer stops, retrieve the hard copy (Figure 1–71).

Q&A Do I have to wait until my worksheet is complete to print it?

No, you can follow these steps to print a document at any time while you are creating it.

Q&A What if I want to print an electronic image of a worksheet instead of a hard copy?

You would click the Printer Status button in the Print gallery and then select the desired electronic image option such as a Microsoft XPS Document Writer, which would create an XPS file.

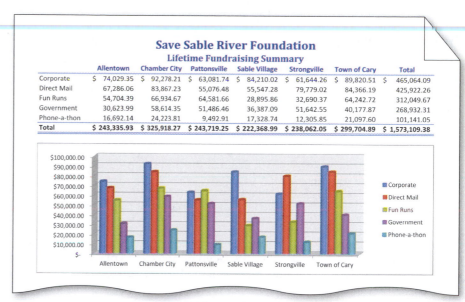

Figure 1–71

To Quit Excel

This Save Sable River Foundation workbook now is complete. The following steps quit Excel if only one workbook is open. For a detailed example of the procedure summarized below, refer to the Office 2010 and Windows 7 chapter at the beginning of this book.

1 If you have one Excel workbook open, click the Close button on the right side of the title bar to close the document and quit Excel; or if you have multiple Excel workbooks open, click File on the Ribbon to open the Backstage view and then click the Exit button to close all open workbooks and quit Excel.

2 If a Microsoft Office Excel dialog box appears, click the Save button to save any changes made to the workbook since the last save.

Starting Excel and Opening a Workbook

Once you have created and saved a workbook, you may need to retrieve it from your storage medium. For example, you might want to revise a worksheet or reprint it. Opening a workbook requires that Excel is running on your computer.

To Start Excel

1 Click the Start button on the Windows 7 taskbar to display the Start menu.

2 Type `Microsoft Excel` as the search text in the 'Search programs and files' text box and watch the search results appear on the Start menu.

3 Click Microsoft Excel 2010 in the search results on the Start menu to start Excel and display a new blank workbook in the Excel window.

4 If the Excel window is not maximized, click the Maximize button next to the Close button on its title bar to maximize the window.

BTW

Managing Versions
Excel automatically saves your work, even when you have not saved a file. If you inadvertently close a file without saving it, you can recover your work by clicking Info in the Backstage view and then clicking the Manage Versions button. On the Manage Versions list, click Recover Unsaved Workbooks to display the Open dialog box. Select the file you want to recover and then click the Open button (Open dialog box) to display the file. You also can click the file to recover in the Versions list next to the Manage Versions button. To delete recent copies of unsaved files, click Delete All Unsaved Workbooks on the Manage Versions list.

To Open a Workbook from Excel

Earlier in this chapter you saved your project on a USB flash drive using the file name, Save Sable River Foundation. The following steps open the Save Sable River Foundation file from the Excel folder in the CIS 101 folder on the USB flash drive. For a detailed example of the procedure summarized below, refer to page OFF 57 in the Office 2010 and Windows 7 chapter at the beginning of this book.

1 With your USB flash drive connected to one of the computer's USB ports, click File on the Ribbon to open the Backstage view.

2 Click Open in the Backstage view to display the Open dialog box.

3 Navigate to the location of the file to be opened (in this case, the USB flash drive, then to the CIS 101 folder [or your class folder], and then to the Excel folder).

4 Click Save Sable River Foundation to select the file to be opened.

5 Click the Open button (Open dialog box) to open the selected file and display the opened workbook in the Excel window.

AutoCalculate

You easily can obtain a total, an average, or other information about the numbers in a range by using the **AutoCalculate area** on the status bar. First, select the range of cells containing the numbers you want to check. Next, right-click the AutoCalculate area to display the Status Bar Configuration shortcut menu (Figure 1–72). The check mark to the left of the active functions (Average, Count, and Sum) indicates that the sum, count, and average of the selected range are displayed in the AutoCalculate area on the status bar. The functions of the AutoCalculate commands on the Status Bar Configuration shortcut menu are described in Table 1–4.

BTW

AutoCalculate
Use the AutoCalculate area on the status bar to check your work as you enter data in a worksheet. If you enter large amounts of data, you select a range of data and then check the AutoCalculate area to provide insight into statistics about the data you entered. Often, you will have an intuitive feel for whether the numbers are accurate or if you may have made a mistake while entering the data.

Table 1–4 AutoCalculate Shortcut Menu Commands	
Command	**Function**
Average	AutoCalculate area displays the average of the numbers in the selected range
Count	AutoCalculate area displays the number of nonblank cells in the selected range
Numerical Count	AutoCalculate area displays the number of cells containing numbers in the selected range
Minimum	AutoCalculate area displays the lowest value in the selected range
Maximum	AutoCalculate area displays the highest value in the selected range
Sum	AutoCalculate area displays the sum of the numbers in the selected range

To Use the AutoCalculate Area to Determine a Maximum

The following steps display the largest amounts of funds raised for any city for the Fun Runs fundraising activity.

1
- Select the range B6:G6 and then right-click the AutoCalculate area on the status bar to display the Customize Status Bar shortcut menu (Figure 1–72).

What is displayed on the Customize Status Bar shortcut menu?

This shortcut menu includes several commands that allow you to control the items displayed on the Customize Status Bar shortcut menu. The AutoCalculate area includes six commands as well as the result of the associated calculation on the right side of the menu.

Figure 1–72

2
- Click Maximum on the shortcut menu to display the Maximum value in the range B6:G6 in the AutoCalculate area of the status bar.

Figure 1–73

- Click anywhere on the worksheet to cause the shortcut menu to disappear (Figure 1–73).

3
- Right-click the AutoCalculate area and then click Maximum on the shortcut menu to cause the Maximum value to no longer appear in the AutoCalculate area.

- Click anywhere on the worksheet to cause the shortcut menu to disappear.

Correcting Errors

You can correct errors on a worksheet using one of several methods. The method you choose will depend on the extent of the error and whether you notice it while typing the data or after you have entered the incorrect data into the cell.

Correcting Errors While You Are Typing Data into a Cell

If you notice an error while you are typing data into a cell, press the BACKSPACE key to erase the incorrect characters and then type the correct characters. If the error is a major one, click the Cancel box in the formula bar or press the ESC key to erase the entire entry and then reenter the data from the beginning.

BTW

Quick Reference
For a table that lists how to complete the tasks covered in this book using the mouse, Ribbon, shortcut menu, and keyboard, see the Quick Reference Summary at the back of this book, or visit the Excel 2010 Quick Reference Web page (scsite.com/ex2010/qr).

BTW

In-Cell Editing
An alternative to double-clicking the cell to edit it is to select the cell and then press the F2 key.

Correcting Errors After Entering Data into a Cell

If you find an error in the worksheet after entering the data, you can correct the error in one of two ways:

1. If the entry is short, select the cell, retype the entry correctly, and then click the Enter box or press the ENTER key. The new entry will replace the old entry.

2. If the entry in the cell is long and the errors are minor, using Edit mode may be a better choice than retyping the cell entry. Use the Edit mode as described below.

   a. Double-click the cell containing the error to switch Excel to Edit mode. In **Edit mode**, Excel displays the active cell entry in the formula bar and a flashing insertion point in the active cell (Figure 1–74). With Excel in Edit mode, you can edit the contents directly in the cell — a procedure called **in-cell editing**.

   b. Make changes using in-cell editing, as indicated below.

      (1) To insert new characters between two characters, place the insertion point between the two characters and begin typing. Excel inserts the new characters at the location of the insertion point.

      (2) To delete a character in the cell, move the insertion point to the left of the character you want to delete and then press the DELETE key or place the insertion point to the right of the character you want to delete and then press the BACKSPACE key. You also can use the mouse to drag through the character or adjacent characters you want to delete and then press the DELETE key or click the Cut button (Home tab | Clipboard group).

      (3) When you are finished editing an entry, click the Enter box or press the ENTER key.

Figure 1–74

BTW

Editing the Contents of a Cell
Rather than using in-cell editing, you can select the cell and then click the formula bar to edit the contents.

When Excel enters the Edit mode, the keyboard usually is in Insert mode. In **Insert mode**, as you type a character, Excel inserts the character and moves all characters to the right of the typed character one position to the right. You can change to Overtype mode by pressing the INSERT key. In **Overtype mode**, Excel overtypes, or replaces, the character to the right of the insertion point. The INSERT key toggles the keyboard between Insert mode and Overtype mode.

While in Edit mode, you may have reason to move the insertion point to various points in the cell, select portions of the data in the cell, or switch from inserting characters to overtyping characters. Table 1–5 summarizes the more common tasks performed during in-cell editing.

Table 1–5 Summary of In-Cell Editing Tasks

	Task	Mouse	Keyboard
1	Move the insertion point to the beginning of data in a cell.	Point to the left of the first character and click.	Press HOME
2	Move the insertion point to the end of data in a cell.	Point to the right of the last character and click.	Press END
3	Move the insertion point anywhere in a cell.	Point to the appropriate position and click the character.	Press RIGHT ARROW or LEFT ARROW
4	Highlight one or more adjacent characters.	Drag the mouse pointer through adjacent characters.	Press SHIFT+RIGHT ARROW or SHIFT+LEFT ARROW
5	Select all data in a cell.	Double-click the cell with the insertion point in the cell if there are no spaces in the data in the cell.	
6	Delete selected characters.	Click the Cut button (Home tab | Clipboard group)	Press DELETE
7	Delete characters to the left of the insertion point.		Press BACKSPACE
8	Delete characters to the right of the insertion point.		Press DELETE
9	Toggle between Insert and Overtype modes.		Press INSERT

BTW

Excel Help
At any time while using Excel, you can find answers to questions and display information about various topics through Excel Help. Used properly, this form of assistance can increase your productivity and reduce your frustrations by minimizing the time you spend learning how to use Excel. For instruction about Excel Help and exercises that will help you gain confidence in using it, read the Office 2010 and Windows 7 chapter at the beginning of this book.

Undoing the Last Cell Entry

Excel provides the Undo command on the Quick Access Toolbar (Figure 1–75), which allows you to erase recent cell entries. Thus, if you enter incorrect data in a cell and notice it immediately, click the Undo button and Excel changes the cell entry to what it was prior to the incorrect data entry.

Figure 1–75

Excel remembers the last 100 actions you have completed. Thus, you can undo up to 100 previous actions by clicking the Undo button arrow to display the Undo list and then clicking the action to be undone (Figure 1–75). You can drag through several actions in the Undo list to undo all of them at once. If no actions are available for Excel to undo, then the Undo button is dimmed and inoperative.

The Redo button, next to the Undo button on the Quick Access Toolbar, allows you to repeat previous actions.

Clearing a Cell or Range of Cells

If you enter data into the wrong cell or range of cells, you can erase, or clear, the data using one of the first four methods listed below. The fifth method clears the formatting from the selected cells.

TO CLEAR CELL ENTRIES USING THE FILL HANDLE

1. Select the cell or range of cells and then point to the fill handle so the mouse pointer changes to a crosshair.
2. Drag the fill handle back into the selected cell or range until a shadow covers the cell or cells you want to erase. Release the mouse button.

TO CLEAR CELL ENTRIES USING THE SHORTCUT MENU

1. Select the cell or range of cells to be cleared.
2. Right-click the selection.
3. Click Clear Contents on the shortcut menu.

TO CLEAR CELL ENTRIES USING THE DELETE KEY

1. Select the cell or range of cells to be cleared.
2. Press the DELETE key.

TO CLEAR CELL ENTRIES AND FORMATTING USING THE CLEAR BUTTON

1. Select the cell or range of cells to be cleared.
2. Click the Clear button (Home tab | Editing group) (Figure 1–75 on the previous page).
3. Click Clear Contents on the menu.

TO CLEAR FORMATTING USING THE CELL STYLES BUTTON

1. Select the cell or range of cells from which you want to remove the formatting.
2. Click the Cell Styles button (Home tab | Styles group) and point to Normal.
3. Click Normal in the Cell Styles Gallery.

The Clear button (Home tab | Editing group) is the only command that clears both the cell entry and the cell formatting. As you are clearing cell entries, always remember that you should *never press the* SPACEBAR *to clear a cell*. Pressing the SPACEBAR enters a blank character. A blank character is text and is different from an empty cell, even though the cell may appear empty.

Clearing the Entire Worksheet

If the required worksheet edits are extremely extensive, you may want to clear the entire worksheet and start over. To clear the worksheet or delete an embedded chart, you would use the following steps.

TO CLEAR THE ENTIRE WORKSHEET

1. Click the Select All button on the worksheet (Figure 1–75).
2. Click the Clear button (Home tab | Editing group) and then click Clear All on the Clear menu to delete both the entries and formats.

The Select All button selects the entire worksheet. Instead of clicking the Select All button, you can press CTRL+A. To clear an unsaved workbook, click the workbook's Close Window button or click the Close button in the Backstage view. Click the No button if the Microsoft Excel dialog box asks if you want to save changes. To start a new, blank workbook, click the New button in the Backstage view.

BTW

Getting Back to Normal
If you accidentally assign unwanted formats to a range of cells, you can use the Normal cell style selection in the Cell Styles gallery. Click Cell Styles (Home tab | Styles group) and then click Normal in the Cell Styles gallery. Doing so changes the format to Normal style. To view the characteristics of the Normal style, right-click the style in the Cell Styles gallery and then click Modify or press ALT+APOSTROPHE (').

BTW

Certification
The Microsoft Office Specialist (MOS) program provides an opportunity for you to obtain a valuable industry credential — proof that you have the Excel 2010 skills required by employers. For more information, visit the Excel 2010 Certification Web page (scsite.com/ex2010/cert).

To delete an embedded chart, you would complete the following steps.

BTW

Quitting Excel
Do not forget to remove your USB flash drive from the USB port after quitting Excel, especially if you are working in a laboratory environment. Nothing can be more frustrating than leaving all of your hard work behind on a USB flash drive for the next user.

TO DELETE AN EMBEDDED CHART

1. Click the chart to select it.
2. Press the DELETE key.

To Quit Excel

The project now is complete. The following steps quit Excel. For a detailed example of the procedure summarized below, refer to the Office 2010 and Windows 7 chapter at the beginning of this book.

1 If you have one Excel workbook open, click the Close button on the right side of the title bar to close the document and quit Excel; or if you have multiple Excel workbooks open, click File on the Ribbon to open the Backstage view and then click Exit in the Backstage view to close all open workbooks and quit Excel.

2 If a Microsoft Office Excel dialog box appears, click the Save button to save any changes made to the document since the last save.

Chapter Summary

In this chapter you have learned how to enter text and numbers to create a worksheet, how to select a range, how to use the Sum button, format cells, insert a chart, and preview and print a worksheet. The items listed below include all the new Excel skills you have learned in this chapter.

1. To Start Excel (EX 6)
2. Enter the Worksheet Titles (EX 8)
3. Enter Column Titles (EX 10)
4. Enter Row Titles (EX 12)
5. Enter Numbers (EX 13)
6. Sum a Column of Numbers (EX 15)
7. Copy a Cell to Adjacent Cells in a Row (EX 17)
8. Determine Multiple Totals at the Same Time (EX 18)
9. Save a Workbook (EX 20)
10. Change a Cell Style (EX 22)
11. Change the Font (EX 24)
12. Bold a Cell (EX 25)
13. Increase the Font Size of a Cell Entry (EX 26)
14. Change the Font Color of a Cell Entry (EX 27)
15. Center Cell Entries Across Columns by Merging Cells (EX 28)
16. Format Column Titles and the Total Row (EX 29)
17. Format Numbers in the Worksheet (EX 31)
18. Adjust the Column Width (EX 33)
19. Use the Name Box to Select a Cell (EX 34)
20. Add a Clustered Cylinder Chart to the Worksheet (EX 38)

21. Change the Worksheet Names (EX 42)
22. Change Document Properties (EX 43)
23. Save an Existing Workbook with the Same File Name (EX 45)
24. Preview and Print a Worksheet in Landscape Orientation (EX 46)
25. Quit Excel (EX 47)
26 Start Excel (EX 47)
27. Open a Workbook from Excel (EX 48)
28. Use the AutoCalculate Area to Determine a Maximum (EX 49)
29. Clear Cell Entries Using the Fill Handle (EX 52)
30. Clear Cell Entries Using the Shortcut Menu (EX 52)
31. Clear Cell Entries Using the DELETE Key (EX 52)
32. Clear Cell Entries and Formatting Using the Clear Button (EX 52)
33. Clear Formatting Using the Cell Styles Button (EX 52)
34. Clear the Entire Worksheet (EX 52)
35. Delete an Embedded Chart (EX 53)

If you have a SAM 2010 user profile, your instructor may have assigned an autogradable version of this assignment. If so, log into the SAM 2010 Web site at www.cengage.com/sam2010 to download the instruction and start files.

Learn It Online

Test your knowledge of chapter content and key terms.

Instructions: To complete the Learn It Online exercises, start your browser, click the Address bar, and then enter the Web address **scsite.com/ex2010/learn**. When the Excel 2010 Learn It Online page is displayed, click the link for the exercise you want to complete and then read the instructions.

Chapter Reinforcement TF, MC, and SA
A series of true/false, multiple choice, and short answer questions that test your knowledge of the chapter content.

Flash Cards
An interactive learning environment where you identify chapter key terms associated with displayed definitions.

Practice Test
A series of multiple choice questions that test your knowledge of chapter content and key terms.

Who Wants To Be a Computer Genius?
An interactive game that challenges your knowledge of chapter content in the style of a television quiz show.

Wheel of Terms
An interactive game that challenges your knowledge of chapter key terms in the style of the television show *Wheel of Fortune*.

Crossword Puzzle Challenge
A crossword puzzle that challenges your knowledge of key terms presented in the chapter.

Apply Your Knowledge

Reinforce the skills and apply the concepts you learned in this chapter.

Changing the Values in a Worksheet

Instructions: Start Excel. Open the workbook Apply 1–1 Clothes Campus Third Quarter Expenses (Figure 1–76a). See the inside back cover of this book for instructions for downloading the Data Files for Students, or see your instructor for information on accessing the files required in this book.

1. Make the changes to the worksheet described in Table 1–6 so that the worksheet appears as shown in Figure 1–76b. As you edit the values in the cells containing numeric data, watch the totals in row 7, the totals in column F, and the chart change.

2. Change the worksheet title in cell A1 to the Title cell style and then merge and center it across columns A through F. Use buttons in the Font group on the Home tab on the Ribbon to change the worksheet subtitle in cell A2 to 16-point Cambria red, bold font and then center it across columns A through F. Use the Red, Accent 2 theme color (column 6, row 1 on the Font gallery) for the red font color.

3. Apply the worksheet name, Third Quarter Expenses, to the sheet tab and apply the Red, Accent 2 theme color to the sheet tab.

4. Change the document properties as specified by your instructor. Save the workbook using the file name, Apply 1–1 Clothed for Campus Third Quarter Expenses. Submit the revised workbook as specified by your instructor.

Table 1–6 New Worksheet Data	
Cell	**Change Cell Contents To**
A1	Clothed for Campus
B4	7829.50
C4	19057.83
D5	24217.92
E5	25859.62
E6	35140.84

(a) Before

(b) After

Figure 1–76

Extend Your Knowledge

Extend the skills you learned in this chapter and experiment with new skills. You may need to use Help to complete the assignment.

Formatting a Worksheet and Adding Additional Charts

Instructions: Start Excel. Open the workbook Extend 1–1 Pack Right Moving Supplies. See the inside back cover of this book for instructions for downloading the Data Files for Students, or see your instructor for information on accessing the files required in this book. Perform the following tasks to format cells in the worksheet and to add two charts to the worksheet.

1. Use the commands in the Font group on the Home tab on the Ribbon to change the font of the title in cell A1 to 22-point Arial Black, green, bold, and the subtitle of the worksheet to 14-point Arial, red, bold.

2. Select the range A3:G8, click the Insert tab on the Ribbon, and then click the Dialog Box Launcher in the Charts group on the Ribbon to open the Insert Chart dialog box. If necessary, drag the lower-right corner of the Insert Chart dialog box to expand it (Figure 1–77).

Figure 1–77

3. Insert a Stacked Area in 3-D chart by clicking the Stacked Area in 3-D chart in the gallery and then clicking the OK button. You may need to use the scroll box on the right side of the Insert Chart dialog box to view the Area charts in the gallery. Move the chart either below or to the right of the data in the worksheet. Click the Design tab and apply a chart style of your choice to the chart.

4. Deselect the chart and reselect the range A3:G8, and then follow Step 3 above to insert a Clustered Horizontal Cone chart in the worksheet. Move the chart either below or to the right of the data so that each chart does not overlap the Stacked Area in 3-D chart. Make sure to make the values on the horizontal axis readable by expanding the size of the chart. Choose a different chart style for this chart than the one you selected for the Stacked Area in 3-D chart.

5. Resize each chart so that each snaps to the worksheet gridlines. You may need to scroll the worksheet to resize and view the charts. Preview the worksheet.

6. Apply a worksheet name to the sheet tab and apply a color of your choice to the sheet tab.

7. Change the document properties as specified by your instructor. Save the workbook using the file name, Extend 1–1 Pack Right Moving Supplies Charts. Submit the revised workbook as specified by your instructor.

Make It Right

Analyze a workbook and correct all errors and/or improve the design.

Fixing Formatting Problems and Data Errors in a Worksheet

Instructions: Start Excel. Open the workbook Make It Right 1–1 Pets. See the inside back cover of this book for instructions for downloading the Data Files for Students, or see your instructor for information on accessing the files required for this book. Correct the following formatting problems and data errors (Figure 1–78) in the worksheet, while keeping in mind the guidelines presented in this chapter.

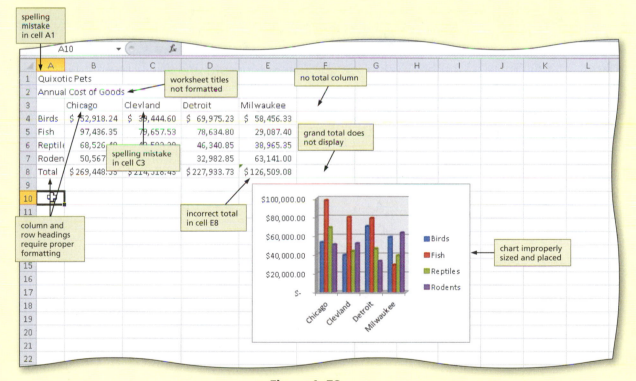

Figure 1–78

1. Merge and center the worksheet title and subtitle appropriately.

2. Format the worksheet title with a cell style appropriate for a worksheet title.

3. Format the subtitle using commands in the Font group on the Home tab on the Ribbon and apply the Red, Accent 2 color to the subtitle.

4. Correct the spelling mistake in cell A1 by changing Quixotic to Exotic. Correct the spelling mistake in cell C3 by changing Clevland to Cleveland.

Continued >

Make It Right *continued*

5. Add a column header for totals in column F and create the necessary totals in row 8.

6. Apply proper formatting to the column headers and total row, including centering the column headers.

7. Adjust the column sizes so that all data in each column is visible.

8. Create the grand total for the annual cost of goods.

9. The SUM function in cell E8 does not sum all of the numbers in the column. Correct this error by editing the range for the SUM function in the cell.

10. Resize and move the chart so that it is below the worksheet data and does not extend past the right edge of the worksheet data. Be certain to snap the chart to the worksheet gridlines by holding down the ALT key as you resize the chart to the right edge of column F and the bottom of row 22.

11. Apply a worksheet name to the sheet tab and apply the Aqua, Accent 5 color to the sheet tab.

12. Change the document properties as specified by your instructor. Save the workbook using the file name, Make It Right 1–1 Exotic Pets Annual Cost of Goods. Submit the revised workbook as specified by your instructor.

In the Lab

Design and/or create a workbook using the guidelines, concepts, and skills presented in this chapter. Labs 1, 2, and 3 are listed in order of increasing difficulty.

Lab 1: Annual Revenue Analysis Worksheet

Problem: You work as a spreadsheet specialist for A Healthy Body Shop, a high-end total fitness center franchise. Your manager has asked you to develop an annual revenue analysis worksheet similar to the one shown in Figure 1–79.

Figure 1–79

Instructions: Perform the following tasks.

1. Start Excel. Enter the worksheet title, A Healthy Body Shop, in cell A1 and the worksheet subtitle, Annual Revenue Analysis, in cell A2. Beginning in row 3, enter the franchise locations, fitness activities, and annual revenues shown in Table 1–7.

Table 1–7 A Healthy Body Shop Annual Revenues

	Atlanta	Boston	New York	Phoenix	Portland
Aquatics	72528.50	53461.85	88367.00	87288.00	65367.37
Cardiovascular	65371.00	92549.86	78345.85	91692.21	58936.63
Dance	53187.96	45493.24	72808.19	57019.34	70114.93
Weight Training	45910.25	85703.71	78719.20	88500.60	47105.30
Yoga & Stretching	58292.50	66884.85	74348.30	76219.00	57390.23

2. Create totals for each franchise location, fitness activity, and company grand total.

3. Format the worksheet title with the Title cell style. Center the title across columns A through G. Do not be concerned if the edges of the worksheet title are not displayed.

4. Format the worksheet subtitle to 14-point Constantia dark blue, bold font, and center it across columns A through G.

5. Use Cell Styles to format the range A3:G3 with the Heading 3 cell style, the range A4:G8 with the 40% - Accent 6 cell style, and the range A9:G9 with the Total cell style. Center the column headers in row 3. Apply the Accounting Number format to the range B4:G4 and the range B9:G9. Apply the Comma Style to the range B5:G8. Adjust any column widths to the widest text entry in each column.

6. Select the range A3:F8 and then insert a Clustered Cylinder chart. Apply the Style 26 chart style to the chart. Move and resize the chart so that it appears in the range A11:G24. If the labels along the horizontal axis (x-axis) do not appear as shown in Figure 1–79, then drag the right side of the chart so that it is displayed in the range A11:G24.

7. Apply the worksheet name, Annual Revenue Analysis, to the sheet tab and apply the Orange, Accent 6, Darker 25% color to the sheet tab. Change the document properties, as specified by your instructor.

8. Save the workbook using the file name Lab 1-1 A Healthy Body Shop Annual Revenue Analysis.

9. Preview and print the worksheet in landscape orientation.

10. Make the following two corrections to the sales amounts: 62,675.45 for New York Weight Training (cell D7), 67,238.56 for Portland Cardiovascular (cell F5). After you enter the corrections, the company totals in cell G8 should equal $1,723,864.05.

11. Preview and print the revised worksheet in landscape orientation. Close the workbook without saving the changes.

12. Submit the assignment as specified by your instructor.

In the Lab

Lab 2: Semiannual Sales Analysis Worksheet

Problem: As the chief accountant for Play 'em Again, a reseller of cell phones, DVDs, electronic games, MP3 players, and accessories, you have been asked by the vice president to create a worksheet to analyze the semiannual sales for the company by products across sales channels (Figure 1–80 on the following page). The sales channels and corresponding revenue by product for the year are shown in Table 1–8.

Continued >

In the Lab *continued*

Figure 1–80

Instructions: Perform the following tasks.

1. Create the worksheet shown in Figure 1–80 using the data in Table 1–8.

2. Use the SUM function to determine total revenue for the three sales channels, the totals for each product, and the company total. Add column and row headings for the totals row and totals column, as appropriate.

Table 1–8 Play 'em Again Semiannual Revenue

	Mail	Store	Web
Accessories	378512.09	20380.80	24257.51
Cell Phones	124118.00	366216.77	32333.20
CDs	47055.42	311570.23	427261.96
Controllers	409368.32	118871.41	36140.54
DSs	281443.97	472259.61	431317.79
DVDs	311004.73	109971.82	21209.46
Games	413265.32	112511.16	151722.44
iPods	149327.59	358232.57	37465.90
Other	254398.60	126224.85	298479.20
PlayStation 3s	253917.77	173103.58	293961.01
PSPs	469556.54	136579.71	163465.19
Wiis	495690.83	10169.70	130150.03
XBoxes	456773.97	169627.11	145925.85

3. Format the worksheet title with the Title cell style and center it across columns A through E. Use the Font group on the Ribbon to format the worksheet subtitle to 16-point Cambria red, bold font. Center the title across columns A through E.

4. Format the range B3:E3 with the Heading 3 cell style and center the text in the cells. Format the range A4:E16 with the 20% - Accent 4 cell style, and the range A17:E17 with the Total cell style. Format cells B4:E4 and B17:E17 with the Accounting Number Format and cells B5:E16 with the Comma Style numeric format.

5. Create a pie chart that shows the revenue contributions of each sales channel. Chart the sales channel names (B3:D3) and corresponding totals (B17:D17). That is, select the range B3:D3, and then while holding down the CTRL key, select the range B17:D17. Insert the Pie in 3-D chart, as shown in Figure 1–80, by using the Pie button (Insert tab | Charts group). Use the chart location F3: K17.

6. Apply the worksheet name, Semiannual Revenue, to the sheet tab and apply the Purple, Accent 4, Lighter 80% color to the sheet tab. Change the document properties, as specified by your instructor.

7. Save the workbook using the file name, Lab 1-2 Play 'em Again Semiannual Revenue. Print the worksheet in landscape orientation.

8. Two corrections to the figures were sent in from the accounting department. The correct revenue is $118,124.45 for Cell Phones sold through the mail (cell B5) and $43,573.67 for iPods sold over the Web (cell D11). After you enter the two corrections, the company total in cell E17 should equal $8,723,956.77. Print the revised worksheet in landscape orientation.

9. Use the Undo button to change the worksheet back to the original numbers in Table 1–8. Use the Redo button to change the worksheet back to the revised state.

10. Close Excel without saving the latest changes. Start Excel and open the workbook saved in Step 7. Double-click cell E6 and use in-cell editing to change the PSPs revenue (cell C14) to $128,857.32. Write the company total in cell E17 at the top of the first printout. Click the Undo button.

11. Click cell A1 and then click the Merge & Center button on the Home tab on the Ribbon to split cell A1 into cells A1, B1, C1, D1, and E1. To merge the cells into one again, select the range A1:E1 and then click the Merge & Center button.

12. Close the workbook without saving the changes. Submit the assignment as specified by your instructor.

In the Lab

Lab 3: Projected College Cash Flow Analysis Worksheet

Problem: Attending college is an expensive proposition and your resources are limited. To plan for your four-year college career, you have decided to organize your anticipated resources and expenses in a worksheet. The data required to prepare your worksheet is shown in Table 1–9.

Table 1–9 College Cost and Resources

Resources	Freshman	Sophomore	Junior	Senior
529 Plans	2700.00	2889.00	3091.23	3307.62
Financial Aid	5250.00	5617.50	6010.73	6431.48
Job	3100.00	3317.00	3549.19	3797.63
Parents	3700.00	3959.00	4236.13	4532.66
Savings	4250.00	4547.50	4865.83	5206.43
Other	1100.00	1177.00	1259.39	1347.55
Expenses	**Freshman**	**Sophomore**	**Junior**	**Senior**
Activities Fee	500.00	535.00	572.45	612.52
Books	650.00	695.50	744.19	796.28
Clothes	750.00	802.50	858.68	918.78
Entertainment	1650.00	1765.50	1889.09	2021.32
Room & Board	7200.00	7704.00	8243.28	8820.31
Tuition	8250.00	8827.50	9445.43	10106.60
Miscellaneous	1100.00	1177.00	1259.39	1347.55

Continued >

In the Lab *continued*

Instructions Part 1: Using the numbers in Table 1–9, create the worksheet shown in columns A through F in Figure 1–81. Format the worksheet title as Calibri 24-point bold purple. Merge and center the worksheet title in cell A1 across columns A through F. Format the worksheet subtitles in cells A2 and A11 as Calibri 16-point bold red. Format the ranges A3:F3 and A12:F12 with the Heading 2 cell style and center the text in the cells. Format the ranges A4:F9 and A13:F19 with the 20% - Accent 2 cell style, and the ranges A10:F10 and A20:F20 with the Total cell style.

Change the name of the sheet tab and apply the Purple color from the Standard Colors area to the sheet tab. Update the document properties, including the addition of at least one keyword to the properties, and save the workbook using the file name, Lab 1-3 Part 1 College Resources and Expenses. Print the worksheet. Submit the assignment as specified by your instructor.

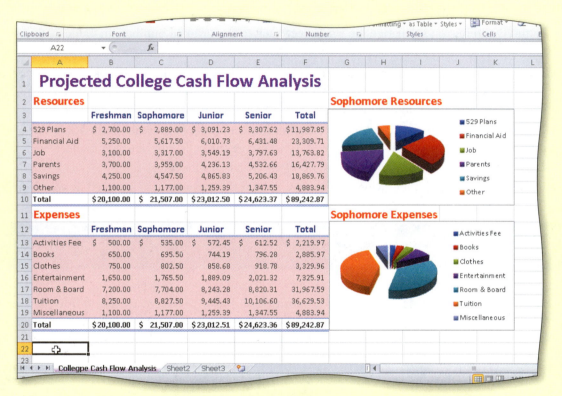

Figure 1–81

After reviewing the numbers, you realize you need to increase manually each of the Sophomore-year expenses in column C by $400, except for the Activities Fee. Change the Sophomore-year expenses to reflect this change. Manually change the Parents resources for the Sophomore year by the amount required to cover the increase in costs. The totals in cells F10 and F20 should equal $91,642.87. Print the worksheet. Close the workbook without saving changes.

Instructions Part 2: Open the workbook Lab 1-3 Part 1 College Resources and Expenses and then save the workbook using the file name, Lab 1-3 Part 2 College Resources and Expenses. Insert an Exploded pie in 3-D chart in the range G3:K10 to show the contribution of each category of resources for the Freshman year. Chart the range A4:B9 and apply the Style 26 chart style to the chart. Add the Pie chart title as shown in cell G2 in Figure 1–81. Insert an Exploded pie in 3-D chart in the range G12:K20 to show the contribution of each category of expenses for the Freshman year. Chart the range A13:B19 and apply the Style 26 chart style to the chart. Add the Pie chart title shown in cell G11 in Figure 1–81. Save the workbook. Print the worksheet in landscape orientation. Submit the assignment as specified by your instructor.

Instructions Part 3: Open the workbook Lab 1-3 Part 2 College Resources and Expenses and then save the workbook using the file name, Lab 1-3 Part 3 College Resources and Expenses. A close inspection of Table 1–9 shows that both cost and financial support figures increase 7% each year. Use Excel Help to learn how to enter the data for the last three years using a formula and the Copy and Paste buttons (Home tab | Clipboard group). For example, the formula to enter in cell C4 is =B4*1.07. Enter formulas to replace all the numbers in the range C4:E9 and C13:E19. If necessary, reformat the tables, as described in Part 1. The worksheet should appear as shown in Figure 1–81, except that some of the totals will be off by approximately 0.01 due to rounding errors. Save the workbook. Submit the assignment as specified by your instructor. Close the workbook without saving changes.

Cases and Places

Apply your creative thinking and problem solving skills to design and implement a solution.

1: Analyzing Quarterly Expenses

Academic

To estimate the funds needed by your school's Travel Club to make it through the upcoming quarter, you decide to create a report for the club itemizing the expected quarterly expenses. The anticipated expenses are listed in Table 1–10. Use the concepts and techniques presented in this chapter to create the worksheet and an embedded Clustered Cylinder chart. Be sure to use an appropriate chart style that compares the quarterly cost of each expense. Total each expense item and each quarter. Include a grand total for all of the expenses. Use the AutoCalculate area to determine the average amount spent per quarter on each expense. Manually insert the averages with appropriate titles in an appropriate area on the worksheet.

Table 1–10 Travel Club Quarterly Expenses				
	1st Quarter	**2nd Quarter**	**3rd Quarter**	**4th Quarter**
Copies and Supplies	75	50	80	150
Meeting Room Rent	400	425	400	425
Miscellaneous	150	100	175	70
Refreshments	130	155	150	225
Speaker Fees	200	200	400	500
Travel	450	375	500	375

2: Create an Exploded Pie in 3-D Chart to Summarize Property Values

Personal

Your wealthy Aunt Nicole owns several properties of varying value. She would like to see the values of the properties in a worksheet and chart that helps her to better understand her investments. She has asked you to develop a worksheet totaling the values of the properties and also to include other relevant statistics. The property values are: Property 1, $56,671.99; Property 2, $82,276.58; Property 3, $60,135.45; Property 4, $107,373.39; and Property 5, $87,512.82. Create an Exploded pie in 3-D chart to illustrate the relative property values. Use the AutoCalculate area to find the average, maximum, and minimum property values and manually enter them and their corresponding identifiers in an appropriate area of the worksheet. Use the Sum button to total the property values.

Continued >

Cases and Places *continued*

3: Analyzing Historical Yearly Sales

Business

You are working part-time for Noble's Mobile Services. Your manager has asked you to prepare a worksheet to help her analyze historical yearly sales by type of product (Table 1–11). Use the concepts and techniques presented in this chapter to create the worksheet and an embedded 3-D Clustered Column chart that includes proper numerical formatting, totaling, and formatting of the worksheet.

Table 1–11 Noble's Mobile Services Historical Yearly Sales				
	2008	**2009**	**2010**	**2011**
Camera Phones	92598	10487	136791	176785
Headsets	9035	8909	4886	6512
Music Phones	57942	44923	54590	67696
Other Accessories	27604	38793	24483	33095
Satellite Radios	17161	19293	30763	44367
Standard Mobile Phones	8549	9264	7600	6048
Wireless PDAs	57963	68059	103025	87367

1 Databases and Database Objects: An Introduction

Objectives

You will have mastered the material in this chapter when you can:

- Design a database to satisfy a collection of requirements
- Describe the features of the Access window
- Create a database
- Create tables in Datasheet and Design views
- Add records to a table
- Close a database
- Open a database
- Print the contents of a table
- Create and use a query
- Create and use a form
- Create and print custom reports
- Modify a report in Layout view

1 | Databases and Database Objects: An Introduction

Introduction

The term **database** describes a collection of data organized in a manner that allows access, retrieval, and use of that data. Microsoft Access 2010, usually referred to as simply Access, is a database management system. A **database management system**, such as Access, is software that allows you to use a computer to create a database; add, change, and delete data in the database; ask and answer questions concerning the data in the database; and create forms and reports using the data in the database.

Project Planning Guidelines

> The process of developing a database that communicates specific information requires careful analysis and planning. As a starting point, establish why the database is needed. Once the purpose is determined, analyze the intended users of the database and their unique needs. Then, gather information about the topic and decide what to include in the database. Finally, determine the database design and style that will be most successful at delivering the message. Details of these guidelines are provided in Appendix A. In addition, each project in this book provides practical applications of these planning considerations.

Project — Database Creation

Camashaly Design Group is a small company that provides custom marketing solutions for the service, nonprofit, and retail sectors. Alyssa Morgan, Camden Scott, and Ashton James started the business after they graduated from a local university. The three owners, all computer graphics design majors and business minors, worked on a service learning project during college that produced a Web site for a nonprofit organization. Alyssa, Camden, and Ashton worked well together. Upon researching the local area for competing businesses, they decided to form their own company. The company specializes in designing and maintaining Web sites and using social networking Web sites for online marketing. They also conduct market research and develop printed media. Camashaly already has received one award for its design work. Camashaly is also recognized for its efforts in providing work opportunities to individuals who want flexible schedules and to student interns.

BTW

BTWs
For a complete list of the BTWs found in the margins of this book, visit the Access 2010 BTW Web page (scsite.com/ac2010/btw).

Camashaly uses business analysts to work collaboratively with clients. Business analysts are employees who translate business requirements into marketing specifications and serve as the interface between clients and Camashaly. Business analysts are paid a base salary and can earn incentive pay for maintaining and expanding client relationships.

Camashaly charges a one-time fee for Web site development. Clients can pay for Web site maintenance by contracting for a specified number of hours or can pay for maintenance on an hour-by-hour basis. Other fees vary depending on the specific scope of work.

To ensure that operations run smoothly, Camashaly organizes data on its clients and business analysts in a database managed by Access. In this way, Camashaly keeps its data current and accurate while the owners can analyze the data for trends and produce a variety of useful reports. In this chapter, you will create the Camashaly database.

In a **relational database** such as those maintained by Access, a database consists of a collection of tables, each of which contains information on a specific subject. Figure 1–1 shows the database for Camashaly Design. It consists of two tables: the Client table (Figure 1–1a) contains information about the clients to whom Camashaly provides services, and the Business Analyst table (Figure 1–1b) contains information about the business analysts to whom these clients are assigned.

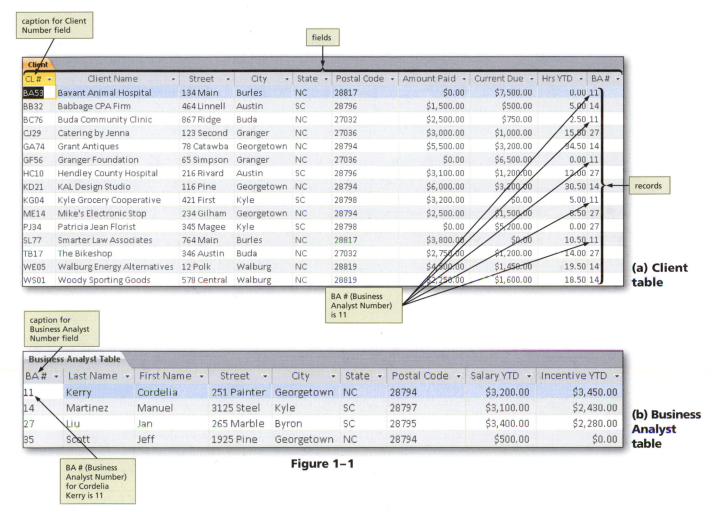

Figure 1–1

The rows in the tables are called **records**. A record contains information about a given person, product, or event. A row in the Client table, for example, contains information about a specific client, such as the client's name, address information, and other data.

The columns in the tables are called fields. A **field** contains a specific piece of information within a record. In the Client table, for example, the fourth field, City, contains the name of the city where the client is located.

The first field in the Client table is CL #, which is an abbreviation for Client Number. Camashaly Design assigns each client a client number. As is common to the way in which many organizations format client numbers, Camashaly Design calls it a number, although it actually contains letters. The Camashaly client numbers consist of two uppercase letters followed by a two-digit number.

The client numbers are unique; that is, no two clients are assigned the same number. Such a field can be used as a **unique identifier**. A unique identifier, as its name suggests, is a way of uniquely identifying each record in the database. A given client number will appear only in a single record in the table. Only one record exists, for example, in which the client number is BB32. A unique identifier also is called a **primary key**. Thus, the Client Number field is the primary key for the Client table.

The next eight fields in the Client table are Client Name, Street, City, State, Postal Code, Amount Paid, Current Due, and Hrs YTD, which is an abbreviation for Contract Hours YTD. YTD is an abbreviation for year to date. The Amount Paid column contains the amount that the client has paid Camashaly Design YTD prior to the current period. The Current Due column contains the amount due to Camashaly for the current period. The Hrs YTD column contains the number of hours the client has contracted for Web site maintenance so far this year. For example, client BB32 is Babbage CPA Firm. The address is 464 Linnell in Austin, South Carolina. The postal code is 28796. The client has paid $1,500.00 for services so far this year. The amount due for the current period is $500.00. The client has contracted for 5.00 hours of Web site maintenance.

Camashaly assigns a single business analyst to work with each client. The last column in the Client table, BA #, which is an abbreviation for Business Analyst Number, gives the number of the client's business analyst.

The first field in the Business Analyst table is also BA #, an abbreviation for Business Analyst Number. The business analyst numbers are unique, so the Business Analyst Number field is the primary key of the Business Analyst table.

The other fields in the Business Analyst table are Last Name, First Name, Street, City, State, Postal Code, Salary YTD, and Incentive YTD. The Salary YTD field gives the salary paid to the analyst thus far this year. The Incentive YTD gives the incentive for which the analyst qualified thus far this year. For example, business analyst 14 is Manuel Martinez. His address is 3125 Steel in Kyle, South Carolina. The Postal Code is 28797. So far this year, he has been paid $3,100.00 in salary. He has earned $2,430.00 in incentive pay.

The business analyst number appears in both the Client table and the Business Analyst table, and relates clients and business analysts. For example, in the Client table, you see that the business analyst number for client Babbage CPA Firm is 14. To find the name of this business analyst, look for the row in the Business Analyst table that contains 14 in the BA # column. After you have found it, you know the client is assigned to Manuel Martinez. To find all the clients assigned to Cordelia Kerry, you would first look in the Business Analyst table to find that her number is 11. You would then look through the Client table for all the clients that contain 11 in the BA # column. Her clients are BA53 (Bavant Animal Hospital), BC76 (Buda Community Clinic), GF56 (Granger Foundation), KG04 (Kyle Grocery Cooperative), and SL77 (Smarter Law Associates).

The last business analyst in the Business Analyst table, Jeff Scott, has not been assigned any clients yet; therefore, his business analyst number, 35, does not appear on any row in the Client table.

Overview

As you read this chapter, you will learn how to create the database shown in Figure 1–1 by performing these general tasks:

- Design the database.
- Create a new blank database.
- Create a table and add the records.
- Preview and print the contents of a table.
- Create a second table and import the records.
- Create a simple query.
- Create a simple form.
- Create and modify a report.

Database Design Guidelines

**Plan
Ahead**

Database design refers to the arrangement of data into tables and fields. In the example in this chapter, the design is specified, but in many cases, you will have to determine the design based on what you want the system to accomplish.

When designing a database to satisfy a given set of requirements, the actions you take and the decisions you make will determine the tables and fields that will be included in the database. As you create a database, such as the one shown in Figure 1–1 on page AC 3, you should follow these general guidelines:

1. **Identify the tables.** Examine the requirements for the database to identify the main objects that are involved. There will be a table for each object you identify.

    In one database, for example, the main objects might be departments and employees. Thus, there would be two tables: one for departments and the other for employees. In another database, the main objects might be clients and business analysts. In this case, there also would be two tables: one for clients and the other for business analysts. In still another database, the main objects might be books, publishers, and authors. This database would require three tables: one for books, a second for publishers, and a third for authors.

2. **Determine the primary keys.** Recall that the primary key is the unique identifier for records in the table. For each table, determine the unique identifier. In a Department table, for example, the unique identifier might be the Department Code. For a Book table, the unique identifier might be the ISBN.

3. **Determine the additional fields.** The primary key will be a field or combination of fields in a table. A table typically will contain many additional fields, each of which contains a type of data. Examine the project requirements to determine these additional fields. For example, in an Employee table, the additional fields might include such fields as Employee Name, Street Address, City, State, Postal Code, Date Hired, Salary, and so on.

4. **Determine relationships between the tables.** Examine the list of tables you have created to see which tables are related. When you determine that two tables are related, include matching fields in the two tables. For example, in a database containing employees and departments, there is a relationship between the two tables because one department can have many employees assigned to it. Department Code could be the matching field in the two tables.

5. **Determine data types for the fields.** For each field, determine the type of data the field can contain. One field, for example, might contain only numbers. Another field might contain currency amounts, while a third field might contain only dates. Some fields contain text data, meaning any combination of letters, numbers, and special characters (!, ;, ', &, and so on). For example, in an Employee table, the Date Hired field would contain dates, the Salary field would contain currency amounts, and the Hours Worked field would contain numbers. The other fields in the Employee table would contain text data, such as Employee Name and Department Code.

6. **Identify and remove any unwanted redundancy.** Redundancy is the storing of a piece of data in more than one place. Redundancy usually, but not always, causes problems, such as wasted space, difficulties with update, and possible data inconsistency. Examine each table you have created to see if it contains redundancy and, if so, determine whether the redundancy causes the problems described. If it does, remove the redundancy by splitting the table into two tables. For example, you might have a single table of employees. In addition to typical employee data (name, address, earnings, and so on), the table might contain Department Number and Department Name. If so, the Department Name could repeat multiple times. Every employee whose department number is 12, for example, would have the same department name. It would be better to split the table into two tables: one for Employees and one for Department. In the Department table, the Department Name is stored only once.

7. **Determine a storage location for the database.** The database you have designed will be stored in a single file. You need to determine a location in which to store the file.

8. **Determine additional properties for fields.** Before creating the database, determine any other properties you should specify for the fields. These could include a field size, which is

(continued)

Plan Ahead

(continued)

the maximum number of characters that can be stored in the field. If you want something other than the field name to appear at the top of a column (such as an abbreviation), you can change the caption to the desired heading. You also can add a description, which is a message that appears on the screen concerning a field whenever the field is selected.

9. **Determine the best method for distributing the database objects.** The traditional method of distributing database objects uses a printer to produce a hard copy of a table or report on paper. You also can distribute the table as an electronic image that mirrors the original table's appearance.

When necessary, more specific details concerning the above guidelines are presented at appropriate points in the chapter. The chapter also will identify the actions performed and decisions made regarding these guidelines during the creation of the database shown in Figure 1–1 on page AC 3.

Designing a Database

This section illustrates the database design process by showing how you would design the database for Camashaly Design from a set of requirements. In this section, you will use commonly accepted shorthand to represent the tables and fields that make up the database as well as the primary keys for the tables. For each table, you give the name of the table followed by a set of parentheses. Within the parentheses is a list of the fields in the table separated by columns. You underline the primary key. For example,

Product (<u>Product Code</u>, Description, On Hand, Price)

represents a table called Product. The Product table contains four fields: Product Code, Description, On Hand, and Price. The Product Code field is the primary key.

Database Requirements

The Camashaly Design database must maintain information on both clients and business analysts. The business currently keeps this data in two Word tables and two Excel workbooks, as shown in Figure 1–2. They use Word tables for address information and Excel workbooks for financial information.

Client Number	Client Name	Street	City	State	Postal Code
BA53	Bavant Animal Hospital	134 Main	Burles	NC	28817
BB32	Babbage CPA Firm	464 Linnell	Austin	SC	28796
BC76	Buda Community Clinic	867 Ridge	Buda	NC	27032
CJ29	Catering by Jenna	123 Second	Granger	NC	27036
GA74	Grant Antiques	78 Catawba	Georgetown	NC	28794
GF56	Granger Foundation	65 Simpson	Granger	NC	27036
HC10	Hendley County Hospital	216 Rivard	Austin	SC	28796
KD21	KAL Design Studio	116 Pine	Georgetown	NC	28794
KG04	Kyle Grocery Cooperative	421 First	Kyle	SC	28798
ME14	Mike's Electronic Stop	234 Gilham	Georgetown	NC	28794
PJ34	Patricia Jean Florist	345 Magee	Kyle	SC	28798
SL77	Smarter Law Associates	764 Main	Burles	NC	28817
TB17	The Bikeshop	346 Austin	Buda	NC	27032
WE05	Walburg Energy Alternatives	12 Polk	Walburg	NC	28819
WS01	Woody Sporting Goods	578 Central	Walburg	NC	28819

Figure 1–2   (a) Client Address Information (Word Table)

	A	B	C	D	E	F	G	H
1	Client Number	Client Name	Amount Paid	Current Due	Contract Hours YTD			
2	BA53	Bavant Animal Hospital	0.00	7,500.00	0			
3	BB32	Babbage CPA Firm	1,500.00	500.00	5			
4	BC76	Buda Community Clinic	2,500.00	750.00	2.5			
5	CJ29	Catering by Jenna	3,000.00	1,000.00	15.5			
6	GA74	Grant Antiques	5,500.00	3,200.00	34.5			
7	GF56	Granger Foundation	0.00	6,500.00	0			
8	HC10	Hendley County Hospital	3,100.00	1,200.00	12			
9	KD21	KAL Design Studio	6,000.00	3,200.00	30.5			
10	KG04	Kyle Grocery Cooperative	3,200.00	0.00	5			
11	ME14	Mike's Electronic Stop	2,500.00	1,500.00	8.5			
12	PJ34	Patricia Jean Florist	0.00	5,200.00	0			
13	SL77	Smarter Law Associates	3,800.00	0.00	10.5			
14	TB17	The Bikeshop	2,750.00	1,200.00	14			
15	WE05	Walburg Energy Alternatives	4,500.00	1,450.00	19.5			
16	WS01	Woody Sporting Goods	2,250.00	1,600.00	18.5			

Figure 1–2 (b) Client Financial Information (Excel Worksheet)

Business Analyst Number	Last Name	First Name	Street	City	State	Postal Code
11	Kerry	Cordelia	251 Painter	Georgetown	NC	28794
14	Martinez	Manuel	3125 Steel	Kyle	SC	28797
27	Liu	Jan	265 Marble	Byron	SC	28795
35	Scott	Jeff	1925 Pine	Georgetown	NC	28794

Figure 1–2 (c) Business Analyst Address Information (Word Table)

	A	B	C	D	E	F	G	H	I
1	Business Analyst Number	Last Name	First Name	Salary YTD	Incentive YTD				
2	11	Kerry	Cordelia	3,200.00	3,450.00				
3	14	Martinez	Manuel	3,100.00	2,430.00				
4	27	Liu	Jan	3,400.00	2,280.00				
5	35	Scott	Jeff	500.00	0.00				

Figure 1–2 (d) Business Analyst Financial Information (Excel Worksheet)

For clients, Camashaly needs to maintain address data. It currently keeps this address data in a Word table (Figure 1–2a). It also maintains financial data for each client. This includes the amount paid, current amount due, and contract hours YTD for the client. It keeps these amounts, along with the client name and number, in the Excel workbook shown in Figure 1–2b.

Camashaly keeps business analyst address data in a Word table, as shown in Figure 1–2c. Just as with clients, it keeps financial data for business analysts, including their salary YTD and incentive YTD, in a separate Excel workbook, as shown in Figure 1–2d.

Finally, it keeps track of which clients are assigned to which business analysts. Each client is assigned to a single business analyst, but each business analyst might be assigned many clients. Currently, for example, clients BA53 (Bavant Animal Hospital), BC76 (Buda Community Clinic), GF56 (Granger Foundation), KG04 (Kyle Grocery Cooperative), and SL77 (Smarter Law Associates) are assigned to business analyst 11 (Cordelia Kerry). Clients BB32 (Babbage CPA Firm), GA74 (Grant Antiques), KD21 (KAL Design Studio), WE05 (Walburg Energy Alternatives), and WS01 (Woody Sporting Goods) are assigned to business analyst 14 (Manuel Martinez). Clients CJ29 (Catering by Jenna), HC10 (Hendley County Hospital), ME14 (Mike's Electronic Stop), PJ34 (Patricia Jean Florist), and TB17 (The Bikeshop) are assigned to business analyst 27 (Jan Liu). Camashaly has an additional business analyst, Jeff Scott, whose number has been assigned as 35, but who has not yet been assigned any clients.

BTW

Additional Data for Camashaly

There are many other types of data that Camashaly could include in a database. For example, they might keep all employee information in a database as well as information on client contracts and an inventory of hardware and software.

Naming Tables and Fields

In designing your database, you must name the tables and fields. Thus, before beginning the design process, you must understand the rules Access applies to table and field names. These rules are:

1. Names can be up to 64 characters in length.
2. Names can contain letters, digits, and spaces, as well as most of the punctuation symbols.
3. Names cannot contain periods (.), exclamation points (!), accent graves (`), or square brackets ([ ]).
4. The same name cannot be used for two different fields in the same table.

The approach to naming tables and fields used in this text is to begin the names with an uppercase letter and to use lowercase for the other letters. In multiple-word names, each word begins with an uppercase letter, and there is a space between words (for example, Client Number). You should know that other approaches exist, all of which are acceptable in Access. Some people omit the space (ClientNumber). Still others use an underscore in place of the space (Client_Number). Finally, some use an underscore in place of a space, but use the same case for all letters (CLIENT_NUMBER or client_number).

Identifying the Tables

Now that you know the rules for naming tables and fields, you are ready to begin the design process. The first step is to identify the main objects involved in the requirements. For the Camashaly Design database, the main objects are clients and business analysts. This leads to two tables, which you must name. Reasonable names for these two tables are:

Client

Business Analyst

Determining the Primary Keys

The next step is to identify the fields that will be the unique identifiers, or primary keys. Client numbers uniquely identify clients, and business analyst numbers uniquely identify business analysts. Thus, the primary key for the Client table is the client number, and the primary key for the Business Analyst table is the business analyst number. Reasonable names for these fields would be Client Number and Business Analyst Number, respectively. Adding these primary keys to the tables gives:

Client (<u>Client Number</u>)
Business Analyst (<u>Business Analyst Number</u>)

Determining Additional Fields

After identifying the primary keys, you need to determine and name the additional fields. In addition to the client number, the Client Address Information shown in Figure 1–2a on page AC 6 contains the client name, street, city, state, and postal code. These would be fields in the Client table. The Client Financial Information shown in Figure 1–2b also contains the client number and client name, which are already included in the Client table. The financial information also contains the amount paid, current due, and contract hours YTD. Adding the amount paid, current due, and contract hours YTD fields to those already identified in the Client table and assigning reasonable names gives:

Client (<u>Client Number</u>, Client Name, Street, City, State, Postal Code,
     Amount Paid, Current Due, Contract Hours YTD)

Similarly, examining the Business Analyst Address Information in Figure 1–2c adds the last name, first name, street, city, state, and postal code fields to the Business Analyst table. In addition to the business analyst number, last name, and first name, the Business Analyst Financial Information in Figure 1–2d would add the salary YTD and Incentive YTD. Adding these fields to the Business Analyst table and assigning reasonable names gives:

Business Analyst (<u>Business Analyst Number</u>, Last Name, First Name, Street, City, State, Postal Code, Salary YTD, Incentive YTD)

Determining and Implementing Relationships Between the Tables

Plan Ahead

> **Determine relationships between the tables.**
> The most common type of relationship you will encounter between tables is the **one-to-many relationship**. This means that each row in the first table may be associated with many rows in the second table, but each row in the second table is associated with only one row in the first. The first table is called the "one" table and the second is called the "many" table. For example, there may be a relationship between departments and employees, in which each department can have many employees, but each employee is assigned to only one department. In this relationship, there would be two tables, Department and Employee. The Department table would be the "one" table in the relationship. The Employee table would be the "many" table.
>   To determine relationships between tables, you can follow these general guidelines:
>
> - Identify the "one" table.
>
> - Identify the "many" table.
>
> - Include the primary key from the "one" table as a field in the "many" table.

According to the requirements, each client has one business analyst, but each business analyst can have many clients. Thus, the Business Analyst table is the "one" table, and the Client table is the "many" table. To implement this one-to-many relationship between business analysts and clients, add the Business Analyst Number field (the primary key of the Business Analyst table) to the Client table. This produces:

Client (<u>Client Number</u>, Client Name, Street, City, State, Postal Code, Amount Paid, Current Due, Contract Hours YTD, Business Analyst Number)
Business Analyst (<u>Business Analyst Number</u>, Last Name, First Name, Street, City, State, Postal Code, Salary YTD, Incentive YTD)

BTW

Database Design Language (DBDL)
DBDL is a commonly accepted shorthand representation for showing the structure of a relational database. You write the name of the table and then within parentheses you list all the columns in the table. If the columns continue beyond one line, indent the subsequent lines.

Determining Data Types for the Fields

Each field has a **data type**. This indicates the type of data that can be stored in the field. Three of the most commonly used data types are:

1. **Text** — The field can contain any characters. A maximum number of 255 characters is allowed in a field whose data type is Text.

2. **Number** — The field can contain only numbers. The numbers either can be positive or negative. Fields are assigned this type so they can be used in arithmetic operations. Fields that contain numbers but will not be used for arithmetic operations (such as postal codes) usually are assigned a data type of Text.

3. **Currency** — The field can contain only monetary data. The values will appear with currency symbols, such as dollar signs, commas, and decimal points, and with two digits following the decimal point. Like numeric fields, you can use currency fields in arithmetic operations. Access assigns a size to currency fields automatically.

BTW

Data Types
Different database management systems have different available data types. Even data types that are essentially the same can have different names. The Currency data type in Access, for example, is referred to as Money in SQL Server.

Table 1–1 shows the other data types that are available in Access.

Table 1–1 Additional Data Types	
Data Type	**Description**
Memo	Field can store a variable amount of text or combinations of text and numbers where the total number of characters may exceed 255.
Date/Time	Field can store dates and times.
AutoNumber	Field can store a unique sequential number that Access assigns to a record. Access will increment the number by 1 as each new record is added.
Yes/No	Field can store only one of two values. The choices are Yes/No, True/False, or On/Off.
OLE Object	Field can store an OLE object, which is an object linked to or embedded in the table.
Hyperlink	Field can store text that can be used as a hyperlink address.
Attachment	Field can contain an attached file. Images, spreadsheets, documents, charts, and so on can be attached to this field in a record in the database. You can view and edit the attached file.
Calculated	Field specified as a calculation based on other fields. The value is not actually stored.

In the Client table, because the Client Number, Client Name, Street, City, and State can all contain letters, their data types should be Text. The data type for Postal Code is Text instead of Number because postal codes are not used in arithmetic operations; you do not add postal codes or find an average postal code, for example. The Amount Paid and Current Due fields both contain monetary data, so their data types should be Currency. The Contract Hours YTD field contains a number that is not a currency amount, so its data type should be Number.

Similarly, in the Business Analyst table, the data type for the Business Analyst Number, Last Name, First Name, Street, City, State, and Postal Code fields all should be Text. The Salary YTD and Incentive YTD fields both contain monetary amounts, so their data types should be Currency.

Fields whose data type is Number often require you to change the field size, which is the storage space assigned to the field by Access. Table 1–2 shows the possible field sizes for Number fields. If the size were Byte, Integer, or Long Integer, for example, only integers could be stored. If you try to store a value that has decimal places, such as 2.50, the portion to the right of the decimal point would be removed, giving a result of 2. To address this problem, you would change to a size such as Single.

Table 1–2 Field Sizes for Number Fields	
Field Size	**Description**
Byte	Integer value in the range of 0 to 255
Integer	Integer value in the range of −32,768 to 32,767
Long Integer	Integer value in the range of −2,147,483,648 to 2,147,483,647
Single	Numeric values with decimal places to seven significant digits — requires 4 bytes of storage
Double	Numeric values with decimal places to more accuracy than Single — requires 8 bytes of storage
Replication ID	Special identifier required for replication
Decimal	Numeric values with decimal places to more accuracy than Single or Double — requires 12 bytes of storage.

Identifying and Removing Redundancy

Redundancy means storing the same fact in more than one place. It usually results from placing too many fields in a table — fields that really belong in separate tables — and often causes serious problems. If you had not realized there were two objects, clients and business analysts, for example, you might have placed all the data in a single Client table. Figure 1–3 shows an example of a table that includes both client and business analyst information. Notice that the data for a given business analyst (number, name, address, and so on) occurs on more than one record. The data for analyst 11, Cordelia Kerry, is repeated in the figure.

Client Table

Client Number	Client Name	Street	...	Business Analyst Number	Last Name	First Name	...
BA53	Bavant Animal Hospital	134 Main	...	11	Kerry	Cordelia	...
BB32	Babbage CPA Firm	464 Linnell	...	14	Martinez	Manuel	...
BC76	Buda Community Clinic	867 Ridge	...	11	Kerry	Cordelia	...
...	...	...	...	...	...	.	...

business analyst numbers are 11

name of business analyst 11 appears more than once

Figure 1–3

Storing this data on multiple records is an example of redundancy, which causes several problems, including:

1. Wasted storage space. The name of business analyst 11, Cordelia Kerry, for example, should be stored only once. Storing this fact several times is wasteful.

2. More difficult database updates. If, for example, Cordelia Kerry's name is spelled wrong and needs to be changed in the database, her name would need to be changed in several different places.

3. A possibility of inconsistent data. Nothing prohibits the business analyst's last name from being Kerry on client BA53's record and Bronson on client BC76's record. The data would be inconsistent. In both cases, the business analyst number is 11, but the last names are different.

The solution to the problem is to place the redundant data in a separate table, one in which the data no longer will be redundant. If, for example, you place the data for business analysts in a separate table (Figure 1–4), the data for each business analyst will appear only once.

Client Table

Client Number	Client Name	Street	...	Business Analyst Number
BA53	Bavant Animal Hospital	134 Main	...	11
BB32	Babbage CPA Firm	464 Linnell	...	14
BC76	Buda Community Clinic	867 Ridge	...	11
...	...	...		

business analyst numbers are 11

Business Analyst Table

Business Analyst Number	Last Name	First Name	...
11	Kerry	Cordelia	...
14	Martinez	Manuel	...
...	...		...

name of business analyst 11 appears only once

Figure 1–4

BTW

Postal Codes

Some organizations with customers throughout the country have a separate table of postal codes, cities, and states. When placing an order, you typically are asked for your postal code (or ZIP code), rather than city, state, and postal code. You then are asked to confirm that the city and state correspond to that postal code.

Notice that you need to have the business analyst number in both tables. Without it, there would be no way to tell which business analyst is associated with which client. The remaining business analyst data, however, was removed from the Client table and placed in the Business Analyst table. This new arrangement corrects the problems of redundancy in the following ways:

1. Because the data for each business analyst is stored only once, space is not wasted.

2. Changing the name of a business analyst is easy. You have only to change one row in the Business Analyst table.

3. Because the data for a business analyst is stored only once, inconsistent data cannot occur. Designing to omit redundancy will help you to produce good and valid database designs.

You should always examine your design to see if it contains redundancy. If it does, you should decide whether you need to remove the redundancy by creating a separate table.

If you examine your design, you'll see that there is one area of redundancy (see the data in Figure 1–1 on page AC 3). Cities and states are both repeated. Every client whose postal code is 28794, for example, has Georgetown as the city and NC as the state. To remove this redundancy, you would create a table whose primary key is Postal Code and that contains City and State as additional fields. City and State would be removed from the Client table. Having City, State, and Postal Code in a table is very common, however, and usually you would not take such action. No other redundancy exists in your tables.

For an introduction to Windows 7 and instruction about how to perform basic Windows 7 tasks, read the Office 2010 and Windows 7 chapter at the beginning of this book, where you can learn how to resize windows, change screen resolution, create folders, move and rename files, use Windows Help, and much more.

To Start Access

If you are using a computer to step through the project in this chapter and you want your screens to match the figures in this book, you should change your screen's resolution to 1024×768. For information about how to change a computer's resolution, refer to the Office 2010 and Windows 7 chapter at the beginning of this book.

The following steps, which assume Windows 7 is running, start Access based on a typical installation. You may need to ask your instructor how to start Access for your computer. For a detailed example of the procedure summarized below, refer to the Office 2010 and Windows 7 chapter.

1 Click the Start button on the Windows 7 taskbar to display the Start menu.

2 Type **Microsoft Access** as the search text in the 'Search programs and files' text box and watch the search results appear on the Start menu.

3 Click Microsoft Access 2010 in the search results on the Start menu to start Access and display the Backstage view for Access.

4 If the Access window is not maximized, click the Maximize button next to the Close button on its title bar to maximize the window.

Creating a Database

In Access, all the tables, reports, forms, and queries that you create are stored in a single file called a database. Thus, you first must create the database to hold the tables, reports, forms, and queries. You can use either the Blank database option or a template to create a new database. If you already know the tables and fields you want in your database, you would use the Blank database option. If not, you can use a template. Templates can guide you by suggesting some commonly used databases.

Determine a storage location for the database.
When creating a database, you must decide which storage medium to use.

If you always work on the same computer and have no need to transport your database to a different location, then your computer's hard drive will suffice as a storage location. It is a good idea, however, to save a backup copy of your database on a separate medium in case the file becomes corrupted or the computer's hard drive fails.

If you plan to work on your database in various locations or on multiple computers, then you can consider saving your projects on a portable medium, such as a USB flash drive or CD. The projects in this book are stored on a USB flash drive, which saves files quickly and reliably and can be reused. CDs are easily portable and serve as good backups for the final versions of projects because they generally can save files only one time.

Plan Ahead

For an introduction to Office 2010 and instruction about how to perform basic tasks in Office 2010 programs, read the Office 2010 and Windows 7 chapter at the beginning of this book, where you can learn how to start a program, use the Ribbon, save a file, open a file, quit a program, use Help, and much more.

To Create a Database

Because you already know the tables and fields you want in the Camashaly Design database, you would use the Blank database option rather than using a template. The following steps assume you already have created folders for storing your files, for example, a CIS 101 folder (for your class) that contains an Access folder (for your assignments). Thus, these steps save the document in the Access folder in the CIS 101 folder on a USB flash drive using the file name, Camashaly Design. For a detailed example of the procedure summarized below, refer to the Office 2010 and Windows 7 chapter at the beginning of this book.

1 With a USB flash drive connected to one of the computer's USB ports, ensure the New tab is selected in the Backstage view and that Blank database is selected in the New gallery.

2 Click the Browse button in the right pane of the New gallery to display the File New Database dialog box.

3 Type **Camashaly Design** in the File New Database dialog box to change the file name. Do not press the ENTER key after typing the file name.

4 Navigate to the desired save location (in this case, the Access folder in the CIS 101 folder [or your class folder] on the USB flash drive).

5 Click the OK button, which returns you to the New gallery. (Your screen may show Camashaly Design.accdb.)

6 Click the Create button in the right pane of the New gallery to create the database on the selected drive with the entered file name (Figure 1–5).

BTW

Q&As
For a complete list of the Q&As found in many of the step-by-step sequences in this book, visit the Access 2010 Q&A Web page (scsite.com/ac2010/qa).

Q&A

The title bar for my Navigation Pane contains All Tables rather than All Access Objects, as in the figure. Is that a problem?

It is not a problem. The title bar indicates how the Navigation Pane is organized. You can carry out the steps in the text with either organization. To make your screens match the ones in the text, click the Navigation Pane arrow and then click Object Type.

Q&A

I do not have the Search bar that appears on the figure. Is that a problem?

It is not a problem. If your Navigation Pane does not display a Search bar and you want your screens to match the ones in the text, right-click the Navigation Pane title bar arrow to display a shortcut menu, and then click Search Bar.

Figure 1–5

TO CREATE A DATABASE USING A TEMPLATE

Ideally, you will design your own database, create a blank database, and then create the tables you have determined that your database should contain. If you are not sure what database design you will need, you could use a template. Templates can guide you by suggesting some commonly used databases. To create a database using a template, you would use the following steps.

1. After starting Access, be sure the Backstage view is open. If it is not, click File on the Ribbon to open it.

2. Click the New tab if it is not already selected.

3. Click Sample templates to display a list of templates stored locally or search Microsoft Office online for additional templates.

4. Click the template you want to use.

5. Enter a file name (or accept the suggested file name) and select a location for the database.

6. Click the Create button to create the database or the Download button to download the database and create the database, if necessary.

BTW

Available Templates
The Blank web database button on the New tab in the Backstage view allows you to create a database that you can publish to a SharePoint server running Access Services. Access 2010 also includes five Web-based templates. To display previously used templates, click the My templates button.

The Access Window

The Access window consists of a variety of components to make your work more efficient and documents more professional. These include the Navigation Pane, Access work area, Ribbon, shortcut menus, and Quick Access Toolbar. Some of these components are common to other Microsoft Office 2010 programs; others are unique to Access.

Navigation Pane and Access Work Area

You work on objects such as tables, forms, and reports in the **Access work area**. In the work area in Figure 1–5, a single table, Table1, is open in the work area. **Object tabs** for the open objects appear at the top of the work area. If you have multiple objects open at the same time, you can select one of the open objects by clicking its tab. To the left of the work area is the Navigation Pane. The **Navigation Pane** contains a list of all the objects in the database. You use this pane to open an object. You also can customize the way objects are displayed in the Navigation Pane.

The **status bar**, located at the bottom of the Access window, presents information about the database object, the progress of current tasks, and the status of certain commands and keys; it also provides controls for viewing the object. As you type text or perform certain commands, various indicators may appear on the status bar. The left edge of the status bar in Figure 1–5 shows that the table object is open in Datasheet view. Toward the right edge are View buttons, which you can use to change the view that currently is displayed.

Creating a Table

To create a table, you must describe the structure of the table to Access. That is, you must describe all the fields that make up the table and their characteristics. You must also indicate the primary key.

In Access, you can use two different views to create a table: Datasheet view and Design view. In **Datasheet view**, the data in the table is presented in rows and columns, similar to a spreadsheet. Although the main reason to use Datasheet view is to add or update records in a table, you can also use it to create a table or to later modify its structure. The other view, **Design view**, is only used to create a table or to modify the structure of the table.

As you might expect, Design view has more functionality for creating a table than Datasheet view. That is, there are certain actions that can only be performed in Design view. If creating your table requires such actions, you must use Design view. If not, you can choose either view. In this chapter, you will create the first table, the Business Analyst table, in Datasheet view. You will create the second table, the Client table, in Design view.

Whichever view you choose to use, before creating the table, you need to determine the names and data types of the fields that will make up the table. You already have determined the types for the Camashaly fields. You also need to determine additional properties for the fields.

**Plan
Ahead**

> **Determine additional properties for fields.**
>
> - **Determine if a special caption is warranted.** Normally, the field name will appear as the label for a field on a form or report and as the column name in Datasheet view. If you would rather have a different name appear, you can change the field's caption to the desired name. One common use of captions is to shorten the column heading. If the data in a column is considerably shorter than the column heading, you could change the caption to a shorter heading. This would enable you to reduce the width of the column and yet still be able to see the entire column heading.
>
> - **Determine if a special description is warranted.** Determine whether to include a description that would appear in the status bar whenever the field is selected.
>
> - **Determine field sizes.** For Text fields, determine the field size; that is, the maximum number of characters that can be entered in the field. Users will be prohibited from entering a value that has more characters than the field size.
>
> - **Determine formats.** Determine whether the data in the field should be formatted in any particular way. You could, for example, specify that a number field is to be formatted with precisely two decimal places.

BTW

Naming Tables
Database users typically have their own guidelines for naming tables. Some use the singular version of the object being described while others use the prefix tbl with a table name. This book uses the singular version of the object (Client, Business Analyst) but adds the word Table to the name for the Business Analyst table to illustrate another possible approach. Including the word Table can assist visually impaired users when viewing the Navigation Pane.

The results of these decisions for the fields in the Business Analyst table are shown in Table 1–3. The table also shows the data types and field sizes of the fields as well as any special properties that need to be changed. The Business Analyst Number field has a caption of BA #, enabling the width of the Business Analyst Number column to be reduced in the datasheet.

Table 1–3 Structure of Business Analyst Table			
Field Name	**Data Type**	**Field Size**	**Description**
Business Analyst Number	Text	2	**Primary Key** **Description:** Business Analyst Number **Caption:** BA #
Last Name	Text	15	
First Name	Text	15	
Street	Text	15	
City	Text	15	
State	Text	2	
Postal Code	Text	5	
Salary YTD	Currency		
Incentive YTD	Currency		

To Modify the Primary Key

When you first create your database, Access automatically creates a table for you. You can immediately begin defining the fields. If, for any reason, you do not have this table or inadvertently delete it, you can create the table by clicking Create on the Ribbon and then clicking the Table button (Create tab | Tables group). In either case, you are ready to define the fields.

The following steps define the first field, the Business Analyst Number field, which is the primary key. Access has already created a primary key field, which it has named ID. Thus, the steps will change the name, data type, and other properties of this field to match the Business Analyst field in Table 1–3.

1

● Right-click the column heading for the ID field to display a shortcut menu (Figure 1–6).

Q&A Why does my shortcut menu look different?

You right-clicked within the column instead of right-clicking the column heading.

Figure 1–6

2

● Click Rename Field on the shortcut menu to highlight the current name.

● Type **Business Analyst Number** to assign a name to the new field.

● Click the white space immediately below the field name to complete the addition of the field (Figure 1–7).

Figure 1–7

Q&A Why does the name not appear in its entirety?

The default column size is not large enough for Business Analyst Number to appear in its entirety. You will address this issue in later steps.

3

- Because the data type needs to be changed from AutoNumber to Text, click the Data Type box arrow (Table Tools Fields tab | Formatting group) to display a menu of available data types (Figure 1–8).

Figure 1–8

4

- Click Text to select the data type for the field (Figure 1–9).

Figure 1–9

5

- Click the Field Size text box (Table Tools Fields tab | Properties group) to select the current field size, use either the DELETE or BACKSPACE keys to erase the current field size, and then type **2** as the new field size.

- Click the Name & Caption button (Table Tools Fields tab | Properties group) to display the Enter Field Properties dialog box.

- Click the Caption text box (Enter Field Properties dialog box), and then type **BA #** as the caption.

- Click the Description text box, and then type **Unique identifier of business analyst** as the description (Figure 1–10).

Figure 1–10

6

- Click the OK button (Enter Field Properties dialog box) to change the caption and description (Figure 1–11).

Figure 1–11

To Define the Remaining Fields in a Table

To define an additional field, you click the Click to Add column heading, select the data type, and then type the field name. This is different from the process you used to modify the ID field, which was an existing field. The following steps define the remaining fields shown in Table 1–3 on page AC 16.

- Click the Click to Add column heading to display a menu of available data types (Figure 1–12).

Q&A Why did I follow a different process when I renamed this field?

The ID field was an existing field, created automatically by Access. For a new field, you need to click the Click to Add heading.

Figure 1–12

2

- Click Text in the menu of available data types to select the Text data type.

- Type Last Name to enter a field name.

- Click the white space below the field name to complete the change of the name. Click the white space a second time to select the field (Figure 1–13).

Q&A I realized after I entered the field name that I selected the wrong data type. How can I correct it?

Click the Data Type box arrow and then select the correct type.

Q&A I inadvertently clicked the white space before entering the field name. How can I correct the name?

Right-click the field name, click Rename Field on the shortcut menu, and then type the new name.

Figure 1–13

- Change the field size to 15 just as you changed the field size of the Business Analyst Number field.

- Using the same technique, add the remaining fields in the Business Analyst table. For the First Name, Street, City, State, and Postal Code fields, the Text data type is correct, but you will need to change the field size to match Table 1–3. For the Salary YTD and Incentive YTD fields, you need to change the data type to Currency. Before defining the Incentive YTD field, you may need to click the right scroll arrow to bring the column for the field to the screen (Figure 1–14).

Figure 1–14

Q&A Why does Currency appear twice?

The second Currency is the format, which indicates how the data will be displayed. For the Currency data type, Access automatically sets the format to Currency, which is usually what you would want. You could change it to something else, if desired, by clicking the arrow and selecting the desired format.

Q&A I have an extra row between the row containing the field names and the row that begins with the asterisk. What happened? Is this a problem? If so, how do I fix it?

You inadvertently added a record to the table by pressing some key. Even pressing the SPACEBAR would add a record. You now have a record you do not want. To fix it, you need to delete the record, which you will do in Step 4.

4

- If you have an additional record between the field names and the asterisk, press the ESC key to delete the record.

Making Changes to the Structure

When creating a table, check the entries carefully to ensure they are correct. If you discover a mistake while still typing the entry, you can correct the error by repeatedly pressing the BACKSPACE key until the incorrect characters are removed. Then, type the correct characters. If you do not discover a mistake until later, you can use the following techniques to make the necessary changes to the structure:

- To undo your most recent change, click the Undo button on the Quick Access Toolbar. If there is nothing that Access can undo, this button will be dim, and clicking it will have no effect.
- To delete a field, right-click the column heading for the field (the position containing the field name), and then click Delete Field on the shortcut menu.
- To change the name of a field, right-click the column heading for the field, click Rename Field on the shortcut menu, and then type the desired field name.
- To insert a field as the last field, click the Click to Add column heading, click the appropriate data type on the menu of available data types, type the desired field name, and, if necessary, change the field size.
- To insert a field between existing fields, right-click the column heading for the field that will follow the new field, and then click Insert Field on the shortcut menu. Right-click the column heading for the field, click Rename Field on the shortcut menu, and then type the desired field name.
- To move a field, click the column heading for the field to be moved to select the field, and then drag the field to the desired position.

As an alternative to these steps, you may want to start over. To do so, click the Close button for the table, and then click the No button in the Microsoft Access dialog box. Click Create on the Ribbon and then click the Table button to create a table. You then can repeat the process you used earlier to define the fields in the table.

To Save a Table

The Business Analyst table structure now is complete. The final step is to save the table within the database. As part of the process, you will give the table a name. The following steps save the table, giving it the name, Business Analyst Table.

1
- Click the Save button on the Quick Access Toolbar to display the Save As dialog box (Figure 1–15).

Figure 1–15

2
- Type **Business Analyst Table** to change the name to be assigned to the table.

- Click the OK button (Save As dialog box) to save the table (Figure 1–16).

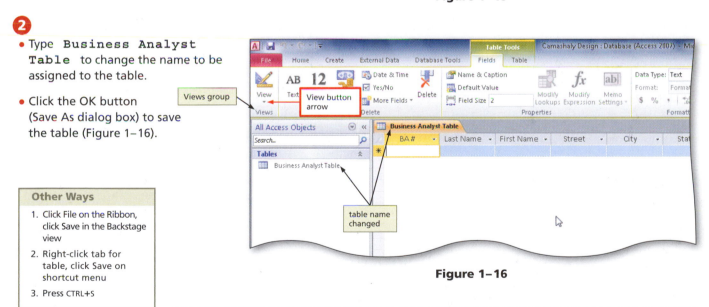

Other Ways

1. Click File on the Ribbon, click Save in the Backstage view
2. Right-click tab for table, click Save on shortcut menu
3. Press CTRL+S

Figure 1–16

To View the Table in Design View

Even when creating a table in Datasheet view, Design view can be helpful. You should view the fields, data types, and properties to ensure you have entered them correctly. This viewing is easier to do in Design view. It is also easier to determine the primary key in Design view. The following steps view the structure of the Business Analyst Table in Design view so that you can verify the design is correct.

1

- Click the View button arrow (Table Tools Fields tab | Views group) to display the View button menu (Figure 1–17).

Q&A

Could I just click the View button rather than the arrow?

Yes. Clicking the button is equivalent to clicking the command represented by the icon currently appearing on the button. Because the icon on the button in Figure 1–17 is the icon for Design view, clicking the button would display the table in Design view. If you are uncertain, you can always click the arrow and select from the menu.

Figure 1–17

2

- Click Design View on the View button menu to view the table in Design view (Figure 1–18).

Figure 1–18

Other Ways

1. Click Design View button on status bar

Checking the Structure in Design View

You should use Design view to carefully check the entries you have made. In Figure 1–18, for example, you can see that the Business Analyst Number field is the primary key of the Business Analyst Table by the key symbol in front of the field name. If your table does not have a key symbol, you can click the Primary Key button (Table Tools Design tab | Tools group) to designate the field as the primary key. You also can check that the data type, the description, the field size, and the caption are all correct.

For the other fields, you can see the field name, data type, and description without taking any special action. To see the field size and/or caption for a field, click the field's **row selector**, the small box that precedes the field. Clicking the row selector for the Last Name field, for example, displays the field properties for the field (Figure 1–19). You then can check to see that the field size is correct. In addition, if the field has a caption, you can check to see if that is correct as well. If you find any mistakes, you can make the necessary corrections on this screen. When you have finished, you would click the Save button to save your changes.

To Close the Table

Once you are sure that your entries are correct and you have saved your changes, you can close the table. The following step closes the table.

- Click the Close button for the Business Analyst Table to close the table (Figure 1–19).

Figure 1–19

Other Ways

1. Right-click tab for table, click Close on shortcut menu

To Add Records to a Table

Creating a table by building the structure and saving the table is the first step in a two-step process. The second step is to add records to the table. To add records to a table, the table must be open. When making changes to tables, you work in Datasheet view. In Datasheet view, the table is represented as a collection of rows and columns called a **datasheet**.

You often add records in phases. For example, you might not have enough time to add all the records in one session. The following steps open the Business Analyst Table in Datasheet view and then add the first two records in the Business Analyst Table (Figure 1–20).

BA #	Last Name	First Name	Street	City	State	Postal Code	Salary YTD	Incentive YTD
11	Kerry	Cordelia	251 Painter	Georgetown	NC	28794	$3,200.00	$3,450.00
14	Martinez	Manuel	3125 Steel	Kyle	SC	28797	$3,100.00	$2,430.00

Figure 1–20

- Right-click the Business Analyst Table in the Navigation Pane to display the shortcut menu (Figure 1–21).

Figure 1–21

2

- Click Open on the shortcut menu to open the table in Datasheet view.

Q&A What if I want to return to Design view?

You can open Design view by clicking Design View on the shortcut menu.

- Click the Shutter Bar Open/Close Button to close the Navigation Pane (Figure 1–22).

Figure 1–22

3

- Click the BA # field if necessary to display an insertion point, and type **11** to enter the first business analyst number (Figure 1–23).

Figure 1–23

4

- Press the TAB key to move to the next field.

- Enter the last name, first name, street, city, state, and postal code by typing the following entries, pressing the TAB key after each one: **Kerry** as the last name, **Cordelia** as the first name, **251 Painter** as the street, **Georgetown** as the city, **NC** as the state, and **28794** as the postal code.

- Type **3200** in the Salary YTD field (Figure 1–24).

Figure 1–24

Q&A Do I need to type a dollar sign?

You do not need to type dollar signs or commas. In addition, because the digits to the right of the decimal point are both zeros, you do not need to type either the decimal point or the zeros.

5

- Press the TAB key to complete the entry for the field.

- Type 3450 in the Incentive YTD field, and then press the TAB key to complete the entry of the first record (Figure 1–25).

Q&A

How and when do I save the record?

As soon as you have entered or modified a record and moved to another record, the original record is saved. This is different from other applications. The rows entered in an Excel worksheet, for example, are not saved until the entire worksheet is saved.

Figure 1–25

6

- Use the techniques shown in Steps 3 through 5 to enter the data for the second record (Figure 1–26).

Experiment

- Click the Salary YTD field on either of the records. Be sure the Table Tools Fields tab is selected. Click the Format box arrow and then click each of the formats in the Format box menu to see the effect on the values in the Salary YTD field. When finished, click Currency in the Format box menu.

Figure 1–26

Making Changes to the Data

As you enter data, check your entries carefully to ensure they are correct. If you make a mistake and discover it before you press the TAB key, correct it by pressing the BACKSPACE key until the incorrect characters are removed, and then type the correct characters. If you do not discover a mistake until later, you can use the following techniques to make the necessary corrections to the data:

- To undo your most recent change, click the Undo button on the Quick Access Toolbar. If there is nothing that Access can undo, this button will be dimmed, and clicking it will have no effect.

- To add a record, click the New (blank) record button, click the position for the Business Analyst Number field on the first open record, and then add the record. Do not worry about it being in the correct position in the table. Access will reposition the record based on the primary key, in this case, the Business Analyst Number.

BTW

Adding Records
You can add records in any order. When you close a table and reopen it, the records will be in order by primary key.

- To delete a record, click the record selector, shown in Figure 1–26, for the record to be deleted. Then press the DELETE key to delete the record, and click the Yes button when Access asks you to verify that you do indeed want to delete the record.

- To change the contents of one or more fields in a record, the record must be on the screen. If it is not, use any appropriate technique, such as the UP ARROW and DOWN ARROW keys or the vertical scroll bar, to move to it. If the field you want to correct is not visible on the screen, use the horizontal scroll bar along the bottom of the screen to shift all the fields until the one you want appears. If the value in the field is currently highlighted, you can simply type the new value. If you would rather edit the existing value, you must have an insertion point in the field. You can place the insertion point by clicking in the field or by pressing F2. You then can use the arrow keys, the DELETE key, and the BACKSPACE key for making the correction. You also can use the INSERT key to switch between Insert and Overtype mode. When you have made the change, press the TAB key to move to the next field.

If you cannot determine how to correct the data, you may find that you are "stuck" on the record, in which case Access neither allows you to move to another record nor allows you to close the table until you have made the correction. If you encounter this situation, simply press the ESC key. Pressing the ESC key will remove from the screen the record you are trying to add. You then can move to any other record, close the table, or take any other action you desire.

To Close a Table

Now that you have created and saved the Business Analyst Table, you can close it. The following step closes the table.

1 Click the Close button for the Business Analyst Table, shown in Figure 1–26, to close the table (Figure 1–27).

Figure 1–27

To Quit Access

The following steps quit Access. For a detailed example of the procedure summarized below, refer to the Office 2010 and Windows 7 chapter at the beginning of this book.

1 Click the Close button on the right side of the title bar to quit Access.

2 If a Microsoft Access dialog box appears, click the Save button to save any changes made to the object since the last save.

Break Point: If you wish to take a break, this is a good place to do so. To resume at a later time, continue following the steps from this location forward.

Starting Access and Opening a Database

Once you have created and later closed a database, you will need to open it in the future in order to use it. Opening a database requires that Access is running on your computer.

To Start Access

1 Click the Start button on the Windows 7 taskbar to display the Start menu.

2 Type `Microsoft Access` as the search text in the 'Search programs and files' text box and watch the search results appear on the Start menu.

3 Click Microsoft Access 2010 in the search results on the Start menu to start Access.

To Open a Database from Access

Earlier in this chapter, you saved your database on a USB flash drive using the file name, Camashaly Design. The following steps open the Camashaly Design database from the Access folder in the CIS 101 folder on the USB flash drive. For a detailed example of the procedure summarized below, refer to the Office 2010 and Windows 7 chapter at the beginning of this book.

1 With your USB flash drive connected to one of the computer's USB ports, click File on the Ribbon to open the Backstage view, if necessary.

2 Click Open in the Backstage view to display the Open dialog box.

3 Navigate to the location of the file to be opened (in this case, the USB flash drive, then to the CIS 101 folder [or your class folder], and then to the Access folder).

4 Click Camashaly Design to select the file to be opened.

5 Click the Open button (Open dialog box) to open the selected file and display the opened database in the Access window.

6 If a Security Warning appears, click the Enable Content button (Figure 1–28).

BTW

Organizing Files and Folders
You should organize and store files in folders so that you easily can find the files later. For a discussion of folders and detailed examples of creating folders, refer to the Office 2010 and Windows 7 chapter at the beginning of this book.

Q&A

When would I not want to enable the content?

You would want to disable the content if you suspected that your database might contain harmful content or damaging macros. Because you are the one who created the database and no one else has used it, you should have no such suspicions.

Figure 1–28

Other Ways

1. Click File on the Ribbon, click Recent in the Backstage view, click file name

To Add Additional Records to a Table

You can add records to a table that already contains data using a process almost identical to that used to add records to an empty table. The only difference is that you place the insertion point after the last record before you enter the additional data. To do so, use the **Navigation buttons**, which are buttons used to move within a table, found near the lower-left corner of the screen when a table is open. The purpose of each of the Navigation buttons is described in Table 1–4.

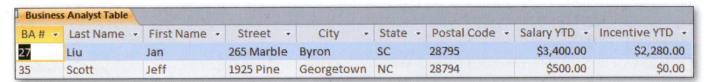

Table 1–4 Navigation Buttons in Datasheet View	
Button	**Purpose**
First record	Moves to the first record in the table
Previous record	Moves to the previous record
Next record	Moves to the next record
Last record	Moves to the last record in the table
New (blank) record	Moves to the end of the table to a position for entering a new record

The following steps add the remaining records (Figure 1–29) to the Business Analyst table.

Figure 1–29

- If the Navigation Pane is closed, click the Shutter Bar Open/ Close Button, shown in Figure 1–27, to open the Navigation Pane (Figure 1–30).

Figure 1–30

- Right-click the Business Analyst Table in the Navigation Pane to display a shortcut menu.

- Click Open on the shortcut menu to open the table in Datasheet view.

- Close the Navigation Pane by clicking the Shutter Bar Open/Close Button (Figure 1–31).

Figure 1–31

● Click the New (blank) record button to move to a position to enter a new record (Figure 1–32).

Q&A

Could you just click the Business Analyst Number (BA #) on the first open record and then add the record?

Yes, but it is a good habit to use the New (blank) Record button. Once a table contains more records than will fit on the screen, it is easier to click the New (blank) record button.

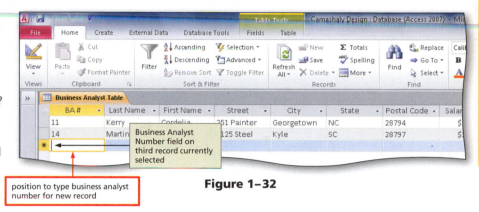

Figure 1–32

● Add the records shown in Figure 1–29, using the same techniques you used to add the first two records (Figure 1–33).

Figure 1–33

Other Ways

1. Click New button (Home tab | Records group)
2. Press CTRL+PLUS SIGN (+)

To Resize Columns in a Datasheet

Access assigns default column sizes, which do not always allow all the data in the field to appear. In some cases, the data might appear but not the entire field name. You can correct this problem by **resizing** the column (changing its size) in the datasheet. In some instances, you may want to reduce the size of a column. The State field, for example, is short enough that it does not require all the space on the screen that is allotted to it. Changing a column width changes the **layout**, or design, of a table.

The following steps resize the columns in the Business Analyst table and save the changes to the layout.

● Point to the right boundary of the field selector for the Business Analyst (BA #) field (Figure 1–34) so that the mouse pointer becomes a two-headed arrow.

Figure 1–34

2

● Double-click the right boundary of the field selector to resize the field so that it best fits the data.

● Use the same technique to resize all the other fields to best fit the data (Figure 1–35).

3

● Save the changes to the layout by clicking the Save button on the Quick Access Toolbar (Figure 1–35).

● Click the table's Close button (shown in Figure 1–33) to close the table.

Q&A What if I closed the table without saving the layout changes?

You would be asked if you want to save the changes.

Figure 1–35

Other Ways

1. Right-click field name, click Field Width

Plan Ahead

Determine the best method for distributing the database objects.

The traditional method of distributing database objects uses a printer to produce a hard copy of a table. A **hard copy** or **printout** is information that exists on a physical medium such as paper. For users who can receive fax documents, you can elect to print a hard copy on a remote fax machine. Hard copies can be useful for the following reasons:

● Many people prefer proofreading a hard copy of a document rather than viewing it on the screen to check for errors and readability.

● Hard copies can serve as reference material if your storage medium is lost or becomes corrupted and you need to re-create the document.

Instead of distributing a hard copy, users can choose to distribute the document as an electronic image that mirrors the original document's appearance. The electronic image of the document can be e-mailed, posted on a Web site, or copied to a portable medium such as a USB flash drive. Two popular electronic image formats, sometimes called fixed formats, are PDF by Adobe Systems and XPS by Microsoft. In Access, you can create PDF and XPS files through the External Data tab on the Ribbon. Electronic images of documents, such as PDF and XPS, can be useful for the following reasons:

● Users can view electronic images of documents without the software that created the original document (i.e., Access). Specifically, to view a PDF file, you use a program called Acrobat Reader, which can be downloaded free from Adobe's Web site. Similarly, to view an XPS file, you use a program called an XPS Viewer, which is included in the latest versions of Windows and Internet Explorer.

● Sending electronic documents saves paper and printer supplies. Society encourages users to contribute to **green computing**, which involves reducing the environmental waste generated when using a computer.

BTW

Changing Printers
To change the default printer that appears in the Print dialog box, click File on the Ribbon, click the Print tab in the Backstage view, click Print in the Print gallery, then click the Name box arrow and select the desired printer.

Previewing and Printing the Contents of a Table

When working with a database, you often will need to print a copy of the table contents. Figure 1–36 shows a printed copy of the contents of the Business Analyst table. (Yours may look slightly different, depending on your printer.) Because the Business Analyst table is substantially wider than the screen, it also will be wider than the normal printed page in portrait orientation. **Portrait orientation** means the printout is across the width of the page. **Landscape orientation** means the printout is across the height of the page. Thus, to print the wide database table, you might prefer to use landscape orientation. A convenient way to change to landscape orientation is to preview what the printed copy will look like by using Print Preview. This allows you to determine whether landscape orientation is necessary and, if it is, to change the orientation easily to landscape. In addition, you also can use Print Preview to determine whether any adjustments are necessary to the page margins.

			Business Analyst Table						4/12/2012
BA #	Last Name	First Name	Street	City	State	Postal Code	Salary YTD	Incentive YTD	
11	Kerry	Cordelia	251 Painter	Georgetown	NC	28794	$3,200.00	$3,450.00	
14	Martinez	Manuel	3125 Steel	Kyle	SC	28797	$3,100.00	$2,430.00	
27	Liu	Jan	265 Marble	Byron	SC	28795	$3,400.00	$2,280.00	
35	Scott	Jeff	1925 Pine	Georgetown	NC	28794	$500.00	$0.00	

Figure 1–36

To Preview and Print the Contents of a Table

The following steps use Print Preview to preview and then print the contents of the Business Analyst table.

1

- If the Navigation Pane is closed, open the Navigation Pane by clicking the Shutter Bar Open/Close Button.

- Be sure the Business Analyst table is selected.

Q&A

Why do I have to be sure the Business Analyst table is selected? It is the only object in the database.

When the database contains only one object, you do not have to worry about selecting the object. Ensuring that the correct object is selected is a good habit to form, however, to make sure that the object you print is the one you want.

Figure 1–37

- Click File on the Ribbon to open the Backstage view.

- Click the Print tab in the Backstage view to display the Print gallery (Figure 1–37).

2

- Click the Print Preview button in the Print gallery to display a preview of what the table will look like when printed.

- Close the Navigation Pane to free up more of the screen for the preview (Figure 1–38).

Q&A

I cannot read the table. Can I magnify a portion of the table?

Yes. Point the mouse pointer, whose shape will change to a magnifying glass, at the portion of the table that you want to magnify, and then click. You can return the view of the table to the one shown in the figure by clicking a second time.

Figure 1–38

Q&A

3

• Click the mouse pointer in the position shown in Figure 1–38 to magnify the upper-right section of the table (Figure 1–39).

My table was already magnified in a different area. How can I see the area shown in the figure?

One way is to use the scroll bars to move to the desired portion of the table. You also can click the mouse pointer anywhere in the table to produce a screen like the one in Figure 1–38, and then click in the location shown in the figure.

Figure 1–39

4

• Click the Landscape button to change to landscape orientation (Figure 1–40).

• Click the Print button (Print Preview tab | Print group) to display the Print dialog box.

• Click the OK button (Print dialog box) to print the table.

• When the printer stops, retrieve the hard copy of the Business Analyst Table.

• Click the Close Print Preview button (Print Preview tab | Close Preview group) to close the Print Preview window.

Figure 1–40

Other Ways

1. Press CTRL+P, click OK button (Print dialog box)

Creating Additional Tables

The Camashaly Design database contains two tables, the Business Analyst table and the Client table. You still need to create the Client table and add records to it. You created the Business Analyst table in Datasheet view. You will create the Client table in Design view.

Recall that the fields for the Client table are Client Number, Client Name, Street, City, State, Postal Code, Amount Paid, Current Due, Contract Hours YTD, and Business Analyst Number. The details that must be entered for these fields are shown in Table 1–5. The Client Number is the primary key. The Client Number field and the Business Analyst Number fields have both descriptions and captions. The Contract Hours YTD field has a caption.

Because the values in the Contract Hours YTD field have decimal places, only Single, Double, or Decimal would be possible field size choices. (See Table 1–2 on Page AC 10 for a description of the possible field sizes for Number fields.) The difference between these choices concerns the amount of accuracy. Double is more accurate than Single, for example, but requires more storage space. Because the rates are only two decimal places, Single is a perfectly acceptable choice.

In addition to changing the field size for the Contract Hours YTD, you will also change the format to Fixed (a fixed number of decimal places) and the number of decimal places to 2.

Table 1–5 Structure of Client Table			
Field Name	**Data Type**	**Field Size**	**Notes**
Client Number	Text	4	**Primary Key** **Description:** Client Number (two uppercase letters followed by 2-digit number) **Caption:** CL #
Client Name	Text	30	
Street	Text	15	
City	Text	15	
State	Text	2	
Postal Code	Text	5	
Amount Paid	Currency		
Current Due	Currency		
Contract Hours YTD	Number	Single	**Caption:** Hrs YTD **Format:** Fixed **Decimal Places:** 2
Business Analyst Number	Text	2	**Caption:** BA # **Description:** Business Analyst Number (number of business analyst for client)

To Create a Table in Design View

The next step in creating the table is to define the fields by specifying the required details in Design view. You will make entries in the Field Name, Data Type, and Description columns and enter additional information in the Field Properties box in the lower portion of the Table window. As you define the fields, the row selector (Figure 1–19 on page AC 23) indicates the field you currently are describing. Clicking the row selector selects the entire row. It is positioned on the first field, indicating Access is ready for you to enter the name of the first field in the Field Name column.

The following steps use Design view to define the fields in the table.

1
- Open the Navigation Pane.
- Click Create on the Ribbon to display the Create tab (Figure 1–41).

Figure 1–41

2

- Click the Table Design button (Create tab | Tables group) to create a new table in Design view (Figure 1–42).

Q&A

Could I save the table now so I can assign it the name I want, rather than Table1?

You certainly could. Be aware, however, that you will still need to save it again once you have added all your fields.

Figure 1–42

3

- Type **Client Number** (the name of the first field) in the Field Name column and then press the TAB key to accept the field name and move to the Data Type column (Figure 1–43).

Figure 1–43

4

- Because the Client Number field is the primary key, click the Primary Key button (Table Tools Design tab | Tools group) to designate the Client Number field as the primary key (Figure 1–44).

Figure 1–44

5

- Press the TAB key to move to the Description column, and then type **Client Number (two uppercase letters followed by a two-digit number)** as the description.

- Click the Field Size text box in the Field Properties pane to produce an insertion point, use either the BACKSPACE or DELETE key as necessary to erase the current entry (255), and then type **4** to change the field size.

- Click the Caption text box to produce an insertion point, and then type **CL #** to enter a caption (Figure 1–45).

Figure 1–45

6

- Click the Field Name column on the second row to produce an insertion point and then make the entries for the Client Name field.

- Use the techniques illustrated in Steps 1 through 5 to make the entries for the remaining fields in the Client table structure, shown in Table 1–5 on page AC 33, up through and including the name of the Amount Paid field.

- Click the Data Type box arrow to display a menu of available data types (Figure 1–46).

Figure 1–46

7

- Click Currency to select the data type.

- Enter the Current Due field and select the Currency data type.

- Enter the Contract Hours YTD field and select the Number data type (Figure 1–47).

Figure 1–47

8

- Click the Field Size box to display the Field Size box arrow.

- Click the Field Size box arrow to display the Field Size box menu (Figure 1–48).

What would happen if I left the field size set to Integer?

If the field size is Integer, no decimal places can be stored. Thus a value of 2.50 would be stored as 2.

If you enter your hours and none of the values have decimal places, probably you did not change the field size.

Figure 1–48

9

- Click Single to select single precision as the field size.

- Click the Format box to display the Format box arrow.

- Click the Format box arrow to display the Format box menu (Figure 1–49).

Figure 1–49

10

- Click Fixed to select fixed as the format.

- Click the Decimal Places box to display the Decimal Places box arrow.

- Click the Decimal Places box arrow to enter the number of decimal places.

- Click 2 to select 2 as the number of decimal places.

- Click the Caption text box to produce an insertion point, and then type `Hrs YTD` to enter a caption (Figure 1–50).

Figure 1–50

11

- Enter the Business Analyst Number field from Table 1–5. Be sure to change the description, field size, and caption to the ones shown in the table.

- Click the Save button on the Quick Access Toolbar to display the Save As dialog box, type Client as the name of the table, and then click the OK button (Save As dialog box) to save the table (Figure 1–51).

Figure 1–51

Correcting Errors in the Structure

When creating a table, check the entries carefully to ensure they are correct. If you make a mistake and discover it before you press the TAB key, you can correct the error by repeatedly pressing the BACKSPACE key until the incorrect characters are removed. Then, type the correct characters. If you do not discover a mistake until later, you can click the entry, type the correct value, and then press the ENTER key. You can use the following techniques to make changes to the structure:

- If you accidentally add an extra field to the structure, select the field by clicking the row selector (the leftmost column on the row that contains the field to be deleted). Once you have selected the field, press the DELETE key. This will remove the field from the structure.

- If you forget to include a field, select the field that will follow the field you want to add by clicking the row selector, and then press the INSERT key. The remaining fields move down one row, making room for the missing field. Make the entries for the new field in the usual manner.

- If you made the wrong field a primary key field, click the correct primary key entry for the field and then click the Primary Key button (Table Tools Design tab | Tools group).

- To move a field, click the row selector for the field to be moved to select the field, and then drag the field to the desired position.

As an alternative to these steps, you may want to start over. To do so, click the Close button for the window containing the table, and then click the No button in the Microsoft Access dialog box. Click Create on the Ribbon and then click the Table Design button to create a table. You then can repeat the process you used earlier to define the fields in the table.

BTW

AutoCorrect Feature
The AutoCorrect feature of Access corrects common mistakes when entering text in a cell. AutoCorrect corrects two capital letters by changing the second letter to lowercase and capitalizes the first letter in the names of days. It also corrects more than 400 commonly misspelled words.

BTW

Other AutoCorrect Options
Using the Office AutoCorrect feature, you can create entries that will replace abbreviations with spelled-out names and phrases automatically. To specify AutoCorrect rules, click File on the Ribbon to open the Backstage view, click Options, and then click Proofing in the Access Options dialog box.

To Close the Table

Now that you have completed and saved the Client table, you can close it. The following step closes the table.

1 Click the Close button for the Client table (see Figure 1–51) to close the table.

Importing Data from Other Applications to Access

Now that you have created the Client table, you could add the records to it just as you did with the Business Analyst table. Access provides an alternative, however, that is available because Camashaly Design has already stored the necessary data in an Excel workbook (Figure 1–52). The data is stored in the form of an Excel **list**; that is, the first row contains column headings describing the data in each of the columns, and the remaining rows contain the data. Camashaly can **import** the data, which means to make a copy of the data in a table in the Access database.

When importing data, you have two choices. You can create a new table, in which case the column headings in the worksheet become the field names in the table. Access will attempt to assign appropriate data types. You would need to review the data types, adjust field sizes, captions, descriptions, and formats after the data was imported. The other option is to add the records to an existing table. This method is appropriate if you have already created the table, provided the column headings in the worksheet match the field names in the table, as they do in the case of the Client table.

	A	B	C	D	E	F	G	H	I	J	K
1	Client Number	Client Name	Street	City	State	Postal Code	Amount Paid	Current Due	Contract Hours YTD	Business Analyst Number	
2	BA53	Bavant Animal Hospital	134 Main	Burles	NC	28817	$0.00	$7,500.00	0.00	11	
3	BB32	Babbage CPA Firm	464 Linnell	Austin	SC	28796	$1,500.00	$500.00	5.00	14	
4	BC76	Buda Community Clinic	867 Ridge	Buda	NC	27032	$2,500.00	$750.00	2.50	11	
5	CJ29	Catering by Jenna	123 Second	Granger	NC	27036	$3,000.00	$1,000.00	15.50	27	
6	GA74	Grant Antiques	78 Catawba	Georgetown	NC	28794	$5,500.00	$3,200.00	34.50	14	
7	GF56	Granger Foundation	65 Simpson	Granger	NC	27036	$0.00	$6,500.00	0.00	11	
8	HC10	Hendley County Hospital	216 Rivard	Austin	SC	28796	$3,100.00	$1,200.00	12.00	27	
9	KD21	KAL Design Studio	116 Pine	Georgetown	NC	28794	$6,000.00	$3,200.00	30.50	14	
10	KG04	Kyle Grocery Cooperative	421 First	Kyle	SC	28798	$3,200.00	$0.00	5.00	11	
11	ME14	Mike's Electronic Stop	234 Gilham	Georgetown	NC	28794	$2,500.00	$1,500.00	8.50	27	
12	PJ34	Patricia Jean Florist	345 Magee	Kyle	SC	28798	$0.00	$5,200.00	0.00	27	
13	SL77	Smarter Law Associates	764 Main	Burles	NC	28817	$3,800.00	$0.00	10.50	11	
14	TB17	The Bikeshop	346 Austin	Buda	NC	27032	$2,750.00	$1,200.00	14.00	27	
15	WE05	Walburg Energy Alternatives	12 Polk	Walburg	NC	28819	$4,500.00	$1,450.00	19.50	14	
16	WS01	Woody Sporting Goods	578 Central	Walburg	NC	28819	$2,250.00	$1,600.00	18.50	14	
17											

Figure 1–52

The process of importing into an Access database uses a wizard. Specifically, if the data is imported from an Excel worksheet, the process will use the Import Spreadsheet Wizard. The wizard takes you through some basic steps, asking a few simple questions. After you have answered the questions, the wizard will import or link the data.

To Import an Excel Worksheet

To import the data in the Camashaly Client Data workbook, you use the Import Spreadsheet Wizard to place the rows from an Excel worksheet into an existing table. The following steps import the Camashaly Client Data Excel workbook, which is provided as a data file. See the inside back cover of this book for instructions on downloading the Data Files for Students, or contact your instructor for more information about accessing the required files.

1

- Click External Data on the Ribbon to display the External Data tab (Figure 1–53).

Figure 1–53

2

- Click the Excel button (External Data tab | Import & Link group) to display the Get External Data – Excel Spreadsheet dialog box.

- Click the Browse button (Get External Data – Excel Spreadsheet dialog box) to display the File Open dialog box.

- Navigate to the USB flash drive (or the location of your data files).

- Double-click your USB flash drive, and then click Camashaly Client Data to select the file to be opened.

- Click the Open button (File Open dialog box), which will return you to the Get External Data dialog box with the Camashaly Client Data workbook selected.

3

- Click the option button to append a copy of records to a table (Figure 1–54).

What happens if I select the option button to import records into a new table?

Instead of the records being added to an existing table, they will be placed in a new table. Access will assign all the data types. You would then need to ensure they are correct. You also would need to change any field sizes, descriptions, captions, formats, or number of decimal places to the ones you want.

Figure 1–54

4

• Click the arrow to produce a menu of available tables.

• Click the Client table to select the table to which a copy of the records will be appended (Figure 1–55).

Figure 1–55

5

• Click the OK button to move to the next Import Spreadsheet Wizard screen (Figure 1–56).

Q&A

The First Row Contains Column Headings check box is checked, but it is dimmed. What if I want to remove the check mark?

When you are appending records to an existing table, the first row must contain column headings. If instead you were creating a new table, the first row might not contain column headings. In that case, you would have control over this check box.

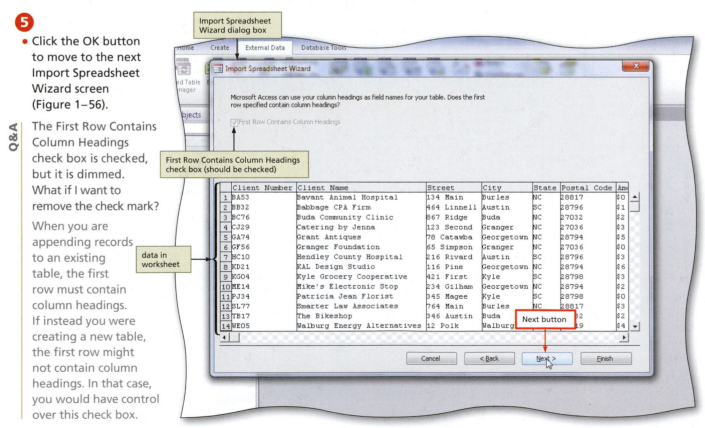

Figure 1–56

6

- Click the Next button to move to the next Import Spreadsheet Wizard screen (Figure 1–57).

 What happens if I later realize I have selected the wrong table?

If you have not yet clicked the Finish button, you can click the Back button to return to the screen where you selected the table, and then select the correct table.

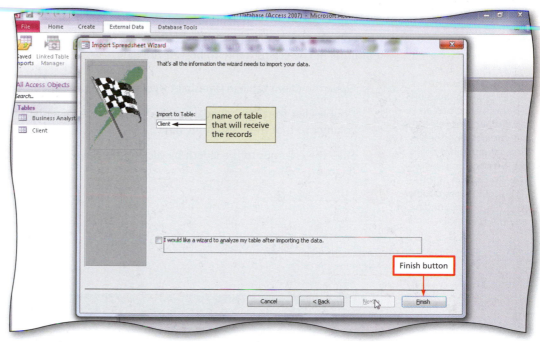

Figure 1–57

7

- Because the table name is correct, click the Finish button to import the data (Figure 1–58).

 I got an error message that stated that a particular field did not exist in the Client table. What did I do wrong? How do I fix it?

When you created the table, you did not name that particular field correctly. Open the table in Design view and change the field name to the correct name. Check other field names as well. When you are done, save and close the table. Then, repeat the import process.

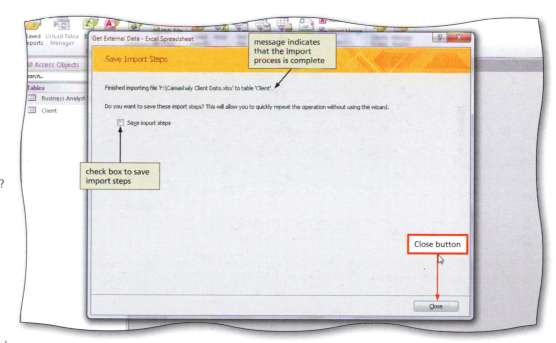

Figure 1–58

8

- Because you will not save the import steps, click the Close button.

 When would I save the import steps?

If you think you might need to repeat these steps in the future, you can save time by saving the steps.

Other Ways

1. Right-click table in Navigation Pane, click Import on shortcut menu

To Resize Columns in a Datasheet

You can resize the columns in the datasheet for the Client table just as you resized the columns in the datasheet for the Business Analyst table. The following steps resize the columns in the Client table to best fit the data.

BTW

Resizing Columns
To resize all columns in a datasheet to best fit simultaneously, select the column heading for the first column, hold down the SHIFT key and select the last column in the datasheet. Then, double-click the right boundary of any field selector.

1 Open the Client table in Datasheet view and then close the Navigation Pane.

2 Double-click the right boundary of the field selectors of each of the fields to resize the columns so that they best fit the data.

3 Save the changes to the layout by clicking the Save button on the Quick Access Toolbar (Figure 1–59).

4 Close the table.

Figure 1–59

Break Point: If you wish to take a break, this is a good place to do so. You can quit Access now. To resume at a later time, start Access, open the database called Camashaly Design, and continue following the steps from this location forward.

Additional Database Objects

A computerized database such as Access contains many types of objects. Tables are the objects you use to store and manipulate data. Access supports other important types of objects as well; each of these objects has a specific purpose that assists in maximizing the benefits of a database. Through queries (questions), Access makes it possible to ask complex questions concerning the data in the database and then receive instant answers. Access also allows the user to produce attractive and useful forms for viewing and updating data. Additionally, Access includes report creation tools that make it easy to produce sophisticated reports for presenting data.

To Use the Simple Query Wizard to Create a Query

Queries are simply questions, the answers to which are in the database. Access contains a powerful query feature that helps you find the answers to a wide variety of questions. Once you have examined the question you want to ask to determine the fields involved in the question, you can begin creating the query. If there are no restrictions involved in the query, nor any special order or calculations, you can use the Simple Query Wizard.

The following steps use the Simple Query Wizard to create a query that Camashaly Design might use to obtain financial information on its clients. The query displays the number, name, amount paid, current due, contract hours YTD, and business analyst number of all clients.

1
- If the Navigation Pane is closed, click the Shutter Bar Open/Close Button to open the Navigation Pane.

- Be sure the Client table is selected.

- Click Create on the Ribbon to display the Create tab.

- Click the Query Wizard button (Create tab | Queries group) to display the New Query dialog box (Figure 1–60).

Figure 1–60

2
- Be sure Simple Query Wizard is selected, and then click the OK button (New Query dialog box) to display the Simple Query Wizard dialog box (Figure 1–61).

Q&A
What would happen if the Business Analyst Table were selected instead of the Client table?

The list of available fields would contain fields from the Business Analyst Table rather than the Client table.

Q&A
If the list contained Business Analyst Table fields, how could I make it contain Client table fields?

Click the arrow in the Tables/Queries box and then click the Client table in the list that appears.

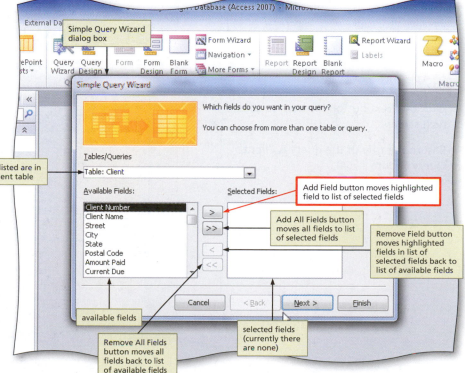

Figure 1–61

3

- With the Client Number field selected, click the Add Field button to add the field to the query.

- With the Client Name field selected, click the Add Field button a second time to add the field.

- Click the Amount Paid field, and then click the Add Field button to add the field.

- In a similar fashion, add the Current Due, Contract Hours YTD, and Business Analyst Number fields (Figure 1–62).

Figure 1–62

4

- Click the Next button to move to the next screen.

- Ensure that the Detail (shows every field of every record) option button is selected (Figure 1–63).

Q&A

What is the difference between Detail and Summary?

Detail shows all the records and fields. Summary only shows computations (for example, the total amount paid).

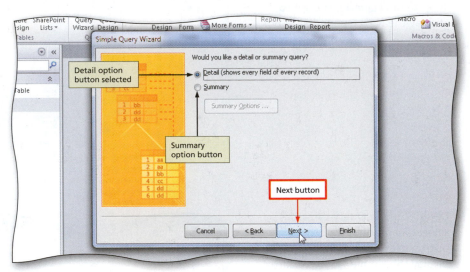

Figure 1–63

5

- Click the Next button to move to the next screen.

- Ensure the title of the query is Client Query (Figure 1–64).

Figure 1–64

6

- Click the Finish button to create the query (Figure 1–65).

- Click the Close button for the Client Query to remove the query results from the screen.

If I want to use this query in the future, do I need to save the query?

Normally you would. The one exception is a query created by the wizard. The wizard automatically saves the query it creates.

CL #	Client Name	Amount Paid	Current Due	Hrs YTD	BA #
BA53	Bavant Animal Hospital	$0.00	$7,500.00	0.00	11
BB32	Babbage CPA Firm	$1,500.00	$500.00	5.00	14
BC76	Buda Community Clinic	$2,500.00	$750.00	2.50	11
CJ29	Catering by Jenna	$3,000.00	$1,000.00	15.50	27
GA74	Grant Antiques	$5,500.00	$3,200.00	34.50	14
GF56	Granger Foundation	$0.00	$6,500.00	0.00	11
HC10	Hendley County Hospital	$3,100.00	$1,200.00	12.00	27
KD21	KAL Design Studio	$6,000.00	$3,200.00	30.50	14
KG04	Kyle Grocery Cooperative	$3,200.00	$0.00	5.00	11
ME14	Mike's Electronic Stop	$2,500.00	$1,500.00	8.50	27
PJ34	Patricia Jean Florist	$0.00	$5,200.00	0.00	27
SL77	Smarter Law Associates	$3,800.00	$0.00	10.50	11
TB17	The Bikeshop	$2,750.00	$1,200.00	14.00	27
WE05	Walburg Energy Alternatives	$4,500.00	$1,450.00	19.50	14
WS01	Woody Sporting Goods	$2,250.00	$1,600.00	18.50	14

Figure 1–65

Using Queries

After you have created and saved a query, Access stores it as a database object and makes it available for use in a variety of ways:

- To view the results of the query, open it by right-clicking the query in the Navigation Pane and clicking Open on the shortcut menu.

- To print the results with the query open, click File on the Ribbon, click the Print tab, and then click either Print or Quick Print.

- If you want to change the design of the query, right-click the query in the Navigation Pane and then click Design View on the shortcut menu to open the query in Design view.

- To print the query without first opening it, be sure the query is selected in the Navigation Pane and click File on the Ribbon, click the Print tab, and then click either Print or Quick Print.

You can switch between views of a query using the View button (Home tab | Views group). Clicking the arrow in the bottom of the button produces the View button menu. You then click the desired view in the menu. The two query views you will use in this chapter are Datasheet view (see the results) and Design view (change the design). You also can click the top part of the View button, in which case, you will switch to the view identified by the icon on the button. In the figure, the button contains the icon for Design view, so clicking the button would change to Design view. For the most part, the icon on the button represents the view you want, so you can usually simply click the button.

To Use a Criterion in a Query

After you have determined the fields to be included in a query, you will determine whether there are any restrictions on the records that are to be included. For example, you might only want to include those clients whose business analyst number is 14. In such a case, you need to enter the 14 as a **criterion**, which is a condition that the records to be included must satisfy. To do so, you will open the query in Design view, enter the criterion below the appropriate field, and then view the results of the query. The following steps enter a criterion to include only the clients of business analyst 14 and then view the query results.

• Right-click the Client Query in the Navigation Pane to produce a shortcut menu (Figure 1–66).

Figure 1–66

• Click Design View on the shortcut menu to open the query in Design view (Figure 1–67).

Figure 1–67

3

- Click the Criteria row in the Business Analyst Number column of the grid, and then type **14** as the criterion (Figure 1–68).

Q&A

The Business Analyst Number field is a text field. Do I need to enclose the value for a text field in quotation marks?

You could, but it is not necessary, because Access inserts the quotation marks for you automatically.

Figure 1–68

4

- Click the View button to display the query results in Datasheet view (Figure 1–69).

Q&A

Could I click the View button arrow and then click Datasheet view?

Yes, if the icon representing the view you want appears on the View button; however, it is easier just to click the button.

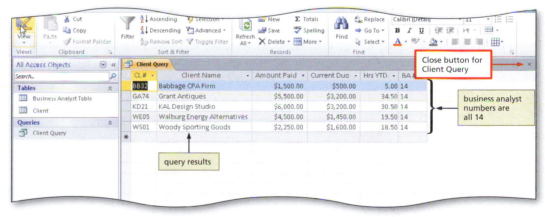

Figure 1–69

5

- Click the Close button for the Client Query to close the query.

- When asked if you want to save your changes, click the No button.

Q&A

If I saved the query, what would happen the next time I ran the query?

You would see only clients of business analyst 14.

Q&A

Could I save the query with another name?

Yes. To save the query with another name, click File on the Ribbon, click Save Object As, enter a new file name in the Save As dialog box and click the OK button (Save As dialog box).

Other Ways

1. Click Run button (Query Tools Design tab | Results group)
2. Click Datasheet View button on status bar

To Print the Results of a Query

The following steps print the results of a saved query.

1 With the Client Query selected in the Navigation Pane, click File on the Ribbon to open the Backstage view.

2 Click the Print tab in the Backstage view to display the Print gallery.

3 Click the Quick Print button to print the query.

Creating and Using Forms

In Datasheet view, you can view many records at once. If there are many fields, however, only some of the fields in each record might be visible at a time. In **Form view**, where data is displayed in a form on the screen, you usually can see all the fields, but only for one record.

To Create a Form

Like a paper form, a **form** in a database is a formatted document with fields that contain data. Forms allow you to view and maintain data. Forms also can be used to print data, but reports are more commonly used for that purpose. The simplest type of form in Access is one that includes all the fields in a table stacked one above the other. The following steps create a form, use the form to view records, and then save the form.

1
- Select the Client table in the Navigation Pane.

- If necessary, click Create on the Ribbon to display the Create tab (Figure 1–70).

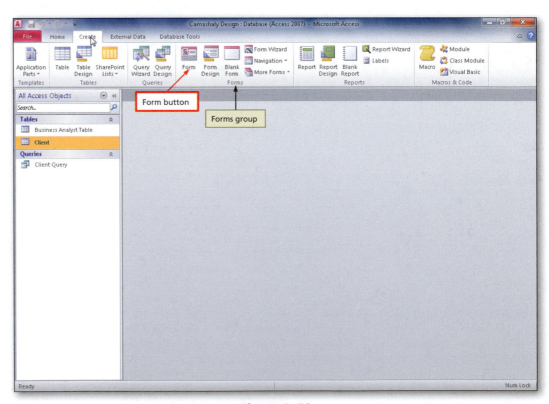

Figure 1–70

2

• Click the Form button (Create tab | Forms group) to create a simple form (Figure 1–71).

Q&A

A Field list appeared on my screen. What should I do?

Click the Add Existing Fields button (Form Layout Tools Design tab | Tools group) to remove the Field list from the screen.

Figure 1–71

3

• If the form appears in Layout view, click the Form View button on the Access status bar to display the form in Form view.

Q&A

How can I recognize Layout view?

Access identifies Layout view in three ways. The left side of the status bar will contain the words Layout View; there will be shading around the outside of the selected field in the form; and the Layout View button will be selected on the right side of the status bar.

• Click the Next Record button three times to move to record 4 (Figure 1–72).

Figure 1–72

4

- Click the Save button on the Quick Access Toolbar to display the Save As dialog box (Figure 1–73).

Figure 1–73

Q&A

Did I have to click the Next Record button before saving?

No. The only reason you were asked to click the button was so that you could experience navigation within the form.

5

- Type **Client Form** as the form name, and then click the OK button to save the form.

- Click the Close button for the form to close the form.

Other Ways

1. Click View button (Form Layout Tools Design tab | Views group)

Using a Form

After you have saved a form, you can use it at anytime by right-clicking the form in the Navigation Pane and then clicking Open in the shortcut menu. In addition to viewing data in the form, you can also use it to enter or update data, a process that is very similar to updating data using a datasheet. If you plan to use the form to enter or revise data, you must ensure you are viewing the form in Form view.

Creating and Printing Reports

Camashaly Design wants to create the Client Financial Report shown in Figure 1–74. Just as you can create a form containing all fields by clicking a single button, you can click a button to create a report containing all the fields. Doing so will not match the report shown in Figure 1–74, however, which does not contain all the fields. Some of the column headings are different. In addition, some of the headings in the report in Figure 1–74 are split over multiple lines, whereas the ones in the report created by clicking the button will not be split. Fortunately, you can later modify the report design to make it precisely match the figure. To do so, you use Layout view for the report.

Client Financial Report

Thursday, April 12, 2012
5:17:00 PM

Client Number	Client Name	Amount Paid	Current Due	Hrs YTD	Business Analyst Number
BA53	Bavant Animal Hospital	$0.00	$7,500.00	0.00	11
BB32	Babbage CPA Firm	$1,500.00	$500.00	5.00	14
BC76	Buda Community Clinic	$2,500.00	$750.00	2.50	11
CJ29	Catering by Jenna	$3,000.00	$1,000.00	15.50	27
GA74	Grant Antiques	$5,500.00	$3,200.00	34.50	14
GF56	Granger Foundation	$0.00	$6,500.00	0.00	11
HC10	Hendley County Hospital	$3,100.00	$1,200.00	12.00	27
KD21	KAL Design Studio	$6,000.00	$3,200.00	30.50	14
KG04	Kyle Grocery Cooperative	$3,200.00	$0.00	5.00	11
ME14	Mike's Electronic Stop	$2,500.00	$1,500.00	8.50	27
PJ34	Patricia Jean Florist	$0.00	$5,200.00	0.00	27
SL77	Smarter Law Associates	$3,800.00	$0.00	10.50	11
TB17	The Bikeshop	$2,750.00	$1,200.00	14.00	27
WE05	Walburg Energy Alternatives	$4,500.00	$1,450.00	19.50	14
WS01	Woody Sporting Goods	$2,250.00	$1,600.00	18.50	14
		$40,600.00	$34,800.00	176.00	

Figure 1–74

To Create a Report

You will first create a report containing all fields. The following steps create and save the initial report. They also modify the report title.

1
- Be sure the Client table is selected in the Navigation Pane.
- Click Create on the Ribbon to display the Create tab (Figure 1–75).

Q&A Why do I need to select the Client table prior to clicking Create on the Ribbon?

You do not need to select it at that point. You do need to select it prior to clicking the Report button at the next step because Access will include all the fields in whichever table or query is currently selected.

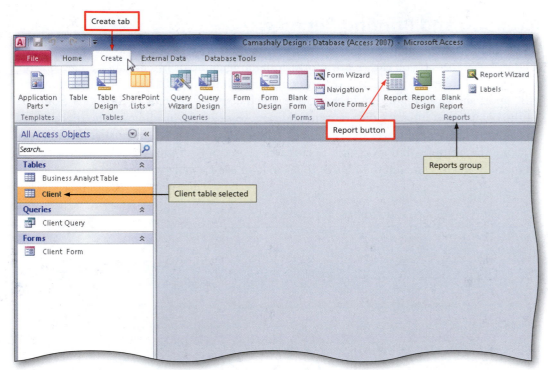

Figure 1–75

2
- Click the Report button (Create tab | Reports group) to create the report (Figure 1–76).

Q&A Why is the report title Client?

Access automatically assigns the name of the table or query as the title. It also automatically includes the date. You can change either of these later.

Figure 1–76

3

- Click the Save button on the Quick Access Toolbar to display the Save As dialog box and then type **Client Financial Report** as the name of the report (Figure 1–77).

Figure 1–77

4

- Click the OK button (Save As dialog box) to save the report (Figure 1–78).

Q&A

The name of the report changed. Why did the report title not change too?

The report title just happens to begin with the same name as the report. If you change the name of the report, Access will not change the report title. You can change it at any time to any title you like.

Figure 1–78

5

- Close the report by clicking its Close button.

Using Layout View in a Report

When working with a report in Access, there are four different ways to view the report. They are Report view, Print Preview, Layout view, and Design view. Report view shows the report on the screen. Print Preview shows the report as it will appear when printed. Layout view is similar to Report view in that it shows the report on the screen, but it also allows you to make changes to the report. It is usually the easiest way to make such changes. Design view also allows you to make changes, but it does not show you the actual report. It is most useful when the changes you need to make are especially complex. In this chapter, you will use Layout view to modify the report.

To Modify Column Headings and Resize Columns

To make the report match the one in Figure 1–74, you need to change the title, remove some columns, modify the column headings, and also resize the columns. The following steps use Layout view to make the necessary modifications to the report.

- Right-click Client Financial Report in the Navigation Pane, and then click Layout View on the shortcut menu to open the report in Layout view.

- If a Field list appears, click the Add Existing Fields button (Report Layout Tools Design tab | Tools group) to remove the Field list from the screen.

- Close the Navigation Pane.

- Click the report title once to select it.

- Click the report title a second time to produce an insertion point (Figure 1–79).

Figure 1–79

Q&A

I clicked at a different position in the title and my insertion point is in the middle of Client. How do I produce an insertion point at the position shown in the figure?

You can use the RIGHT ARROW key to move the insertion point to the position in the figure or you can click the desired position.

2

- Press the SPACEBAR to insert a space and then type **Financial Report** to complete the title.

- Click the column heading for the Street field to select it.

- Hold the SHIFT key down and then click the column headings for the City field, the State field, and the Postal Code fields to select multiple column headings.

Q&A

What happens if I do not hold down the SHIFT key?

As soon as you click the column heading, it will be the only one that is selected. To select multiple objects, you need to hold the SHIFT key down for every object after the first one.

Figure 1–80

I selected the wrong collection of objects. What should I do?

You can click somewhere else on the report so that the objects you want are not selected, and then begin the process again. Alternatively, you can repeatedly click the Undo button on the Quick Access Toolbar to undo your selections. Once you have done so, you can select the objects you want.

- Click Arrange on the Ribbon to display the Arrange tab (Figure 1–80).

3
- Click the Select Column button (Report Layout Tools Arrange tab | Rows & Columns group) to select the entire columns corresponding to the column headings you selected in the previous step.

- Press the DELETE key to delete the columns.

- Click the column heading for the Client Number field twice, once to select it and the second time to produce an insertion point (Figure 1–81).

I inadvertently selected the wrong field. What should I do?

Click somewhere outside the various fields to deselect the one you have selected. Then, click the Client Number field twice.

Figure 1–81

4
- Use the DELETE or BACKSPACE keys as necessary to erase the current entry and then type **Client Number** as the new entry.

- Click the heading for the Business Analyst Number field twice, erase the current entry, and then type **Business Analyst Number** as the new entry.

- Click the Client Number field heading to select it, point to the lower boundary of the heading for the Client Number field so that the mouse pointer changes to a two-headed arrow and then drag the lower boundary to the approximate position shown in Figure 1–82 to expand the column headings.

Figure 1–82

Do I have to be exact?

No. If you are in a slightly different position, your report would look a little different from the one in the figure, but the difference would not be significant.

5

- Point to the right boundary of the heading for the Client Number field so that the mouse pointer changes to a two-headed arrow and then drag the right boundary to the approximate position shown in Figure 1–83 to reduce the width of the column.

Q&A

Do I have to be exact?

No. Again, if you are in a slightly different position, the difference between your report and the one in the figure would not be significant.

Figure 1–83

6

- Using the same technique, resize the other columns to the sizes shown in Figure 1–84.

Figure 1–84

To Add Totals to a Report

The report in Figure 1–74 contains totals for the Amount Paid, Current Due, and Hrs YTD columns. You can use Layout view to add these totals. The following steps use Layout view to include totals for these three columns.

1

- Click the Amount Paid field heading (shown in Figure 1–84) to select the field.

Q&A
Do I have to click the heading? Could I click the field on one of the records?

You do not have to click the heading. You also could click the Amount Paid field on any record.

- Click Design on the Ribbon to display the Design tab.

- Click the Totals button (Report Layout Tools Design tab | Grouping & Totals group) to display the list of available calculations (Figure 1–85).

Figure 1–85

2

- Click Sum to calculate the sum of the amount of paid values.

Q&A
Is Sum the same as Total?

Yes.

- Using the same technique, add totals for the Current Due and Hrs YTD columns.

- Scroll down to the bottom of the report to verify that the totals are included. If necessary, expand the size of the total controls so they appear completely.

- Click the Page number to select it and then drag it to the approximate position shown in Figure 1–86.

Figure 1–86

Q&A Why did I need to move the page number?

The dotted line near the right-hand edge of the screen indicates the right-hand border of the available space on the printed page, based on whatever margins and orientation are currently selected. A portion of the page number extends beyond this border. By moving the page number, it no longer extends beyond the border.

3

- Click the Save button on the Quick Access Toolbar to save your changes to the report layout.
- Close the report.

To Print a Report

The following steps print the report.

1 With the Client Financial Report selected in the Navigation Pane, click File on the Ribbon to open the Backstage view.

2 Click the Print tab in the Backstage view to display the Print gallery.

3 Click the Quick Print button to print the report.

Q&A How can I print multiple copies of my report?

Click File on the Ribbon to open the Backstage view. Click the Print tab, click Print in the Print gallery to display the Print dialog box, increase the number in the Number of Copies box, and then click the OK button (Print dialog box).

Q&A How can I print a range of pages rather than printing the whole report?

Click File on the Ribbon to open the Backstage view. Click the Print tab, click Print in the Print gallery to display the Print dialog box, click the Pages option button in the Print Range area, enter the desired page range, and then click the OK button (Print dialog box).

BTW

Tabbed Documents Versus Overlapping Windows
By default, Access 2010 displays database objects in tabbed documents instead of overlapping windows. If your database is in overlapping windows mode, click File on the Ribbon, click Options in the Backstage view, click Current Database in the Access Options dialog box, and select the Display Document Tabs check box and the Tabbed Documents option button.

Database Properties

Access helps you organize and identify your databases by using **database properties**, which are the details about a file. Database properties, also known as **metadata**, can include such information as the file's author, title, or subject. **Keywords** are words or phrases that further describe the database. For example, a class name or database topic can describe the file's purpose or content.

Five different types of document properties exist, but the more common ones used in this book are standard and automatically updated properties. **Standard properties** are associated with all Microsoft Office documents and include author, title, and subject. **Automatically updated properties** include file system properties, such as the date you create or change a file, and statistics, such as the file size.

To Change Database Properties

The Database Properties dialog box contains areas where you can view and enter database properties. You can view and change information in this dialog box at anytime while you are working on your database. It is a good idea to add your name and class name as database properties. You also can add keywords that further describe your database. The following steps use the Properties dialog box to change database properties.

1

- Click File on the Ribbon to open the Backstage view.

- If necessary, click the Info tab in the Backstage view to display the Info gallery (Figure 1–87).

Q&A

How do I close the Backstage view?

Click File on the Ribbon or click the preview of the document in the Info gallery to return to the Access database window.

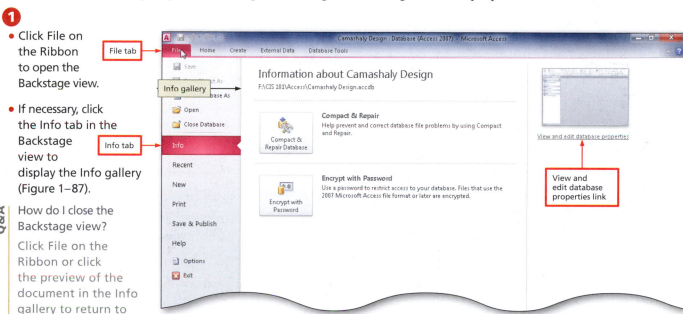

Figure 1–87

2

- Click the 'View and edit database properties' link in the right pane of the Info gallery to display the Camashaly Design.accdb Properties dialog box (Figure 1–88).

Q&A

Why are some of the database properties in my Properties dialog box already filled in?

The person who installed Microsoft Office 2010 on your computer or network may have set or customized the properties.

Figure 1–88

- If necessary, click the Summary tab.

- Click the Subject text box, if necessary delete any existing text, and then type **CIS 101, Section 20** as the Subject property.

- Click the Author text box and then type **Trevor Wilkins** as the Author property. If a name already is displayed in the Author text box, delete it before typing the new name.

- Click the Keywords text box, if necessary delete any existing text, and then type **online marketing, Web site design** as the Keywords property (Figure 1–89).

Q&A

What types of properties does Access collect automatically?

Access records such details as when the database was created, when it was last modified, total editing time, and the various objects contained in the database.

Figure 1–89

- Click the OK button to save your changes and remove the Camashaly Design.accdb Properties dialog box from the screen.

To Quit Access

The following steps quit Access.

1 Click the Close button on the right side of the title bar to quit Access.

2 If a Microsoft Access dialog box appears, click the Save button to save any changes made to the object since the last save.

Special Database Operations

The special operations involved in maintaining a database are backup, recovery, compacting a database, and repairing a database.

Backup and Recovery

It is possible to damage or destroy a database. Users can enter data that is incorrect; programs that are updating the database can end abnormally during an update; a hardware problem can occur; and so on. After any such event has occurred, the database may contain invalid data. It even might be totally destroyed.

Obviously, you cannot allow a situation in which data has been damaged or destroyed to go uncorrected. You must somehow return the database to a correct state. This process is called recovery; that is, you recover the database.

The simplest approach to recovery involves periodically making a copy of the database (called a **backup copy** or a **save copy**). This is referred to as **backing up** the database. If a problem occurs, you correct the problem by copying this backup copy over the actual database, often referred to as the **live database**.

To back up the database that is currently open, you use the Back Up Database command on the Save & Publish tab in the Backstage view. In the process, Access suggests a name that is a combination of the database name and the current date. For example, if you back up the Camashaly Design database on April 20, 2012, Access will suggest the name, Camashaly Design_2012-04-20. You can change this name if you desire, although it is a good idea to use this name. By doing so, it will be easy to distinguish between all the backup copies you have made to determine which is the most recent. In addition, if you discover that a critical problem occurred on April 18, 2012, you may want to go back to the most recent backup before April 18. If, for example, the database was not backed up on April 17 but was backed up on April 16, you would use Camashaly Design_2012-04-16.

To Back Up a Database

You would use the following steps to back up a database to a file on a hard disk or high-capacity removable disk.

1. Open the database to be backed up.
2. Click File on the Ribbon to open the Backstage view, and then click the Save & Publish tab.
3. With Save Database As selected in the File Types area, click Back Up Database in the Save Database As area, and then click the Save As button.
4. Selected the desired location in the Save As box. If you do not want the name Access has suggested, enter the desired name in the File name text box.
5. Click the Save button to back up the database.

Access creates a backup copy with the desired name in the desired location. Should you ever need to recover the database using this backup copy, you can simply copy it over the live version.

Compacting and Repairing a Database

As you add more data to a database, it naturally grows larger. When you delete an object (records, tables, forms, or queries), the space previously occupied by the object does not become available for additional objects. Instead, the additional objects are given new space; that is, space that was not already allocated. To remove this wasted space from the database, you must **compact** the database. The same option that compacts the database also repairs problems that might have occurred in the database.

To Compact and Repair a Database

You would use the following steps to compact and repair a database.

1. Open the database to be compacted.
2. Click File on the Ribbon to open the Backstage view, and then, if necessary, select the Info tab.
3. Click the Compact & Repair Database button in the Info gallery to compact and repair the database.

The database now is the compacted form of the original.

BTW

Access Help
At any time while using Access, you can find answers to questions and display information about various topics through Help. Used properly, this form of assistance can increase your productivity and reduce your frustrations by minimizing the time you spend learning how to use Access. For instruction about Access Help and exercises that will help you gain confidence in using it, read the Office 2010 and Windows 7 chapter at the beginning of this book.

Additional Operations

Additional special operations include opening another database, closing a database without quitting Access, and saving a database with another name. They also include deleting a table (or other object) as well as renaming an object. Finally, you can change properties of a table or other object, such as the object's description.

When you open another database, Access will automatically close the database that previously was open. Before deleting or renaming an object, you should ensure that the object has no dependent objects; that is, other objects that depend on the object you want to delete.

TO OPEN ANOTHER DATABASE

To open another database, you would use the following steps.

1. Click File on the Ribbon to open the Backstage view.
2. Click Open.
3. Select the database to be opened.
4. Click the Open button.

TO CLOSE A DATABASE WITHOUT QUITTING ACCESS

You would use the following steps to close a database without quitting Access.

1. Click File on the Ribbon to open the Backstage view.
2. Click Close Database.

BTW

Certification
The Microsoft Office Specialist (MOS) program provides an opportunity for you to obtain a valuable industry credential — proof that you have the Access 2010 skills required by employers. For more information, visit the Access 2010 Certification Web page (scsite.com/ac2010/cert).

TO SAVE A DATABASE WITH ANOTHER NAME

To save a database with another name, you would use the following steps.

1. Click File on the Ribbon to open the Backstage view, and then select the Save & Publish tab.
2. With Save Database As selected in the File Types area and Access Database selected in the Save Database As area, click the Save As button.
3. Enter a name and select a location for the new version.
4. Click the Save button.

TO DELETE A TABLE OR OTHER OBJECT IN THE DATABASE

You would use the following steps to delete a database object.

1. Right-click the object in the Navigation Pane.
2. Click Delete on the shortcut menu.
3. Click the Yes button in the Microsoft Access dialog box.

BTW

Quick Reference
For a table that lists how to complete the tasks covered in this book using the mouse, Ribbon, shortcut menu, and keyboard, see the Quick Reference Summary at the back of this book, or visit the Access 2010 Quick Reference Web page (scsite.com/ac2010/qr).

TO RENAME AN OBJECT IN THE DATABASE

You would use the following steps to rename a database object.

1. Right-click the object in the Navigation Pane.
2. Click Rename on the shortcut menu.
3. Type the new name and press the ENTER key.

Chapter Summary

In this chapter you have learned to design a database, create an Access database, create tables and add records to them, print the contents of tables, create queries, create forms, and create reports. You also have learned how to change database properties. The items listed below include all the new Access skills you have learned in this chapter.

1. Start Access (AC 12)
2. Create a Database (AC 13)
3. Create a Database Using a Template (AC 14)
4. Modify the Primary Key (AC 16)
5. Define the Remaining Fields in a Table (AC 19)
6. Save a Table (AC 21)
7. View the Table in Design View (AC 21)
8. Close the Table (AC 23)
9. Add Records to a Table (AC 23)
10. Quit Access (AC 26)
11. Open a Database from Access (AC 27)
12. Add Additional Records to a Table (AC 28)
13. Resize Columns in a Datasheet (AC 29)
14. Preview and Print the Contents of a Table (AC 31)
15. Create a Table in Design View (AC 33)
16. Import an Excel Worksheet (AC 38)
17. Use the Simple Query Wizard to Create a Query (AC 43)
18. Use a Criterion in a Query (AC 46)
19. Print the Results of a Query (AC 48)
20. Create a Form (AC 48)
21. Create a Report (AC 52)
22. Modify Column Headings and Resize Columns (AC 54)
23. Add Totals to a Report (AC 57)
24. Change Database Properties (AC 59)
25. Back Up a Database (AC 61)
26. Compact and Repair a Database (AC 61)
27. Open Another Database (AC 62)
28. Close a Database without Quitting Access (AC 62)
29. Save a Database with Another Name (AC 62)
30. Delete a Table or Other Object in the Database (AC 62)
31. Rename an Object in the Database (AC 62)

 If you have a SAM 2010 user profile, your instructor may have assigned an autogradable version of this assignment. If so, log into the SAM 2010 Web site at www.cengage.com/sam2010 to download the instruction and start files.

Learn It Online

Test your knowledge of chapter content and key terms.

Instructions: To complete the Learn It Online exercises, start your browser, click the Address bar, and then enter the Web address **scsite.com/ac2010/learn**. When the Access 2010 Learn It Online page is displayed, click the link for the exercise you want to complete and then read the instructions.

Chapter Reinforcement TF, MC, and SA
A series of true/false, multiple choice, and short answer questions that test your knowledge of the chapter content.

Flash Cards
An interactive learning environment where you identify chapter key terms associated with displayed definitions.

Practice Test
A series of multiple choice questions that test your knowledge of chapter content and key terms.

Who Wants To Be a Computer Genius?
An interactive game that challenges your knowledge of chapter content in the style of a television quiz show.

Wheel of Terms
An interactive game that challenges your knowledge of chapter key terms in the style of the television show *Wheel of Fortune*.

Crossword Puzzle Challenge
A crossword puzzle that challenges your knowledge of key terms presented in the chapter.

Apply Your Knowledge

Reinforce the skills and apply the concepts you learned in this chapter.

Adding a Caption, Creating a Query, Creating a Form, and Creating a Report

Instructions: Start Access. Open the Babbage CPA Firm database. See the inside back cover of this book for instructions for downloading the Data Files for Students, or see your instructor for information on accessing the files required in this book.

The Babbage CPA Firm employs bookkeepers who maintain the books for those clients who need bookkeeping services. The Babbage CPA Firm has a database that keeps track of its bookkeepers and clients. Each client is assigned to a single bookkeeper, but each bookkeeper may be assigned many clients. The database has two tables. The Client table contains data on the clients who use the bookkeeping services of the Babbage CPA Firm. The Bookkeeper table contains data on the bookkeepers employed by Babbage CPA Firm.

Perform the following tasks:

1. Open the Bookkeeper table in Design view and add BKR # as the caption for Bookkeeper Number. Save the changes to the table.

2. Open the Bookkeeper table in Datasheet view and resize all columns to best fit the data. Save the changes to the layout of the table.

3. Use the Simple Query Wizard to create a query for the Client table that contains the Client Number, Client Name, Amount Paid, and Balance Due. Use the name, Client Query, for the query.

4. Create a simple form for the Bookkeeper table. Use the name, Bookkeeper, for the form.

5. Close the Bookkeeper form.

6. Create the report shown in Figure 1–90 for the Client table. The report includes totals for both the Amount Paid and Balance Due fields. Be sure the totals appear completely. You might need to expand the size of the controls. Move the page number so that it is within the margins.

7. Compact the database.

8. Back up the database.

9. Change the database properties, as specified by your instructor. Submit the revised database in the format specified by your instructor.

Client Financial Report

Thursday, April 12, 2012
8:38:16 PM

Client Number	Client Name	Amount Paid	Balance Due	Bookkeeper Number
A54	Afton Mills	$575.00	$315.00	22
A62	Atlas Suppliers	$250.00	$175.00	24
B26	Blake-Scripps	$875.00	$250.00	24
D76	Dege Grocery	$1,015.00	$325.00	22
G56	Grand Cleaners	$485.00	$165.00	24
H21	Hill Shoes	$0.00	$285.00	34
J77	Jones Plumbing	$685.00	$0.00	22
M26	Mohr Crafts	$125.00	$185.00	24
S56	SeeSaw Industries	$1,200.00	$645.00	22
T45	Tate Repair	$345.00	$200.00	34
W24	Woody Sporting Goods	$975.00	$0.00	34
C29	Catering by Jenna	$0.00	$250.00	34
		$6,530.00	$2,795.00	

Figure 1–90

Extend Your Knowledge

Extend the skills you learned in this chapter and experiment with new skills. You may need to use Help to complete the assignment.

Using a Database Template to Create a Students Database

Instructions: Access includes a number of templates that you can use to create a beginning database that can be modified to meet your specific needs. You will create a Students database using the Students template. The database includes sample tables, queries, forms, and reports. You will change the database and create the Student Birthdays Query, shown in Figure 1–91.

Figure 1–91

Perform the following tasks:

1. Start Access.

2. With a USB flash drive connected to one of the computer's USB ports, ensure the New tab is selected in the Backstage view and select Sample templates in the New gallery.

3. Select the Students template and create a new database on your USB drive with the file name, Students.

4. Close the Student List form and change the organization of the Navigation Pane to Tables and Related Views .

5. Delete the Student Details form.

6. Use the Query Wizard to create the query shown in Figure 1–91. Save the query as Student Birthdays Query.

7. Open the Student Phone List in Layout view and use the tools on the Format tab to make the Student Phone List title bold and change the font size to 24. Delete the control containing the time.

8. Save your changes to the report.

9. Compact the database.

10. Change the database properties, as specified by your instructor. Submit the revised database in the format specified by your instructor.

Make It Right

Analyze a database and correct all errors and/or improve the design.

Correcting Errors in the Table Structure

Instructions: Start Access. Open the Beach Rentals database. See the inside back cover of this book for instructions for downloading the Data Files for Students, or see your instructor for information on accessing the files required in this book.

Beach Rentals is a database containing information on rental properties available at a beach resort. The Rentals table shown in Figure 1–92 contains a number of errors in the table structure. You are to correct these errors before any additional records can be added to the table. The Rental Code field is a Text field that contains a maximum of three characters. The field Address was omitted from the table. The Address field is a Text field with a maximum of 20 characters. It should appear after Rental Code. Only whole numbers should be allowed in the Bedrooms and Bathrooms fields. The column heading Weakly Rental is misspelled, and the field should contain monetary values. The Distance field represents the walking distance from the beach; the field should display two decimal places. The table name should be Rental Units, not Rentals.

Change the database properties, as specified by your instructor. Submit the revised database in the format specified by your instructor.

Figure 1–92

In the Lab

Design, create, modify, and/or use a database using the guidelines, concepts, and skills presented in this chapter. Labs are listed in order of increasing difficulty.

Lab 1: Creating Objects for the ECO Clothesline Database

Problem: ECO Clothesline is a local company that designs and manufactures eco-friendly casual wear, yoga clothing, and fitness apparel. All clothes are made from earth-friendly fabrics, such as bamboo, hemp, organic cotton, and natural silk. The company recently decided to store its customer and sales rep data in a database. Each customer is assigned to a single sales rep, but each sales rep may be assigned many customers. The database and the Customer table have been created, but there is no data in the Customer table. The Sales Rep table has not been created. The company plans to import the Customer data from an Excel workbook, shown in Figure 1–93a. The other Excel workbook (Figure 1–93b) contains information on the sales representatives that ECO employs. ECO would like to finish storing this data in a database and has asked for your help.

Instructions: Perform the following tasks: Start Access and open the ECO Clothesline database. See the inside back cover of this book for instructions for downloading the Data Files for Students, or see your instructor for information on accessing the files required in this book.

1. Import the Lab 1-1 Customer Data workbook into the Customer table.

2. Add the captions Cust # to the Customer Number field and SR # to the Sales Rep Number field in the Customer table and save the changes.

3. Open the Customer table in Datasheet view and resize the columns to best fit the data. Save the changes to the layout of the table.

4. Use Datasheet view to create a table in which to store the data related to sales reps. Use the name Sales Rep for the table. The fields and the data for the Sales Rep table are shown in Figure 1–93b.

	A	B	C	D	E	F	G	H	I	J	K
1	Customer Number	Customer Name	Street	City	State	Postal Code	Balance	Amount Paid	Sales Rep Number		
2	AM23	Amy's Store	223 Johnson	Oxford	TN	37021	195.00	1,695.00	44		
3	BF34	Barbara's Fashions	1939 Jackson	Lowton	TN	37001	150.00	0.00	51		
4	BL15	Blondie's on Main	3294 Main	Oxford	TN	37021	555.00	1,350.00	49		
5	CM09	Casual by Marie	3140 Halsted	Ashton	VA	20123	295.00	1,080.00	51		
6	CY12	Curlin Yoga Studio	1632 Clark	Georgetown	NC	28794	145.00	710.00	49		
7	DG14	Della's Designs	312 Gilham	Granger	NC	27036	340.00	850.00	44		
8	EC07	Environmental Casual	1805 Broadway	Pineville	VA	22503	0.00	1,700.00	44		
9	FN19	Fitness Counts	675 Main	Oxford	TN	37021	345.00	1,950.00	51		
10	JN34	Just Natural	2200 Lawrence	Ashton	VA	20123	360.00	700.00	49		
11	LB20	Le Beauty	13 Devon	Lowton	TN	37084	200.00	1,250.00	49		
12	NC25	Nancy's Place	1027 Wells	Walburg	NC	28819	240.00	550.00	44		
13	RD03	Rose's Day Spa	787 Monroe	Pineville	VA	22503	0.00	975.00	51		
14	TT21	Tan and Tone	1939 Congress	Ashton	VA	20123	160.00	725.00	44		
15	TW56	The Workout Place	34 Gilham	Granger	NC	27036	680.00	125.00	51		
16	WS34	Woody's Sporting Goods	578 Central	Walburg	NC	28819	1,235.00	0.00	49		
17											

(a) Customer Data (Excel Workbook)

	A	B	C	D	E	F	G	H	I	J
1	Sales Rep Number	Last Name	First Name	Street	City	State	Postal Code	Base Pay YTD	Comm Rate	
2	44	Jones	Pat	43 Third	Oxford	TN	37021	13,000.00	0.05	
3	49	Gupta	Pinn	678 Hillcrest	Georgetown	NC	28794	15,000.00	0.06	
4	51	Ortiz	Gabe	982 Victoria	Ashton	VA	20123	12,500.00	0.05	
5	55	Sinson	Terry	45 Elm	Walburg	NC	28819	500.00	0.04	
6										

(b) Sales Rep Data (Excel Workbook)

Figure 1–93

The primary key for the Sales Rep table is Sales Rep Number. Assign the caption SR # to the Sales Rep Number field. Comm Rate is a Number field, and Base Pay YTD is a Currency data type. The field size for Sales Rep Number is 2. The State field size is 2, and the Postal Code field size is 5. All other text fields have a field size of 15.

5. Open the Sales Rep table in Design view and change the field size for the Comm Rate field to Single, the format to Fixed, and the Decimal Places to 2.

6. Add the data shown in Figure 1–93b to the Sales Rep table. Resize the columns to best fit the data. Save the changes to the layout of the table.

7. Create a query using the Simple Query Wizard for the Customer table that displays the Customer Number, Customer Name, Balance, Amount Paid, and Sales Rep Number fields. Use the name Customer Query.

8. Create and save the report shown in Figure 1–94 for the Customer table. The report should include Customer Number, Customer Name, Balance, and Sales Rep Number fields. Include a total for the Balance field.

9. Change the database properties, as specified by your instructor. Submit the revised database in the format specified by your instructor.

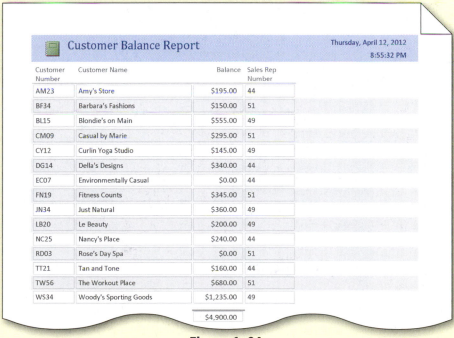

Customer Balance Report   Thursday, April 12, 2012
                                                8:55:32 PM

Customer Number	Customer Name	Balance	Sales Rep Number
AM23	Amy's Store	$195.00	44
BF34	Barbara's Fashions	$150.00	51
BL15	Blondie's on Main	$555.00	49
CM09	Casual by Marie	$295.00	51
CY12	Curlin Yoga Studio	$145.00	49
DG14	Della's Designs	$340.00	44
EC07	Environmentally Casual	$0.00	44
FN19	Fitness Counts	$345.00	51
JN34	Just Natural	$360.00	49
LB20	Le Beauty	$200.00	49
NC25	Nancy's Place	$240.00	44
RD03	Rose's Day Spa	$0.00	51
TT21	Tan and Tone	$160.00	44
TW56	The Workout Place	$680.00	51
WS34	Woody's Sporting Goods	$1,235.00	49

$4,900.00

Figure 1–94

In the Lab

Lab 2: Creating the Walburg Energy Alternatives Database

Problem: Walburg Energy Alternatives is a nonprofit organization that promotes the use of energy alternatives such as solar power and wind power. The organization provides a variety of services and funds itself through donations. Recently, the organization decided to sell a small number of items in its education center to help fund programs. The store purchases the items from vendors that deal in energy-saving products. Currently, the information about the items and vendors is stored in the Excel workbook shown in Figure 1–95. Each item is assigned to a single vendor, but each vendor may be assigned many items. You volunteer part-time at the store, and the store manager has asked you to create a database that will store the item and vendor information. You have already determined that you need two tables in which to store the information: an Item table and a Vendor table.

Instructions: Perform the following tasks:

1. Design a new database in which to store all the objects related to the items for sale. Call the database Walburg Energy Alternatives.

2. Use the information shown in the Excel workbook in Figure 1–95 to determine the primary keys and determine additional fields. Then, determine the relationships between tables, the data types, and the field sizes.

3. Create the Item table using the information shown in Figure 1–95.

4. Create the Vendor table using the information shown in Figure 1–95. Be sure that the field size for the Vendor Code in the Item table is identical to the field size for the Vendor Code in the Vendor table. Add the caption, Phone, for the Telephone Number field.

Figure 1–95

5. Add the appropriate data to the Item table. Resize the columns to best fit the data and save the changes to the layout.

6. Add the appropriate data to the Vendor table. Resize the columns to best fit the data and save the changes to the layout.

7. Create a query for the Item table. Include the Item Number, Description, Cost, Selling Price, and Vendor Code in the query. Save the query as Item Query.

8. Open the Item Query and add a criterion to limit retrieval to those items supplied by Scryps Distributors. Save the query as Item-Scryps Query.

9. Create a simple form for the Item table. Use the name, Item, for the form.

10. Create the report shown in Figure 1–96 for the Item table. Do not add any totals.

11. Change the database properties, as specified by your instructor. Submit the database in the format specified by your instructor.

Inventory Status Report

Thursday, April 12, 2012
8:56:19 PM

Item Number	Description	On Hand	Cost
3663	Air Deflector	8	$5.45
3673	Energy Booklet	25	$2.70
4553	Energy Saving Kit	7	$42.75
4573	Faucet Aerator	20	$0.89
4583	Fluorescent Light Bulb	18	$4.50
5923	Low Flow Shower Head	11	$8.75
6185	Luminescent Night Light	12	$3.75
6234	Programmable Thermostat	3	$34.25
6345	Rain Gauge	16	$2.89
7123	Retractable Clothesline	10	$13.25
7934	Shower Timer	15	$2.45
8136	Smoke Detector	10	$6.10
8344	Toilet Tank Water Saver	18	$3.35
8590	Water Conservation Kit	8	$13.45
9458	Windows Insulator Kit	10	$4.95

Figure 1–96

In the Lab

Lab 3: Creating the Philamar Training Database

Problem: Philamar Training provides business processes and information technology training to various companies and organizations. Philamar employs trainers who work with individual companies to determine training needs and then conduct the training. Currently, Philamar keeps data on clients and trainers in two Word documents and two Excel workbooks. Philamar also keeps track of which clients are assigned to which trainers. Each client is assigned to a single trainer, but each trainer might be assigned many clients. Currently, clients BS27, FI28, and MC28 are assigned to trainer 42, Belinda Perry. Clients CE16, CP27, FL93, HN83, and TE26 are assigned to trainer 48, Michael Stevens. Clients EU28 and PS82 are assigned to trainer 53, Manuel Gonzalez. Philamar has an additional trainer, Marty Danville, who has been assigned trainer number 67, but who has not yet been assigned any clients.

Instructions: Using the data shown in Figure 1–97 and the information in the previous paragraph, design the Philamar Training database. The data shown in Figure 1–97 is included in the Data Files for Students in the following files: Lab 1-3a.docx, Lab 1-3b.docx, Lab 1-3c.xlsx, and Lab 1-3d.xlsx. Use the database design guidelines in this chapter to help you in the design process.

Client Number	Client Name	Address	City	State	Postal Code
BS27	Blant and Sons	4806 Park	Kingston	TX	76653
CE16	Center Services	725 Mitchell	San Rita	TX	78364
CP27	Calder Plastics	7300 Cedar	Kingston	TX	76653
EU28	Elba's Furniture	1445 Hubert	Tallmadge	TX	77231
FI28	Farrow-Idsen	829 Wooster	Cedar Ridge	TX	79342
FL93	Fairland Lawn	143 Pangborn	Kingston	TX	76653
HN83	Hurley National	3827 Burgess	Tallmadge	TX	77231
MC28	Morgan-Alyssa	923 Williams	Crumville	TX	76745
PS82	PRIM Staffing	72 Crestview	San Rita	TX	78364
TE26	Telton-Edwards	5672 Anderson	Dunston	TX	77893

(a) Client Address Information (Word Table)

	A	B	C	D	E
1	Client Number	Client Name	Amount Paid	Current Due	
2	BS27	Blant and Sons	$11,876.00	$892.50	
3	CE16	Center Services	$12,512.00	$1,672.00	
4	CP27	Calder Plastics	$5,725.00	$0.00	
5	EU28	Elba's Furniture	$3,245.00	$202.00	
6	FI28	Farrow-Idsen	$8,287.50	$925.50	
7	FL93	Fairland Lawn	$976.00	$0.00	
8	HN83	Hurley National	$0.00	$0.00	
9	MC28	Morgan-Alyssa	$3,456.00	$572.00	
10	PS82	PRIM Staffing	$7,500.00	$485.00	
11	TE26	Telton-Edwards	$6,775.00	$0.00	
12					

(c) Client Financial Information (Excel Workbook)

Trainer Number	Last Name	First Name	Address	City	State	Postal Code
42	Perry	Belinda	261 Porter	Burdett	TX	76734
48	Stevens	Michael	3135 Gill	Rockwood	TX	78884
53	Gonzalez	Manuel	265 Maxwell	Camino	TX	76574
67	Danville	Marty	1827 Maple	Dunston	TX	77893

(b) Trainer Address Information (Word Table)

	A	B	C	D	E
1	Trainer Number	Last Name	First Name	Hourly Rate	YTD Earnings
2	42	Perry	Belinda	$23.00	$17,620.00
3	48	Stevens	Michael	$21.00	$13,567.50
4	53	Gonzalez	Manuel	$24.00	$19,885.00
5	67	Danville	Marty	$20.00	$0.00
6					

(d) Trainer Financial Information (Excel Workbook)

Figure 1–97

When you have completed the database design, create the database, create the tables, and add the data to the appropriate tables. Be sure to determine the correct data types and field sizes.

Finally, prepare the Client Query shown in Figure 1–98 and the Client Status Report shown in Figure 1–99. The report does not include totals. Change the database properties, as specified by your instructor. Submit the database in the format specified by your instructor.

Figure 1–98

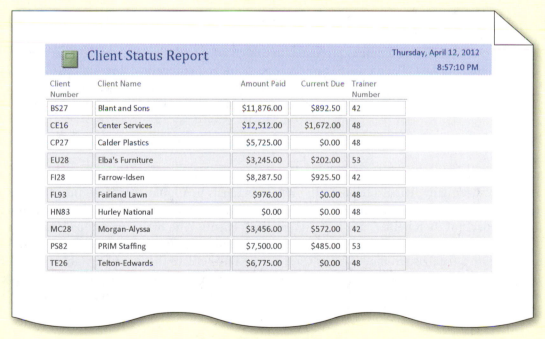

Figure 1–99

Cases and Places

Apply your creative thinking and problem solving skills to design and implement a solution.

See the inside back cover of this book for instructions for downloading the Data Files for Students, or see your instructor for information on accessing the files required in this book.

1: Design and Create an Advertising Database

Academic

You are a Marketing major currently doing an internship with the Chamber of Commerce in a local city. The Chamber publishes a Newcomer's Guide that contains advertisements from local businesses. Ad reps contact the businesses to arrange for advertising. Each advertiser is assigned to a single ad rep, but each ad rep may be assigned many advertisers. The Chamber would like your help in creating a database of advertisers and advertising representatives.

Based on the information in the Case 1-1 Chamber of Commerce workbook, use the concepts and techniques presented in this chapter to design and create a database to store the data that the Chamber needs. Submit your assignment in the format specified by your instructor.

2: Design and Create a Consignment Database

Personal

You are involved in a volunteer organization that provides clothing and school supplies to needy children. Recently, the Board of Directors decided to open a consignment shop as a way to raise additional funds. In a consignment shop, individuals bring in unwanted items, and the shop sells the items. Proceeds are split between the seller and the shop. The database must keep track of the items for sale in the shop as well as maintain data on the sellers. Each item is assigned to a single seller, but each seller may be assigned many items. The Board has asked you to create a database to store information about the consignment items.

Use the concepts and techniques presented in this chapter to design and create a database to store the consignment data. Then create the necessary tables and enter the data from the Case 1-2 Consignment workbook. Create an Available Items Report that lists the item number, description, price, and seller code. Submit your assignment in the format specified by your instructor.

3: Design and Create a Senior Care Database

Professional

You are co-owner of a company, Senior Care, that provides nonmedical services to older adults who need assistance with daily living. Helpers will drive individuals to appointments, do the grocery shopping, fill prescriptions, help with personal care, and provide companionship. Each client is assigned to a single helper, but each helper may be assigned many clients. The other owners have asked you to create a database of clients and helpers. Use the concepts and techniques presented in this chapter to design and create a database to meet Senior Care needs. Then create the necessary tables and enter the data from the Case 1-3 Senior Care workbook. Create a Client Report that lists each client's client number, client last name, client first name, balance, and helper number. Submit your assignment in the format specified by your instructor.

NOTES

NOTES

NOTES

NOTES

Project Planning Guidelines

Using Project Planning Guidelines

The process of communicating specific information to others is a learned, rational skill. Computers and software, especially Microsoft Office 2010, can help you develop ideas and present detailed information to a particular audience.

Using Microsoft Office 2010, you can create projects such as Word documents, PowerPoint presentations, Excel spreadsheets, and Access databases. Productivity software such as Microsoft Office 2010 minimizes much of the laborious work of drafting and revising projects. Some communicators handwrite ideas in notebooks, others compose directly on the computer, and others have developed unique strategies that work for their own particular thinking and writing styles.

No matter what method you use to plan a project, follow specific guidelines to arrive at a final product that presents information correctly and effectively (Figure A–1). Use some aspects of these guidelines every time you undertake a project, and others as needed in specific instances. For example, in determining content for a project, you may decide that a chart communicates trends more effectively than a paragraph of text. If so, you would create this graphical element and insert it in an Excel spreadsheet, a Word document, or a PowerPoint slide.

Determine the Project's Purpose

Begin by clearly defining why you are undertaking this assignment. For example, you may want to track monetary donations collected for your club's fund-raising drive. Alternatively, you may be urging students to vote for a particular candidate in the next election. Once you clearly understand the purpose of your task, begin to draft ideas of how best to communicate this information.

Analyze Your Audience

Learn about the people who will read, analyze, or view your work. Where are they employed? What are their educational backgrounds? What are their expectations? What questions do they have?

PROJECT PLANNING GUIDELINES

1. DETERMINE THE PROJECT'S PURPOSE
Why are you undertaking the project?

2. ANALYZE YOUR AUDIENCE
Who are the people who will use your work?

3. GATHER POSSIBLE CONTENT
What information exists, and in what forms?

4. DETERMINE WHAT CONTENT TO PRESENT TO YOUR AUDIENCE
What information will best communicate the project's purpose to your audience?

Figure A–1

Design experts suggest drawing a mental picture of these people or finding photos of people who fit this profile so that you can develop a project with the audience in mind.

By knowing your audience members, you can tailor a project to meet their interests and needs. You will not present them with information they already possess, and you will not omit the information they need to know.

Example: Your assignment is to raise the profile of your college's nursing program in the community. How much do they know about your college and the nursing curriculum? What are the admission requirements? How many of the applicants admitted complete the program? What percent pass the state board exams?

Gather Possible Content

Rarely are you in a position to develop all the material for a project. Typically, you would begin by gathering existing information that may reside in spreadsheets or databases. Web sites, pamphlets, magazine and newspaper articles, and books could provide insights of how others have approached your topic. Personal interviews often provide perspectives not available by any other means. Consider video and audio clips as potential sources for material that might complement or support the factual data you uncover.

Determine What Content to Present to Your Audience

Experienced designers recommend writing three or four major ideas you want an audience member to remember after reading or viewing your project. It also is helpful to envision your project's endpoint, the key fact you wish to emphasize. All project elements should lead to this ending point.

As you make content decisions, you also need to think about other factors. Presentation of the project content is an important consideration. For example, will your brochure be printed on thick, colored paper or posted on the Web? Will your PowerPoint presentation be viewed in a classroom with excellent lighting and a bright projector, or will it be viewed on a notebook computer monitor? Determine relevant time factors, such as the length of time to develop the project, how long readers will spend reviewing your project, or the amount of time allocated for your speaking engagement. Your project will need to accommodate all of these constraints.

Decide whether a graph, photo, or artistic element can express or emphasize a particular concept. The right hemisphere of the brain processes images by attaching an emotion to them, so audience members are more apt to recall these graphics long term rather than just reading text.

As you select content, be mindful of the order in which you plan to present information. Readers and audience members generally remember the first and last pieces of information they see and hear, so you should place the most important information at the top or bottom of the page.

Summary

When creating a project, it is beneficial to follow some basic guidelines from the outset. By taking some time at the beginning of the process to determine the project's purpose, analyze the audience, gather possible content, and determine what content to present to the audience, you can produce a project that is informative, relevant, and effective.

Appendix B

Publishing Office 2010 Web Pages Online

With Office 2010 programs, you use the Save As command in the Backstage view to save a Web page to a Web site, network location, or FTP site. **File Transfer Protocol** (**FTP**) is an Internet standard that allows computers to exchange files with other computers on the Internet.

You should contact your network system administrator or technical support staff at your Internet access provider to determine if their Web server supports Web folders, FTP, or both, and to obtain necessary permissions to access the Web server.

Using an Office Program to Publish Office 2010 Web Pages

When publishing online, someone first must assign the necessary permissions for you to publish the Web page. If you are granted access to publish online, you must obtain the Web address of the Web server, a user name, and possibly a password that allows you to connect to the Web server. The steps in this appendix assume that you have access to an online location to which you can publish a Web page.

TO CONNECT TO AN ONLINE LOCATION

To publish a Web page online, you first must connect to the online location. To connect to an online location using Windows 7, you would perform the following steps.

1. Click the Start button on the Windows 7 taskbar to display the Start menu.
2. Click Computer in the right pane of the Start menu to open the Computer window.
3. Click the 'Map network drive' button on the toolbar to display the Map Network Drive dialog box. (If the 'Map network drive' button is not visible on the toolbar, click the 'Display additional commands' button on the toolbar and then click 'Map network drive' in the list to display the Map Network Drive dialog box.)
4. Click the 'Connect to a Web site that you can use to store your documents and pictures' link (Map Network Drive dialog box) to start the Add Network Location wizard.
5. Click the Next button (Add Network Location dialog box).
6. Click 'Choose a custom network location' and then click the Next button.
7. Type the Internet or network address specified by your network or system administrator in the text box and then click the Next button.
8. Click 'Log on anonymously' to deselect the check box, type your user name in the User name text box, and then click the Next button.
9. If necessary, enter the name you want to assign to this online location and then click the Next button.
10. Click to deselect the Open this network location when I click Finish check box, and then click the Finish button.

11. Click the Cancel button to close the Map Network Drive dialog box.

12. Close the Computer window.

TO SAVE A WEB PAGE TO AN ONLINE LOCATION

The online location now can be accessed easily from Windows programs, including Microsoft Office programs. After creating a Microsoft Office file you wish to save as a Web page, you must save the file to the online location to which you connected in the previous steps. To save a Microsoft Word document as a Web page, for example, and publish it to the online location, you would perform the following steps.

1. Click File on the Ribbon to display the Backstage view and then click Save As in the Backstage view to display the Save As dialog box.

2. Type the Web page file name in the File name text box (Save As dialog box). Do not press the ENTER key because you do not want to close the dialog box at this time.

3. Click the 'Save as type' box arrow and then click Web Page to select the Web Page format.

4. If necessary, scroll to display the name of the online location in the navigation pane.

5. Double-click the online location name in the navigation pane to select that location as the new save location and display its contents in the right pane.

6. If a dialog box appears prompting you for a user name and password, type the user name and password in the respective text boxes and then click the Log On button.

7. Click the Save button (Save As dialog box).

The Web page now has been published online. To view the Web page using a Web browser, contact your network or system administrator for the Web address you should use to connect to the Web page.

Appendix C

Saving to the Web Using Windows Live SkyDrive

Introduction

Windows Live SkyDrive, also referred to as **SkyDrive**, is a free service that allows users to save files to the Web, such as documents, presentations, spreadsheets, databases, videos, and photos. Using SkyDrive, you also can save files in folders, providing for greater organization. You then can retrieve those files from any computer connected to the Internet. Some Office 2010 programs including Word, PowerPoint, and Excel can save files directly to an Internet location such as SkyDrive. SkyDrive also facilitates collaboration by allowing users to share files with other SkyDrive users (Figure C−1).

Figure C−1

Note: An Internet connection is required to perform the steps in this appendix.

To Save a File to Windows Live SkyDrive

You can save files directly to SkyDrive from within Word, PowerPoint, and Excel using the Backstage view. The following steps save an open Word document (Koala Exhibit Flyer, in this case) to SkyDrive. These steps require you to have a Windows Live account. Contact your instructor if you do not have a Windows Live account.

1

- Start Word and then open a document you want to save to the Web (in this case, the Koala Exhibit Flyer).

- Click File on the Ribbon to display the Backstage view (Figure C–2).

Figure C–2

- Click the Save & Send tab to display the Save & Send gallery (Figure C–3).

Figure C–3

3

- Click Save to Web in the Save & Send gallery to display information about saving a file to the Web (Figure C–4).

Figure C–4

4

- Click the Sign In button to display a Windows Live login dialog box that requests your e-mail address and password (Figure C–5).

Q&A What if the Sign In button does not appear?

If you already are signed into Windows Live, the Sign In button will not be displayed. Instead, the contents of your Windows Live SkyDrive will be displayed. If you already are signed into Windows Live, proceed to Step 6.

Figure C–5

5

- Enter your Windows Live e-mail address in the E-mail address box (Windows Live login dialog box).

- Enter your Windows Live password in the Password text box.

- Click the OK button to sign into Windows Live and display the contents of your Windows Live SkyDrive in the right pane of the Save & Send gallery.

- If necessary, click the My Documents folder to set the save location for the document (Figure C–6).

Q&A What if the My Documents folder does not exist?

Click another folder to select it as the save location. Record the name of this folder so that you can locate and retrieve the file later in this appendix.

Q&A My SkyDrive shows personal and shared folders. What is the difference?

Personal folders are private and are not shared with anyone. Shared folders can be viewed by SkyDrive users to whom you have assigned the necessary permissions.

Figure C–6

6

● Click the Save As button in the right pane of the Save & Send gallery to contact the SkyDrive server (which may take some time, depending on the speed of your Internet connection) and then display the Save As dialog box (Figure C–7).

Figure C–7

7

● Type **Koala Exhibit Web** in the File name text box to enter the file name and then click the Save button (Save As dialog box) to save the file to Windows Live SkyDrive (Figure C–8).

Q&A

Is it necessary to rename the file?

It is good practice to rename the file. If you download the file from SkyDrive to your computer, having a different file name will preserve the original file.

Figure C–8

8

● If you have one Word document open, click the Close button on the right side of the title bar to close the document and quit Word; or if you have multiple Word documents open, click File on the Ribbon to open the Backstage view and then click Exit in the Backstage view to close all open documents and quit Word.

Web Apps

Microsoft has created a scaled-down, Web-based version of its Microsoft Office suite, called **Microsoft Office Web Apps,** or **Web Apps**. Web Apps contains Web-based versions of Word, PowerPoint, Excel, and OneNote that can be used to view and edit files that are saved to SkyDrive. Web Apps allows users to continue working with their files even while they are not using a computer with Microsoft Office installed. In addition to working with files located on SkyDrive, Web Apps also enables users to create new Word documents, PowerPoint presentations, Excel spreadsheets, and OneNote notebooks. After returning to a computer with the Microsoft Office suite, some users choose to download files from SkyDrive and edit them using the associated Microsoft Office program.

Note: As with all Web applications, SkyDrive and Office Web Apps are subject to change. Consequently, the steps required to perform the actions in this appendix might be different from those shown.

To Download a File from Windows Live SkyDrive

Files saved to SkyDrive can be downloaded from a Web browser using any computer with an Internet connection. The following steps download the Koala Exhibit Web file using a Web browser.

- Click the Internet Explorer program button pinned on the Windows 7 taskbar to start Internet Explorer.

- Type **skydrive.live.com** in the Address bar and then press the ENTER key to display a SkyDrive Web page requesting you sign in to your Windows Live account (Figure C–9). (If the contents of your SkyDrive are displayed instead, you already are signed in and can proceed to Step 3 on the next page.)

Q&A Why does the Web address change after I enter it in the Address bar?

The Web address changes because you are being redirected to sign into Windows Live before you can access SkyDrive.

Q&A Can I open the file from Microsoft Word instead of using the Web browser?

If you are opening the file on the same computer from which you saved it to the SkyDrive, click File on the Ribbon to open the Backstage view. Click the Recent tab and then click the desired file name (Koala Exhibit Web, in this case) in the Recent Documents list, or click Open and then navigate to the location of the saved file (for a detailed example of this procedure, refer to the Office 2010 and Windows 7 chapter at the beginning of this book).

Figure C–9

- Click the Sign in link to display the Windows Live ID and Password text boxes (Figure C–10).

Q&A Why can I not locate the Sign in link?

If your computer remembers your Windows Live sign in credentials from a previous session, your e-mail address already may be displayed on the SkyDrive Web page. In this case, point to your e-mail address to display the Sign in button, click the Sign in button, and then proceed to Step 3. If you cannot locate your e-mail address or Sign in link, click the Sign in with a different Windows Live ID link and then proceed to Step 3.

Figure C–10

● If necessary, enter your Windows Live ID and password in the appropriate text boxes and then click the Sign in button to sign into Windows Live and display the contents of your SkyDrive (Figure C–11).

Q&A

What if my screen shows the contents of a particular folder, instead of all folders?

To display all folders on your SkyDrive, point to Windows Live in the upper-left corner of the window and then click SkyDrive on the Windows Live menu.

Figure C–11

● Click the My Documents folder, or the link corresponding to the folder containing the file you wish to open, to select the folder and display its contents (Figure C–12).

Figure C–12

5
- Point to the Koala Exhibit Web file to select the file and display commands associated with the file.
- Click the More link to display the More menu (Figure C–13).

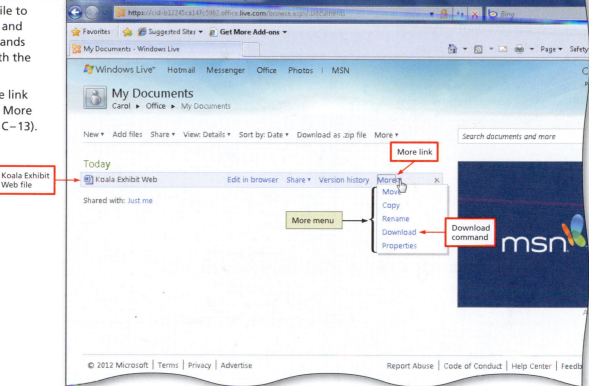

Figure C–13

6
- Click Download on the More menu to display the File Download dialog box (Figure C–14).

Figure C–14

- Click the Save button (File Download dialog box) to display the Save As dialog box (Figure C–15).

- Navigate to the desired save location.

- Click the Save button to save the file on your computer's hard disk or other storage device connected to the computer.

Figure C–15

Collaboration

In today's workplace, it is common to work with others on projects. Collaborating with the members of your team often requires sharing files. It also can involve multiple people editing and working with a certain set of files simultaneously. Placing files on SkyDrive in a public or shared folder enables others to view or modify the files. The members of the team then can view and edit the files simultaneously using Web Apps, enabling the team to work from one set of files (Figure C–16). Collaboration using Web Apps not only enables multiple people to work together, it also can reduce the amount of time required to complete a project.

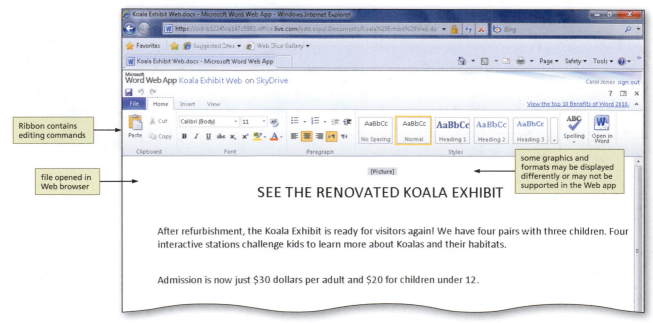

Figure C–16

Index

A

Access, **OFF 53**
See also databases
features and operations, OFF 54–56
Help, AC 62
importing data from other
applications to, AC 38–42
overview of, OFF 53–56
quitting, OFF 58, AC 26, AC 60
starting, OFF 53, AC 12, AC 27
window, Navigation Pane, work
area, AC 15
Access work area, **AC 15**, **OFF 54**
Accounting Number format,
EX 32–33
Acrobat Reader, EX 45
actions, undoing and redoing,
WD 23
active cell (Excel), **OFF 49**
active tabs, **OFF 16**
adding
content to Title Slide, OFF 40,
OFF 43
page borders, WD 41–43
records to tables, AC 23–25,
AC 28–29
slides to presentations, PPT 14–20,
PPT 21–24
text to documents, OFF 20
text to slides, PPT 40–42
totals to reports, AC 56
transitions between slides,
PPT 43
Address bar, **OFF 24**
Aero, OFF 2–3, OFF 27
aligning
numbers, EX 14
paragraphs, WD 13
photographs, PPT 36–38
snapping charts, EX 40
text, EX 12
All Programs list, OFF 10
animations, adding slide transitions,
PPT 43–45
apostrophes (')
entering numbers as text, EX 16
viewing style characteristics,
EX 52
application software, **OFF 2**
applications, importing data to
Access from, AC 38–42
area charts, EX 36

B

arranging slides, PPT 39–40
arrow keys, completing entry in
adjacent cells, EX 11
asterisk (*) and file, folder names,
OFF 22, OFF 28
audience, analyzing, APP 1–2
Auto Fill options, EX 18
AutoCalculate, using, EX 48–49
AutoCalculate area, **EX 48**
AutoCorrect feature, **EX 9**
AutoCorrect options, AC 37
automatically updated properties,
WD 49, **PPT 45**, **EX 43**, **AC 58**
AutoPlay window, opening,
OFF 22

backing up (database), **AC 61**
backslash (\) and file, folder names,
OFF 22, OFF 28
BACKSPACE key, to correct errors,
EX 49
Backstage view, **OFF 35**
closing, EX 43, WD 49, AC 59
closing Office files using, OFF 44
creating new Office documents
from, OFF 41–43
opening recent Office files using,
OFF 45
saving files to SkyDrive, APP 5–8
backup copy, **AC 61**
Basic, Windows 7, OFF 2–3
Blank Database option, OFF 55
Blank layout, PPT 21
blank lines, inserting, WD 7
body copy, **WD 5**
bold, **EX 25**
cell entries, EX 25
making text, WD 28, PPT 19–20
borders
adding page, WD 41–43
printing, WD 53
BTW Web page, PPT 4
bubble charts, EX 37
bulleted lists, **WD 22–23**,
PPT 14–15
bullets
removing, WD 23
using, WD 13
buttons, removing from Quick
Access Toolbar, OFF 19

C

calculating
with AutoCalculate, EX 48, EX 49
sums, EX 15–16
Cancel box, formula bar, **EX 8**
Cancel button, OFF 35
capitalization, WD 18, EX 9
category axis, **EX 40**
cell reference (Excel), **OFF 49**
Cell Styles button EX 52
cells
active, OFF 49
bolding entries, EX 25
calculating sums, EX 15–16
centering entries across columns,
EX 28–29
changing font colors of entries,
EX 27
changing styles, EX 22–23
clearing, EX 52
completing entry in previously
selected cells, EX 14
completing entry with arrow keys,
EX 11
copying to adjacent cells, EX 16–18
correcting errors while you type,
EX 49–51
editing contents of, EX 50
increasing font size of entries,
EX 26
merging, EX 28–29
selecting, EX 6, EX 34–35
splitting merged, EX 29
undoing last entry, EX 51
values and charting, EX 37
centered, **WD 14**
centering
cell entries across columns,
EX 28–29
page contents vertically, WD 40
paragraphs, WD 14
certification, Microsoft Office
Specialist (MOS), WD 44,
EX 52, AC 62
certifications, PPT 50
changing
data in tables, AC 25–26
database properties, AC 59–60
document properties, WD 49–50,
PPT 45–47, EX 43–44
file names, OFF 52
font colors of cell entries, EX 27

fonts in worksheets, EX 24–25
screen resolution, OFF 33–34,
    WD 4, PPT 4, EX 5
table structure, AC 20–22
text color, PPT 13
text fonts, case, WD 17–18
worksheets names, EX 42–43
character formatting, **WD 12**
characters
    deleting, WD 47
    formatting, WD 12–30, PPT 12–14
    nonprinting, WD 7
    variable character fonts, WD 10
charting
    Excel feature, **OFF 46**
    PowerPoint feature, OFF 36
charts
    cell values and charting, EX 37
    embedded, **EX 36**
    legends, **EX 41**
    resizing, EX 40
    types of, EX 36–37
clearing cells, ranges, worksheets,
    EX 52–53
clip art
    inserting into slides, PPT 26–33
    resizing, PPT 33–36
Clip Art task pane, **PPT 26–31**
clips, **PPT 26**
    copyright regulations, PPT 27
    inserting into slides, PPT 27–31
    moving, PPT 36–38
    properties, PPT 29
Close button, OFF 35
closing
    Backstage view, WD 49, PPT 46,
        EX 43, AC 59
    databases, AC 62
    Office files, OFF 44, OFF 56
    programs, OFF 35
    tables, AC 26
closing slide, ending slide shows
    with, PPT 38–40
Clustered Cylinder charts, EX 37–42
collaboration using SkyDrive,
    APP 12
collapsing folders, OFF 26
collections, PPT 26
colon (:) and file, folder names,
    OFF 22, OFF 28
color themes, **WD 28–29**
colors
    of bullets, PPT 17
    cell entry font, EX 27
    font, **PPT 10, EX 22**

shading, WD 20
text, WD 24–25, PPT 12–13
using in flyer, WD 13
using in presentations, PPT 9
column charts, EX 37
column heading (Excel), **OFF 49**
columns, EX 5
    adjusting widths, EX 33–34
    centering cell entries across,
        EX 28–29
    entering titles, EX 10–11
    formatting titles, EX 29–31
    resizing, AC 54–56
    resizing datasheet, AC 29–30,
        AC 42
Comma Style format, EX 32
Command bar, **OFF 24**
commands, **OFF 10**
    See also specific command
    adding to Quick Access Toolbar,
        OFF 19
    AutoCalculate shortcut menu
        (table), EX 48
    cell selection, EX 35
    on Ribbon, OFF 14–15
comments, adding to presentations,
    PPT 24
common dialog boxes, **OFF 8**
compact (database), **AC 61**
Comparison slide layout, PPT 21,
    PPT 23
compressing file size, PPT 31
computers
    changing screen resolution,
        OFF 31–34
    logging on to, OFF 6–7
connecting to online location,
    APP 3–4
conserving ink, toner, WD 51
content
    changing slide text, PPT 40–42
    standard layouts for, PPT 21
contextual tabs, EX 39
copy area, **EX 17**
copying
    cells to adjacent cells, EX 16–18
    slides, PPT 38–39
copyright regulations, PPT 27
creating
    bulleted lists, PPT 14–15
    databases, OFF 55–56, AC 13
    documents, OFF 20
    folders, OFF 22–25
    forms, AC 48–50
    new paragraphs, OFF 20, WD 6

Office documents, OFF 41–43,
    OFF 47
Publisher documents,
    OFF 60–61
reports, AC 51–58
tables, AC 15–20, AC 32–37
title slides, PPT 7–8
criterion, using in queries,
    AC 46–47
Currency data type, **AC 9**, AC 20
currency symbols, AC 20
custom layouts, **PPT 21**
customizing
    Quick Access Toolbar, OFF 19
    Ribbon, OFF 49
cylinder charts, EX 37

D

data types, **AC 9**
    available in Access (table), AC 10
    determining, AC 5
database design, **AC 5**
database management systems
    (DBMSs), **OFF 53**, AC 2
database properties, changing,
    AC 58–60
databases, **AC 2, OFF 53**
    backup and recovery, AC 60–62
    closing, AC 62
    compacting, AC 61
    creating, OFF 55–56, AC 13
    creating using templates, AC 14
    design guidelines, AC 5–6
    opening, OFF 57, AC 27, AC 62
    overview, components of,
        AC 2–12
    relational, **AC 3**
    tables. *See* tables
Datasheet view, **AC 15**, AC 48
datasheets
    described, **AC 23**
    resizing columns in, AC 29–30,
        AC 42
DELETE key, clearing cell entries,
    EX 52
deleting
    bullets from slides, PPT 18
    databases, database objects,
        AC 62
    embedded charts, EX 53
    files, folders, OFF 64–65
    records, AC 20, AC 26
    text from documents, WD 47
    text from slides, PPT 40–42

demoting (text), **PPT 17**
Design view, **AC 15**, AC 21–22
  creating tables in, AC 33–37
  opening, AC 24
  for reports, AC 53
designing databases, AC 5–12
desktop, Windows, OFF 7
desktop publishing. *See* Publisher
destination area, **EX 17**
Dialog Box Launcher, **OFF 15**
dialog boxes
  common, described, **OFF 8**
  navigating, OFF 30
displaying
  formatting marks, WD 7
  hidden windows, OFF 67
  Mini toolbar, PPT 13
  PowerPoint window, PPT 48
  Ribbon, OFF 17
  Ribbon tabs, OFF 16
  Start menu, OFF 10–11
  user icons, OFF 6
Document Information Panel,
  WD 49, **EX 43**
  changing document properties
    using, EX 43–44
  using, PPT 46–47
document properties, **WD 49**,
  PPT 45, **EX 43**
  changing, WD 49–50, PPT 45–47,
    EX 43–44
  printing, WD 49, EX 45
document themes, **PPT 5–6**
document window components,
  OFF 12–16
documents
  choosing themes, PPT 5–6
  correcting errors, WD 44
  creating from Backstage view,
    OFF 41–43
  creating new, OFF 20
  creating Publisher, OFF 60–61
  deleting text from, WD 47
  formatting generally, WD 12–13
  inserting pictures in, WD 30–32,
    WD 35
  inserting text, WD 46
  navigating, WD 11
  opening from PowerPoint,
    PPT 50–51
  planning, WD 4
  printing, WD 51–52, PPT 53
  quitting Office program with open,
    OFF 35
  saving, WD 12

saving, organizing, OFF 21–30
saving Office, OFF 51–52
tabbed, AC 58
  zooming, WD 33, WD 45
.docx files, OFF 21, WD 14
dollar sign ($), entering, EX 13
doughnut charts, EX 37
download described, **WD 30**
drag and drop
  to delete text, PPT 41–42
  method described, **PPT 39**
  moving items using, PPT 39–40
drag-and-drop editing, **WD 47**
dragging
  to move windows, OFF 66–67
  to resize windows, OFF 67
drawing (PowerPoint feature),
  OFF 36
drives, organizing files and
  folders on, OFF 21–30
duplicating. *See* copying

E

Ease of Access Center, OFF 6
Edit mode, **EX 50**
editing
  drag-and-drop, WD 47
  in-cell, EX 50
effects
  applying picture, WD 38–39
  applying text, WD 19–20
electronic mail, **OFF 58**
e-mail
  See also Outlook
  described, **OFF 58**
e-mailing PowerPoint presentations,
  OFF 36
embedded charts, **EX 36**, EX 53
energy-saving information, PPT 2
Enhanced ScreenTips, **OFF 15**
Enter box, formula bar, **EX 8**
ENTER key, WD 8
ergonomics, *preventing wrist
  injuries*, OFF 4
errors
  See also mistakes
  correcting in documents, WD 44
  correcting text input, OFF 20
  methods of correcting,
    EX 49–53
Excel, **OFF 46**
  See also workbooks, worksheets
  creating documents from Windows
    Explorer, OFF 47

features and operations, OFF 49–52
importing worksheets into Access,
  AC 38–42
Excel 2010
  Help, EX 51
  new features, EX 4
  opening workbook from, EX 47–48
  quitting, EX 47
  starting, EX 5
  window, OFF 49–50
expanding folders, OFF 26

F

Favorites area, **OFF 24**
fields, **AC 3**
  determining special properties for,
    AC 16
  naming, AC 8
  renaming, AC 19
  selecting, deselecting, AC 55
file formats
  .docx files, OFF 21
  for importing, PPT 32
  recognized by PowerPoint (table),
    PPT 31
file management
  described, **OFF 62**
  moving, renaming, deleting files,
    OFF 63–65
file names
  changing, OFF 52
  described, **OFF 21**
File Transfer Protocol (FTP),
  APP 3
files, **OFF 7**
  See also specific file type
  closing, OFF 56
  collaboration using SkyDrive,
    APP 12
  compressing size of, PPT 31
  creating through Backstage view,
    OFF 42
  deleting, OFF 64–65
  document properties, using,
    PPT 45
  moving, OFF 64
  opening existing Office, OFF 57
  opening from SkyDrive,
    APP 9–12
  opening recent Office, using
    Backstage view, OFF 45
  organizing, WD 12, EX 20
  PDFs, EX 45
  renaming, OFF 63, APP 8

saving, organizing, OFF 21–30
saving in folders, OFF 27–28
saving presentation, OFF 41,
  PPT 47
saving to SkyDrive, APP 5–8
fill handles, **EX 17**
  clearing cell entries, EX 52
  copying cells to adjacent cells using,
    EX 16–18
folder windows, **OFF 24**
folders, **OFF 10**
  creating, OFF 22–23
  creating within folders,
    OFF 24–25
  deleting, OFF 65
  expanding, collapsing, navigating,
    OFF 26
  Microsoft Office, OFF 11
  organizing, WD 12, PPT 14,
    EX 20
  personal vs. shared, APP 7
  private, APP 10
  saving, organizing files in,
    OFF 21–30, OFF 41, OFF 44
folders (OneNote), **OFF 62**
font color, **EX 22**
Font gallery, EX 24
font size, **WD 12, EX 22**
  changing, WD 16, WD 21–22
  increasing cell entry, EX 26
font style, **EX 22**
fonts, **WD 12, PPT 10, EX 22**
  changing, WD 13, WD 17,
    EX 24–25
  coloring, WD 24–25
  increasing size, PPT 11,
    PPT 20
  size, in presentations, PPT 9
  variable character, WD 10
Form view, **AC 48**, AC 50
format described, **WD 12,**
  PPT 10, EX 22
formatting
  charts, EX 37
  paragraphs, WD 12–15,
    WD 22–23
  text in presentations, PPT 9
  using Mini toolbar, WD 26
  words, PPT 20
  worksheets, EX 22–34
formatting marks, displaying,
  WD 7
forms, creating, using, **AC 48–50**
formula bar, **OFF 50**, OFF 51,
  EX 8

G

galleries, **OFF 14**
grammar and spelling check,
  WD 9–11
graphics, resizing, WD 34–35,
  WD 36
greater than symbol (>) and file,
  folder names, OFF 22, OFF 28
green computing, **EX 45, AC 30**
gridlines (Excel), **OFF 49**
groups on Ribbon, OFF 17
guidelines, project planning,
  APP 1–2

H

hard copy, **AC 30**
hardcopies, **EX 45**
headings
  levels of, EX 30
  report columns, changing,
    AC 54–56
  row and column, OFF 49, EX 5
headlines, **WD 5**
health, preventing wrist injuries,
  OFF 4, WD 11
Help, WD 35, EX 51, AC 62
  obtaining for Windows 7, OFF 5
  obtaining using links, OFF 70
  PowerPoint, PPT 45
  searching for, OFF 68–70
  Table of Contents, OFF 71
  Windows Help and Support,
    OFF 73–74
  Word, OFF 66
hiding
  Mini toolbar, OFF 15
  ruler, WD 5
  spelling errors, WD 9
Home tab
  described, **OFF 14**
  displaying, using, OFF 17

I

icons
  See also specific icon
  content-insertion, PPT 16
  folder, OFF 22
images
  clips. *See* clips
  copyright regulations, PPT 27
Import Spreadsheet Wizard,
  AC 38–42

importing, **AC 38**
  data from other applications to
    Access, AC 38–42
  file types, PPT 32
in-cell editing, **EX 50**, EX 51
increasing font size, PPT 20
ink, conserving, WD 51
Insert mode, **EX 50**
Insert tab, EX 36
inserting
  See also adding
  blank lines, WD 7
  clip art, photographs into slides,
    PPT 26–33
  photographs into presentations,
    PPT 31–32
  pictures in documents, WD 30–32,
    WD 35
  text into documents, WD 46
insertion point, OFF 20, WD 11,
  EX 8
italicized text, **WD 24, PPT 13**
italicizing text, WD 24

K

keyboard
  document navigation with, WD 11
  KeyTips, **OFF 16**
keyboard shortcuts, **OFF 4–5,**
  EX 35
keywords, **PPT 45, EX 43, AC 58**

L

landscape orientation, **OFF 39,**
  PPT 7, EX 46, **AC 30**
Layout gallery, **PPT 21**
Layout view, AC 49, AC 53–58
layouts, **OFF 39, PPT 21, AC 29**
  changing slide, PPT 21–24
  custom, **PPT 21**
left-aligned text, WD 14
legends, chart, **EX 41**
less than symbol (<) and file, folder
  names, OFF 22, OFF 28
levels (paragraph), **PPT 8**
libraries, **OFF 24**
Libraries area, **OFF 24**
line charts, EX 36
lines
  inserting blank, WD 7
  selecting, WD 15, WD 21
links, Help, OFF 70
lists (Excel), **AC 38**

lists, creating bulleted, PPT 14–15
live database, **AC 61**
live preview, **OFF 14**, OFF 27
lock icon, APP 10
logging on to computers, **OFF 5–7**

M

magnifying text. *See* zooming
maximizing windows, **OFF 12**
maximums, calculating using
    AutoCalculate, EX 49
menus, **OFF 10**
  See also specific menu
  using shortcut, OFF 18
Merge & Center button, Home tab,
    EX 28
merging cells, **EX 28–29**
metadata, **EX 43**, **PPT 45**, **AC 58**
Microsoft Access 2010
  See also Access
  described, **OFF 8**, **OFF 53**
Microsoft Certified Application
    Specialist (MCAS), PPT 50
Microsoft Clip Organizer, **PPT 26**,
    PPT 27–31
Microsoft Communicator, **OFF 8**
Microsoft Excel 2010
  See also Excel
  described, **OFF 8**
Microsoft InfoPath 2010, **OFF 8**
Microsoft Office 2010, **OFF 7**
  introduction to, PPT 8
  publishing Web pages online,
    APP 3–4
  programs, OFF 8
Microsoft Office folder, OFF 11
Microsoft Office Specialist (MOS),
    WD 44, EX 52, AC 62
Microsoft Office suites, OFF 8–9
Microsoft Office Web Apps,
    APP 8
Microsoft OneNote 2010, **OFF 8**
Microsoft Outlook 2010, **OFF 8**
Microsoft PowerPoint 2010
  See also PowerPoint
  described, **OFF 8**
Microsoft Publisher 2010, **OFF 8**,
    OFF 59–61
Microsoft SharePoint Workspace
    2010, **OFF 8**
Microsoft Web Apps, **OFF 8**
Microsoft Word 2010
  See also Word
  described, **OFF 8**

Mini toolbar
  described, using, **OFF 15**, WD 16,
    WD 26
  displaying, PPT 13
minimalist style, PPT 35
minimized windows, **OFF 30**
minimizing
  Ribbon, OFF 17
  windows, OFF 30–31
mistakes
  AutoCorrect feature, **EX 9**
  automatic spelling correction,
    WD 9
  correcting errors in documents,
    WD 44
  correcting table structure errors,
    AC 37
  correcting typing, WD 6,
    PPT 8–9
  methods of correcting errors,
    EX 49–53
  undoing, EX 8, AC 20
  using AutoCalculate to avoid,
    EX 48
mouse
  document navigation with,
    WD 11
  operations (table), OFF 4
  using, OFF 2
  using in Excel, OFF 49
moving
  clips, PPT 36–38
  files, OFF 64
  manually through slides in slide
    shows, PPT 49
  text, WD 47–48
  windows, OFF 66–67
multi-level bulleted list slides,
    adding, **PPT 15–18**
multimedia, using in PowerPoint
    presentations, OFF 36
My Collections, **PPT 26**

N

Name box
  formula bar, **OFF 50**
  selecting cell using, EX 34–35
names
  fields, AC 8
  file, **OFF 21**, OFF 27–28, OFF 52
  folder, OFF 22–23
  tables, AC 8
  user, **OFF 5**
  worksheets, EX 42–43

navigating
  described, **OFF 30**
  dialog boxes, OFF 30
  documents, WD 11
  using mouse, OFF 2–4
Navigation Pane, **OFF 24**, OFF 54,
    AC 14, **AC 15**
nonprinting characters, displaying,
    WD 7
Normal cell style, EX 52
Normal style, WD 5
Normal view, PPT 21, **PPT 24**,
    PPT 25
notebooks (OneNote), **OFF 62**
Notes Page view, **PPT 24**
Notes pane, **PPT 24**
note-taking program (OneNote),
    OFF 61–62
Number data type, **AC 9**
numbers
  alignment in cells, EX 14
  entering, EX 13–14
  entering as text, EX 16
  formatting in worksheets,
    EX 31–33
  numeric limitations of Excel,
    EX 13
  summing columns of, EX 15–16

O

Object tabs (Access), **AC 15**,
    OFF 54
Office 2010, **OFF 7**, PPT 8,
    APP 3–4
Office Collections, **PPT 26**
Office programs, suites, OFF 8–9
  See also specific program
  obtaining Help, OFF 68–72
  starting from Windows Explorer,
    OFF 48
  Windows Help and Support,
    OFF 73–74
Office Theme, **PPT 5**
OneNote, OFF 61–62
one-to-many relationship, **AC 9**
opening
  AutoPlay window, OFF 22
  Backstage view, OFF 42
  Clip Art task pane, PPT 31
  databases, AC 27, AC 62
  Design view, AC 24
  documents from PowerPoint,
    PPT 50–51
  documents from Word, WD 45

existing files, OFF 57
files from SkyDrive, APP 9–12
forms, AC 50
operating systems, **OFF 2**
organizing files and folders, OFF 21–30, WD 12, PPT 14, EX 20
orientation
landscape, **PPT 7**
portrait page, PPT 22
Outline tab, PPT 21, **PPT 24**
outlining (PowerPoint feature), OFF 36
Outlook, **OFF 58**
Outlook window, OFF 58–59
overlapping windows vs. tabbed documents, AC 58
Overtype mode, **EX 50**

P

pages
See also documents
centering contents vertically, WD 40–41
OneNote, **OFF 62**
viewing single, WD 40–41
panes, **OFF 10**
navigation, OFF 24
task, **OFF 15**
paragraph formatting, **WD 12**
paragraphs, **PPT 8**
centering, WD 14
creating new, OFF 20, WD 6
formatting, WD 12–30
formatting mark (¶), WD 7
selecting, PPT 12
shading, WD 20
spacing before, after, WD 43
using in presentations, PPT 8–9
password text box, OFF 6–7
passwords
described, **OFF 5**
and user accounts, OFF 6–7
paste area, **EX 17**
Paste Options, WD 48
paths, **OFF 21**
paths and corresponding drives, folders, **OFF 21–22**
PDF files
described, **AC 30**
viewing, EX 45
people icon, APP 10

personal folders vs. shared folders, APP 7
photographs
inserting into presentations, PPT 31–32
inserting into slides, PPT 26–33
resizing, PPT 35–36
picture effects, applying, WD 38–39
picture styles, WD 37
Picture Tools Format tab, OFF 14
pictures. *See also* graphics, images, photographs
inserting in documents, WD 30–32, WD 35
wrapping text around, PPT 32
pie charts, EX 36
pixels, screen resolution, OFF 31–32
placeholders, **OFF 39, PPT 7**
deleting text in, PPT 41–42
selecting text, PPT 16
using with slides, PPT 7
planning
databases, AC 2
distribution of worksheets, EX 45
printing of documents, WD 51
projects, WD 2, PPT 2, PPT 4
projects, guidelines, APP 1–2
use of color, WD 24
Word documents, WD 4
worksheets, EX 2
worksheets formatting, EX 22–23
plus sign (+) and shortcut keys, OFF 5
point size, **EX 22**
points (font), **PPT 10**
portrait orientation, **AC 30, OFF 39**, EX 46
portrait page orientation, PPT 22
positioning charts, EX 37
postal codes, AC 12
PowerPoint, **OFF 36–38**
BTW Web page, PPT 4
file formats recognized (table), PPT 31
Help, PPT 45
Office suites (table), **OFF 9**
opening documents from, PPT 50–51
quitting, PPT 50
presentations, overview of, PPT 2–4
Ribbon, OFF 39–40
saving files in folders, OFF 41

starting, OFF 37–38, PPT 4–5, PPT 50
views, using, PPT 24–25
window, OFF 39–40, PPT 48
presentations, **OFF 36–37, PPT 2**
See also slide shows
adding slides to, PPT 14–20
creating title for, PPT 7–8
inserting photographs into, PPT 31–32
printing, PPT 51–53
saving, PPT 14, PPT 47
preview, live, OFF 14
previewing
and printing worksheets, EX 45–47
slide shows, PPT 52
tables, AC 30–32
Previous Locations button, **OFF 24**
primary keys, **AC 3–4**
determining, AC 5, AC 8–9
modifying, AC 16–17
Print Layout view, **OFF 12**, WD 5
Print Preview, AC 53
printing
document properties, WD 49, EX 45
documents, WD 51–52
presentations, PPT 51–53
tables, AC 30–32
worksheets, EX 45–47
printouts, **AC 30, EX 45**
private folders, APP 10
programs
See also specific program
Help, obtaining, OFF 72
Office suites, **OFF 8**
panes, OFF 10
quitting, OFF 35, OFF 45, OFF 52
starting and using, OFF 9–11, OFF 37–38
switching between, OFF 27
tabs in, OFF 14
project planning guidelines, APP 1–2
projects
database creation, AC 2–12
flyer with pictures, WD 2–4
presentation with bulleted lists, clip art, PPT 2–4
worksheet with embedded chart, EX 2–4

promoting (text), **PPT 17**
properties
  See also specific property
  clip, PPT 29
  document, and standard, **EX 43**
  standard, automatically updated,
    WD 49, **PPT 45**
publication types, **OFF 60**
Publisher
  creating documents, OFF 60–61
  described, **OFF 59–60**
publishing Office 2010 Web pages
    online, APP 3–4

Q

queries, **AC 42–43**
  creating, AC 43–45
  saving, AC 47
  using, AC 45–48
  using criterion in, AC 46–47
question mark (?) and file, folder
    names, OFF 22, OFF 28
Quick Access Toolbar, **OFF 16**
  customizing, OFF 19
  using shortcut menus, OFF 18
Quick Reference Web page, PPT 52
quitting
  Access, AC 26, AC 60
  Excel, EX 47
  Office program with open
    document, OFF 35
  Office programs, OFF 45, OFF 52
  PowerPoint, PPT 50
  Word, WD 53
quotation marks (')
  and file, folder names, OFF 22,
    OFF 28
  and text fields, AC 47

R

radar charts, EX 37
ranges, **EX 15**
  clearing, EX 52
  copying one to another, EX 18
records, **AC 3**
  adding to tables, AC 23–25,
    AC 28–29
  deleting, AC 20, AC 26
recover (database), **AC 61**
Recycle Bin, **OFF 7**
Redo command, OFF 19, EX 51
redoing actions, WD 23

redundancy, identifying and
    removing, AC 5, AC 10–12
Refresh button, **OFF 24**
relational databases, **AC 3**
relationships, determining,
    implementing between tables,
    AC 9
relative references, **EX 17**
removing
  See also deleting
  bold styles from cells, EX 25
  bullets, WD 23
  KeyTips from screen, OFF 16
  redundancy, AC 10–12
  styles, PPT 11
renaming
  database objects, AC 62
  fields, AC 19
  files, APP 8, OFF 63
repairing databases, AC 61
replacing slide text content,
    PPT 40–42
Report view, AC 53
reports
  adding totals to, AC 56
  creating, AC 51–53
  Layout view, using in, AC 53–58
repositioning
  clips, PPT 36–38
  slides, PPT 39–40
requirements document, **EX 3**
resizing, **PPT 33**, **WD 34**
  charts, EX 40
  clip art, photographs, PPT 33–36
  datasheet columns, **AC 29–30**,
    AC 42
  graphics, WD 34–36
  report columns, AC 54–56
  windows, OFF 66–67
resolution, screen. *See* screen
    resolution
Restart command, **OFF 6**
restoring
  Ribbon, OFF 17
  windows, OFF 30–31
reversing changes, undoing mistakes,
    PPT 8
Ribbon, **OFF 14–15**
  Access, OFF 54
  appearance of, PPT 15
  customizing, OFF 49
  displaying tabs, minimizing,
    restoring, OFF 16–17
  Excel, OFF 49

PowerPoint, **OFF 40**
  screen resolution and, WD 8
  at various screen resolutions,
    OFF 32–33
rotate handles, WD 37
row heading (Excel), **OFF 49**
row selector, **AC 22**
rows
  copying cells to adjacent cells,
    EX 17–18
  determining contents for, EX 5
  entering titles, EX 12
rulers, showing or hiding, WD 5

S

Save & Send gallery, APP 5–8
Save As command, APP 3
Save As dialog box, OFF 51–52
Save command, OFF 19
save copy, **AC 61**
saving
  backup and recovery operations,
    AC 60–62
  databases, OFF 55, AC 62
  documents, WD 12
  existing document with same
    name, WD 30
  files in folders, OFF 27–29,
    OFF 41
  files in Office programs,
    OFF 8
  files to SkyDrive, APP 5–8
  import steps, AC 41
  Office documents with same file
    name, OFF 51
  and organizing files, OFF 21–30
  presentations, PPT 14, PPT 47
  queries, AC 47
  records, AC 25
  tables, AC 21
  Web pages to online location,
    APP 3–4
  workbooks, EX 20, EX 45
screen resolution
  changing, OFF 33–34, WD 4,
    EX 5
  described, **OFF 31–32**, PPT 4
ScreenTips, Enhanced, **OFF 15**
scroll arrows, **OFF 4**
scroll bars, **OFF 4**, OFF 12–13
scroll box, **OFF 4**
scrolling through folder contents,
    OFF 26

search box
  described, **OFF 24**
  starting programs using,
    OFF 37–38
searching for Help topics,
  OFF 68–70
Section Header slide layout,
  PPT 21
sections (OneNote), **OFF 62**
selecting
  cells, EX 6, EX 34–35
  lines, WD 15, WD 21
  paragraphs, PPT 10
  text placeholders, PPT 16
  words, WD 27–28, PPT 12,
    PPT 19
selection rectangles, **WD 32,**
  PPT 33
shade, applying, **WD 20**
Shared Collections, **PPT 26**
shared folders vs. personal folders,
  APP 7
sheet tab (Excel), **OFF 49**
shortcut keys, **OFF 4–5**
shortcut menus, using, **OFF 18,**
  OFF 33–34
Shut down command, **OFF 6**
Shutter Bar Open/Close button,
  OFF 54
shutting down Windows 7,
  OFF 6
signature lines, **WD 5**
signing in to Windows Live, APP 7,
  APP 9–10
Simple Query Wizard, AC 43–45
size, font, **EX 22**
sizing
  See also resizing
  charts, EX 40
  font size, **WD 12,** WD 13
  fonts, WD 16
sizing handles, OFF 40,
  PPT 33
SkyDrive, **APP 5**
  collaboration using, APP 12
  opening files from, APP 9–12
  saving files to, APP 5–8
  Web Apps, APP 8
slash (/) and file names, OFF 28
Sleep command, **OFF 6**
slide indicator, **PPT 25**
Slide pane, **PPT 24**
Slide Show toolbar, PPT 49
Slide Show view, **PPT 47–50**

slide shows, **OFF 36–37, PPT 2**
  See also presentations
  ending with closing slide,
    PPT 38–40
  Title Slide, OFF 39–40
slide transitions, **PPT 43**
sliders, using, OFF 34
slides, **OFF 39**
  adding to presentations,
    PPT 14–20, PPT 21–24
  changing layouts, PPT 21–24
  changing text content,
    PPT 40–42
  closing, PPT 38–40
  copying, PPT 38–39
  creating title, PPT 7–8
  editing text in, PPT 40–42
  emphasis, adding, PPT 12
  inserting clip art, photographs into,
    PPT 26–33
  moving to another, in Normal view,
    PPT 24
  multi-level bulleted list,
    PPT 15–18
  in presentations generally, PPT 2
  spell-checking, PPT 40
Slides tab, **PPT 24**
snaps described, **EX 40**
software. *See specific program*
source area, **EX 17**
spacing before, after paragraphs,
  WD 43
spelling check, WD 9–11, PPT 40,
  EX 9
splitting merged cells, EX 29
spreadsheets. *See* worksheets
Standard Colors, PPT 13
standard properties, **WD 49,**
  PPT 45, EX 43, AC 58
Start button, **OFF 10**
Start menu, starting programs using,
  OFF 10–11
starting
  Access, AC 12, AC 27
  Excel, OFF 48, EX 5, EX 47
  PowerPoint, PPT 4–5, PPT 50
  programs, OFF 9–11, OFF 37–38
  Publisher, OFF 60
  slide shows, PPT 47–48
  Windows 7, OFF 5–7
  Windows Help and Support,
    OFF 73–74
  Word, WD 4–5, WD 45
Status bar, **OFF 13, AC 15**

Status Bar Configuration shortcut
  menu, EX 48–49
stock charts, EX 36–37
storage for databases, AC 13
styles, **WD 37**
  See also specific style
  applying picture, WD 37
  changing cell, EX 22–23
  font, PPT 12–14, **EX 22**
  minimalist, PPT 35
  Normal, WD 5
subtitles, worksheet, EX 7
suites, **OFF 8**
SUM function, **EX 15–16**
sums
  calculating, EX 15–16, AC 56
  determining multiple totals at same
    time, EX 18–19
surface charts, EX 37
switching between programs,
  OFF 27

T

tabbed documents, AC 58
tables, **OFF 46**
  See also databases
  adding records to, AC 23–25,
    AC 28–29
  changing structure of, AC 20–22,
    AC 37
  checking structure in Design view,
    AC 22
  closing, AC 23, AC 26
  creating, AC 15–20, AC 32–37
  determining relationships between,
    AC 9
  identifying, AC 5
  naming, AC 8
  previewing, printing, AC 30–32
  saving, AC 21
tabs
  changing Ribbon, OFF 16–17,
    OFF 49
  contextual, EX 39
  on Ribbon, **OFF 14**
Tabs pane, PPT 21
task panes, **OFF 15**
templates
  creating databases using, AC 14
  publication types, OFF 60
text, **EX 7**
  applying text effects, WD 20
  changing font, WD 17

changing font size, WD 21–22
changing slide content, PPT 40–42
choosing for slides, PPT 7
colored, PPT 12–13
correcting errors in documents,
    WD 44
deleting from documents, WD 47
elements of, WD 13
entering, WD 5–8, EX 12
entering in documents, OFF 20
entering numbers as, EX 16
in Excel, **OFF 50**
inserting into documents, WD 46
italicizing, WD 24, PPT 13
making bold, WD 28, PPT 19–20
moving, WD 47–48
selecting, WD 27–28
spelling and grammar check,
    WD 9–11
standard layouts for, PPT 21
underlining, WD 27
wordwrap, WD 8
wrapping around pictures, PPT 32
text boxes, OFF 6
Text data type, **AC 9**
text effects, applying, WD 19–20
text placeholders, selecting, PPT 16
text slides, creating with multi-level
    bulleted list, PPT 15–18
Theme Colors, PPT 13
themes, **WD 12**, EX 22, **EX 24**
  color, **WD 28–29**
  document, **PPT 5–6**
title bars, **OFF 11**
Title Only slide layout, PPT 21–22
Title Slides
  creating, PPT 7–8
  entering content in, OFF 40,
    OFF 43
  layout, **OFF 39**, PPT 21
titles
  entering column, EX 10–11
  entering row, EX 12
  entering worksheet, OFF 50–51,
    EX 8
  formatting column, EX 29–31
  report, AC 52–53
  worksheet, EX 7
toner, conserving, WD 51
tool tabs, **OFF 14**
toolbars
  Mini toolbar, **OFF 15**
  Quick Access Toolbar, **OFF 16**
  Slide Show, PPT 49

totals
  adding to reports, AC 56
  determining multiple at same time,
    EX 18–19
transitions, adding slide, **PPT 43**

U

underlining
  spelling, grammar errors, WD 9
  text, WD 27
Undo command, OFF 19, EX 51
undoing
  actions, WD 23
  changes in tables, AC 25
  input mistakes, AC 20
  last cell entry, EX 51
  mistakes, EX 8, PPT 8, PPT 34
  picture formatting, WD 38
  typing mistakes, WD 6
unique identifiers, **AC 3–4**
USB flash drives
  saving files on, OFF 21–22,
    OFF 27–29, OFF 44
  storing databases on, AC 13
  storing files, folders on, OFF 22–23
user accounts, **OFF 5**
user icons, **OFF 5**, OFF 6
user names, **OFF 5**

V

value axis, **EX 37**
verifying saved files, OFF 30
vertical bar (|) and file, folder names,
    OFF 28
viewing
  presentations in Slide Show view,
    PPT 47–50
  single page, WD 40–41
views
  See also specific view
  Access, AC 15
  PowerPoint, PPT 24–25
  for reports, AC 53
  switching between query, AC 45

W

Web, Excel support, OFF 46
Web Apps, **APP 8**
Web Collections, **PPT 26**
Web pages, publishing Office 2010
    online, APP 3–4

Web-based templates, AC 14
Welcome screen, **OFF 5–6**
windows, **OFF 11**
  Access, AC 15
  Excel, OFF 49–50
  folder, OFF 24–25
  maximizing, **OFF 12**
  minimizing, restoring,
    OFF 30–31
  moving, OFF 66–67
  OneNote, OFF 62
  Outlook, OFF 58–59
  overlapping, vs. tabbed documents,
    AC 58
  PowerPoint, OFF 39–40
  Publisher, OFF 60
  resizing, OFF 66–67
  Word, WD 5
Windows 7, **OFF 2**
  starting, logging on, OFF 5–7
  Windows Help and Support,
    OFF 73–74
Windows 7 Aero, OFF 2–3
Windows 7 Basic, OFF 2–3
Windows desktop, OFF 7
Windows Explorer
  creating Office document from,
    OFF 47
  moving, renaming, deleting files,
    OFF 62–65
  starting Office program using,
    OFF 48
Windows Help and Support,
    OFF 73–74
Windows Live SkyDrive
  See also SkyDrive
  described, **APP 5**
Word, OFF 9
  Help, OFF 66, OFF 68–72,
    WD 35
  Office suites (table), **OFF 9**
  opening documents from,
    WD 45
  quitting, WD 44, WD 53
  saving files to SkyDrive, APP 5–8
  starting, WD 4–5, WD 45
word processing
  PowerPoint feature, OFF 36
  Word. *See* Word
Word window, OFF 12–16, WD 5
words
  formatting, PPT 20
  selecting, PPT 12, PPT 19
wordwrap, **WD 8**

workbooks, **OFF 46**
  opening from Excel, EX 48
  saving, EX 20
worksheets, **OFF 46**
  See also cells, columns, rows
  adding Clustered Cylinder chart to,
    EX 38–42
  adjusting column widths,
    EX 33–34
  changing fonts, EX 24–25
  changing names, EX 42–43
  clearing, EX 52–53
  components, navigation of,
    OFF 49
  development cycle, EX 4

entering titles, EX 8–9, OFF 50–51
formatting, EX 22–34
formatting in worksheets, EX 31–33
importing into Access, AC 38–42
planning, EX 2–6
printing, EX 45–47
titles, subtitles, EX 7
wrapping text around pictures,
    PPT 32
wrist injuries, minimizing, WD 11

X

X Y (scatter) charts, EX 36
x-axis, **EX 40**

XPS files, **AC 30**, EX 47
XPS Viewer, EX 45

Y

y-axis, **EX 37**

Z

zooming
  described, WD 5
  documents, WD 33, WD 45

Quick Reference Summary

Table 1: Microsoft Word 2010 Quick Reference Summary

Task	Page Number	Mouse	Ribbon	Shortcut Menu	Keyboard Shortcut
Bold	WD 28	Bold button on Mini toolbar	Bold button (Home tab | Font group)	Font, Font tab (Font dialog box)	CTRL+B
Bullets, Apply	WD 22		Bullets button (Home tab | Paragraph group)	Bullets	* (ASTERISK), SPACEBAR
Center	WD 14	Center button on Mini toolbar	Center button (Home tab | Paragraph group)	Paragraph, Indents and Spacing tab (Paragraph dialog box)	CTRL+E
Change Case	WD 18		Change Case button (Home tab | Font group)	Font, Font tab (Font dialog box)	SHIFT+F3
Change Spacing before or after Paragraph	WD 43		Spacing Before or Spacing After box arrow (Page Layout tab | Paragraph group)	Paragraph, Indents and Spacing tab (Paragraph dialog box)	
Color Text	WD 25	Font Color button on Mini toolbar	Font Color button arrow (Home tab | Font group)		
Document Properties, Change	WD 49		Properties button (File tab | Info tab)		
Font Size, Change	WD 16	Font Size box arrow on Mini toolbar	Font Size box arrow (Home tab | Font group)	Font, Font tab (Font dialog box)	CTRL+D
Font, Change	WD 17	Font box arrow on Mini toolbar	Font box arrow (Home tab | Font group)	Font, Font tab (Font dialog box)	CTRL+D
Formatting Marks	WD 7		Show/Hide ¶ button (Home tab | Paragraph group)		CTRL+SHIFT+*
Graphic, Resize	WD 34	Drag sizing handle	Shape Height and Shape Width text boxes (Picture Tools Format tab | Size group)	Size and Position, Size tab (Layout dialog box)	
Insertion Point, Move Down/Up One Line	WD 11				DOWN ARROW/ UP ARROW
Insertion Point, Move Down/Up One Paragraph	WD 11				CTRL+DOWN ARROW/ CTRL+UP ARROW

Table 1: Microsoft Word 2010 Quick Reference Summary *(continued)*

Task	Page Number	Mouse	Ribbon	Shortcut Menu	Keyboard Shortcut
Insertion Point, Move Down/Up One Screen	WD 11				PAGE DOWN/ PAGE UP
Insertion Point, Move Left/ Right One Character	WD 11				LEFT ARROW/ RIGHT ARROW
Insertion Point, Move Left/ Right One Word	WD 11				CTRL+LEFT ARROW/ CTRL+RIGHT ARROW
Insertion Point, Move to Beginning/End of Document	WD 11				CTRL+HOME/ CTRL+END
Insertion Point, Move to Beginning/End of Line	WD 11				HOME/ END
Insertion Point, Move to Bottom of Document Window	WD 11				ALT+CTRL+PAGE DOWN/ ALT+CTRL+PAGE UP
Italicize	WD 24	Italic button on Mini toolbar	Italic button (Home tab | Font group)	Font, Font tab (Font dialog box)	CTRL+I
Move Text	WD 47	Drag and drop selected text	Cut button (Home tab | Clipboard group); Paste button (Home tab | Clipboard group)	Cut; Paste	CTRL+X; CTRL+V
Open a Document	WD 45		Open (File tab)		CTRL+O
Page Border, Add	WD 41		Page Borders button (Page Layout tab | Page Background group)		
Picture Style, Apply	WD 37		More button in Picture Styles gallery (Picture Tools Format tab | Picture Styles group)		
Picture Effects, Apply	WD 38		Picture Effects button (Picture Tools Format tab | Picture Styles group)	Format Picture	
Picture, Insert	WD 31		Insert Picture from File button (Insert tab | Illustrations group)		
Print Document	WD 51		Print button (File tab | Print tab)		CTRL+P
Quit Word	WD 44	Close button on title bar	Exit (File tab)		ALT+F4
Redo	WD 23	Redo button on Quick Access Toolbar			CTRL+Y
Save New Document	WD 12	Save button on Quick Access Toolbar	Save or Save As (File tab)		F12
Save Document, Same File Name	WD 30	Save button on Quick Access toolbar	Save (File tab)		CTRL+S
Scroll, Up/Down One Line	WD 11	Click scroll arrow at top/bottom of vertical scroll bar			
Scroll, Up/Down One Screen	WD 11	Click above/below scroll box on vertical scroll bar			
Select Block of Text	WD 30	Click beginning, SHIFT-click end			
Select Character(s)	WD 30	Drag through characters			SHIFT+RIGHT ARROW or SHIFT+LEFT ARROW

Table 1: Microsoft Word 2010 Quick Reference Summary (continued)

Task	Page Number	Mouse	Ribbon	Shortcut Menu	Keyboard Shortcut
Select Entire Document	WD 30	In left margin, triple-click	Select button arrow (Home tab | Editing group)		CTRL+A
Select Graphic	WD 30	Click graphic			
Select Group of Words	WD 27	Drag mouse pointer through words			CTRL+SHIFT+RIGHT ARROW
Select Line	WD 15	Click in left margin			SHIFT+DOWN ARROW
Select Multiple Lines	WD 21	Drag mouse pointer in left margin			SHIFT+DOWN ARROW
Select Nonadjacent Items	WD 15	Select first item, hold down CTRL key while selecting item(s)			
Select Paragraph	WD 30	Triple-click paragraph			CTRL+SHIFT+DOWN ARROW or CTRL+ SHIFT+UP ARROW
Select Sentence	WD 30	CTRL-click			
Select Word	WD 30	Double-click word			CTRL+SHIFT+RIGHT ARROW or CTRL+ SHIFT+LEFT ARROW
Shade Paragraph	WD 20		Shading button arrow (Home tab | Paragraph group)		
Spelling, Check as You Type	WD 9	Click word, Spelling and Grammar Check icon on status bar		Right-click error, click correct word on shortcut menu	
Text Effect, Apply	WD 19		Text Effects button (Home tab | Font group)		
Theme Colors, Change	WD 28		Change Styles button (Home tab | Styles group)		
Underline	WD 27	Underline button on Mini toolbar	Underline button (Home tab | Font group)	Font, Font tab (Font dialog box)	CTRL+U
Undo	WD 23	Undo button on Quick Access Toolbar			CTRL+Z
Zoom Document	WD 33	Zoom Out or Zoom In button on status bar	Zoom button (View tab | Zoom group)		
Zoom One Page	WD 41		One Page button (View tab | Zoom group)		

Table 2: Microsoft PowerPoint 2010 Quick Reference Summary

Task	Page Number	Mouse	Ribbon	Shortcut Menu	Keyboard Shortcut
Clip Art, Insert	PPT 27	Clip Art icon in slide	Clip Art button (Insert tab | Images group)		
Clip Art, Photo, or Shape, Move	PPT 36	Drag			ARROW KEYS move selected image in small increments
Document Properties, Change	PPT 46		Properties button (File tab | Info tab)		
Document Theme, Choose	PPT 5		More button (Design tab | Themes group)		

Table 2: Microsoft PowerPoint 2010 Quick Reference Summary (continued)

Task	Page Number	Mouse	Ribbon	Shortcut Menu	Keyboard Shortcut
Font Size, Increase	PPT 11	Increase Font Size button or Font Size box arrow on Mini toolbar	Increase Font Size button or Font Size box arrow (Home tab | Font group)		CTRL+SHIFT+>
Font, Change Color	PPT 13	Font Color button or Font Color button arrow on Mini toolbar	Font Color button or Font Color button arrow (Home tab | Font group)	Font, Font tab (Font dialog box)	CTRL+SHIFT+F
List Level, Increase	PPT 17	Increase List Level button on Mini toolbar	Increase List Level button (Home tab | Paragraph group)		TAB or ALT+SHIFT+RIGHT ARROW
List Level, Decrease	PPT 18	Decrease List Level button on Mini toolbar	Decrease List Level button (Home tab | Paragraph group)		SHIFT+TAB or ALT+SHIFT+LEFT ARROW
Next Slide	PPT 25	Next Slide button on vertical scroll bar or next slide thumbnail on Slides tab			PAGE DOWN
Open Presentation	PPT 50		Open (File tab)		CTRL+O
Photo, Insert	PPT 32	Insert Picture from File icon on slide or Insert Clip Art icon on slide	Picture button or Clip Art button (Insert tab | Images group)		
Previous Slide	PPT 26	Previous Slide button on vertical scroll bar or click previous slide thumbnail on Slides tab			PAGE UP
Print a Presentation	PPT 51		Print button (File tab | Print tab)		CTRL+P
Quit PowerPoint	PPT 50	Close button on title bar	Exit (File tab)	Right-click Microsoft PowerPoint button on taskbar, click Close window	ALT+F4
Resize	PPT 33	Drag sizing handles	Enter height and width values (Picture Tools Format tab | Size group or Drawing Tools Format tab | Size group)	Format Picture or Format Shape, Size tab; or enter height and width in Shape Height and Shape Width boxes	
Save a Presentation	PPT 14	Save button on Quick Access Toolbar	Save or Save As (File tab)		CTRL+S or F12
Slide, Add	PPT 14		New Slide button (Home tab | Slides group)		CTRL+M
Slide, Arrange	PPT 39	Drag slide in Slides tab or Outline tab to new position, or in Slide Sorter view drag to new position			
Slide, Duplicate	PPT 38		New Slide arrow (Home tab | Slides group), Duplicate Selected Slides		

Table 2: Microsoft PowerPoint 2010 Quick Reference Summary (continued)

Task	Page Number	Mouse	Ribbon	Shortcut Menu	Keyboard Shortcut
Slide, Select Layout	PPT 21		Layout button or New Slide arrow (Home tab | Slides group)		
Slide Show View	PPT 47	Slide Show button at lower-right PowerPoint window	Slide Show button (Slide Show tab | Start Slide Show group)		F5
Slide Show, End	PPT 49	Click black ending slide		End Show	ESC or HYPHEN
Text, Bold	PPT 20	Bold button on Mini toolbar	Bold button (Home tab | Font group)	Font, Font tab (Font dialog box)	CTRL+B
Text, Change Color	PPT 13	Font Color button or Font Color button arrow on Mini toolbar	Font Color button or Font Color button arrow (Home tab | Font group)	Font, Font tab (Font dialog box)	
Text, Delete	PPT 41		Cut button (Home tab | Clipboard group)	Cut	DELETE or CTRL+X or BACKSPACE
Text, Italicize	PPT 11	Italic button on Mini toolbar	Italic button (Home tab | Font group)	Font, Font tab (Font dialog box)	CTRL+I
Text, Select Paragraph	PPT 10	Triple-click paragraph			SHIFT+DOWN ARROW or SHIFT+UP ARROW
Text, Select Word	PPT 12	Double-click word			CTRL+SHIFT+RIGHT ARROW or CTRL+SHIFT+LEFT ARROW
Transition, Add	PPT 43		Transitions tab | Transition to This Slide group		ALT+A , T

Table 3: Microsoft Excel 2010 Quick Reference Summary

Task	Page Number	Mouse	Ribbon	Shortcut Menu	Keyboard Shortcut
All data in a cell, Select	EX 51	Double-click if there are no spaces in data			
Auto Fill	EX 18	Drag fill handle	Auto Fill Options button (Home tab | Editing group)		
AutoCalculate	EX 48	Select range | right-click AutoCalculate area | click calculation			
Bold	EX 25	Bold button on Mini toolbar	Bold button (Home tab | Font group)	Format Cells on shortcut menu | Font tab | Bold	CTRL+B
Cell Entries, Clear Selected	EX 52	Drag fill handle from empty cell through cells with entries	Clear button (Home tab | Editing group) | Clear Contents	Clear Contents on shortcut menu	DELETE
Cell Style, Change	EX 52		Cell Styles button (Home tab | Styles group)		
Cell, Highlight	EX 19	Drag mouse pointer			

Table 3: Microsoft Excel 2010 Quick Reference Summary (continued)

Task	Page Number	Mouse	Ribbon	Shortcut Menu	Keyboard Shortcut
Cell, Select	EX 34	Click cell or click Name box, type cell reference, press ENTER			Use arrow keys
Cells, Merge and Center	EX 28	Merge & Center button on Mini toolbar	Merge & Center button (Home tab | Alignment group)	Format Cells on shortcut menu | Alignment tab	
Characters to left of insertion point, Delete	EX 50				BACKSPACE
Characters to right of insertion point, Delete	EX 50				DELETE
Characters, Highlight	EX 51	Drag through adjacent characters			SHIFT+RIGHT ARROW or SHIFT+LEFT ARROW
Chart, Add	EX 38		Charts group | Insert tab		
Color Text	EX 27	Font Color button on Mini toolbar	Font Color button arrow (Home tab | Font group)		
Column Width	EX 33	Drag column heading boundary		Column Width on shortcut menu	
Complete an Entry	EX 8	Click Enter box			Press ENTER
Document Properties, Change	EX 43		Properties button (File tab | Info tab)		
Document Properties, Print	EX 45		File tab | Print tab, first box arrow (Settings area)		
Document Properties, Set or View	EX 43		File | Info tab		
Entry, Complete	EX 8	Click Enter box			Press ENTER
Font Color	EX 27	Font Color box arrow on Mini toolbar	Font Color button arrow (Home tab | Font group)	Format Cells on shortcut menu | Font tab	
Font Size, Decrease	EX 26	Font Size box arrow on Mini toolbar	Decrease Font Size button (Home tab | Font group)	Format Cells on shortcut menu | Font tab	
Font Size, Increase	EX 26	Font Size box arrow on Mini toolbar	Increase Font Size button (Home tab | Font group)	Format Cells | Font Tab	
Font Type	EX 24	Font box arrow on Mini toolbar	Font box (Home tab | Font group)	Format Cells | Font tab	
Font, Change	EX 24	Font Size box arrow on Mini toolbar	Font box arrow (Home tab | Font group)	Format Cells | Font tab	
Highlight Cells	EX 18	Drag mouse pointer			SHIFT+ARROW KEY
In-Cell Editing	EX 50	Double-click cell			F2
Insert and Overtype modes, Toggle between	EX 50				INSERT
Insertion point, Move	EX 8	Click			Use arrow keys
Insertion point, move to beginning of data in cell	EX 51	Point to left of first character and click			HOME
Insertion point, move to ending of data in cell	EX 51	Point to right of last character and click			END

Table 3: Microsoft Excel 2010 Quick Reference Summary (continued)

Task	Page Number	Mouse	Ribbon	Shortcut Menu	Keyboard Shortcut
Numbers, Format	EX 31	Accounting Number Format, Percent Style, or Comma Style button on Mini toolbar	Cell Styles button (Home tab | Styles group) or Accounting Number Format, Percent Style, or Comma Style button (Home tab | Number group), or Format Cells: Number dialog box launcher | Accounting, or Percentage or Number Format list arrow | Accounting or Percentage		
Open a Workbook	EX 48		Open or Recent (File tab)		CTRL+O
Print Worksheet	EX 46		File tab | Print tab		CTRL+P
Quit Excel	EX 47	Close button on right side of title bar	Exit (File tab)		
Range, Deselect	EX 18	Click outside range			
Range, Select	EX 28	Drag fill handle through range			
Redo	EX 51	Redo button on Quick Access Toolbar			CTRL+Y
Save Workbook	EX 20	Save button on Quick Access Toolbar	Save (File tab | Save button)		CTRL+S
Save Workbook, New Name	EX 20	Save button on Quick Access Toolbar			
Save Workbook, Same Name	EX 20	Save button on Quick Access Toolbar	Save (File tab | Save button)		CTRL+S
Select Cell	EX 7	Click cell or click Name box, type cell reference, press ENTER			Use arrow keys
Select Entire Worksheet	EX 52	Click Select All button			CTRL+A
Selected characters, Delete	EX 50		Cut button (Home tab | Clipboard group)		DELETE
Selected Chart, Delete	EX 53				DELETE
Sheet Name, Change	EX 42	Double-click type name		Rename on shortcut menu	
Sum	EX 15	Click Insert Function button in formula bar | SUM in Select a function list | OK | range | OK	Sum button (Home tab | Editing group)		ALT+EQUAL SIGN (=) twice
Text, Delete after typing but before pressing the ENTER key	EX 8	Click Cancel box in formula bar			Press ESC
Text, Delete while typing	EX 8				Press BACKSPACE
Undo	EX 51	Undo button on Quick Access Toolbar			CTRL+Z
Worksheet Name, Change	EX 42	Double-click sheet tab, type name		Rename on shortcut menu	
Worksheet, Clear	EX 52		Select All button | Clear button (Home tab | Editing group)		CTRL A, press DELETE
Worksheet, Preview	EX 46		File tab | Print tab		CTRL+P

Table 4: Microsoft Access 2010 Quick Reference Summary

Task	Page Number	Mouse	Ribbon	Shortcut Menu	Keyboard Shortcut
Close Object	AC 23	Close button for object		Right-click item, Close	
Column Headings, Modify	AC 54			Right-click field name, Rename Field	
Column, Resize	AC 54, AC 55	Double-click right boundary of field selector in datasheet		Right-click field name, Field Width	
Criterion, Use	AC 46	Right-click query, Design View, Criteria row			
Data, Import	AC 38		Button for imported data format (External Data tab | Import & Link group)	Right-click object, click selected format on Import menu	
Database Properties, Change	AC 59		View and edit database properties link (File tab | Info tab)		
Database, Create	AC 13		Blank database button (File tab | New tab)		
Form, Create	AC 48		Form button (Create tab | Forms group)		
Open Database	AC 27		Open button (File tab)		
Open Table	AC 24	Double-click table in Navigation Pane		Right-click table in Navigation Pane, click Open in shortcut menu	
Preview or Print Object	AC 31		Print or Print Preview button (File tab | Print tab)		CTRL+P, ENTER
Query, Create using Simple Query Wizard	AC 43		Query Wizard button (Create tab | Queries group)		
Record, Add	AC 28	New (blank) record button in Navigation buttons	New button (Home tab | Records Group)		CTRL+PLUS SIGN (+)
Remaining Fields in Table, Define	AC 19	In Datasheet view, click Click to Add field (Fields tab)			
Report, Create	AC 52		Report button (Create tab | Reports group)		
Save Object	AC 21	Save button on Quick Access Toolbar	File tab, Save		CTRL+S
Table, Create in Design View	AC 33		Table Design button (Create tab | Tables group)		
Table, View in Design View	AC 21		View button arrow (Table Tools Fields tab | Views group), Design View		
Totals, Add to a Report	AC 57		Totals button (Report Layout Tools Design tab | Grouping & Totals group)		